MULTILINGUAL MATTERS 36
Series Editor: Derrick Sharp

The Use of Welsh
A Contribution to Sociolinguistics

Edited by
Martin J. Ball

MULTILINGUAL MATTERS LTD
Clevedon · Philadelphia

I *NICOLE*

Nid cymin ar y min mau
Blys gwin a blas i genau

Library of Congress Cataloging-in-Publication Data

The Use of Welsh : a contribution to sociolinguistics.
  Includes index.
  1. Welsh language—Variation. 2. Welsh language—
Usage. I. Ball, Martin.
PB2114.U84 1988   491.6'6'019   87-32530
ISBN 0-905028-99-6
ISBN 0-905028-98-8 (pbk.)

British Library Cataloguing in Publication Data

The Use of Welsh: a contribution to
  sociolinguistics. —— (Multilingual
  matters ; 36).
  1. Welsh language —— Dialects
  2. Sociolinguistics
  I. Ball, Martin, J.
  491.6'6   PB2196

ISBN 0-905028-99-6
ISBN 0-905028-98-8 Pbk

Multilingual Matters Ltd.

Bank House, 8a Hill Road,   & 242 Cherry Street,
Clevedon, Avon BS21 7HH   Philadelphia PA 19106-1906,
England.   U.S.A.

Cover design by John Kempster.
Typeset by Photo·Graphics, Honiton, Devon.
Printed and bound in Great Britain by Short Run Press Ltd.,
Exeter EX2 7LW.

Multilingual Matters

Please contact us for the latest book information:
Multilingual Matters, Bank House, 8a Hill Road,
Clevedon, Avon BS21 7HH, England.

Contents

Preface

In this book is presented a collection of chapters by specialist authors covering aspects of contemporary usage of the Welsh language. Welsh is the most vigorous of the surviving Celtic tongues, and has been the subject of many recent linguistic works. These have covered its syntax, such as Awbery (1976), and Jones & Thomas (1977), and its phonetics and phonology, such as Ball & Jones (1984), and Ball (forthcoming). Political and cultural aspects have been dealt with in Stephens (1979), and the bilingual situation in Wales is discussed in Baker (1985). No book, however, has been produced up to now that has specifically dealt with the use of Welsh, that is the patterns of variation in language governed by regional, social and stylistic factors. This book is an attempt to fill this gap; it is intended as a contribution to Welsh sociolinguistics.

However, I have tried to ensure that this is not simply a book for the academic linguist or Celticist. To this end, many of the important concepts used in linguistics, and the necessary terminology that goes with them, are briefly and simply introduced in relevant places for the benefit of the general reader. These explanations are not given too much space, as I have recognized the need not to distract the more knowledgeable reader, and where necessary references to fuller accounts available in the literature are provided.

The book is divided into six parts, each containing several chapters. Part I is intended as an introduction to the fact that a language is not a homogeneous entity as many grammarians would have us believe, but that there are patterns of variation, and that linguists have attempted various ways to account for them. The introductory chapter presents some conflicting opinions on the usage of a particular aspect of Welsh, and asks the question, "How should the linguist describe this usage?". The next two chapters outline the fields of dialectology and sociolinguistics, and the advantages and disadvantages of these approaches.

Part II is concerned with defining the different levels of language. Patterns of usage vary dependent upon whether we are talking about vocabulary, pronunication or grammar. Each of these topics is given a chapter, with examples drawn from Welsh. Also included is a chapter on consonant mutations, features peculiar to the Celtic languages, which seem to form a bridge over the three levels of language previously discussed.

Part III contains accounts of three dialect studies. Many authorities recognize two main geographical varieties of Welsh — North and South — with Mid-Wales forming a transition between them. Following this, I have included work by specialists on a northern dialect (Pwllheli), a Mid-Wales dialect (Breconshire), and a southern one (Swansea Valley). Due to limitations of space, these studies are not intended to be comprehensive, but they do provide a good deal of information on the Welsh spoken in these areas.

However, as stressed earlier in the book, regional variation is not the only factor affecting the use of Welsh. Part IV tackles some of the non-geographical varieties of the language, commencing with a major study of literary Welsh, which has had such an influence on the development of "high" varieties of the language. Literary and official Welsh are closely related forms which provide the language with a standard dialect, so necessary if the status of the language is to be improved in the minds of speakers. Broadcast Welsh, on the other hand, might be expected to reflect the patterns of usage noted elsewhere in the book. The part of the chapter discussing radio notes this, while the television section discusses the problems of the standard of Welsh to be used, and the use of English in certain Welsh language programmes, from two different viewpoints: the linguist and the producer. The final chapter of this section describes a form of Welsh that sometimes appears far removed from the literary Welsh of the earlier chapter. This is *Cymraeg Byw*, the variety specially drawn up to aid second language learners.

Part V turns attention to the use of Welsh by children, an area much neglected in Welsh lingustics. The acquisition of the language is tackled in the first chapter, with more specific areas being studied thereafter. These cover the use of pronouns of address, of mutations, and the patterns of phonological disorder that may occur in children with speech problems.

The final section of the book is perhaps more theoretical than some of the other chapters. The first topic that is tackled is the problem of describing linguistic change in progress. Using data from the Welsh speakers of Y Wladfa, Patagonia, it is shown how non-linguistic factors are important in determining when linguistic change takes place, and who leads it. The final chapter returns to the problem of the mutations discussed in earlier contributions. A method of incorporating the variability shown in the use of these features into a theoretical description of Welsh is proposed.

Where necessary in this book, use has been made of the phonetic symbols of the International Phonetic Association. For readers unused to this alphabet, I will end this preface with a list of the symbols used in transcribing Welsh consonants, vowels and diphthongs, with accompanying words in ordinary orthography to show the correspondence between symbol and pronunciation. The symbol usage follows the guidelines proposed in Ball (forthcoming). Using this list the values of the symbols should be clear.

Phonetic symbols used in transcription

Consonants

/p/	*p*en	e*p*a	ma*p*
/b/	*b*ach	e*b*ol	ma*b*
/t/	*t*ad	e*t*o	he*t*
/d/	*d*awn	ta*d*au	ta*d*
/k/	*c*ig	ti*c*ian	to*c*
/g/	*g*ardd	te*g*an	ci*g*
/tʃ/	*tsh*ips	ma*ts*ys	ma*ts*
/dʒ/	*j*wg		
/m/	*m*êl	a*m*au	ca*m*
/n/	*n*aw	e*nn*ill	u*n*
/ŋ/	'*ng*ardd	cy*ng*or	i*ng*
/f/	*ff*a	u*ff*ern	rha*ff*
/v/	*f*ory	hu*f*en	ha*f*
/θ/	*th*ema	a*th*ro	gwr*th*
/ð/	*dd*oe	a*dd*o	har*dd*
/s/	*s*âl	a*s*e*s*u	o*s*
/ʃ/	*si*arad	pa*si*o	i*s* (in some areas: /is/)
/x/	*ch*i	a*ch*au	uw*ch*
/h/	*h*af	bi*h*afio	
/ɬ/	*ll*an	ga*ll*u	gwe*ll*
/l/	*l*an	ta*l*u	tâ*l*

| /r̥ʰ/ - /r̥/ | *rh*ew | | |
| /r/ | *r*adio | a*r*aith | mô*r* |

| /w/ | *w*iwer | wi*w*er |
| /j/ | *i*aith | fforddi*o* |

Vowels

* represents a southern form   † represents a northern form

/i/	t*i*	*t*ŷ*
/ɪ/	p*i*ll	*p*u*mp
/e/	p*ê*l	
/ɛ/	p*e*n	
/a/	m*a*m	
/ɑ/	m*â*n	
/ɔ/	ff*o*n	
/o/	ff*ô*n	
/ʊ/	m*w*ng	
/u/	m*ŵ*g	
/ɨ/	†t*ŷ*	
/ɹ/	†p*u*mp	
/ə/	*y*n	

Diphthongs

* represents a southern form   † represents a northern form

/aɪ/	g*ai*r	*aer	*aur
/ɔɪ/	tr*oi*	*oer	
/ʊɪ/	*ll*wy*		
/əɪ/	t*ei*	*lle*u*ad	
/ɪʊ/	ll*iw*	*ll*yw*	
/ɛʊ/	ll*ew*		
/aʊ/	ll*au*		
/əʊ/	ll*y*wydd		
/ɨʊ/	†ll*yw*		
/aɹ/	†*au*r		
/ɑɨ/	†*ae*r		
/ɔɹ/	†*oe*r		
/ʊɹ/	†ll*wy*		
/əɹ/	†lle*u*ad		

Part I:
Linguistic Variation and Welsh

1 Introduction

MARTIN J. BALL

One task which the linguist may decide to undertake is to describe the patterns of linguistic usage of speakers of a particular language. This may result in pedagogical grammars (which in turn may or may not be prescriptive in their approach) or theoretical treatises, using the language data as examples. A major problem arises, however, if the speakers of the language are not consistent in their usage of any particular feature. The problem posed by this has been answered in several ways: it can be ignored altogether, and solely one form described (this is basically similar to the prescriptivist approach, where one form is prescribed as desirable, any others criticized as undesirable); secondly all variation can be put down to fluctuations in performance, the innate linguistic competence (or knowledge) of the speakers lacking such variation. Alternatively, casual or "free" variation can be assumed, with no reason why any one form need be chosen by the speaker. Another way round the problem is to assume there may well be a reason (linguistic or non-linguistic) why one form is used on one occasion or by one speaker, and another used elsewhere or by other speakers. This book will examine a number of aspects of variation in Welsh, and attempt to account for them.

To take one example of linguistic variation in Welsh, we can quote from various pedagogical grammars of Welsh on the subject of the use of the initial consonant mutations of Welsh (see Chapters 7 and 20 for further details of these features). Evans (1974: 13–14) for example states,

> "*Nasal mutation*
> (i) After the personal pronoun *fy* (my). . .
> (ii) After the preposition *yn*. . .
>
> *Aspirate (spirant) mutation*
> (1) After the feminine pronouns *ei*, *'i*, *'w*. (her). . .
> (2) After the prepositions *gyda*, *efo* (with). . .
> (3) After the conjunctions *â* (as), *a* (and), *na* (neither, nor). . .

(4) After the negatives *ni*, *na*, (not) which are omitted, *na* (than). . ."

And later, "These are the mutations after numerals . . . Aspirate [after] *tri*, *chwe*" (Evans, 1974: 53).

On the other hand, Uned Iaith Genedlaethol Cymru (UIGC = Welsh National Language Unit) (1976: 121) for the same group of mutations, make the following comments,

"*Nasal Mutation*
(1) After the personal pronoun *fy*... .
(2) After the preposition *yn*. . ."

While this agrees with Evans (1974), their account of aspirate mutation does not.

"*Aspirate mutation*
(1) After the personal pronouns *ei*, '*i* (b) and '*w* (b). . .
(2) After the prepositions *â*, *gyda*, *tua*. . . This rule does not apply in many dialects. . .
(3) After the conjunction *a*. . . This rule does not apply in many dialects.
(4) Negative forms of the inflected verb. . .
(5) Comparison of adjectives — after *â* in the equative and *na* in the comparative . . . These rules do not apply in many dialects. . .
(6) After the negative form of the relative pronoun *na*. . .
(7) After *tra*. . . This usage is mainly found in literary Welsh." (UIGC, 1976: 120–21).

Elsewhere in the text further comment is added to these notes concerning variation in usage: for example on *gyda* and *tua*, "These mutations are still found in some dialects and in literary Welsh but are not used in this text book" (UIGC, 1976: 58); concerning *a*, *na*, "In literary Welsh and in some dialects [they cause] aspirate mutation of c, p, t. . . However, in other dialects, this rule no longer operates and this text book follows that practise" (p. 63). And, concerning the numerals, "In literary Welsh *tri* and *chwe* are followed by the aspirate mutation, but this rule is generally broken in speech. . ." (p. 20). The differences between these two texts is the more surprising as both claim to be describing *Cymraeg Byw*, the form of Welsh especially devised for second language learners.

The previous work then appears to be assigning variation in the use of mutations to dialectology, that is, claiming that different regional forms of Welsh have different usage patterns. What is the response of dialectologists to this claim? C. Thomas (1979: 137) reviewed the grammar referred to (UIGC, 1976), and asks, "Why was it chosen to follow the vernacular language (the dialects) in the case of the aspirate mutation *only*, and why were they so selective in this task?".[1] She points out numerous examples where certain dialects do not use mutations (aspirate in negative sentences, nasal after *yn*) which UIGC (1976) does not mention, and quotes evidence to show that many areas still use mutations where UIGC avoid them. Thomas concludes "Developments like [changes in the soft mutation] are on the same level as the tendency to avoid the aspirate mutation under certain circumstances, and if we accept one tendency into the language system generally we must accept them all" (C. Thomas, 1979: 139).[2] However, Thomas admits that she does not know the reason for the variation in aspirate mutation, "speakers . . . choosing it sometimes, and avoiding it at others in a way in which it is not possible to see a system" (C. Thomas, 1979: 139).[3]

In a traditional grammar such as Williams (1980) we would expect to find mutations described as being invariable, and a full list of where the mutations are found in the standard language is given (Williams, 1980: 174–77). The following comment is also made. "In some dialects there is a tendency to keep the radical after *yn*, and even to substitute the soft for the nasal mutation. Careful speakers shun such irregularities" (p. 175). No mention is made of any other possible variation.

On the other hand, another guide to learning Welsh, Rhys Jones (1977: 331) also notes the tendency to variable usage of mutations — assigning this to stylistic reasons (spoken *versus* written) rather than to regional differences.

"The Aspirate Mutation which formerly occurred after *â*, 'with', *gyda*, 'together with', and *tua*, 'towards', and which is still observed in written Welsh, is generally omitted in speech. . . The Aspirate Mutation after *a*, 'and', also tends to disappear."

Concerning numerals, Rhys Jones (1977: 332) states, "The masculine numerals *tri*, 'three', and the numeral *chwe* will cause Aspirate Mutation, but in speech this is mainly reserved for *cant* and *ceiniog*"; and for negative verbs, "verbs beginning with c, p, t, take the Aspirate Mutation. . . There is a marked tendency in colloquial speech for this mutation to be replaced by the Soft Mutation, by analogy with words beginning with g, b, d etc." (pp. 335–36).

However, a regional difference is attributed to variable use of the nasal mutation:

> "*yn*, 'in', is followed by the Nasal Mutation. . . There is a tendency in many areas to use the Soft Mutation rather than the Nasal after *yn*. . . and even not to mutate T and D at all. . ." (Rhys Jones, 1977: 331).

With all the conflicting evidence presented in these accounts, it is obvious that a full review of studies of varieties of Welsh is needed, together with an examination of how to treat linguistic variation. Then data from native speakers need to be collected and analysed so that the variable usage may be freshly examined along with its relation to other factors. By doing this we may be able to account for the variation and to integrate it into a theoretical description of Welsh. This then is the way in which this book approaches the problem of variation in Welsh.

Notes to Chapter 1

1. In the original: "pam y dewiswyd dilyn yr iaith lafar (tafodieithoedd) ynglŷn â'r treiglad llaes *yn unig* a phaham y buwyd mor ddewisol wrth y gwaith".
2. In the original: "Y mae datblygiadau fel yr uchod ar yr un tir â'r duedd i hepgor treiglad llaes o dan rai amodau, ac os derbyniwn un duedd i mewn i sistem yr iaith yn gyffredinol rhaid derbyn y cyfan".
3. In the original: "siaradwyr yn. . . ei ddewis weithiau a'i hepgor dro arall mewn ffordd nad oes modd gweld sistem ynddi".

2 Accounting for linguistic variation: Dialectology

MARTIN J. BALL

Introduction

Traditionally, linguists have viewed variation in language usage as being due to geographical factors, and the study of this area is termed *dialectology*. Dialectology has a comparatively long history in the Western European linguistic tradition, with the earliest recognized dialectological work being carried out in Germany in 1876. Interest in this study soon led to similar research throughout Western Europe and North America.

In Britain, the most important work in dialectology was the *Survey of English Dialects* (usually known as *SED*), begun under the direction of Eugen Dieth and Harold Orton in 1948, and completed in 1978, three years after Orton's death (see Orton *et al.*, 1978). In the United States the *Linguistic Atlas of the United States and Canada* was begun in 1930, and although atlases for several regions have appeared, much still remains unpublished. Closer to home, linguistic atlases of Scotland, covering both Scots and Gaelic have appeared in recent years. More information on the development of dialectology can be found in Chambers and Trudgill (1980) and Petyt (1980). Trudgill (1986) explores the fascinating area of dialects in contact.

Throughout most of its history, dialectology has concentrated on rural speakers, and has been monostylistic: that is to say has recorded only one style of speech from informants. In this it differs markedly from the approach of *sociolinguistics* (described in Chapter 3) which has been interested mainly in urban speech, and has investigated stylistic differences. This chapter will examine firstly the methodology of dialect studies, and then go on to look at this tradition in the Welsh context.

The methodology of dialectology

Although not all dialect studies have adopted precisely identical methodological approaches, a large number of them did share certain features in common. Here we can examine the aspects of selecting the informants (i.e. the speakers chosen to provide the samples of dialect), data collection (i.e. the methods used to prompt or elicit the necessary speech sample, and how it is recorded), and data analysis (what has been done with the data collected in order to illustrate the characteristics of the dialect).

Before we turn to these points, however, we must firstly clarify what aspects of language a dialect study is in fact investigating. As we will see in Part II of this book, language can be examined on several levels. Linguists (i.e. scholars of linguistics) recognize the following main areas of study:

(a) *Phonetics*. That is, the study of speech sounds: how they are made, how they are perceived, and their acoustic characteristics.

(b) *Phonology*. This is the study of how speech sounds are organized in language, often in a particular language or dialect.

(These first two areas would come under the general heading of pronunciation in the non-linguist's terms.)

(c) *Lexis*. This is the study of vocabulary, and links in with the study of morphology and semantics discussed below.

(d) *Morphology*. This area of study also investigates words, but whereas lexis is concerned with listing whole words, morphology is concerned with looking at how words are built up from smaller units of meaning, such as prefixes and suffixes.

(e) *Syntax*. This level goes beyond morphology — the study of the structure of words — and is the study of the structure of sentences.

(Morphology and syntax are often classed together by the linguist as *grammar*.)

(f) *Semantics*, or meaning. The final "core-area" of linguistics is concerned with the meaning of both individual words, and of longer utterances, such as sentences.

In theory, a dialect study can investigate any or all of these areas of linguistics. However, for reasons often to do with ease of transcription and analysis, dialectology has traditionally concentrated on phonetics/ phonology and on lexis, with the occasional minimal reference to morphology, and even less often, syntax. Lexical semantics may be subsumed under the heading of lexis, although lexical studies are often simple lists of dialect words, with little attempt to see whether the meaning of words common to the dialect and the standard language differ at all.

As we will see, traditional data collection techniques in dialectology are suited to the recording of lexical items (for use in both vocabulary and pronunciation studies), but present serious problems for the study of other linguistic areas. These techniques also do not exploit the full range of speakers' styles, and therefore are rejected in modern sociolinguistic investigations as described in the following chapter.

Selecting informants

Many dialectologists have seen their task as one of recording the old rural dialects before they die out. This attitude has coloured the dialectologist's view of which speakers to choose as informants. Naturally, informants had to originate in the rural area under study; but further, it was usually stipulated that they should have spent all, or the great majority, of their lives in the same area. This was laid down to avoid any "contamination" of the speaker's dialect through contact with speakers from other areas. However, "contamination" from educated forms of the language in question could pose a similar threat to the "purity" of the dialect concerned, so dialectologists would, where possible, select inform-ants who had received the minimum of formal education, as well as being untravelled.

Further requirements of the researchers meant that where possible informants were chosen from amongst the older inhabitants of the dialect area. For example, the *Survey of English Dialects* (referred to above) stipulated that informants should be at least 60, and many were consider-ably older. We have already mentioned the dialectologists' desire to describe the oldest forms of dialects which might be thought to be dying out. It naturally followed from this that informants from the oldest gener-ation were most likely still to retain these forms.

The final notable characteristic of subjects chosen in traditional dialectology concerns sex. The majority of informants chosen in most studies were male. Chambers & Trudgill (1980: 35) note that this decision was reached "because in the western nations women's speech tends to be more self-conscious and class-conscious than men's". Interestingly enough, this is one assertion that seems to have been confirmed empirically, in many cases, through sociolinguistic studies (see Chapter 3).

The main characteristics of subjects chosen as informants for dialect studies, then, are that they be non-mobile, old, rural males. The acronym NORMS has been coined from these characteristics (see Chambers & Trudg-ill, 1980: 33). However, the NORM is not representative of the speech of a dialect area as a whole. As Chambers & Trudgill point out, the greatest proportion of the population of Britain, for example, today is the opposite of the NORM: mobile, young, urban and female. Traditional dialectology has increasingly been seen as "linguistic archaeology" of little relevance to today's speakers. This lack of representativeness is indeed one of the reasons for the increasing lack of interest in this area, concomitant with a growth in popularity in sociolinguistic studies.

Data collection

Having selected informants, the dialectologist next needed to devise a method of collecting the dialect material. How this was done depended to some extent on what language areas were being investigated. Face-to-face interviews (latterly involving the use of tape recorders) were necessary if phonetic and phonological information were required. However, postal questionnaires could be utilized for lexical and grammatical surveys.

Whether live or postal, some kind of questionnaire was usually drawn up to ensure that all subjects were asked the same thing, thereby making the results strictly comparable. For lexical and phonological studies, questions leading to one word answers were adequate. For grammatical investigations, whole or part sentences would be required as answers.

Questions in a questionnaire could be either direct or indirect. Direct questioning involved using the standard word/pronunciation while asking the informant for the dialect version, e.g. "What do you call a haystack?" Eventually, this method was replaced by the indirect method to avoid any bias in the answers which the use of the standard form might create. Examples of indirect questions might include "What do you call this [picture of haystack]?", or "What do you call the thing you build out of cut hay?" Various types of indirect question were devised for the *SED*, and are described in detail in Chambers & Trudgill (1980: 25–26).

The disadvantage of indirect questioning is the length of time involved in completing the questionnaire. For example, the *SED* had a questionnaire of about 1,200 items, which generally took over 20 hours to complete. This led in turn to incomplete questionnaires, or examples where more than one informant was used to complete one questionnaire.

Another disadvantage of this approach was that it was generally monostylistic. Formal questioning, with little opportunity for informal chatting, leads to a generally formal style. The time restrictions naturally counted against any chance for the researcher to record instances of casual speech.

The replies given by informants were generally transcribed into the phonetic alphabet of the International Phonetic Association (IPA), except where no phonetic or phonological information was required, when ordinary orthography would be employed. In early dialect studies this transcription was done "live", later on transcription via tape recordings became the normal practice. As Chambers & Trudgill (1980) point out, the use of the tape recorder did not often in fact free dialectologists of the artificiality of the indirect question, as this part of the methodology appeared to have become too firmly entrenched.

Data analysis

As dialectology saw itself as investigating the geography of linguistics, mapping was an obvious way of displaying its results, and was in fact the most popular. Indeed, some dialect surveys (such as that in the United States) went under the name of "linguistic atlas" surveys.

Two main ways of plotting dialect information onto maps may be noted: direct and interpretative. The direct method shows, by means of symbols, the response given in each locality sampled, to one particular question on the questionnaire. This, of course, could involve the use of many symbols and be difficult to read easily. Interpretative maps attempted to alleviate this problem by grouping answers together into a small number of categories. For example, there might be two or three main answers (with their closely related variants) which could easily be illustrated as areas on a map with boundary-lines dividing the areas from each other. Lesser used or exceptional forms would be noted in footnotes only.

A development of these basic maps were ones designed to show major dialect boundaries. Boundary-lines on a map (known as *isoglosses*) link together the farthest locations where a particular form occurred. Where several isoglosses come together to form a *bundle*, we often find a major dialect boundary. Chambers & Trudgill (1980, Chapter 7) discuss dialect mapping in some detail, including the famous example of the Rhenish Fan. In Northern Germany, a bundle of isoglosses separated the Northern "Low German" dialect from the Southern "High German". These isoglosses however diverge markedly in the Rhine valley, so in this area the major dialect boundary collapses (see Figure 2.1).

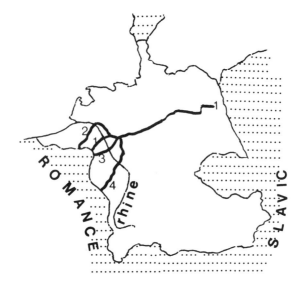

FIGURE 2.1   *The Rhenish Fan (after Bloomfield, 1933)*

Key: Isogloss 1, maken/maxen;
        Isogloss 2, ik/ix;
        Isogloss 3, dorp/dorf;
        Isogloss 4, dat/das,

First variant found north of each isogloss.

As noted earlier, dialectology came to prominence in the last quarter of the nineteenth century, and enjoyed great popularity with linguists for nearly a hundred years. However, as described in Chapter 3, interest in studying the complex patterns of urban speech, coupled with dissatisfaction with the methodology of dialectology, lead to the growth of sociolinguistics and the eclipse of dialect studies. The remainder of this chapter will examine the background to dialectology in Wales.

Dialectology in Wales

Early work

The first major piece of dialectological work in Wales is undoubtedly Sweet's (1884) comprehensive study of the Welsh of the Gwynant valley in Gwynedd. Sweet makes it clear in his introduction that the account following was drawn from his own fieldwork: "The following is a description of the sounds and forms of Welsh as spoken in the valley of Gwynant in Carnarvonshire, based on personal obsevations" (Sweet, 1884: 1). Unfortunately, little description is given of how his data were collected. He does state, however, that "every sentence here givn has been writn down directly from the mouths of the peple, and repeatedly revized" (Sweet, 1884: 43), which suggests live transcription of spontaneous speech. The texts themselves cover numerous topics, the majority appearing to be unprompted.

Sweet's work is self-contained, in that it is a complete description of a single dialect (indeed, it seems to have set the pattern for many such dialect monographs in Welsh dialectology). Many dialect studies, of course, have been concerned with delineating one dialect from another; pointing to similarities or differences between them. The nearest Sweet gets to this is the occasional comparison to literary Welsh that he includes. For example, he includes literary Welsh equivalents to his colloquial texts. Another example is that of mutations (see Chapters 1 and 7), where Sweet (1884: 24) notes, "the aspirate mutation of *m* and *n* are not admitted in the literary language, and again:

> "The laws of mutation are carried out with the same strictness in the dialect as in the literary language, and follow, in the main, the principles laid down in the grammars, tho there is divergence in detail". (Sweet, 1884: 25).

Following Sweet's work, the main trend in dialect studies was compiling vocabularies or collections of idioms peculiar to a particular area. Again, this is not part of the main tradition of dialectology described earlier in this chapter, but much of this work is of value in that it has recorded local forms of lexis that may well have died out by now.

The best known, and one of the earliest, of these studies was Fynes-Clinton's (1913) "Welsh Vocabulary of the Bangor District". In his preface, the author notes that "My aim in the present book has been to make an accurate record of the words in colloquial use in one clearly defined district in Wales" (p. i). He goes on to state that his vocabulary is not restricted to dialect words alone, but includes all the words noted in colloquial speech whether localized or not.

The book contains a lengthy introduction, giving much phonological and a little morphological information on the dialect. The remainder of the book is given over to the vocabulary. The words are written in a phonetic transcription, and the entries include not only meanings, but instances of usage.

Again, little information is given on data collection, though the author suggests in the description of his informants, that the obtaining of specialized vocabulary may have been accomplished through direct questioning. Four main informants were used, with several more friends and relatives of the author helping peripherally. It is somewhat sobering to realize that this book records the vocabulary of speakers born between 1835 and 1859.

In the same tradition as Fynes-Clinton, though undertaken in a less scholarly manner, are the slightly earlier works of Myrddin Bardd (1907), and Morris (1910). The former contains a list of dialect words, followed by a list of dialect idioms of Caernarvonshire. The latter (in English) is a dictionary of dialect words only from north Pembrokeshire. Again, little is mentioned on how the words were collected: Morris (1910: 8) states, "all the examples illustrative of the use of words have been taken down from the mouth of the people", though he does not note how many informants were used.

The first notable dialect study within the mainstream of dialectology is probably Sommerfelt (1925). This work is an investigation of the dialect of Cyfeiliog (in the Dyfi valley), and is subtitled "A Contribution to Welsh Dialectology". Sommerfelt notes the use of a questionnaire, though unfortunately does not reproduce it. He does, however, fully list his subjects. These numbered 14, of which only two were women. The average age of the subjects was 52, which is lower than in many dialect studies. However, out of the total, several informants were over 70, and only one was under 30.

The work is extremely comprehensive, covering the phonetics, phonology, morphology, syntax and lexis of the dialect. Sommerfelt also attempts to describe some of the non-linguistic factors which had contributed to the particular nature of the local dialect. He notes the geography of the area that had helped to keep it "a region set apart from its neighbours" (p. 2), but also social factors such as "the advent of the railway with its too slavish concomitant homage to things English" (p. 3). He also describes "the lively social life of the people [that] keeps the language strong. Prayer meetings are numerous and Welsh literary societies frequent" (p. 4).

Sommerfelt's work is also interesting in that it is one of the earliest to use any kind of instrumental phonetic devices. Included in the book are traces from a "Rousselot inscriptor". This device displays frequencies of the mouth air-flow and vocal cord vibrations. In subsequent studies the use of other instrumentation is sometimes seen.

Sommerfelt also includes a map of his district with the boundaries of two phonological features. His work was not primarily concerned with mapping features of Cyfeiliog Welsh, and indeed the boundaries are not derived from his own work. He included them primarily to show how Cyfeiliog fitted into the North, Mid, South divide of Welsh dialects. The boundaries are derived from work by Darlington (1902). His was one of the earliest attempts at 'mapping' dialect boundaries in Welsh (although his actual paper includes only verbal directions for the boundaries, not maps). Two of the important features he discusses (those taken up by Sommerfelt) are the /ɨ/ – /i/ boundary, and the [a] – [æ] boundary, see Figure 2.2 (see also this volume, Chapter 9).

The first of these is a north–south distinguisher. In north Welsh *u* and, in certain syllables, *y* are pronounced with a high central vowel /ɨ/. In South Welsh, these along with *i* are all pronounced /i/. Therefore, *tŷ*, 'house', and *ti*, 'thou, you', are contrasted in the north, but not in the south. Darlington established the boundary for this difference, at the turn of the century, to run from just north of Tywyn, south of Corris, up to Aberangell and across to Llanerfyl. Sommerfelt, in his area of study (which is south of this line) encountered some evidence of transitional forms. It has been suggested (Sommerfelt, 1925; Ball, 1976, etc.) that this boundary is likely to be moving further north, as the southern form gains ground.

The second boundary marks off an area of Mid Wales where *â* is pronounced as a raised and fronted [æ] instead of the usual northern and southern [a]. The northern boundary for this in Darlington's day was reckoned to run from just north of Harlech, north of Trawsfynydd, then south of Bala, and along the Berwyn mountains. The southern boundary starts north of Aberystwyth, then south at Plynlymon and south of Llangurig. It seems likely that the area of this feature has also been contracting.

If Darlington's work was the beginning of dialect mapping in Welsh, little more work was done in this field until A. R. Thomas published his *Linguistic Geography of Wales* (1973). This is discussed further below (and see Chapter 4). However, studies of individual dialects continued apace, usually in the form of theses presented to the University of Wales for higher degrees. These are discussed in the following section.

Later work

More recent work in Welsh dialectology is divided between that concerned with describing the dialect situation of Wales as a whole, and

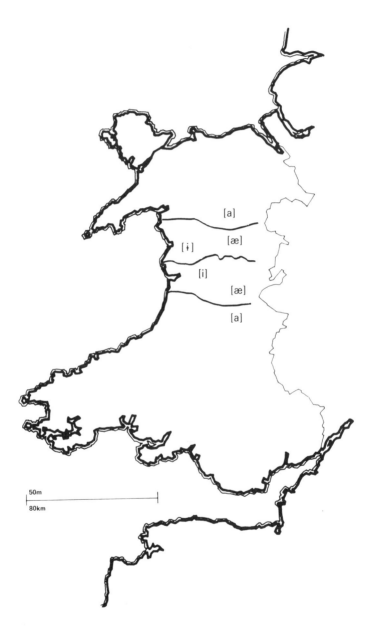

FIGURE 2.2   *Darlington's boundaries*

studies of individual dialects in depth. We will consider these two approaches in turn.

The dialects of Wales

The traditional view of the dialectal divisions of Welsh can be found, for example, in Morris-Jones (1913). He states (p. 8):

The spoken language has four main dialects as follows:

(1) Venedotian, the dialect of Gwynedd or North-west Wales (Gwynedd dialect).
(2) Powysian, the dialect of Powys, or North-east Wales. (Powys dialect).
(3) Demetian, the dialect of Dyfed or South-west Wales.
(4) Gwentian, the dialect of Gwent and Morgannwg, or South-east Wales.

These four areas are shown in Figure 2.3.
Not all authors have used these terms; for example, Sir John Rhys (quoted in Thomas, 1973) substitutes *Ordovic* for Powysian, and *Silurian* for Gwentian.

As noted above, Darlington was one of the first to conduct work on dialect boundaries in Wales. However, interest in dialect areas predates his work. Sir John Rhys, working in the last quarter of the nineteenth century, drew a map to illustrate his main areas (see A. R. Thomas, 1973: iv, and Figure 2.3), though it is doubtful whether this was based on anything more than casual observation and traditional, historical views of dialect areas.

Thorne (1984) discusses in detail some of the work of scholars in the first decades of this century who attempted to correlate dialect boundaries and medieval administrative boundaries. He presents more recent evidence for various parts of Wales, some of it based on his own in-depth research in south-west Wales.

However, despite this work, no-one had attempted for Wales the sort of linguistic atlas study that we have seen were conducted elsewhere. The desirability for such a study was discussed by Watkins (1955). He noted that an initial attempt to undertake such a survey had been started by the Guild of Graduates of the University of Wales at the beginning of the century, and he references the various publications that came out of this work. The final report appeared in 1935, though little work was in fact done after 1910.

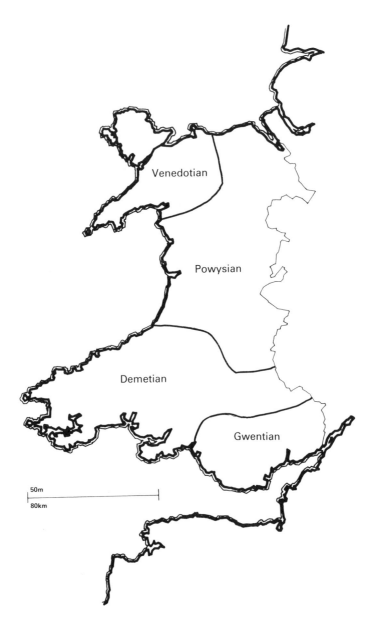

FIGURE 2.3   *Morris-Jones' dialect areas*

Watkins describes a proposed survey, using traditional dialectology methods. He describes his proposal as being based to some extent on the *SED* and on the Breton atlas (Le Roux, 1924). Interestingly enough, Watkins' questionnaire contained questions framed in Welsh alone. This was done to avoid the formality that might be engendered by translating from English: "when the informant was asked to translate, the examination-like atmosphere created tended to make the informant (in spite of himself) give us standard forms in reply" (Watkins, 1955: 41).

The plans proposed by Watkins never came to fruition, but re-emerged in a slightly different form in the work of A. R. Thomas (1973). This major work — *The Linguistic Geography of Wales* — is described in more detail in Chapter 4, but we can briefly describe aspects of the work here. Thomas' aims are described as follows:

"to assemble detailed information on the distribution of well over a thousand Welsh dialect forms; and, on the basis of that information, to illustrate the major speech areas which emerge." (A. R. Thomas, 1973: ix).

The survey is mainly lexical, though some morphological and phonological variables are also included.

In the questionnaire used for this survey, translating from English *was* employed. Thomas does not discuss the dangers of formality through this usage. He does note the possibility that it might cause an overuse of English loan words, though finds that this does not in fact occur.

Interestingly, the major speech areas which Thomas describes do not always concur with the traditional areas described above. He finds (A. R. Thomas, 1973: 14) three overall areas (north, midlands and south), each divisible into east and west (see Figure 2.4). Below these (p. 15) 16 minor speech areas can also be identified.

Since the publication of his *Linguistic Geography*, Thomas has published much work on how his dialect material can be mapped, particularly using computer analysis. This work is reported in A. R. Thomas (1975; 1977; 1978 and 1980).

Dialect monographs

As noted above, many of the single dialect studies of Welsh have been presented as theses for higher degrees of the University of Wales. Naturally, smaller studies of certain aspects of various dialects have appeared in academic journals, or edited collections (see for example Ball

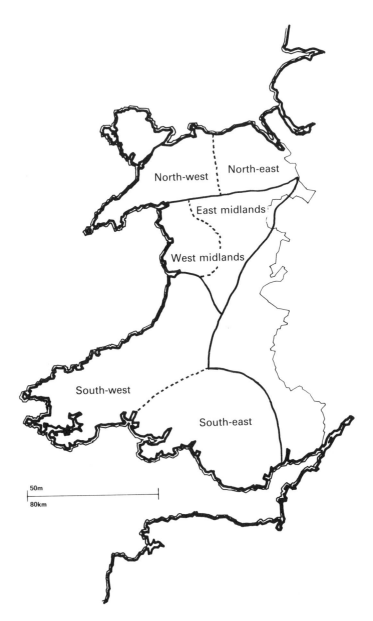

FIGURE 2.4   *Thomas' dialect areas*

& Jones, 1984). The most useful journals for the researcher in this area are *The Bulletin of the Board of Celtic Studies, Cardiff Working Papers in Welsh Linguistics*, and *Studia Celtica*.

One of the earliest of the theses is that by Angharad Morris-Jones (1926), daughter of the eminent Celticist John Morris-Jones. Her thesis was a study of Anglesey Welsh (an area since much neglected). The most influential study of this early period was J. J. Glanmor Davies' (1934) study of the Welsh of Ceinewydd (New Quay) in Ceredigion. This included phonetic, phonological, grammatical and lexical information. Some early phonetic instrumentation was employed in this study. A particularly valuable aspect of this study is noted by Watkins (1961: 231) "a large number of technical terms were taken into Welsh, coined for the purpose of scientific theses on phonetics".[1]

A complete list of all the monographs on Welsh dialects that appeared before the Ceinewydd study is found in T. Jones (1934). Awbery (1982) lists those undertaken after this date. Below I include a list of the most important dialect theses since 1934, and these are also plotted on a map (see Figure 2.5). They are listed in alphabetical order of author.

(1)   Bevan (1971): Vale of Glamorgan
(2)   E. J. Davies (1955): Llandygwydd and Dihewyd (Ceredigion)
(3)   J. J. G. Davies (1934): Ceinewydd
(4)   L. Davies (1969): Merthyr Tudful
(5)   Griffiths (1975): Llanfair Caereinion
(6)   G. D. Jones (1962): Rhosllanerchrugog
(7)   G. E. Jones (1983): Brycheiniog
(8)   R. O. Jones (1967): Ty Ddewi, Dyffryn Nantlle & Llanfachreth
(9)   R. O. Jones (1983): Patagonia
(10) Lewis (1960): North East Ceredigion
(11) Middleton (1965): Tafarnau Bach
(12) Phillips (1955): Dyffryn Elái
(13) E. Rees (1958): Dyffryn Llwchwr
(14) R. Rees (1936): Dyffryn Aman
(15) A. Roberts (1973): Pwllheli
(16) Ruddock (1969): Hirwaun
(17) Samuel (1971): Y Rhigos
(18) A. Thomas (1958): Dyffryn Wysg
(19) C. Thomas (1961): Nantgarw
(20) Thorne (1971): Llangennech
(21) Thorne (1977b): Carnwyllion
(22) Watkins (1951): Llansamlet

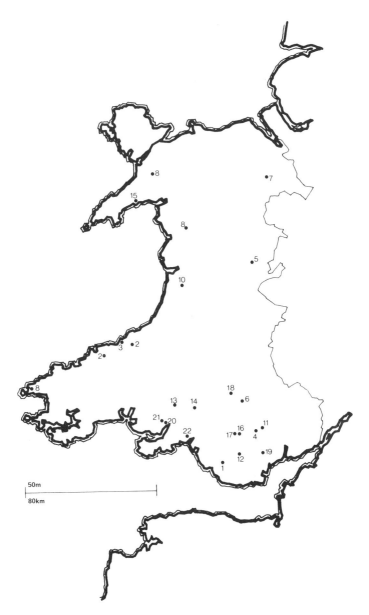

FIGURE 2.5   *Location of studies since 1934*

As can be seen from Figure 2.5, work in north Wales is surprisingly sparse.

Conclusion

Dialectology, as a form of linguistic archaeology, is clearly of value in rescuing localized forms on the verge of dying out. In its traditional form it does not, however, give a comprehensive picture of the linguistic repertoires of an entire speech community. The next chapter, on sociolinguistics, will describe the attempt of linguists to go beyond these limitations.

Notes to Chapter 2

1. In the original: "daeth llu to eiriau technegol i'r Gymraeg wedi'u bathu at bwrpas trafodaethau gwyddonol mewn seineg".

3 Accounting for linguistic variation: Sociolinguistics

MARTIN J. BALL

How can we account for the variable usage of linguistic features within linguistic theory? Do our present grammatical theories permit us to describe features that may or may not be present for no apparent linguistic reason?

Up until the mid-1960s the theoretical explanation most usually provided by linguists for phenomena of variability was the notion of *free variation*. Described by Lyons (1968: 73) as follows, "Units which occur, but are not in contrast with one another, in a given context are in free variation", free variation implies that there is in fact no reason why a choice is made by a speaker to use one variant rather than another out of the total range of variants of a form within that speaker's repertoire. It might be considered that this notion is just another way of saying it is not known why such a choice is made. Fischer (1958) attacks this label in very much the same terms.

Variation in terms of regionally differentiated forms of a language had of course been studied for a long time, under the name of *dialectology* (see Chapter 2). However the interests of dialectologists were concerned mostly with the description of a homogeneous dialect and in describing its geographical aspects (the plotting of isoglosses, etc), and the problem of variable usage by speakers of the dialect itself did not receive a lot of attention, although it was recognized: Gleason (1961: 406) notes, "In any given area, it is possible to recognize and describe a system of SOCIAL DIALECTS. . . there are also differences in LEVELS OF SPEECH [= situationally conditioned variation]". However, although recognized, little descriptive work has been carried out. As Petyt (1980: 108) observes, "Until quite recently, when faced with variation, linguists. . . have simply ignored it. . . [or] the term free variation has been applied".

An advance in the accounting for the problem of variability (against the background of a long tradition of a theoretical linguistics hostile to the notion of heterogeneity) was through the notion of the use of differing systems by speakers. It was not however implied that variation was due to casual, *ad hoc* borrowing from a different dialect. D. Jones (1950) proposed the concept of the *diaphone*, which was considered to be a group of phonetic variants all in a non-contrastive relationship, yet not in complementary distribution. This was a grouping then that could account for a number of variant forms in a particular language, including forms that seemed to differ regionally (e.g. /əʊ/ in received pronunciation (R.P.) compared with /o:/ in Scots) or socially (e.g. /h/ in higher class speech compared with zero in lower in many areas) (D. Jones, 1950: 195–98).

From the concept of the diaphone was worked out the notion of the co-existent system or *diasystem*, although this was also suggested to some extent by Bloch (1948) and Fries & Pike (1949). The first person to set out the theory was Weinreich (1953, 1954) — and this approach to variability has become known as *structural dialectology*. It was proposed that speakers had command over more than one system (that two or more systems were co-existent) and that these systems could be equated with regional factors. This was to account for both productive and receptive abilities of speakers. Most of the work done concerned phonology, though Weinreich claimed (1954: 310ff) that it would be equally applicable to lexis and grammar. Variation is then accounted for as the use of one or other of the co-existent systems, and presumably the occasional borrowing of certain items from one system when the other happens to be in use.

The theory relied a lot on the novelty of its schematic display of the relationships between systems, but as Chambers & Trudgill (1980: 45) point out, the theory could "handle inventory differences succssfully, but it can deal with incidence and distribution differences only with difficulty". Furthermore, the theory is mainly concerned with variation as seen by traditional dialectologists, that is regional variation, and has little to say in respect of defining the various systems: there is not a great deal said on the effect of other non-linguistic variables on the choice of a particular form. Weinreich (1954: 317) only briefly notes, "In the domain of dialect sociology, . . . the use of extra-linguistic correlations and statistical sampling techniques offers promising possibilities of research in an almost untrodden field". To include such information, it can be argued, would so increase the number of systems required to be in a co-existent state, as to prove completely unworkable.

Although structural dialectology presented some new insights it was nevertheless part of the dialectology tradition, and as Dittmar (1976: 116) points out, dialectology suffers from three main weaknesses:

"(1) It was limited to phonology and grammar.
(2) Linguistic variation was related only to geographical conditions. . .; finally, even dialectologists became increasingly aware that speech variation is a result of the processes of interaction of a series of factors. . . other than geography.
(3) Dialectology was unable to develop a comprehensive theory capable of explaining speech variation."

The growing awareness noted above of non-geographical factors influencing language variation was the impetus to the development of sociolinguistics described in the next section.

Since its early development this field has proved of enormous interest to many linguists, so much so that a look through the literature might suggest the necessity for the institution of a prize for the best book entitled *Sociolinguistics* (e.g. Fishman, 1970; Pride & Holmes, 1972; Trudgill, 1974a; Bell, 1976; Dittmar, 1976; Hudson, 1980). Also, sociolinguistics covers a wide area of linguistic interest (the relations between language and culture; speech as social interaction; language and social inequality, *viz.* Hudson, 1980) not all of which are of direct relevance to the study of variability in Welsh. It is not proposed therefore that this chapter should be a complete review of all work undertaken under the heading of sociolinguistics, this being both impractical and unnecessary. Nor is it intended to look at the attempts to provide theoretical accounts of variability that are basically outside mainstream sociolinguistic approaches (e.g. generative dialectology, polylectal grammars; see Chambers & Trudgill, 1980). Rather, those areas of especial importance for this book will be examined, including the development of sociolinguistics, some important concepts, and the methodology used in sociolinguistic investigations.

It is not intended to include in this chapter a review of any of the ways in which sociolinguists have attempted to account for their findings formally, within the framework of a theory of grammar, as this will be dealt with in Chapter 20.

The development of sociolinguistics

It is generally recognized that the term *sociolinguistics* was coined by Currie (1952) in an article exploring the relationship of speech to social status, which is of course still one of the main aims of the field. Currie's paper does not present any new data, but is basically a discussion of how some of the trends then present in linguistics, especially in dialectology, could be developed into a new field of investigation. Currie concludes that his paper "has emphasized the persisting interest in the relationship of oral English and social status. . . Specifically, a field for quite conscious study here called socio-linguistics has been envisioned. . ." (p. 47).

Currie had correctly noted a trend in American dialectology where, unlike Europe, work was not restricted to rural areas. It may be that the urban situation prompted more forcefully the realization of the importance of social factors. However this may be, McDavid (1948) published a study of postvocalic-r usage in South Carolina, that contained information on social differences. At the time this was not seen as an end in itself: he comments, "A social analysis proved necessary because the data proved too complicated to be explained by merely a geographical statement. . ." (reported in Petyt, 1980:133). This clearly implies that at this stage the social analysis was not the primary impetus behind the study, but this attitude gradually changed over the following 15 years or so.

In the mid-1950s attacks on the traditional methods of dialectology were being made by sociologists who had developed a refined methodology for sampling and investigating communities. Pickford (1956) particularly pointed out the use such a methodology would be to dialectologists, criticizing their current findings on grounds of lacking reliability and validity.

As reported in Petyt (1980), studies of urban communities became more frequent, including Putnam & O'Hern (1955) who investigated black speech in Washington; De Camp (1958–9) who worked in San Francisco; and Levine & Crockett (1967) on North Carolina speech. This last study was conducted earlier than the publication date suggests, and showed considerable methodological advances over previous studies. Sampling and fieldwork techniques were much more rigorously designed, bearing in mind the contributions of sociology, and laying down the framework for many future studies. As noted in Petyt (1980: 136), Levine & Crockett found considerable variation in the use of postvocalic-r in North Carolina, and were able to correlate this variation with both linguistic and social factors — something that became a major concern in sociolinguistics.

Another important paper of this period was Fischer (1958). As noted above, he criticized the term free variation as an explanation of variation in language. He concluded that many examples of what was then generally termed as free variation were in fact "socially conditioned variants" (p. 51).

Sociolinguistics came to a much greater degree of prominence (and subsequently, popularity) within linguistics with the work of Labov in the mid-1960s. The work on Martha's Vinyard (1963), and New York (1966a) developed and refined methodology and analysis, and laid the foundations for the explosion of work in this field. Many of the concepts and techniques developed by Labov will be discussed in the remaining sections of this chapter, although there will be no description of the studies themselves (see Labov, 1972a, for further details of these studies).

Concepts of sociolinguistics

Variability

This section will examine some of the main sociolinguistic concepts, especially those of relevance to this study. Firstly, one of the most basic concepts underlying sociolinguistics will be considered: variability or heterogeneity. Any linguist with reasonable powers of observation will note that language is variable, in that different speakers may use different varieties of a language, and that individual speakers may vary particular forms from moment to moment. In other words variability is both inter- and intra-idiolectal (taking idiolect here to be that form of a language spoken by a particular individual, cf. Bell, 1976: 35–36).

However, although variability should be clear to linguists, for most of the history of modern linguistics "linguists have tended to act as if language were not variable" (Chambers & Trudgill, 1980: 145). To some extent this is understandable, for as Bell (1976: 19) notes, language can be seen both as "a highly structured and abstract system. . . and at the same time prone to capricious idiosyncrasy". The tendency among linguists has been until recently to concentrate on describing the homogeneous abstract, structured aspects of language, and as noted above, to assign variability to free variation, or indeed to ignore it altogether.

A major problem with this approach was in the area of data collection. If one attempts to describe an abstract, idealized form of language (the *langue* of Saussure), one has only the data collected in real-life language situations complete with its inherent variability (i.e. the *parole* of Saussure). This is of course one of the reasons why Chomsky (1957) abandoned the structuralist discovery procedures.

Despite this problem, linguists have been urged to avoid the problems posed by variability, rather than to attempt to answer them. For example, Hockett (1958: 1) urges his readers to exclude "variations of. . . pattern from individual to individual, or from group to group, within a speech community"; and Gleason (1955: 391) asks us to "eliminate certain types of variation of minor interest. . . by restricting attention. . . to utterances produced by one speaker under a single set of circumstances". Finally, Harris (1951: 11) notes that we can assume that "all styles within a dialect may be roughly described by a single structural system".

This approach to variability in language is often termed homogeneous (*viz*. Chambers & Trudgill, 1980: 145), and the major change of approach provided by sociolinguistics is arguably the change of focus of linguistics towards heterogeneity or variability: the necessity for accounting for variation in linguistic description. As Dittmar (1976: 106–7) notes, "Speech communities are. . . rarely homogeneous. In most cases they are composed of varieties which are connected with the speech community as a whole by a number of shared social norms".[1] Dittmar further notes a classification of varieties (a neutral term adopted by many sociolinguists in preference to dialect or accent, etc.) into four main groups (p. 107):

"(1) Standard variety,
(2) regional variety,
(3) social variety, and
(4) functional variety."

Of these, regional variation, under the heading of dialectology had of course received much attention from linguistics, but as noted above, only in terms of homogeneous dialects, ignoring the possibility of inter-dialectal variation. It was left to sociolinguistics to explore fully these different varieties and the relationships between them.

Variables

With the recognition of variability as an aspect of language needing to be described came the problem of adequate linguistic constructs and terminology with which to attempt this. As variation can occur on different linguistic levels (phonetic, phonological, morphological, syntactic and presumably semantic) a construct was developed that was independent of previous terminology that might have been overly associated with one particular level (e.g. diaphone).

The term *linguistic variable* was first used by Labov (1963), and described by him as "a linguistic feature with. . . [a] range of variation" (Labov, 1972a: 7); implying by this a feature that may be realized in a number of different ways while preserving the same meaning. Hudson (1980: 157) points out the difficulties involved in attempting a rigorous definition of the term ("it is hard to be clear about what counts as the same meaning"), concluding that as the variable is simply one of the sociolinguist's tools, a precise definition is unnecessary.

Labov also introduced the practice of enclosing variables in round brackets, to distinguish them from phonemes or morphemes; he notes: "the parentheses indicate a different approach to the analysis of variation. Whereas / / means that internal variation is to be disregarded as insignificant, ( ) indicates that this variation is the prime focus of the study" (Labov, 1972a: 11). Any linguistic variable has of course at least two realizations (often many more), and following Labov (1963) these realizations have come to be termed *variants*.

In some instances the definition of the variants is a simple matter. For example, Labov's (1966a) study included the variable (r) (= postvocalic-r). This had only two possible variants: [r], or zero (Labov, 1972a: 73). However variability in vowel realizations is much more difficult to characterize in terms of variants. Usually a number of approximate phonetic qualities are established as variants, and actual occurrences matched to the nearest variant. For example, in the same 1966 study, Labov established a variable (eh) consisting of five separate variants.

Using variables, consisting of variants, scores can be worked out for individual informants, and then for specific groups of informants. Usually a numerical value is assigned to each variant and average scores established for each variable, though researchers differ in exactly how these averages are calculated (cf. Labov, 1966a; Milroy, 1980; or Romaine, 1981).[2] As Trudgill (1974b: 90) points out:

"By means of these scores we are able: (i) to investigate the nature of correlation between realizations of phonological variables and social class; social context and sex; (ii) to discover which variables are subject to social class differentiation and which to stylistic variation; and (iii) to find out which variables are most important in signalling the social context of some linguistic interaction, or the social class of a speaker."

This last comment implies that not all variables have the same social significance, and this will be examined further below.

Before leaving the topic of the variable, it is necessary to examine the non-linguistic or social variable. The term *social variable* is also to be found in Labov (*viz*. Labov, 1972a: 26), though in other works non-linguistic factors may be termed *social phenomena* or *social parameters* (Trudgill, 1974b); *influences on linguistic variables* (Hudson, 1980); *social differences* (Petyt, 1980); or *extra-linguistic variable* (Milroy, 1980). Chambers & Trudgill (1980: 60) however use the term social variable.

The social variable is basically any non-linguistic feature having at least two sub-divisions or categories, that might be found to have a correlation with the use of a particular linguistic variable. For example, if the sex of a speaker is found to have a positive correlation with the choice of a particular variant of a linguistic variable, then sex would be classifiable as a social variable in that instance.

Among social variables that have been investigated are social class membership; regional background; sex of speaker; age of speaker; context of utterance (style); group identity of speaker; though others could of course be incorporated. Below we will be discussing patterns of correlations that have been found between these social and linguistic variables.

The correlation of linguistic and social variables has been one of the main areas of study within sociolinguistics. However, this type of "correlational sociolinguistics" is not without its critics among sociolinguists. Deuchar (1983) for example notes that group-orientated social variables do not always account for data gathered in sociolinguistic studies.

Types of variable

As noted above, it has been found that linguistic variables behave in different ways in relation to social variables. Bell (1976: 33) shows in diagrammatic form these different types: linguistic variables which correlate with social stratification, but not with style shifting are termed *indicators*; while those which correlate with social stratification and style shifting are termed *markers*. Finally, those which correlate only with style shifting are termed *stereotypes*. (These terms were first coined by Labov, 1963; 1966a.)

These differences imply that different linguistic variables have different statuses in the consciousness of speakers. As Chambers & Trudgill (1980: 84) remark, "Speakers appear to be less aware of. . . an indicator than they are of. . . a marker". They go on to suggest that an indicator is a fairly stable feature, while many markers seem to be taking part in linguistic change, termed change from below (i.e. from "below the level of conscious awareness" (Chambers & Trudgill 1980: 88)). The stereotype however is a variety which is consciously known about, and often stigmatized or ridiculed by speakers, and so is being used less often — partaking therefore in change from above the level of conscious awareness (p. 88).

Speech community

There has been much debate about the definition of the term *speech community*, and this debate has its implications for the study to be undertaken. The concept of the speech community is not restricted to sociolinguistics, though it has felt to be particularly important in this area, rather it is a term first used by structuralists. Bloomfield (1933: 42) defined the term as follows, "A speech community is a group of people who interact by speech". Limitations to this definition which imply that speech communities share a common language are found in Hockett (1958: 8) and Lyons (1970: 326); but Gumperz (working broadly within a sociolinguistic framework) felt that speech communities could be monolingual or multilingual (1962). His definition of the term (1968: 381) states:

> "The speech community: any human aggregate characterized by regular and frequent interaction by means of a shared body of verbal signs and set off from similar aggregates by significant differences in language use."

Labov (1972a) slightly alters the emphasis in his definition from shared linguistic behaviour to shared attitudes to language (viz. Hudson, 1980: 27):

> "The speech community is not defined by any marked agreement in the use of language elements, so much as by participation in a set of shared norms . . . observed in overt types of evaluative behavior, and by the uniformity of abstract patterns of variation which are invariant in respect to particular levels of usage." (Labov, 1972a: 120–21).

As Hudson (1980: 27) notes, "This kind of definition puts emphasis on the speech community as a group of people who feel themselves to be a community in some sense, rather than a group only the linguist . . . could know about". And he notes similar definitions in Hymes (1972) and Halliday (1972).[3]

Labov's work led to the use of variable rules (see Chapter 20 below) as a descriptive device in what he terms a community grammar (1972a: 247). The speech community shares both variable rules and norms for using them. As Romaine (1980: 47) notes, Labov's theory concerns "speech communities where all the social groups use the variable in the same way, though not necessarily to the same extent". Romaine attacks this viewpoint pointing out that the data does not always support the idea of an entire speech community using variables in the same way. "Some . . . data show clear interactions between social and linguistic constraints from individual to individual and group to group" (p. 48). Indeed she claims that if linguistic change is to take place within a speech community, there must be times when the community "does not share the same constraints on the application of a rule" (p. 48). Deuchar (1983) shares these doubts, and refers to Cheshire's (1982) study of Reading adolescents.

Romaine's conclusion is that it is not necessary to alter the Labovian definition of speech community radically, but that:

"Speech communities share a socially based organisation of linguistic means which is not necessarily cast in the highly restricted form of variable rules." (Romaine, 1980: 53).

Romaine also notes the term *social network*, which she defines as "a level of abstraction below the speech community" (p. 53), and this concept has been used extensively in recent studies (viz. Milroy, 1980). The social network focuses on the individual within a speech community; the network being the links between that individual and other people with whom he is in contact (i.e. socially, through work, family or neighbourhood association, etc.). High-density networks are those where many of the individual's associates also know each other (i.e. form networks with each other); whereas low-density networks are those where most of the individual's associates do not know each other (viz. Milroy, 1980).

Differences in approach to the speech community may seem disturbing — as it could be felt that agreement would be vital on so basic a concept as the people and their language to be studied. As Hudson (1980: 28) points out, to some extent all the definitions are correct — it is just the sets of people who differ. The importance of this for sociolinguistic studies is that a clear definition must be given by the researcher of what he means by speech community.

The importance of social networks should also be noted, as these smaller groups would appear to be particularly useful in studying speakers of a minority language, as Milroy found them in studying small communities of working-class speakers in Belfast.

Sociolinguistic methodology

Choice of community

This section will briefly discuss some of the methodology used in sociolinguistic studies. Such methodology involves identifying the speech community to be studied; choosing the linguistic and social variables to be concentrated on; choosing a representative sample of subjects; designing a data collection procedure (e.g. interview); analysing the data collected; and finally presenting the results showing what correlations exist, if any, between the social and linguistic variables.

The problem of defining speech community has just been discussed, but the criteria behind the choice of a particular speech community to study by a researcher is of course different, and largely a matter of personal preference. Interest in a particular area, or linguistic problem, together with some initial observations, will lead a researcher to posit certain hypotheses about the relation of linguistic and non-linguistic factors which can best (or only) be tested within a particular speech community. Again, the particular linguistic variables to be studied will be included on the basis of the researcher's own initial observations or pilot study, and also possibly previous studies. The same is true to some extent on the choice of social variables, although it is easy here to extend social variables beyond what has been already observed, simply through the subjects chosen and the design of the interview.

Choice of subjects

The choice of subjects is one area where modern sociolinguists differ clearly from traditional dialectologists. Criticisms of the methodology of dialectology are noted above, and their concentration on old, rural speakers was rejected by sociolinguists in favour of random sampling — a technique already in use by sociologists. A random sample of names from an electoral register (or similar list) is chosen to ensure representativeness. It has been shown statistically (Goode & Hatt, 1952; Moser, 1958) that a sufficiently large sample should ensure representatives from the major social class and age groups etc. It has also been shown (Labov, 1966a) that the sample will not be disturbed by the small number of refusals to participate that is usual. Numerous studies have been carried out using this technique, see for example Labov (1966a), Trudgill (1974b), and of specific Welsh interest, R. O. Jones (1976).

However, random sampling does have its drawbacks. As Milroy (1980: 41) points out, "The population to be studied is usually sampled for isolated individuals . . . who are then recorded out of context of the social networks within which they customarily interact". She goes on to note that a fieldworker's visit is unlikely to produce a large part of the speaker's linguistic repertoire, so "the data obtained are often very sharply limited in their capacity to represent a wide range of speech styles". For this reason, the use of the concept of social network is proposed as a method of choosing subjects, together with the recording of group situations in order to obtain the maximum range of styles.

Manipulating style

The access to different styles is particularly important for the sociolinguist — especially access to the vernacular. As Labov (1972a: 208) comments, the vernacular is the style in which minimum attention is given to the monitoring of speech. "Observation of the vernacular gives us the most systematic data for our analysis of linguistic structure". Milroy (1980: 23) also notes:

> "If information is available only on more careful styles, data may . . . be seriously incomplete so that any description . . . may be quite inadequate."

However, the major problem facing the sociolinguist seeking access to the vernacular is the *observer's paradox*. Labov (1972a: 209) describes this problem as follows:

> "We are then left with the Observer's Paradox: the aim of linguistic research in the community must be to find out how people talk when they are not being systematically observed; yet we can only obtain these data by systematic observation."

To answer this problem attempts have been made to ensure this particular, most informal style can be elicited in interviews. As noted above, Milroy and others (e.g. Blom & Gumperz, 1972) prefer group interview situations. However, the classical Labovian technique divides the individual interview into separate degrees of formality to produce differing styles.

The question-and-answer part of the interview is felt to be formal, producing a formal style. This formality can be progressively increased by the following techniques: the subject reading a prose passage, a list of words, and a list of minimal pairs (where a pair of words differ only in one of the linguistic variables in question).

To obtain casual or vernacular speech involves the asking of questions designed to make the speaker forget the interview situation (e.g. "Were you ever in danger of being killed?" "Have you ever been in a very humorous situation?", etc.). Also, interruptions from a friend or relative, or conversations before the interview officially starts, or after it ends can produce a casual style (see Labov, 1972a: 85ff).

However, as Labov (1972a: 95) notes, it is necessary to check that casual speech has been obtained in these instances, not just formal interview style. He proposes that channel cues will provide this information:

"A change in tempo, a change in pitch range, a change in volume or rate of breathing, form socially significant signs of shift towards a more spontaneous or more casual style of speech."

However, Milroy (1980: 26) notes that not all researchers have found these classical Labovian techniques able to produce casual speech, ". . . the interaction between language and situation is too complex and too little understood for any interviewer to be able to manipulate it reliably" (see also Wolfram & Fasold, 1974: 85 for similar comments). It has also to be acknowledged that to use channel cues to define casual speech is to some extent a circular definition, as the channel cues themselves are described as being characteristics of casual speech. It should also be noted that in later work Labov himself (e.g. Labov, Cohen, Robins & Lewis, 1968) used other methods including group interviews to elicit casual speech.

This is still an ongoing debate, but it will be clearly necessary to consider carefully how to elicit casual speech from informants.

Analysis of data

The material collected by tape-recording from interviews needs to be transcribed, in narrow phonetic transcription if phonological variables are involved. Then the analysis proceeds by noting which variant is used in which situation for all the variables and for all the speakers. The raw data are subjected to statistical analyses if necessary, the results of which will support or otherwise hypotheses about the correlation of linguistic and social variables.

There is some debate as to the validity of simply grouping individual scores together into social groups, or age groups etc., ignoring individual differences. (Cf. Labov, 1972a: 124 with Milroy, 1980: 133, and Romaine, 1981: 102–3. For general discussion see Hudson, 1980: p. 163ff.) Milroy (1980) concludes that examining the data from both standpoints will be profitable, though in some of Labov's studies only grouped results are given. To some extent this also reflects Milroy's use of the social network with its emphasis on networks of individuals.

We have already mentioned that by analysing results linguistic variables have been seen as being indicators, markers or stereotypes. The results will also be able to tell us about the status of social variables. At different times, in different places, different social variables may be seen as having greater or lesser effect, particularly in the area of innovating sound changes. Chambers & Trudgill (1980: 167) note:

"Very often, several of the independent variables combine to identify the innovating group [of speakers] but occasionally, . . . one of the variables clearly takes precedence over all the others. . ."

They then go on to discuss three such examples: class-based, sex-based and age-based.

Studies have shown that the different social variables often do correlate with the choice of linguistic variant (see Labov, 1963; 1966a; Trudgill, 1974b; etc.). The choice of linguistic variant may be governed by social class membership — the higher up the class ladder you are, the more likely are you to be influenced by a standard or prestige linguistic form to produce a variant like that form, or to produce that form more often.

The sex of the speaker often has a role to play, with women appearing more influenced than men by prestige forms. Style or context of utterance has been shown to affect certain linguistic variables: the standard form being used more often in formal situations. Group membership is also sometimes important. As Labov (1963) showed, non-standard forms are often maintained to show group solidarity against outsiders, and this might also explain why some groups of male speakers use more non-standard forms than equivalent groups of women.

Indeed it might be maintained that all these social variables show a dichotomy between the forces of status (making us change towards a standard or prestige variety), and solidarity (making us maintain or move towards non-standard varieties, marking us out as separate).

No detail is given here on how scores for individual variables are worked out, nor the different ways in which results can be displayed (showing up features such as hypercorrection, or the so-called S-curve). These will be found discussed in many of the chapters following.

Conclusions

The purpose of this chapter has been to show that the variation in linguistic usage can be studied in a principled way within linguistics. It will of course be necessary to adapt the concepts and procedures described in this chapter to the particular linguistic character of the Welsh speech community, and this will be dealt with in the following chapters.

Notes to Chapter 3

1. For more discussion of this topic see Weinreich, Labov & Herzog (1968).
2. Criticisms of this scoring method are found in Hudson (1980: 162).
3. See also Labov (1972a: 248, note 40).

Part II:
Variation and Levels
of Language

4 Studying lexical geography

ALAN R. THOMAS

The study of lexical geography is probably the oldest branch of dialectology, and in Wales there has been long-standing interest in recording "different words for the same thing". This has looked pretty well exclusively for differences of usage between geographical regions, which have been regarded as being more evident than those between social classes (though not proven to be so). The first organized attempt to collate a representative archive of regional variants in Welsh dialects was that of the Guild of Graduates of the University of Wales, with listings of regional forms recorded in NLW Mss 2473 and in the Guild's *Proceedings* in the first decade of this century. Useful though these listings are, they lack the one essential element of geographical dialectology — strict comparability of their data.

Comparability

Surveys of geographical variation in lexical usage are, by definition, studies on the macro-level, gathering a limited amount of data from an extensive network of localities. Since the aim of the researcher is to collect regional words for the same items from all localities as far as possible (to maximize comparability of the linguistic data), it follows that the localities themselves will need to be essentially of the same character, in terms of their cultural and commercial make-up. For studies of Welsh, this requirement is best met by setting up a network of rural localities, since even in the industrial south-east, indigenous speakers of the language are found mainly in the valley villages, rather than in the conurbations. For a survey carried out in the 1960s, and reported in A. R. Thomas (1973; 1980), the geographical disposition of the locations used are shown on Figure 4.1.

An essential means of ensuring comparability in the linguistic data collected is the compiling of a questionnaire to be administered at every

41

locality. Responses to precisely the same questions are recorded at every one. Variation is found in all fields of vocabulary, and in general there will be some word for any given item in all parts of the country, as with, for example,

> worktools: N(orthern) *cribyn*, s(outhern) *rhaca*, "rake";
> family relations: N *taid*, s *tadcu*, "grandfather";
> grammatical words: N *allan*, s *mâs*, "out".

The words for such items as these form the bulk of lexical variation in Welsh by today, but our information on its geographical patterning can be reinforced by gleaning information from an area of vocabulary which now contains a large proportion of archaic, obsolete and obsolescent items. This is the terminology of traditional farming practice, with its wealth of variants, as in

> N *tâs*, SE *bera*, SW *rhic*, "hayrick";
> N *trol*, s *cart (gisht)*, Midland *trwmbel*, "light cart";
> N *cwt, cyt*, s *twlc*, "pigsty".

Farming is the only work-related activity which is a productive source of local variants for a macro survey, being the only one which is practised generally throughout the country. The terminology of coal-mining, or any of the other heavy industries which were for so long the occupational backbone of the southern valleys, despite their richness and variety, necessarily give information only on their own restricted geographical area.

The utility of the archaic vocabulary of farming places a restriction on the kind of informant who is likely to be most knowledgeable in the area of traditional farming practice. As modernization of farming practice introduces new methods and machinery with little, if any, variation in terminology in Welsh language usage, we go to older generation speakers who preserve knowledge — and, in the case of many methods and artifacts, memory — of traditional terminology. By this means, we can reinforce our knowledge of *contemporary* lexical variation which occurs widely throughout the population with the historical perspective afforded by a largely obsolescent area of lexicon known principally to older speakers. Because of its archaism, this evidence is particularly valuable in providing a base-line for dialect variation during the first half of this century, against which the extent and nature of change over its second half can be assessed.

To heighten our chances of obtaining genuine localized forms, with no admixture of dialect forms, we can restrict the older generation speakers to those whose families are rooted in their localities for some three generations or so (wherever possible), and who have themselves not lived or worked outside them for extended periods. And to minimize interference from standard usage, the informants can be restricted to those who have had the minimum of formal education.

For the survey reported in A. R. Thomas (1973; 1980), informants completed a written questionnaire, in their own homes. The questions were mainly of two types. They might be asked in Welsh to give their "usual local word" for a concept, as in the kinship relation to them of *mam eich mam*, "your mother's mother". Where it was not so easy to encapsulate a concept concisely in a single line description, an English language equivalent was given, following a general characterization of it in Welsh, as in

> *Coed wedi eu torri yn barod i gynnau tân.* . . FIREWOOD
> "Sticks cut ready to light a fire"

Occasionally, an English word was given alone, where they were asked for their Welsh equivalent for it, as in the word "furniture". In all cases, informants were encouraged to give any other words in less common local usage for the item, and to indicate when they might be used and by whom.

Dialect areas

The notion of dialect "areas" is elusive in purely linguistic terms, because the corpus of data from a dialect survey is too extensive for any analyst to be able to comprehend it in all its variety — even the survey of Welsh dialects referred to here, a relatively small-scale one by European standards, gathered, in all, responses to some 750 questions from 175 localities, providing a potential data-file of 131,250 items. Consequently, dialectologists have frequently adduced ethnographic and anthropological evidence in support of their intuitions about what constitutes a dialect area in particular cases. Thorne (1985: 105–7) makes a suggestive connection along these lines when he points up the close parallels between some of the major dialect areas proposed in A. R. Thomas (1973) and the distribution of regional house types in Wales. However, by today computational procedures have transformed our ability to analyse the masses of survey data, and it is now possible to detect regional distribution patterns, and their strengths relative to each other, from the linguistic data alone,

and it emerges that the major features of regional variation in Wales form
a not unexpected pattern.

If we take the 1,100 regional forms which have clear-cut and internally regular distributions, the picture which emerges is of two major dialect
complexes or continua, each of them considerably diversified internally,
but also revealing striking interdependence of their component parts. As
most linguists would have predicted, there is a bilateral division between
north and south.

There is a core southern area, defined by the distributions of 177 of
the 1,100 regional forms. These forms are strongly distributed throughout
the area to the south of a line drawn from the mouth of the Dyfi, along
its southern watershed and that of the Wye (what we will call the Dyfi-
Wye axis). These are words like

   rhaca, "rake";   *moddion*, "medicine";

but some 16 of them have an extended distribution, stretching to the
southern watershed of the Dee, exemplified by

   copish, "codpiece";   *llaeth*, "milk".

The south has two major sub-dialects, in the east and west, with the Tywi
valley forming a broad area of transition between them, where forms
typical of either south-east or south-west can occur. Forms typical of the
south-east are

   piw, "udder";   *can*, "flour";

and of the south-west

   iet, "gate";   *anner*, "heiffer".

Superimposed on the southern area, there is a weakly distinguished sub-
dialect centred on the Tanat and Fyrnwy valleys in the west midlands.
Forms typical of this sub-dialect are

   blaid, "cowshed";   *ratlin*, "smallest pig in a litter".

Perhaps the most striking feature of the southern dialectal complex
is the result of the encroachment of the English language by geographical
diffusion, resulting in the fulfilment of the process of language shift in the
northern regions of Powys, where there is no longer any indigenous Welsh
spoken. There is evidence, however, of a linguistic link between the
Tanat-Fyrnwy region and the higher reaches of the Wysg, to the immediate
south of the anglicized area. There are words with "split" distributions,
occurring solely in these two locations, suggesting that, in earlier times,

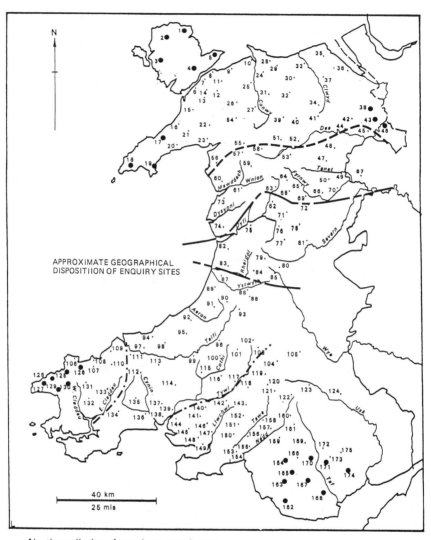

----- Northern limits of southern continuum.
---·-- Southern limits of northern continuum.
—·— Core-area boundaries.

● ● ● ● Sub-dialect nuclei
● ● ●

FIGURE 4.1   Geographical variation in lexicon usage taken from a survey
in the 1960s
Source: A. R. Thomas (1973, 1980).

they occurred throughout an eastern region bounded by the Tanat and the Wysg. Such forms are

weinws, "cart-house";   *tempro*, "air clothes".

The core northern area is defined by 198 forms, which are strongly distributed as far south as the Dyfi, with the exception of some 27 which do not extend to the west of the Clwyd. These are words like

cledr, "palm of hand";   *bwrdd*, "table".

Some 42 reach to the northern watershed of the Aeron and Teifi, while 27 are distributed through various parts of the south, with a concentrated distribution reaching to the mouth of the Cynin — forms like

stôl, "stall";   *brychni haul*, "freckles".

The north has two sub-dialects, in the east and west. Forms typical of the north-eastern variety, like

gwrthban, "blanket";   *cowlas*, "section in a barn"

tend to be confined to the east of the Conwy, but those of the north-west, like

gwana, "hay-swath";   *balog*, "codpiece"

frequently occur to the east of the Conwy. The distribution areas of both sets can reach as far south as the Dyfi for the north-east, and the Wnion for the north-west.

Dialect nuclei

The predominant division between the dialects of Welsh is that between north and south, and none of the sub-dialectal groupings approach these two basic areas in distinctiveness. Within the major sub-dialects described above, however, there are a plethora of local varieties, on the whole weakly distinguished. They form progressively diminishing clusters of localities within a given sub-dialect, each contained within its immediate precursor, until they culminate in a nucleus which contains a small set of localities which are the lexically most distinct within the sub-dialect in question.

As is shown in Figure 4.1 (though with some simplification), these nuclei are at the geographical peripheries of the Welsh language continuum, and for the north-west sub-dialect there are two, in Ynys Môn and LLŷn . This appears to indicate that there has traditionally been no single dominant focal (geographical) area as a determinant of Welsh language usage. And this, in turn, echoes a comment made in E. G. Bowen (1964: 14) that, because of its broken terrain, Wales has never had a single point of political dominance: he goes on to say "in consequence, the salient element which is seen in the history of Wales over the ages is centrifugal rather than centripetal development" (my translation).

The sub-dialect nuclei are revealing of a significant qualitative difference between the northern and southern complexes. We can get a measure of the homogeneity of a dialect area by comparing the number of forms in the nucleus of a sub-dialect *which are exclusive to that sub-dialect*, with the totality of forms which occur there when the core-area forms are added in to their score — that is, we get an indication of the relative independence of the nuclear localities from the core area, north or south. Forms exclusive to the sub-dialects can be expressed as a percentage of the total scores in this way:

North-east:		14%
North-west,	Ynys Môn:	29%
	Llŷn:	25%
South-west:		40%
South-east:		39%

This suggests strongly that the southern complex, in which the nuclei are more evidently independent of features which are common to the whole complex, is more fragmented, less homogeneous than the northern one. In this connection, it is relevant to note that the southern dialects, as a whole, are less conservative and more innovative than their northern counterparts on the phonological level, too (see A. R. Thomas, 1976).

Change

The dialects of Welsh are now in a process of change as dramatic as any in their history. Some localized instances can be deduced from the data collected for this enquiry: the region to the south of the Dyfi-Wye axis constitutes the cantref of Penweddig, described by Lloyd (1911: 257) as the most important of the four cantrefi of mediaeval Ceredigion. Along its southern boundary, to the south of the Ystwyth and Wyre rivers, ran "a pronounced linguistic frontier. . . in the Dark Ages" (E. G. Bowen, 1950). There is now clear evidence that forms indigenous to this region are being displaced by those of the area to its immediate south, for instance

cwtanu, "shorten clothes" by southern *byrhau;*
gwynio, "to ache" by southern *gwynegu*.

There is a more pervasive pair of changes afoot, however. Studies, hitherto unpublished, conducted under the direction of Dr Robert Owen Jones of the Department of Welsh in the University College of Swansea, have revealed a significant generation-related divergence in the nature of lexical change in the dialects of Welsh. In comparing the lexicon of speakers during the last five years with that recorded for informants from the same areas in A. R. Thomas (1973), it was found that a great deal of dialectal lexicon was being lost — for older speakers it involved, primarily, a shift to the corresponding English equivalent; for children of school age, under the influence of Welsh-medium education, it involved a shift from dialectal vocabulary to standard usage. What is not clear is the extent to which social variation is supplanting regional variation.

5 The study of pronunciation patterns

MARTIN J. BALL

Phonetics and phonology

The study of the pronunciation patterns of a language is termed *phonology*. The phonologist establishes the phonology of a language by analysing the raw data on all the speech sounds used in that language, that is the *phonetics* of the language. Phonetics, therefore, is concerned only with a description of speech sounds in terms of their acoustic, articulatory, and auditory characteristics. It makes no assumptions regarding how any particular sound is used in a language. On the other hand, phonology is concerned with just that problem: the use one particular language makes of sounds, and patterns of sounds.

One concern of phonology is to establish the sound units of a language. Let us take an example from the Welsh pronunciation of south Wales. The phonetician will tell us that in that accent there can be distinguished various *t*-like sounds. One of these is articulated as a voiceless, alveolar plosive, which we can symbolise as [t]. Another is articulated further forward: a voiceless, dental plosive, [t̪]. A third is articulated further back: a voiceless, post-alveolar plosive, [t̠]. The phonologist will want to know whether these sounds are totally separate units of Welsh, or whether they can somehow be classed together as variants of an overall "t" unit.

To solve the problem, the phonologist will examine the phonetic contexts where these sounds occur. It turns out that [t̪] only occurs following or preceding dental fricatives (written *th* or *dd* in Welsh). For example:

het dda [hɛt̪ ða].

Furthermore, [t̠] only occurs preceding the post-alveolar liquid sound (written *r*), as in:

trais [t̠ɹaɪs].

The alveolar [t] does not occur in these contexts, so all three "t" types are in mutually exclusive environments. The phonologist states they are in "complementary distribution". Any sounds that are in complementary distribution, and are phonetically similar, are classed together into one phonological unit, termed the *phoneme*. The individual variants of the phoneme are termed *allophones*. To distinguish phonemes from allophones, different brackets are used to enclose the symbols, so for the example we have been examining, we would note that the southern Welsh phoneme /t/ contains the allophones [t], [t̪] and [t̪] amongst others.

A fuller explanation of phonetics and phonology, and the relationship between them can be found in Lass (1984) and Hawkins (1984), and in Welsh in Watkins (1961). The most recent works discussing the phonology of Welsh and how to transcribe it into phonetic symbols are Ball & Jones (1984), and Ball (forthcoming).

The phonology of Welsh

A large number of dialect studies on Welsh have concentrated on analysing the phonology of the Welsh of the various regions concerned. Studies of this sort involve researchers gathering data through recording phonetic data from representative groups of speakers. Before the use of tape recorders became widespread, this recording had to be made directly onto paper by the researcher, using the phonetic symbols of the International Phonetic Association (IPA, 1949). Now the transcription can be made from tape, and various instrumental procedures are available to help resolve any ambiguities.

The phonetic data can then be analysed into phonemic units, as described above. The resulting analysis is usually then compared to standard pronunciations of Welsh. Unlike English with the R.P. accent (see Gimson, 1962), Welsh has no nationally accepted non-regional standard accent (that is to say *pronunciation*; arguably there is a standard *dialect*). However, as described in Ball (forthcoming), there are "standard" pronunciations one can identify. Thus, a standard southern accent would be that used by educated south Walian Welsh speakers in formal contexts, and a similarly defined northern version also exists.

The remainder of this chapter will describe firstly how accents can be compared with each other, and secondly some of the major regional pronunciation differences from standard accents. In order to do this, we need firstly to describe the phonemic units of the northern and southern "standards". To do this we will be using the IPA phonetic symbols referred to above. In the following lists, round brackets enclose any unit whose usage is variable. The theoretical background to the lists is discussed in full in Ball (forthcoming).

Consonants

	South-west							North-west				
p	t	k	b	d	g		p	t	k	b	d	g
	tʃ			dʒ				tʃ			dʒ	
		m	n	ŋ					m	n	ŋ	
f θ s ʃ χ v ð (z) h							f θ s ʃ χ v ð h					
		ɬ		l					ɬ		l	
	(ɹ̥)		r					r̥		r		
		w	j						w	j		

Vowels

South-west: i, ɪ, e, ɛ, a, ɑ, ɔ, o, ʊ, u, ə
North-west: i, ɪ, e, ɛ, a, ɑ, ɔ, o, ʊ, u, ɨ, ɫ,ə

Diphthongs

South-west: aɪ, ɔɪ, ʊɪ, əɪ, ɪʊ, ɛʊ, aʊ, əʊ
North-west: aɪ, ɔɪ, əɪ, ɪʊ, ɛʊ, aʊ, əʊ, iʊ, aɫ, ɑɫ, ɔɫ, ʊɫ, əɫ

The precise relation between the northern and southern vowel and diph-thong system is described in Ball (forthcoming), but can be deduced to some extent from the list showing the correspondence between spelling and pronunciation at the end of the Preface.

Further features of pronunciation, such as stress, length and inton-ation, are not discussed in this chapter. Discussion of them is to be found in both Ball & Jones (1984), and Ball (forthcoming), but it is true to say that little appears to be known on possible patterns of variation in these suprasegmental aspects of speech.

Accent differences

When examining differences between accents, whether regional or social or both, the phonologist can distinguish three or four different categories. It is important to discuss these categories here, as they have implications for the kind of transcription that is needed to capture the differences. In this, and further discussions in this chapter, the term "standard" will be used to describe the northern standard for northern accents, and the southern for southern accents; these two standards having been described in Ball (forthcoming).

The first of these categories is generally termed "realizational differences". These differences are purely phonetic not affecting the phonological system, and so can only be shown in a narrow, or sub-phonemic transcription. This sort of difference can be seen when comparing two equivalent phonemic units of the accents concerned. If the actual phonetic realizations of the two units differ, but no phonemic merger is involved, then this would be a realizational difference. An example from Welsh would be the treatment of fortis stops in Patagonian Welsh as opposed to the standard forms of Welsh. In phonemic terms, both Patagonian and other forms of Welsh have three fortis plosive phonemes: /p, t, k/. However, whereas phonetically the southern standard accent (for example) realizes these as [pʰ, tʰ, kʰ] in the most usual allophones, Patagonian normally realizes them as [p⁼, t⁼, k⁼].

Other examples include the dental-alveolar differences between northern and southern accents in the realizations of the /t/ and /d/ phonemes; the [x] – [χ] differences noted for the back fricative phoneme; and vowel phoneme differences such as [æ] – [ɑ] for /a/.

The second category of accent differences is termed "systemic". This is on a phonemic level, and is therefore reflected in phonemic transcription. Most usually this concerns an accent lacking a phonemic unit present in another, rather than major re-arrangements of an entire system. Examples from Welsh include the absence of an /h/ phoneme in southern accents, along with /h/-related phonemes (/r̥/, and voiceless nasals). Examples with vowels include the lack of /ɨ/ – /ɨ/ in southern accents (together with centralizing diphthongs). Systemic differences operate "across-the-board", in that the absence/presence of a phoneme is not restricted to particular words or phonotactic sequences. For example, the north Pembrokeshire accent as described by Awbery (1984, 1986), virtually lacks the /ə/ phoneme. However, the sound is retained in a few lexical items, so cannot be classed as being totally missing from the accent's system.

For differences of the north Pembrokeshire /ə/ type, we need categories that take into account smaller domains than the entire system: such as the syllable or the word. Our final two categories are of this type, and again the differences are phonemic.

Accent differences that are concerned with phonotactic constraints can be termed "structural". Examples would be found if one accent contained sequences of consonants not permitted in another, or allowed certain vowels in word-final position when the other does not, and so on. Naturally, a systemic difference often results in one accent lacking a phoneme, which in turn cannot be entered into the list of possible phonotactic configurations. Examples of this type need not also be classed as structural differences. This term will be reserved for instances when the phonemes concerned exist in both accents, but the structural possibilities are limited in one case.

Structural differences between Welsh accents are not numerous, the most striking example being dealt with in detail in Awbery (1984). This concerns the constraints surrounding the distribution of phonemically long and short vowels in northern, southern and central accents. Although many similarities exist between these accents, Awbery points to certain consistent differences. Examples of these include vowels before /ɬ/ in monosyllables: these being long in south Wales, short in north. Further, in penultimate syllables we find a three-way split on vowel length in general: short vowels only in north Wales, context-dependent long or short in south Wales, and long and short vowels in free variation in mid-Wales. On the other hand, Awbery notes that many features to do with vowel length are common to all areas (e.g. unstressed vowels being short).

The final category — "distributional differences" — are similar, and indeed are often classed together with structural differences. Here, however, the term is restricted to differences in the distribution of certain phonemes that are not across-the-board, but occur in certain lexical items, or classes of lexical items only. Again the phonemes in question exist in both accents, but their lexical distribution differs. The example of the north Pembrokeshire /ə/ fits well into this category: a large class of words which in other acccents have /ə/ replace this with other vowels (e.g. /'kənar/ → /'kɪnar/), but a small group of lexical items do still retain the schwa vowel. Therefore, /ə/ cannot be viewed as being phontactically banned, but rather distributionally limited.

These four kinds of accent differences will be seen in the following discussion of commonly differing features, and accent descriptions. It must be borne in mind that narrow transcriptions will show all these difference types, whereas a phonemic one will only show the last three.

Main differences

This section will examine phonemic units and combinations noting briefly the main variations that occur in various accents. Consonants and consonant clusters are examined firstly, followed by vowels and diphthongs.

Consonants

All Welsh accents have six plosive phonemes, /p, t, k, b, d, g/ which enter into most permitted consonant clusters. Realization differences, as noted in the previous section, occur in that Patagonian Welsh speakers (particularly younger speakers) realize /p, t, k/ as [p⁼, t⁼, k⁼] rather than [pʰ, tʰ, kʰ]. /t/ and /d/ may be realized as [t̪ʰ] and [d̪] in northern accents rather than [tʰ] and [d]. Certain south-eastern accents have a structural difference from all others, in that medial, intervocalic fortis stops are not permitted, being replaced by lenes (/'ebol//'epol/). In accents border-this area, this process becomes distributional in that it does not affect all lexical items.

All accents of Welsh have three voiced nasal phonemes, /m, n, ŋ/. The /n/ phoneme of northern accents is often [n̪] as opposed to southern [n]. No important phonemic level differences are reported in the literature.

The status of the so-called voiceless nasals, and their phonetic realizations need not be discussed here. This book treats them transcriptionally as clusters of nasal+/h/, so the lack of these in southern accents is accounted for by the lack of /h/.

The affricate phonemes — /tʃ, dʒ/ — are mainly subject to distributional differences. These are manifested in certain northern accents, where although /dʒ/ is present, /tʃ/ is used in many lexical items where southern accents have /dʒ/ (e.g. /'kabaitʃ/ – /'kabaidʒ/). Another difference (perhaps best termed "structural in free variation") is a result of style and perhaps utterance rate. This is when /t/ or /d/ is followed by /j/: the resultant cluster is often realized as /tʃ/ or /dʒ/, for example /'djaʊl/ → /'dʒaʊl/.

The Welsh fricative system shows few realizational differences between accents. Personal differences may be detected in the amount of voicing found in /v/ and /ð/ (see Ball, 1984a), or lip-rounding and palatalization in /ʃ/, but the only important realizational difference is found with /χ/. This is usually described as being realized as [χ], but researchers have

noted that it is usually [x] for some accents (e.g. Usk Valley, though
A. R. Thomas, 1959; 1961 is not consistent on this point; see also R. O.
Jones, 1967). Younger speakers of Patagonian Welsh are noted as using
a [x] realization, which may indeed be very close to [ç]. These Patagonian
speakers also manifest a systemic difference: replacing all examples of /ʃ/
with /s/. Other systemic differences include the loss of /h/, replaced by ∅
in many southern (and Patagonian) accents. Structural differences (in
some accents these may only be distributional) result in the loss of word-
final /v/, and to a lesser extent /ð/. This may be more stylistic than regional.
Finally, G. E. Jones (1984b) notes the idiosyncratic realization of /h/ as
[ħ] in some northern accents.

The liquids show several accent differences. /l/ is nearly always
realized as [l] in southern accents, but may be [ɫ] or [lʲ] in northern. /r/
shows few differences, but may be realized consistently as [ɹ] instead of
as [r] in east Powys. The use of [ɹ] and [ʀ]/[ʁ] appears to be idiosyncratic, though the latter forms are often found in the Bala area. The main
difference with /r̥/ is systemic, in that it is missing from all /h/-less accents
being replaced by /r/.

The glides /w/ and /j/ show few differences between accents, although
in certain mid-Wales accents there is a structural difference in that /w/ is
dropped from ccc clusters, for example /gwliθ/ → /gliθ/.

There are in fact few structural differences affecting consonant clusters between Welsh accents. One minor example concerns initial /χw-/
sequences. These are generally found as /hw-/ sequences in mid-Wales,
and as /w-/ in /h/-less accents. Most of the other examples are reported
more fully in Awbery (1984), but we can give the example of final
fricative+sonorant clusters which are acceptable in northern accents, but
not in southern where an epenthetic vowel is required: /ˈɔvn/ – /ˈovon/.

Vowels

A chapter of this size is not sufficient to go into full details of all
the patterns of difference between accents for vowels and diphthongs, so
the account here is admittedly superficial.

The main regional realizational differences were in fact noted in
Chapter 3. The lax vowels of southern accents are generally realized as
tenser varieties in the north; realizations of /e/ and /o/ tend to differ
between northern and southern accents; centralization of /a/ to [ä] in the
penultima is found in south-eastern accents; and the realization of /ɑ/ as

[æ]/[ae] in central accents. More detailed descriptions of the phonetic realizations of vowels (and diphthongs) are found in the individual dialect studies listed at the end of this chapter.

Systemic differences are found in the lack of /i/ and /ɨ/ in southern and most central accents, though both [i] and [ʉ] seem to occur in some mid-Wales accents, with a distribution limited to a small set of lexical items (see G. E. Jones, 1984b). It would seem best to treat these as realizational variants of /i/. Some accents seem to have an increased vowel system, and one such is discussed in the next section below.

Structural differences are found with respect to restrictions on the occurrence of phonologically long and short vowels. These are described in detail by Awbery (1984), and have been briefly referred to above.

Distributional differences include the restriction on /ə/ in north Pembrokeshire, and the over-extension of /ə/ in south Cardiganshire. Other examples are of minor importance.

Diphthongs

The most important realizational differences are described in Ball (forthcoming), particularly notable is the lengthening of the initial element, in northern accents, of /ɛʊ/, /aʊ/, /ɔɨ/ and /ʊɨ/. Systemic differences include the loss in southern accents of /əɨ, aɨ, ɑɨ, ɔɨ, ʊɨ/ and /iʊ/. These merge with equivalent southern diphthongs with /ɪ/ or /i/, except for /aɨ/, which is stylistically controlled. This is found as /aɪ/ in formal styles, and /ɑ/ in informal ones in stressed syllables in most southern accents. Another stylistically controlled difference results in southern /aɪ/ when from northern /aɨ/ merging with /ɔɪ/. In southern accents, in informal styles, /ɔɪ/ from northern /ɔɨ/ often merges with /ɔ/. Finally, unstressed /aɪ/ often merges with /ɪ/ or /ɛ/, and the plural allomorph /aɨ – aɪ/ merges with /a – ɛ/ in informal styles in most regions.

Few distributional or structural differences have been noted, though reference to the detailed studies should be made here.

Conclusion

In this chapter I have tried to show that studying the pronunciation patterns of different areas of groups of speakers is not simply a matter of direct comparison of the different sounds. The way in which the sounds of any accent are organized into a phonological system means that comparisons are necessary both below and above the phoneme unit, and both in terms of system and structure. This chapter has also attempted to point out some characteristics of northern and southern forms, with occasional reference to other areas. Readers should bear in mind, however, that this treatment has only been superficial. For more detailed descriptions they are urged to consult the works referred to in Chapter 2. For those looking for a recent, theoretical treatment of the phonology of a Welsh accent, Awbery's (1986) work on north Pembrokeshire is recommended. Finally, when looking at any account of regional pronunciation, readers should remember what was said in Chapter 3 about sociolinguistic variation: the pronunciation of any region may well be restricted to certain groups of speakers alone, and they may only use it under certain stylistic conditions.

6 Variation in grammar

MARTIN J. BALL

Morphology

The grammatical level of linguistic description is traditionally held to encompass two distinct areas of study: morphology and syntax.

Morphology is concerned with the analysis of words, not in terms of their pronunciation, but in terms of their construction out of basic word units, or *morphemes*. To clarify this point, let us examine some examples from Welsh. A word like *cath*, "cat" is not divisible into smaller units that bear any kind of meaning. However, the word *cathod*, "cats" can be so divided: into a unit *cath* and a unit *-od*, this latter being interpreted as representing the concept of "plural".

As the above example showed, some morphemes can stand by themselves (*cath*), and so are termed "free morphemes". Others (e.g. *-od*) can only be found attached to another morpheme, and are termed "bound morphemes".

We also find that in words of two or more morphemes, one is usually more central to the overall meaning than the other(s). This one is called "the root", whereas the others are termed "affixes". So in the case of *cathod, cath* is the root, and *-od* is the affix.

Affixes themselves can be divided into two groups: those occurring before a root ("prefixes"), and those following a root ("suffixes"). Examples of these two types can be seen in the following words:
Prefixes: *di*flas, *arch*esgob, *ar*lunio
"distasteful", "archbishop", "to draw".
Suffixes: tad*au*, tad*ol*, coch*i*, rhyn*llyd*, arlun*io*
"fathers", "fatherly", "to redden", "chilly", "to draw".
As can be seen from the second list, suffixes can have a grammatical function (such as plural in *tadau*), or a word-formation function, that is creating a new word as a verb from an adjective (*cochi* from *coch*, "red"). Grammatical suffixes are termed "inflectional", while word-forming suffixes are called "derivational". Compared with English, Welsh has quite

a large number of inflectional suffixes, for example: noun plural, in some cases noun singular, several sets of tense+person suffixes for verbs, degrees of comparison for adjectives, and person endings for prepositions. We will return to some of these at a later stage.

However, the number of derivational endings is much larger. For example, Williams (1980) lists no fewer than 30 endings than can be found converting other words into nouns. Examples of these include *-did* (adjective to noun, as *glendid* from *glan* + *did*, "cleanliness"), and *-iad* (usually verb to noun, or noun to noun, as *cysylltiad* from the verb *cysylltu* + *iad*, "connection", or possibly from the noun *cyswllt* + *iad*).

Finally, we can note that the pronunciation of morphemes may differ in different environments. Sometimes this difference is phonetically conditioned, whereas at other times these differences may appear to be arbitrary. Examples of these differences can be seen if we examine the Welsh plural morpheme. Plurality in Welsh is expressed in a number of different ways (inflectional suffix, internal vowel change, and combinations of these, for example). However, they are all alike in standing for plurality, so must be classed as a single morpheme. Because they differ in form but not in meaning, they are termed *allomorphs* of the plural morpheme (i.e. variants). Williams (1980: 10–11) notes the following basic plural allomorphs in the form of suffixes: *-au*, *-iau*, *-ion*, *-on*, *-i*, *-ydd*, *-edd*, *-oedd*, *-ed*, *-aint*, *-od*, and *-iaid*. Vowel changes, vowel changes plus suffixes, and various other devices add considerably to the number of allomorphs. Allomorphs do exist for other Welsh morphemes, but it is probably true to say that the plural morpheme exhibits the greatest number of such variants.

Before moving on to look at morphological variation in Welsh, let us recapitulate what we have been saying about morphology, in the following diagrams.

(1)

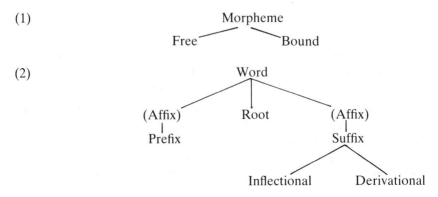

(2)

(3)   Morpheme

                                       Allomorphs

A fuller account of morphology can be found in Matthews (1974), and Watkins (1961). Welsh morphology is discussed in Williams (1980), and Jones & Thomas (1977).

Variation in Welsh morphology

In terms of regional variation, the morphology of Welsh is remarkably stable. Variation in free forms is generally considered under the heading of lexical geography (see Chapter 4), so will not be referred to here. Little variation is noted for the derivational prefixes and suffixes, so we will concentrate in this section on inflectional suffixes.

The main areas of variation are verbal forms, and prepositional forms, and these are the forms that we will look at in more detail. The variation involved in both cases is due to regional factors in some instances, and stylistic (literary *versus* colloquial Welsh) in others.

R. M. Jones & Thomas (1977: 398) note that describing verbal inflections "is a fairly complex task as there is a considerable amount of variation". These two authors list the verb inflections of the regular verb, and of various irregular verbs, showing various kinds of variation. It is not necessary for us to repeat this entire list, but we may usefully look at some of the verb endings of the regular verb, and the copula (*bod*, "to be").

As can be seen from Table 6.1, the morphology of the regular verb varies both in terms of style — literary *versus* colloquial — and in terms of region: northern *versus* southern, though many of these latter are due to phonological factors rather than purely morphological.

The most important features of regional variation in verb morphology are probably the third persons singular, preterite (past) and present/future. In the preterite we find -*odd* in most areas, but -*ws* in many southern varieties (particularly of the south east). The historical distribution of these two forms is explored in Awbery, Jones & Suggett

TABLE 6.1   *Paradigms of the regular verb*

Traditional written Present/future	*Preterite*	*Imperfect*	*Pluperfect*
canaf	cenais	canwn	canaswn
ceni	cenaist	canit	canasit
can	canodd	canai	canasai
canwn	canasom	canem	canasem
cenwch	canasoch	canech	canasech
canant	canasant	canent	canasent

Colloquial spoken Future	*Preterite*	*Conditional*	*Conditional*
gana	ganis/ganes	ganwn	ganswn
gani	ganist/ganest	ganet/ganat	ganset/gansat
ganith/ganiff	ganodd/ganws	gane/gana	ganse/gansa
ganwn/ganan	ganson/ganon	ganen/ganan	gansen/gansan
ganwch	gansoch/ganoch	ganech/ganach	gansech/gansach
ganan	ganson/ganon	ganen/ganan	gansen/gansen

Note: In the colloquial spoken paradigms, northern forms are generally those to the left, although *e/a* distinction is basically one of north-east and south-west *versus* north-west and south-east. There is no functional difference between the two forms of the conditional, both forms being available to many speakers, though the first is probably more common.

(1985) using information from slander cases. In the present/future we find *-iff* as the usual spoken form in southern varieties, with *-ith* being found in the north. Literary Welsh lacks both these endings, and depending on the verb we may find no ending, *-a*, or an internal vowel change.

The copula in Welsh has a series of different paradigms (i.e. sets of endings), depending on the tense. Table 6.2 below sets out just the present tense paradigm. Here again there is variation both in terms of style and region. Here it will be noted that the spoken forms involve various amounts of phonological simplification. The southern forms have taken this process somewhat further by removing in many instances the (originally optional) *yd-* prefix from the copula.

If we examine the person inflections on Welsh prepositions, we see an interesting case of analogic levelling. The literary forms have been simplified in spoken Welsh, and this simplification has involved the reduction of the number of paradigms due to analogy. The paradigm is a concept central to morphology, and in a recent paper, Carstairs (1983: 127) proposes a general principle of "paradigm economy": "that there exists a real tendency. . . towards keeping the total of paradigms. . . close

TABLE 6.2 *Present tense paradigms of* bod, *"to be"*

I	II	III	IV	V
Traditional written				
yr ydwyf fi	nid ydwyf i	ydwyf	yr wyf	ydwyf
yr ydwyt ti	nid ydwyt ti	ydwyt	yr wyt	ydwyt
y mae ef, hi	nid ydyw ef, hi	ydyw	y mae, yw	ydyw
yr ydym ni	nid ydym ni	ydym	yr ym	ydym
yr ydych chwi	nid ydych chwi	ydych	yr ych	ydych
y maent hwy	nid ydynt hwy	ydynt	y maent, ynt	ydynt
Northern colloquial spoken				
'rydw i	'dydw i	ydw i	'dw i	(y)(n)dw
'rwyt ti	'dwyt ti	wyt ti	'ti	wyt
mae o, hi	'dydy o, hi	ydy o, hi	mae/'dy o, hi	(y)(n)dy
'rydan ni	'dydan ni	ydan ni	'dan ni	(y)(n)dan
'rydach chi	'dydach chi	ydach chi	'dach chi	(y)(n)dach
maen nhw	'dydyn nhw	ydyn nhw	maen/'dyn nhw	(y)(n)dyn
Southern colloquial spoken				
rw i	'dw i	w i	w i	ydw
rwyt ti	'dwyt ti	wyt ti	'ti	wyt
ma' e, hi	'dyw e, hi	yw e, hi	ma'/yw e, hi	ydy
ryn ni	'dyn ni	yn ni	'ni	ydyn
rych chi	'dych chi	ych chi	'chi	ydych
ma'n nw	'dyn nw	yn nw	ma'n/yn nw	ydyn

I: Full forms used in positive declaratives.
II: Full forms used in negatives (declaratives or interrogatives).
III: Full forms used in positive interrogatives.
IV: Contracted forms used in positive and negative declaratives and interrogatives (third person alternatives relate to these features)
V: Answer words to yes-no questions.

to the logical minimum". It is further suggested that morphological change will tend to be in the direction of economizing rather than proliferating paradigms. Similarly, analogic levelling is a well-known feature of morphological change (see for example Matthews, 1974: 68f), and this notion can be seen to complement what Carstairs suggests. What we can show here is how the current usage of prepositions in colloquial Welsh is a result of considerable paradigmatic simplification, and we can use this to explore the implications for the principle of paradigm economy.

In the literary language three regular preposition paradigms are found, with one irregular preposition accounted for separately (Uned Iaith Genedlaethol Cymru, 1978). The three paradigms will be termed here

TABLE 6.3   *Prepositional paradigms in standard Welsh*

	-AF	-OF(i)	-OF(ii)	-OF(iii)	-YF	I
1st	-af	-of	-of	-of	-yf	∅
2nd	-at	-ot	-ot	-ot	-yt	∅
3rd	-o/-i	-ddo/-ddi	-to/-ti	-o/-i	-o/-i	-ddo/-ddi
1st	-om	-om	-om	-om	-ym	∅
2nd	-och	-och	-och	-och	-ych	∅
3rd	-ynt	-ddynt	-tynt	-ynt	-ynt	-ddynt

-AF: *at, dan, am(dan), ar(n)*.
-OF(i): *heb, yn, rhag, trwy/drwy, rhwng(rhyng)*; (ii): *tros/dros*; (iii): *o(hon)*.
-YF: *gan, wrth*.

the -AF paradigm, the -OF paradigm and the -YF paradigm, and the suffixes relevant to each one are shown in Table 6.3. The preposition *i*, "to", lies outside these paradigms, and may be termed "defective" as it carries only third singular and third plural endings.

These three regular paradigms do not however reach any great level of paradigm simplicity. The -AF paradigm contains two main suffix vowels: *a* for first and second singular, *o* for first and second plural. The -OF paradigm has three variants, two of which are restricted to single examples. It also has an intrusive consonant at the beginning of the suffix, which is, however, restricted to third singular and third plural. The -YF paradigm is restricted to two examples only, again countering simplicity in the overall system.

If the usual spoken forms of the prepositions are examined (see for example R. M. Jones & Thomas, 1977, or Uned Iaith Genedlaethol Cymru, 1978), it will be seen that analogic levelling of the paradigms has taken place, producing a far simpler system. Not only has the overall number of paradigms been reduced, but the paradigms themselves contain fewer variants. All the paradigms have experienced a levelling of suffix vowels, with the result that, depending on dialect area, first and second singular and first and second plural suffixes all contain *a* throughout or *o* throughout. The -OF paradigm regularizes the intrusive consonant to all persons, thus simplifying the morphology here too (consonant changes throughout the preposition and verbal systems remove the final *f* of first singular, and the final *t* of third plural).

These changes are shown in Table 6.4, and as can be seen, they result in a reduction of the number of paradigms. The vowel levelling

TABLE 6.4   *Prepositional paradigms in spoken Welsh*

	Class 1	Class 2(i)	Class 2(ii)
1st	-a, -o	-a, -o	-a, -o
2nd	-at, -ot	-at, -ot	-at, -ot
3rd	-o/-i	-ddo/-ddi	-to/-ti
1st	-an, -on	-an, -on	-an, -on
2nd	-ach, -och	-ach, -och	-ach, -och
3rd	-yn	-ddyn	-tyn

Class 1: *at, dan, am(dan), ar(n), o(hon), gan*, wrth.*
Class 2(i): *heb, yn, rhag, trwy/drwy, rhwng (rhyng);* (ii): *tros/dros.*
* Other forms exist of *gan,* not fitting into these paradigms.

Note: The added consonants of Class 2 can also be heard in other persons.

leads to a merger of -AF and -YF paradigms (to Class 1 in Table 6.4), thus removing the very small -YF class. These vowel changes also mean that variant (iii) of the -OF paradigm merges with new Class 1. The new Class 2 (the rest of the former -OF) now shows greater regularity in its suffix usage.

The irregular preposition *i* still maintains its defective pattern, though it has been reported (Elwyn Hughes, personal communication) as being used with Class 2 type endings in second singular, and even first and second plural in some areas.

Syntax

While morphology is the study of word structure, syntax is the study of sentence structure. When we analyse a sentence we can consider two distinct levels. Firstly, we can examine the major sentence roles. Following the usage of Quirk, Greenbaum, Leech & Svartvik (1972), these roles will be termed Subject (s), Object (o), Verb (v), Complement (c) and Adverbial (A) (also termed Adjunct). Examples of these sentence roles can be seen in the following sentences:

(1) *Mae'r dyn yn gweld y ci,* "the man is seeing the dog";
     v-   s   -v   o
(2) *Mae Jac yn hapus,* "Jac is happy";
     v   s   c
(3) *Mae e'n siarad yn gyflym,* "he's talking quickly".
     v-   s   -v   A

Many other sentence patterns occur in Welsh, and are discussed more fully in Jones & Thomas (1977).

The analysis of sentences into these major roles is often termed "clause-level analysis". The next level of analysis, termed "phase-level", is concerned with what different units or word categories comprise the subject, object, verb, complement and adverbial roles. For example, sentence (1) above has a subject consisting of *'r dyn*, that is a determiner (*'r*) and a noun (*dyn*). The phrase-level analysis of (1) – (3) above gives:

(1a)   *Mae*   *'r*   *dyn*   *yn*   *gweld*   *y*   *ci;*
        V-   S   -V   O
        aux det noun comp verb det noun
(2a)   *Mae*   *Jac*   *yn*   *hapus;*
        V   S   C
        cop noun comp adjective
(3a)   *Mae*   *e*   *'n*   *siarad*   *yn*   *gyflym;*
        V-   S   -V   A
        aux pron comp verb comp adverb

In these examples, aux is the auxiliary verb; det, the determiner (article); comp, the complementizer; cop, the copular verb; and pron, the pronoun. Again, these sentences include only a few phrase-level categories.

Potentially, therefore, variation in syntax can occur at two levels: clause and phrase. A fuller account of syntax is available in Matthews (1981), in Welsh in Watkins (1961), and on Welsh in Richards (1938), Awbery (1976) and Jones & Thomas (1977).

The rest of this section will look at two areas of syntax, showing in one case many regional variations, and in the other mostly stylistic. Interestingly enough, both cases are on the borderline between clause and phrase levels. The variation manifests itself as a choice of varying phrasal elements, but also has an influence on clausal structure.

Negation

Negation generally affects entire clauses, and so can be considered clausal in that respect. In most languages, however, negation is realized by a negative word being attached to a noun or verb (for example), thus becoming part of a noun phrase or verb phrase respectively. The variation we will be examining here will concern both noun-phrase and verb-phrase negation.

In literary Welsh, the negative particle *nid* is placed before a noun phrase to negate it, for example:

(4) *Nid Siân a welodd y dyn*, "(it was) not Siân who saw the man".

However, as Watkins (1961) pointed out, there are a variety of ways in which noun-phrase negation may be realized in spoken Welsh, and many of these depend on region. One of the regionally restricted forms is *nace*, found in west Glamorgan:

(5) *Nace Siân welodd y dyn.*[1]

More widespread is the use of *dim*, a negative particle also commonly found in verb-phrase negation in spoken Welsh:

(6) *Dim Siân welodd y dyn.*

This form is found in many areas of West and North Wales. Interestingly, *Cymraeg Byw*, the form of Welsh specially developed for learners (see Chapter 14), retains the standard form *nid*, though it is true that this form can still be heard in spoken Welsh in many areas, even if only as a formal variant.

Verb-phrase negation in standard Welsh involves the use of *ni* (*nid* before vowels) placed before the main verb (or before the auxiliary verb if there is one), and the optional use of the emphasizer *ddim* (mutated from *dim*, "anything, nothing") after the subject, for example:

(7) *Ni ddaeth Elwyn (ddim) i'r tŷ*, "Not came Elwyn to the house".

The spoken form of this construction varies little from region to region, and involves the loss of *ni*, and the obligatory use of *ddim*:

(8) *Ddaeth Elwyn ddim i'r tŷ*;

Negation in subordinate clauses differs somewhat in standard Welsh through the use of the particle *na(d)* instead of *ni(d)*. In spoken Welsh, however, the same reduction to *ddim* and loss of negative particle takes place.

Regional variation is found, however, in the case of the negation of the verb *bod* "to be", whether as copula or auxiliary. The standard Welsh example in (9),

(9) *Nid yw Pam yn y gwaith*, "not is Pam in (the) work"

may be found in several forms depending mainly on region:

(10) *Tydi Pam ddim yn y gwaith* (northern);
(11) *Smo/simo Pam yn y gwaith* (south-west);
(12) *Nag yw Pam yn y gwaith* (western);
(13) *Dyw Pam ddim yn y gwaith* (southern).

Pre-sentential particles

This section carries on to some extent from the last examples. Verb-phrase negation in standard Welsh uses a pre-sentential particle, *ni(d)* or *na(d)*. Other such particles are found in standard Welsh, and can be found in all sentences which commence with a main verb or auxiliary verb (i.e. the majority of cases). These particles denote whether the sentence is negative or positive, interrogative or declarative, emphatic or non-emphatic, and whether it is a negative-interrogative. Particles are also used to mark embedded subordinate clauses of various types. A full analysis of these particles is given in R. M. Jones & Thomas (1977: 356f). If we adapt the table on page 356 of that publication, we can display the particles used in main clauses:[2]

TABLE 6.5 *Pre-sentential particles in standard Welsh*

	Positive	Negative
Declarative unemphatic	ø	*ni(d)*
Declarative emphatic	*fe/mi*	*ni(d). . .ddim*
Interrogative	*a*	*oni(d)*
Imperative	ø	*na(c)*

It will be seen from this table that most sentence types are clearly differentiated by the use of these particles. Although positive imperatives and positive unemphatic declaratives are not so distinguished, the former lacks a subject so will not be confused with the latter. Examples of the use of these articles may be seen in the following sentences:

(14) *Daeth Peter i'm gweld*, "Peter came to see me";
(15) *Fe ddaeth Peter i'm gweld*, "Peter *did* come to see me";
(16) *Ni ddaeth Peter i'm gweld*, "Peter didn't come to see me";
(17) *A ddaeth Peter i'm gweld?*, "Did Peter come to see me?";
(18) *Oni ddaeth Peter i'm gweld?*, "Didn't Peter come to see me?";
(19) *Dewch i'm gweld!*, "Come to see me!";
(20) *Na ddewch i'm gweld!* "Don't come to see me!"

It would appear that such a system of pre-sentential particles would be an economical and clear method of marking sentence types. It is all the more surprising then when we find that in most spoken forms of Welsh, this system has almost completely broken down. This is especially true with the regular, main clause particles discussed above. Of Table 6.5 above, the only regularly used particles in spoken Welsh are the declarative emphatics, *fe/mi*. It appears that *fe* is most commonly found in southern varieties, and *mi* in northern, though usage of both by speakers is not uncommon. A third variant, *i*, appears to be a localized form restricted to south-western dialects. Even these emphatic forms are relatively uncommon, but the verb mutation they cause is retained, and indeed is more usual in spoken Welsh than the unmutated form.

From this discussion, we can examine the effect the loss of these particles has on the examples in (14) – (20) above:

(14a) *Ddaeth Peter i 'ngweld i;*
(15a) *Fe ddaeth Peter i 'ngweld i;*
(16a) *Ddaeth Peter ddim i 'ngweld i;*
(17a) *Ddaeth Peter i 'ngweld i?;*
(18a) *Ddaeth Peter ddim i 'ngweld i?;*
(19a) *Dewch i 'ngweld i!;*
(20a) *Peidiwch (â) dod i 'ngweld i!*

These sentences show several changes from the preceding set. All pre-sentential particles (apart from optional *fe/mi*) are dropped. Negatives are distinguished from positives by use of the post-subject *ddim*. Interrogatives and declaratives, however, are not distinguished syntactically at all, and must rely on intonation alone. The negative of imperatives is generally conveyed by the use of the verb *peidio (â)*, "stop, cease", and indeed this can be found often in standard Welsh as well. A slightly different syntax is also found for the final part of these sentences: *i 'ngweld i* for *i'm gweld*, "to see me". This is not connected with the use of particles, however.

The question may be raised here of why such a straightforward system as that found in standard Welsh should break down in spoken forms so completely. Although we cannot be sure, it is possibly the result of two factors. Firstly, with negatives, the increasing use of the optional emphasizer *ddim* would presumably concentrate the intonation pattern of the sentence onto that particle. Heavily stressed *ddim* would result in the loss of stress on *ni(d)*, and its eventual dropping. If one particle were lost, a process of analogy (described above in the morphology section) could well operate, leading to the loss of the others, and an increased reliance on the role of intonation.

The second main factor could be end-focus. It is often argued by linguists that the main information focus of the sentence is at the end. This could mean that the information value of sentence-initial particles gradually diminished. Intonation would have to be used to reinforce the particles, or the use of another particle not restricted to initial position. This also could lead to the eventual abandoning of the pre-sentential particles.

Whatever the cause of the change, it must be remembered that sentence roles in spoken Welsh are readily distinguishable, even if the part played by syntax alone has been reduced.

Conclusion

This chapter has dealt with the two areas of grammar: morphology and syntax. We have only been able to scratch the surface of these topics, and readers especially interested in this area should consult the various dialect studies in detail. Information on these studies is to be found in Chapter 2.

It is true to say that dialect studies in the past have often concentrated on phonology and lexis (vocabulary) to the detriment of morphology and syntax. The study of grammatical usage in Welsh still, therefore, offers profitable research opportunities to those interested in this area.

Notes to Chapter 6

1. The spoken form generally omits the relative pronoun *a*.
2. Different sets of particles are found with the copula, *bod*, "to be".

7 Variation in the use of initial consonant mutations

MARTIN J. BALL

The mutations

As noted in the introduction, the initial consonant mutations of Welsh are prone to variation in usage. Before we can examine this variation in any detail, we must firstly describe what initial consonant mutations are.

Initial consonant mutations in Welsh are a series of synchronic phonological changes affecting word initial consonants. These changes are not caused by the phonological context, but are triggered by the syntactic environment of the word in question. For example, the word *cath*, "cat", is rea¹·ʔed as *gath* in the phrase *ei gath* "his cat"; as *chath* in *ei chath* "her cat"; and as *nghath* in *fy nghath* "my cat". Phonologically, these versions can be transcribed as follows:

cath	/kɑθ/
ei gath	/i gɑθ/
ei chath	/i xɑθ/
fy nghath	/vəŋhɑθ/ or /ŋhɑθ/

As can be seen from the above example, there are three sets of phonological changes called mutations: the soft mutation (or lenition), the aspirate or spirant mutation (spirantization) and the nasal mutation (nasalization). I shall abbreviate these as SM, AM and NM respectively.

The changes with SM convert voiceless plosives to voiced; voiced stops to voiced fricatives; voiceless liquids to voiced; and /m/ to /v/. These changes can be seen below:

p	⟶	b
t	⟶	d
k	⟶	g

b	$\longrightarrow$	v
d	$\longrightarrow$	ð
g	$\longrightarrow$	ø (historically via [ɣ])

| ɬ | $\longrightarrow$ | l |

| r̥ | $\longrightarrow$ | r |

| m | $\longrightarrow$ | v (historically via [ṽ]) |

The changes with AM are the conversion of voiceless plosives to voiceless fricatives:

p	$\longrightarrow$	f
t	$\longrightarrow$	θ
k	$\longrightarrow$	x (phonetically, often [χ])

The changes with NM are the conversion of fortis and lenis plosives to fortis and lenis nasals:[1]

p	$\longrightarrow$	mh
t	$\longrightarrow$	nh
k	$\longrightarrow$	ŋh

b	$\longrightarrow$	m
d	$\longrightarrow$	n
g	$\longrightarrow$	ŋ

As noted above, these three mutations[2] are triggered by a variety of syntactic environments. Many of these are lexical, that is to say the mutation is triggered by a particular word onto a following word. Some are purely syntactic, that is a word is mutated when in a particular syntactic position. Morphology can also have a part to play, as prefixing and compounding can cause mutation, but this becomes word-internal and is not discussed further in this chapter. The historical motivation for the phonological changes of mutation, and the triggers causing them is discussed in detail in Ball (1984b) and need not detain us here.

The full set of triggers for each mutation is listed in traditional grammar books, such as Williams (1980). However, to give a flavour of the type of context occurring as a trigger, we can note some of the common ones for each mutation in Standard Welsh:

SM
Feminine noun after the definite article;
adjective after feminine noun;
noun/adjective following complementizer *yn*;
nouns following certain numerals: *un*, "one" (feminine nouns only),
    dau/dwy, "two";
verbs following various pre-verbal particles;
nouns and verbs after certain possessive pronouns: *dy*, "your", *ei*,
    "his";
verbs following relativizer *a*;
direct object of non-periphrastic (i.e. inflected) verb;
nouns etc. following certain prepositions.

AM
Nouns following certain numerals: *tri* "three", *chwe* "six";
nouns and verbs following possessive pronoun: *ei* "her";
verbs after certain pre-verbal particles;
nouns etc. following certain prepositions: *â*, *gyda*, *efo* "with", *tua*,
    "towards";
nouns etc. following certain conjunctions: *a* "and", *â* "as";
adjectives etc. following the adverb *tra* "very".

NM
Nouns etc. following the preposition *yn*, "in";
nouns and verbs following the possessive pronoun *fy*, "my";
certain fossilized time expressions with the words *blynedd*, *blwydd*,
    "year", *diwrnod*, "day".

As we noted in the introduction, it appears that in modern spoken Welsh, these "rules" of mutation usage are not always adhered to. It appears from previous research described in detail in Ball (1984b) that some speakers do not mutate consistently (or at all) after some of these triggers, or use a different mutation than the standard requires (this usually involves changing AM or NM to SM). The variation reported is variation in which triggers cause a mutation rather than an across-the-board variation in an entire mutation.

The mutations of Welsh, and the other Celtic languages, present an interesting puzzle to students of language use and variation. The previous three chapters have examined lexical, phonological and grammatical variation in Welsh. There is a real sense in which studying mutation usage encompasses all three of these. They are phonological in that the end result of applying a mutation is a phonological change. They are grammatical in that the syntactic position of a word is usually the "reason" why it is mutated. They are lexical in that, as we saw above, it is very often individual lexical items that trigger a mutation.

The final chapter of this book presents one solution of how to describe variable mutation usage within linguistic theory. The rest of this chapter, however, presents an account of an investigation into variation in the use of initial consonant mutations undertaken by the author, appearing in full in Ball (1984b).

Setting up the study

As we noted in Part I, the study of linguistic variation requires that we choose some subjects and record their speech through use of a questionnaire or other similar strategies. The problem I faced when setting up the project to examine mutation usage was not so much to do with choice of subjects, but in the methods used to get the speech sample.

The styles referred to as formal (or interview) and casual in Chapter 3 obviously presented few problems apart from the fact that it could not be guaranteed that examples of all the triggers would occur. The more formal styles of reading passage and word lists presented the major problem, however. It was obviously important to examine the effect formality might have on mutation usage, but these "written" styles would remove choice from the speaker. The mutations are reflected in writing, and so speakers would be most likely simply to follow the written form of the stimulus presented to them (this was confirmed in a pilot study reported in Ball 1984b). To get round this problem, pictures were used to represent the word that would be mutated in standard Welsh, and inserted in prose passages and sentences. A pilot study confirmed the usefulness of this technique, and in the final study numerals (e.g. written as "3") were used as well.

The problem of ensuring enough examples of the triggers in ordinary speech remained. The first step taken was to restrict the triggers to the two mutations most often reported as being subject to variable usage (AM and NM), and to include only those triggers that commonly occur in speech (these are listed below). Secondly, another technique was added to the data collection method: the reporter's test. This test requires the subject to report to an imaginary third person *exactly* what the tester is doing. Various activities were devised, moving coloured shapes, movement of hands and arms etc., which would guarantee utterances from the subject containing mutation triggers. Pilot studies showed that this test produced fairly casual speech, as the subject is so busy attending to the task, he forgets to monitor his speech output too closely (see Ball, 1986).

The variables examined

A set of linguistic and non-linguistic variables was drawn up. The linguistic variables were the commoner triggers of AM and NM, as follows:
AM
(1) *a*, "and";
(2) *â, gyda*, "with";
(3) *tri*, "three";
(4) *chwe*, "six";
(5) *na, tua*, "nor/than", "towards";
(6) *ei*, "her";
(7) negative verb (*ni, na* or ø + non-periphrastic verb form).

NM
(8) *yn*, "in".

With (1) – (6) the variants expected are +AM and radical; with (7) the variants expected are +AM +SM or radical with (8) the variants expected are +NM, +SM or radical. The reasons for grouping some of these triggers is discussed in Ball (1984b) and need not detain us here.

The non-linguistic variables included style. The interview was designed to capture four styles: casual, formal via the conversational part of the interview, reporter's test, and reading passage. In the event, the results divided into two categories: "formal" (formal + reading passage) and non-formal (casual + reporter's test).

The other non-linguistic variables were controlled in terms of the subjects chosen: sex, age and acculturation. The sex variable fortunately presents only the two variants of male and female. The age variable has however been split into many different variants according to different researchers' aims or resources. For this study, in order to keep the number of different variants reasonably low, within the capability of a single researcher project, three age categories only were chosen, and speakers under the age of 20 were not selected as subjects (see Hatton, this volume, Chapter 17 for a study of children's mutation usage). The age ranges chosen were: 20–39; 40–59; 60+.

In previous studies, social class has been widely chosen as a non-linguistic variable. However its operation in the minority language situation is arguably different from a monolingual situation (viz. R. O. Jones, 1976: 54), and in any case the notion has been criticized as being too abstract (Trudgill, 1974b), and as lacking "any kind of objective, or even intersubjective, reality" (Milroy, 1980: 14). R. O. Jones (1976) in the minority language situation constructs groups of speakers according to a general concept of *acculturation*, taking into account such aspects as education, religion, self-evaluation and economic status.

The difficulty in keeping to a social-class analysis in a bilingual situation is that the speakers who are bilingual are liable not to be spread evenly through the classes, especially when the language under investigation is the minority language in the community chosen. Only in areas where Welsh is spoken by a large majority of inhabitants would an even class mix be found. The area chosen for this study was Cwmtawe, the Swansea Valley (see also Siân Thomas, this volume, Chapter 8), which is now a minority Welsh-speaking area. For this reason, social class was not chosen as a variable, but rather use was made of an adapted form of R. O. Jones' acculturation index. This gave two groups: a w-group (acculturated to Welsh) and an E-group (acculturated to English).

The subjects

The subjects were chosen from the Cwmtawe region. One dialect area was chosen in order to avoid the dialect variable, as this would have added extra complexity to the study. A considerable amount of previous research has been done on Cwmtawe Welsh (though little on mutation usage; see Ball 1984b), and this coupled with the fact that I had access to various social networks in the area, led to the choice of area.

Subjects were not chosen by random sample. Instead the concept of the social network (see Chapter 3, and Milroy, 1980) was utilized. Two fairly dense networks were used, and 11 subjects chosen from each. All these subjects were given individual interviews, but in some cases the networks were exploited to obtain group recordings. In one sense, a random sampling of the networks took place, as not all first-order members of the networks were used. However, this was in fact a quasi-random sampling, as I ensured 11 male and 11 female subjects. Full details of these subjects were given in Ball (1984b), but if we examine the speakers in terms of the three age groups, we find that age and acculturation interact. Age Group I (20–39) contained two male and two female speakers, all classed as English-acculturated. At the other extreme, Group III

(60–79) contained four male and four female speakers, all classed as Welsh-acculturated. Only Group II (40–59) had a mixture of acculturation types: two male and three female Welsh-acculturated, and three male and two female English-acculturated.

It is interesting to note that from this quasi-random approach, although both networks had representatives in the three age groups and both acculturation groups, Welsh speakers in the younger age ranges were rare, and were all in the E-acculturation group. Conversely, there was no shortage of older speakers, who in turn were all the W-group. Doubtless younger W-speakers, and older E-speakers could have been found, but as both networks displayed the same characteristics, it was felt that this was representative of a sociolinguistic trend in Cwmtawe.

As we will see later, the acculturation variable was not, in the end, sufficient to capture the grouping of speakers in terms of how they used mutations, and I will argue that what is needed here is a classification in terms of what model of Welsh (standard or dialect) was used by speakers as the prestige version to which they looked, if indeed some speakers had any such model at all.

Results

As noted above, variables (1) – (5) had only two variants, so in these results, percentage non-mutation usage is given. Variable (6), (7) and (8) had three variants, so index scores were calculated for these. For (7), the following values were assigned to each variant: AM (most "standard"), 1; SM, 2; and radical (least standard) 3. For (8), the following values were assigned to each variant: NM, 1; SM, 2; radical, 3. Variable (6) (*ei*, "her") also in fact showed three variants: AM (standard), 1; radical, 2; SM (least standard in this case as *ei* + SM usually means "his"), 3. The method of calculating final scores is to multiply the value of each variant by the number of times it occurs for a subject and divided by the total of instances of the variable. The resultant index score is given numerical value by subtracting 1 and multiplying by 100.

The percentage-scored variables

The results for all speakers for variables (1) – (5) are shown in Figure 7.1. As can be seen the *a* variable approaches nearest to standard

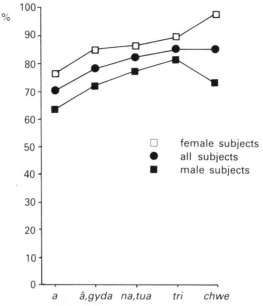

FIGURE 7.1   *The percentage scored variables*

Welsh usage with 70% non-standard forms. The next most standard is *â, gyda*. However, both these are well over the 50% mark. *Na, tua*, appears to fit with *â, gyda* into a medium scoring group (82% and 78% respectively). *Tri* and *chwe* form a high scoring group at 85%. The low and medium groups seem to be related to some extent with the speaker's age, suggesting perhaps the remains of a linguistic change over time; whereas the two numerals did not display this, suggesting a change that has virtually been completed in the dialect.

A linguistic explanation for the differences is also available. The common SM mutation often occurs following prepositions and some conjunctions (e.g. *neu*, "or"). The triggers in the low and medium groups are prepositions and conjunctions. Numerals (apart from *dau/dwy*, "two"; and *un*, "one", when with feminine nouns, all of which cause SM) generally do not trigger mutations. Further, *tair*, the feminine of *tri*, causes no mutation, and *chwech*, the form of *chwe* when not pre-nominal also causes no mutation. *Chwech* is often substituted for *chwe* in Cwmtawe Welsh. It would seem that the greater use of AM after *a* than after the other triggers may be due to the more frequent occurrence of this word, and because many "fossilized" idioms exist with *a* + AM (e.g. *ceffyl a chart*, "horse and cart").

Index-scored variables

The results for all speakers for variables (6) – (8) are shown in Figure 7.2. *Ei* has the result nearest to standard (index score 32; percentage of AM 74%). This must in part be explainable by the semantic load carried by the mutation in distinguishing *ei*, "her", from *ei*, "his". Questioning the subjects also leads me to feel that particular emphasis has been put on the correct usage of the mutation by teachers, parents and so on, because of the semantic aspect.

The next variable is *yn* (index 118; percentage NM: 37%) followed closely by negverb (index 124; percentage AM: 23%). Although both these variables showed some evidence of an expansion of SM, in fact mutation loss is a stronger factor than mutation replacement. *Yn* seems to differ from the AM triggers (apart from *ei*) in the tests of speakers' ability to perceive mutation errors (see Ball, 1985a) which show that, whatever the pattern of usage, the standard form *is* part of nearly all speakers' competence — language ability — whereas the other AM triggers are only peripherally so, if at all, for many speakers.

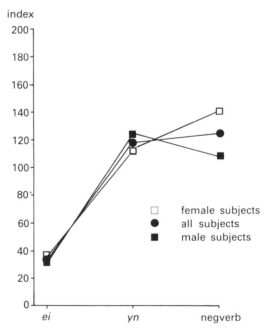

FIGURE 7.2   *The index scored variables*

Non-linguistic variables

Although it is difficult to separate the age variable from acculturation, it does seem that age is a factor in the results, particularly with *a* and *â*, *gyda* as noted above. The acculturation division (w/e) also shows a clear difference for most variables, and by combining the age and acculturation groupings, a consistent, and in some cases statistically significant, difference is found.

With the sex variable, the difference between male and female speakers is generally not statistically significant (though it is with *chwe*). However there is a consistent difference in that female speakers use more non-standard forms than the males. This goes counter to the usual findings (e.g. Trudgill, 1974a, b), that women retain standard forms more than men do. It appears that in this community the men are the ones who are more likely to be exposed to the force of standard Welsh; attending Welsh language activities, and reading and writing Welsh, more than the women do. This pattern of behaviour is also perhaps a reflection of other social patterns which restrict the role of women outside the home among the older members of the community.

The final non-linguistic variable is style. Generally speaking, as expected, the formal style showed greater standard mutation usage, and this was particularly strong with *tri* and *chwe*. This again suggests that these are triggers only known to those who can use standard Welsh. *Yn* (see comments above) also showed considerable style-shifting. Because of methodological problems described in Ball (1984b) the figures for *ei*, negverb, and *na, tua* were not examined in terms of style.

Subjects

The acculturation classification of subjects did not in fact prove totally satisfactory. Although clear differences were found, there were quite a number of cases where previously classed e-subjects seemed to behave like w-ones, and vice versa.

Therefore, it was decided to re-classify subjects into three groups by analysing how they actually used the variables. The scores for each variable could usually be divided into three usage bands (sometimes two). The scores for the bands varied from variable to variable, but it was mostly clear where the divisions should be made. The subjects' scores were averaged out, and subjects assigned to three groups. Table 7.1 shows the

TABLE 7.1   *Scores for variables by groups of speakers*

	a	*â, gyda*	*tri*	*chwe*	*na, tua*	*negverb*	*ei*	*yn*
A	33	37	65	64	43	113	21	61
B	78	96	91	91	100	97	32	134
C	100	100	100	100	100	177	45	158

scores (% and index) of non-standard mutation usage for the three groups. These figures clearly show that the data justify this division of subjects. Indeed, with many of the variables there was little or no overlap between the subjects in these groupings. Statistically, the following variables showed significant differences between the three groups: *a, â, gyda, tri, chwe, na, tua, yn*. Various intergroup differences were also significant.

This grouping does not wholly fit into the age or acculturation differences discussed above. It would appear to me that this division is one that relates to which form of Welsh the speakers use as a model of "correctness". Group A would appear to be those who have standard Welsh as a model, and have had access to Welsh education etc. Group B seem to operate within Cwmtawe Welsh, using the dialect as a standard. The main diagnostic (for AM at least) is that most of this group still have access to *a* + AM, which is still a peripheral feature of the dialect. Group C (consisting mainly of the younger and E-acculturated subjects) appear to have no model for mutation usage, in this respect. While not semi-speakers in all respects, this group also displayed considerable lexical borrowing from English.

Conclusion

This study has shown that variation in mutation usage does exist, but that this variation is in terms of the trigger contexts rather than the sound change in general. We have also seen how speakers in Cwmtawe divide into groups according to their mutation usage.

As with all studies of linguistic variation, the question arises as to how the linguist can capture this variation in the grammatical rules he writes. This problem, in the context of mutation usage, is tackled in Chapter 20 of this book.

Notes to Chapter 7

1. See G. E. Jones (1984b) and Ball (forthcoming) for a discussion of the so-called "voiceless nasals" in Welsh.
2. The so-called "pre-vocalic aspiration" is excluded from this chapter. See Ball (1984b) for a discussion of this feature.

Part III:
Studies of the Use of Welsh

8 A study of *Calediad* in the Upper Swansea Valley

SIÂN ELIZABETH THOMAS

Introduction

My research was centred around the village of Ystalyfera, situated in the Upper Swansea Valley.

During the Industrial Revolution, many families moved from Cardiganshire and Carmarthenshire into the Swansea Valley, searching for work in the coal mines and in the tin works. These people brought with them the traditions and customs of their native areas and the generations that followed were the product of a fusion of two cultures — that of the industrial valley and the rural culture of West Wales.

One of the most important influences on the day-to-day life of the inhabitants was religion. The many chapels in the village were the centre of social life. Almost every chapel had its own drama society, choir, children's choir and recitation party, and the competition between them at the local eisteddfodau was very fierce. The language of each chapel and its activities was Welsh, although some of the annual events were conducted through the medium of English. Little has changed in that respect. With the exception of the United Reformed Church and the Church in Wales, Sunday worship and all the chapel activities are still carried out through the medium of Welsh.

Ystalyfera was also renowned in the Valley for its choral tradition, and many of its choirs were National Eisteddfod winners. For those who were not singers there was always the brass band. The village had, and still has, two brass bands. For those not musically inclined there was sport, with the choice of rugby, cricket and bowls.

There were seven coal mines in the area, but unlike the Rhondda, where villages were built around the mines, all seven at Ystalyfera were outside the village. The iron works were among the first in the country, and until about 15 years ago, traces of the old canal that carried goods to Swansea still remained. Today a by-pass follows the course of the old canal through the village.

The local junior school teaches bilingually. Until pupils reach the age of seven, lessons are almost totally through the medium of Welsh; from eight years of age until they leave the school at the age of eleven, more and more English is introduced. As a result, some families choose to send their children to the Welsh Junior School at Pontardawe, five miles away. At the age of eleven, children have the choice of attending either the English-medium comprehensive school, Cwmtawe, at Pontardawe, or Ysgol Gyfun, Ystalyfera, the Welsh-medium comprehensive school. The last ten years have seen an increase in the number of children entering the Welsh School, and now the children are evenly divided between both English and Welsh comprehensive schools.

About 50 years ago, two council estates were built in Ystalyfera — one above and one below the "old" village. They had the effect of anglicizing the village, although the middle band — the "old" village — has remained strongly Welsh.

This brief history has looked at the cultural and linguistic background of the people of Ystalyfera — a society with a strong but mixed cultural background — and my study concentrated on a cross-section of this society.

Research project

My research concentrated on the devoicing of consonants used in the Welsh spoken by a cross-section of the Welsh speakers of Ystalyfera. This devoicing, or *caledu*, occurs in the middle of a word when one of the voices consonants — [b][d][g] — is situated between two vowels, or between a vowel and [n][l][r], that is

vowel + [b][d][g] + vowel;
vowel + [b][d][g] + [n][l][r].

In the Welsh spoken in a large part of the old County of Glamorgan, the consonants change from being voiced consonants to being voiceless consonants — [p][t][k]. For example:

cegin would become "cekin";
cadair would become "cater/catair";
pysgodyn would become "pysgotyn".

This *calediad* of the consonants is especially strong in the Welsh dialects spoken in the Upper Swansea Valley, and in Ystalyfera in particular. The purpose of my study therefore was to discover whether this was a feature which varied according to age, and the amount of education received by each speaker, and, if so, why?

I looked at many ways of sampling speakers before deciding on "stratified random sampling", or "quasi-random sampling", as the method best suited to my needs.

". . .because the method does improve representativeness, it allows the use of a smaller sample than does simple random sampling, with a greater precision and consequent saving in time and money." (Goode & Hatt, 1952: 221)

I divided the Welsh speaking community into five age groups as follows:

(A) children under the age of 11;
(B) young people between the ages of 11 and 25, (to include those in secondary education, college or university if necessary);
(C) speakers between the ages of 25 and 40;
(D) speakers between the ages of 40 and 70;
(E) speakers over 70 years of age.

After choosing 3% of each group by quasi-random sampling, I was left with a total of 29 speakers. Although I did not wish to complicate the study by using more sub-divisions, I felt that certain factors merited consideration. The sex of the speaker was particularly important when studying Group E — a group in which the male of the family went out to work, leaving the female at home. Two different speech forms were possible in this situation, one for each sex. Education was important in all groups, especially when comparing the limited, English-medium education which the older generation of Group E received, with the choice of Welsh- or English-medium education offered to the younger generation in Groups A, B, C. Family background, social life and occupation were also important. Bearing the words of Milroy in mind, I decided to use 'tokens' to categorize my speakers further:

"No method of analysis in the present state of knowledge is likely to capture completely the complexity of the way speakers use varia- bility; but to add in a necessarily limited way the dimension of individual choice to those variables already considered (which may be seen as lying outside the speakers control), we use here the analytic tool of social network analysis. This allows, to some extent, qualification of the character of an individual's everyday social relationships — the influences to which he is constantly open." (Milroy, 1980: 115)

As well as the questionnaire, that gave me the linguistic information I needed, I had a series of questions to provide the data needed to complete the token grading on each speaker. After completing preliminary interviews with each of my speakers, I was happy that my sample was representative of the Welsh-speaking community of Ystalyfera.

My study was of pronunciation and so a questionnaire that provided oral answers was necessary. The first spontaneous answer was recorded on tape and left me free to concentrate on making the interviewees feel relaxed. I was also able to analyse the interview in detail at home. One interesting point arose from my tape-recording of the interviews — there was a feeling among some of the older speakers that their Welsh was "not good enough" to be recorded! However, after some persuasion, and the reassurance that I would be the only one who would listen to the tapes, they all agreed to be interviewed. Labov (1963), in his study of the language of young males on Martha's Vineyard Island in Massachusetts in the mid-1960s, showed the great difference between formal and informal language. My own study needed to show the differing degrees of *calediad* in formal and informal situations, and so, bearing Labov's study in mind, I made sure that time was left for informal chat at the end of each interview. The informality was often achieved by pretending to switch the recorder off at the end of the formal interview, remembering, of course, to make it clear to each speaker that I had done so before completing the interview.

The questionnaire included a large number of familiar words with sounds in a position to *caledu*, and were simple enough for the youngest speaker to be able to read. These words were: made into word-lists to be read; inserted into a piece of prose, to be read; made into phrases to be translated. Questions were asked where the chosen words would be the answers. There were also individual words to be translated and pictures to describe chosen words; and of course the 'chat' at the end of the interview. I also decided on informal conversation between each section of the interview, trying to direct the conversation to subjects such as birthdays, holidays, favourite food, sport, hobbies, etc.

At the end of the interview I was satisified that I had recorded sufficient samples of both formal and informal speech.

Results of research

An interesting and unexpected factor emerged whilst I was analysing the tapes. I had presumed that the results would be clear-cut; there would either be *caledu* or no *caledu*, but I found that there were two strengths of *caledu*. The Welsh of Ystalyfera, therefore, had three sub-divisions within this one variation — a strong *caledu*, a weaker *caledu*, and no *caledu* whatsoever.

[b][d][g] are lenis unaspirated voiced sounds — sounds that are created by using a weak muscular energy. In order to achieve *caledu*, the lenis unaspirated voiced sound becomes a fortis unaspirated voiceless sound, that is a sound achieved by using a strong muscular energy and more breath. The result is [p][t][k].

The *calediad gwan* (weak) falls somewhere between the two — there is less voice needed. The result is [b̥][d̥][g̥].

(1)   The original [b][d][g] lenis unaspirated voiced;
(2)   *calediad cryf* [p][t][k] fortis unaspirated voiceless;
(3)   *calediad gwan* [b̥][d̥][g̥] lenis unaspirated voiceless.

When *caledu cryf* (strong) is achieved, two phonetic characteristics are changed — lenis to fortis and voiced to voiceless.
When *caledu gwan* (weak) is achieved, only one phonetic characteristic is changed — voiced to voiceless. For example:

ugain, 'twenty'	[igain]:	the original, standard Welsh pronunciation
	[igen]:	how the word is normally pronounced in spoken Welsh;
	[iken]:	the word with *caledu cryf*;
	[i-gen]:	the word with *caledu gwan* and
	[i-gen̥]:	voiceless.

I shall refer to both types of *caledu* as *caledu cryf* and *caledu gwan* for the remainder of this article, and try to explain why this happens, and when. When referring to the general process of *caledu*, I shall use either *caledu* (the verb), or *calediad* (the noun). *Calediad cryf* and *calediad gwan* include both noun and adjective.

Certain results were common to each group, and I feel I must mention these before moving on to the general analysis of results. Only rarely did the consonant [b] *caledu* in each of the five age groups, but especially so in Group D. It is obvious, therefore, that this linguistic variation is gradually disappearing. In my opinion, the [b] will be the first to lose its corresponding sound in *calediad*, that is [p]. This could happen in the near future.

A further point was that almost all the speakers would *caledu* far more frequently as the interview progressed, and as they became more relaxed. When a swear word which contained consonants in a position to *caledu* slipped in, then almost without exception it would happen, for example *diawledig*, "devilish". There was also a tendency in all the speakers to speed up the pace of speech as they became more relaxed and soon forgot the fear of not "speaking properly".

As mentioned earlier, another variation came to light during the interview period, one I had not foreseen. It became obvious that the *calediad gwan* existed. As *calediad* became less and less strong, *calediad cryf* became *calediad gwan*, and then disappeared completely. The finer difference between the two variations are analysed earlier in this article.

The influence of the English speakers in the area was noticeably strong too, especially in Group A — the very young children. In the section of the interview given to translation, and question and answer, I was surprised at the number of speakers who gave me an answer in English. This was even more surprising when one remembers that I had only included every-day words in the whole of the questionnaire.

Interpretation of research

As previously stated, the purpose of my study was to find the degree of *calediad* that existed in the spoken Welsh of the people of Ystalyfera, and to discover whether this variation depended on the speaker's age, education and cultural likes and dislikes. It was particularly interesting to note the difference between Group A and Group E. Both groups were more limited in their possible spectra of speech than the other groups, but there was a difference between these two groups — Group A had only one language variety, whereas Group E was aware of a formal and informal language.

Seventy years or so ago a full formal education was a privilege — something for the very rich or the highly gifted. The vast majority of the population received little or no formal education. In this respect, Ystalyfera was no different from other industrial areas. Generally speaking, only those who entered the ministry to follow a religious calling, or those who trained to become teachers, received higher education. The speakers of Group E would have been youngsters during this period, and this explains why so few of them had received any formal education. Yet they are all intelligent people who show an interest in local activities. They were aware of a formal and informal language, but since education is not the reason for the ability of this group to speak a formal language, what were the other contributing factors?

Religion and the social life that surrounded the chapels were a great influence on this age group, an influence that has become less important over the years. In the chapels — or rather in the Sunday Schools — the villagers received the other, additional education. Here people were taught to read classics written in a formal Welsh — the Bible and hymn books. Chapel members became used to taking part in the services — once again in a formal language — and the language used throughout the services was a formal one too. We are therefore indebted to the chapels for giving the ordinary inhabitants a formal language of a high standard of correctness that has remained part of their speech to this day.

There are, of course, exceptions to every rule. One or two of the speakers in Group E kept their "every-day" language even in the most formal conditions. However, taking the group as a whole, the two forms of language spoken by Group E were made clear in the difference in levels of *caledu* between the more formal sections of the interview and the free speech section.

The average results of Group E in each category are given in Table 8.1. The lack of a formal Welsh was obvious in the speech of those individuals who were not chapel-goers, and also in the speech of those who chose to worship through the medium of English.

TABLE 8.1

	Calediad cryf (%)	Calediad gwan (%)
Word-lists	2.02	16.47
Reading	4.62	21.31
Translating	15.17	21.37
Question and answer	22.38	29.92
Pictures	21.33	29.33
Informal speech	45.28	21.97

One of the speakers in Group E showed the influence of education
on the speech of this age group. She had been a teacher and had therefore
received a good formal college education. Due to her position as a teacher,
her every-day speech had become formal, and *calediad* as a variation of
her formal speech had almost completely disappeared. She was able to
converse on far more subjects through the medium of Welsh than many
of her contemporaries, but she had lost much of her natural dialect.
However, she was found to have a degree of *calediad gwan*. Could this
suggest that, hidden in the formal speech which had become her every-
day speech, there was still a hint of dialect? Her *calediad gwan* reached
its peak in the picture section, 60%, and its lowest in the word-list, 24%.
Religion was of little or no influence on her speech: she attended the
local church and therefore worshipped through the medium of English.

As I moved from group to group — down in age — education
became more and more important, especially so in Groups C, B, A. Each
member of Groups A and B were receiving, or had received, a full
education as required by law, and Group B had been given the opportunity
to receive a full education through the medium of Welsh. Results showed
that their percentage of *calediad*, both *cryf* and *gwan*, remained low in
each section of the interview. It is obvious that *calediad cryf* is rapidly
decreasing in the speech of the younger members of society, and that
education could be the main reason for this. Although the contribution
of the Welsh schools is immeasureable, they are also indirectly responsible
for the decline of local dialect by over-standardizing the language of the
children attending these schools, and for neutralizing their dialect. It is
true that, thanks to the Welsh schools, children are able to converse on
almost any subject in Welsh, but always in formal language. They are
almost equally at home in a variety of linguistic situations and are therefore
less aware of the difference between formal and informal speech. Surely
there must be a way of offering a high standard of education through the
medium of Welsh, and keeping the local dialect, rather than creating a
dialect that is almost unique to that particular school, which is what
happens at the moment.

We are rapidly approaching a bilingual situation within a bilingual
situation, where within the language of the Welsh speakers we have the
Welsh spoken by people who have attended Welsh Schools and the Welsh
spoken by the others. I have already mentioned that *calediad cryf* is
disappearing in the speech of the younger members of the society, but I
must also note that *calediad gwan* is also on the decline. I feel certain
that if the members of Group A were interviewed again in ten years'
time, any *calediad* they still have will have disappeared, leaving their

language formal, correct, but with little trace of local dialect. If only it were possible to encourage local dialect whilst teaching a formal language.

Education, or the lack of it, is very important in the development of a language. Despite the fact that the older speakers had little or no formal education, the society itself was responsible for conditioning their language. I believe that the fact that society itself was culturally very strong must have been responsible for maintaining and strengthening the Welshness of the area, despite outside influences. But the cultural life of the area is not as strong today, and therefore does not influence language as it did. The day-to-day language of the older generation is often more correct than the day-to-day language of the younger speakers, even though they are not as well educated. Their language reflected the society they were part of — a very Welsh society. The language of the younger speakers also reflects the society of which they are part. Generally speaking, the Welsh spoken by those children above the age of eight years, who are not members of the Welsh schools, tends to be of a lower standard than that of the others. There are exceptions of course. If Welsh is the language of the home, then the influence of the school is not as great.

There are three main influences on the Welsh spoken at Ystalyfera — education, religion, and the anglicizing of the social life. Age is a contributing factor to all three.

When the members of Group E were children, Welsh was spoken in all situations — at work and at play. The young are always associated with bringing about change. Over the years, more and more English was introduced into the society of Ystalyfera, and gradually replaced Welsh as the main language. To a large degree, English is now the medium of children's play, mainly due to the influx of non-Welsh speaking families into the village. A large number of the children living in the old section of the village speak Welsh fluently as a first language. Children of non-Welsh speaking families who have moved into the village — mainly into the two council estates — are not Welsh speakers. Both sets of children attend the same village school, and so English becomes the language of play, and, to a great degree, the language of the school. Bearing this in mind, it is surprising that such a large number of the local children still speak Welsh, but it is not surprising that their *calediad* has all but disappeared.

Certain cultural activities in the area are still held through the medium of Welsh, but they are activities that appeal to the older generation. Very little, with the exception of activities arranged by the chapels, is arranged through the medium of Welsh for the young children. All their societies are English — St John's Ambulance, Brownies, Girl Guides, Scouts and Youth Club. There is a local branch of the *Urdd* (the Welsh League of Youth) at Pontardawe, three miles away, but this again caters for those over 11 years of age, not for the very young. Once again we are indebted to the chapels for preserving the Welshness of this generation as well as in previous generations. However, things are getting better. Nursery children now have the opportunity of attending the local branch of *Mudiad Ysgolion Meithrin* — the Welsh medium playgroups. These children were obviously too young to interview, but it is encouraging, and will, hopefully, contribute greatly to the Welshness of the area in future years.

I have concentrated my attention so far on Groups A and E — the oldest and the youngest speakers. It is easier to see the general picture in this way. The other groups fall somewhere between these two. When members of Group E were young, the Welsh language was given a place of importance and respect, and today the language is once again respected and becoming increasingly important, thanks mainly to the increase in the number of Welsh schools. Groups C and D were somewhat mixed linguistically: they worked through the medium of English and socialized through the medium of the language of lesser importance — Welsh. Their speech reflects this — there is no pattern — it is a disorganized mixture of both languages.

Generally speaking, dialect is becoming less and less a part of the speech of the area, and *calediad*, as a variation of dialect, is quickly disappearing too. Many people are of the opinion that Welsh, as a medium of speech for the older generation is old-fashioned, and that English is now the medium of the young and the influential. We turn to the schools for help, but the local school is becoming more and more anglicized, whilst the Welsh taught in Welsh schools is standard but without dialect, and is somewhat unnatural. It is true to say that as educational standards improve, dialects decrease. This is especially true of the younger groups.

Calediad gwan also increased as we move from Group A to B. In Group A we saw the lowest percentage of *calediad cryf* and *calediad gwan*, but by Group D we saw that *calediad gwan* decreased as *calediad cryf* increased.

Groups A and B had two dialect variations — *calediad cryf* or *gwan*, and no *calediad*, whilst Groups C, D and E had three variations — *calediad cryf*, *calediad gwan*, and no *calediad*. The high percentage of *calediad gwan* in each group showed that *calediad* is generally decreasing. Although *calediad* is still strong in the speech of the locals, it is only noticeably so when they are completely at home in a situation speaking to friends. This is something one notices when listening to conversations in local shops.

The average results for each group, given in Table 8.2, when seen side by side, make the picture somewhat clearer.

TABLE 8.2   Calediad *by speaker group in percentages*

	Calediad cryf (%)	Calediad gwan (%)
Group A		
Word-lists	0	9.5
Reading	0	5.5
Translating	0	17.05
Question and answer	6.25	33.00
Pictures	20.83	23.75
Informal speech	18.25	18.25
Group B		
Word-lists	0.83	8.3
Reading	0.98	4.33
Translating	5.18	9.00
Question and answer	7.77	15.89
Pictures	16.44	25.55
Informal speech	22.83	21.05
Group C		
Word-lists	2.3	8.13
Reading	5.7	11.33
Translating	2.21	10.67
Question and answer	20.44	24.74
Pictures	35.55	11.60
Informal speech	58.52	16.00
Group D		
Word-lists	5.63	13.99
Reading	6.13	18.34
Translating	20.46	25.10
Question and answer	26.51	27.80
Pictures	19.48	25.75
Informal speech	39.13	31.12
Group E		
Word-lists	2.02	16.47
Reading	4.62	21.31
Translating	15.17	21.37
Question and answer	22.38	29.92
Pictures	21.33	29.33
Informal speech	45.28	21.97

In conclusion, my particular study made it clear that *calediad* as part of the dialect of Ystalyfera is slowly disappearing, mainly due to the improvement in standards of education, the gradual decline of Welsh activities in the village, the decreasing influence of the chapels, and the increase in English activities in the Valley. Unless we are able to improve and expand Welsh medium education, change the way it is taught, and try to halt the influence of English, I cannot see a long term future for *calediad* as a variation in the dialect of the Welsh-speaking people of Ystalyfera.

Notes to Chapter 8

1. This chapter is based on fieldwork carried out by the author for an MA degree of the University of Wales, 1981–83.

9 Some features of the Welsh of Breconshire

GLYN E. JONES

The territory referred to by the term Breconshire in this description constituted one of the original 13 counties of Wales. This shire unit existed from 1536 until 1974, when, with the re-organization of local government, it was incorporated into the new and larger county of Powys. With minor changes on the southern border, the old Breconshire corresponds to the present-day District of Brecknock within Powys (see H. Griffiths, 1981–86).

The original Breconshire was itself composed of two earlier units, namely Cantref Buellt, the area forming the northern tip of the county, extending from the Epynt mountain to the boundary with Radnorshire, and the *gwlad* of Brycheiniog. The *gwlad* of Brycheiniog was one of the native kingdoms of Wales. It was probably founded in the fourth century (Copplestone-Crow, 1982), and retained its territorial identity, and to some extent, its independence as a native Welsh kingdom, up to the coming of the Normans in the eleventh century. Over the following three centuries, Cantref Buellt and the *gwlad* of Brycheiniog constituted lands which were disputed territories involving, at different times. Llywelyn ap Gruffydd, the English crown, and Norman families such as de Braose, fitz-Herbert, de Bohum, de Clare, Despenser and Mortimer (W. Rees, 1968). Under the terms of the 1536 *Act of Union of England and Wales*, Cantref Buellt and the territory of the former *gwlad* of Brycheiniog were joined to form a new shire unit — Breconshire (Bowen, 1908: 79). Figure 9.1 displays the main areas of the county. The distribution of some lexical items do still seem to reflect the historical territorial divide between the old Cantref Buellt[1] and the *gwlad* of Brycheiniog, but only one item, *bera*, 'a haystack', is known to correlate exclusively with the old *gwlad* of Brycheiniog (see G. E. Jones, 1985b: 69–72).

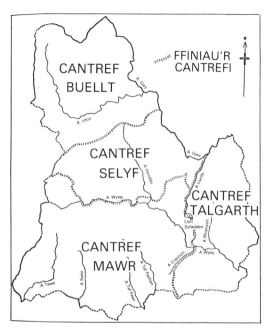

FIGURE 9.1
Source: (*Atlas Brycheiniog* p. 38)

The Welsh language in Breconshire

According to the 1981 Census (Office of Population Censuses and Surveys, 1982), Welsh is spoken by 24.2% of the population of the District of Brecknock.[2] However, the majority of these speakers live in the west of the District, with far fewer speakers living in the east. This west-east divide is well-established in Breconshire. Pryce (1978: 11, Figure 2) has shown that, on the evidence of parochial returns concerning language use in Sunday services, the eastern flank of Breconshire (along with the Welsh border country in general of course) constituted a bilingual language zone in the mid-eighteenth century, whilst the west of the county was Welsh. Southall (1892) in his linguistic map of Wales gave a roughly tripartite division of the county from east to west: the north-eastern edge being English-speaking only; the middle with less than 60% of the population being Welsh-speaking; the west with over 60% of the population being Welsh-speaking.

This description of some of the features of Breconshire Welsh is based on a study (G. E. Jones, 1983) of the Welsh of speakers from the west of the county, mainly from the area extending from Defynnog to Llanwrtyd. This area includes speakers from the scattered communities of Llandeilo'r-fân, Llanfihangel Nant Brân, Tirabad and Llangamarch. All the speakers were from the older age-group (65+), and were all life-long inhabitants of their native areas. Almost all were from an agricultural background, that is they were farmers, sons, daughters, wives of farmers, farm labourers, and women who had been in service on farms. All were of a similar educational background, having completed their formal education between the ages of 13 and 15.

The Welsh of Breconshire

The variety of Welsh spoken in Breconshire is of great interest to the dialectologist. Geographically, Breconshire links south-east Wales, specifically Morgannwg and Gwent, with mid-Wales. South-east Wales has its own distinct variety of Welsh, known since the Middle Ages as *Gwenhwyseg* (see this volume, Chapter 2). Mid-Wales constitutes a highly important and complex transition area between southern and northern varieties of Welsh. Important phonological isoglosses occur here (see for example Darlington, 1902; Awbery, 1984: 76), as well as numerous lexical isoglosses (many described in *The Linguistic Geography of Wales*, here-after *LGW*, A. R. Thomas, 1973 for example, pp. 16, 37–38; see also this volume, Chapter 4). The disappearance of the Welsh language from Radnorshire — the county area immediately to the north of Breconshire — makes the evidence of Breconshire vital for an understanding and knowledge of the characteristics of the Welsh of this lower midland area of mid-Wales.

Interesting examples of the linking function that Breconshire has between the Welsh of the south-east and that of mid-Wales can be seen if we look at the geographical spread of the most salient features of south-east Wales.

Consonantal phonemes

The distribution of the consonantal phonemes /h/, the glottal frica-tive, and /r̥/. the voiceless aspirated alveolar trill. These phonemes do not occur in the Welsh dialects of Glamorgan, the glottal fricative being replaced by ø, and the voiceless aspirated alveolar trill by a voiced alveolar trill [r]. Thus such words as *hapus*, "happy", *heno*, "tonight", *rhif*, "number", *rhwydd*, "easy", are realized as [apɪs, eno, riv, rʊɪð] and not as [hapis, heno, r̥iv, r̥ʊɪð].

An analysis of the occurrence of [h] and [r̥] in the speech of some Breconshire speakers in an area extending from its borders with Glamorganshire across the county to Llanwrtyd in the north (G. E. Jones, 1983: 101–7) showed both variables becoming gradually established with [h] scoring 88% and 90% occurrence in the speech of some informants in the north, and [r̥] 73% and 75% occurrence. Informants in the south of the county had 0% occurrence for [h] and [r̥]. Clearly, Breconshire spans the transition to/from the [h]- and [r̥]-less dialects of south-east Wales.

Provection (see also this volume, Chapter 8)

This feature is the neutralization of the contrast between voiced and voiceless plosives in the penultimate syllable; the voiceless plosives only, [p, t, k], may appear in this position in Glamorgan Welsh. This feature is found in Breconshire, but diminishes as one proceeds northwards across the county, until only a few items such as [ikɛn] < *ugain*, "twenty, a score", [ruprɪd] < *rhywbryd*, "sometimes", [ɔɪtran] < *oedran*, "age", exhibit the feature (see G. E. Jones, 1983: 241–44).

-ws inflection

The third person singular past tense ending *-ws* of the inflected verb (see also this volume, Chapter 6) is the norm in Glamorgan Welsh but proceeding northwards across Breconshire it is replaced by *-odd*. Although the *-ws* ending was not recorded in the speech of informants north of the Epynt mountain (G. E. Jones, 1983: 257), historical evidence suggests that its distribution extended as far north as Radnorshire in the seventeenth and eighteenth centuries (Awbery, Jones & Suggett, 1985: 12–13).

Base forms of irregular verbs

The base forms of the irregular verbs *mynd*, "to go", *dod*, "to come", *cael*, "to get/have", *gwneud*, "to make/do". In Glamorgan dialect, the base forms of these verbs in the imperfect tense are *el-*, *del-*, *cel-*, *gnel-* respectively (C. Thomas, 1974: 273). Thus first-person singular imperfect would be *elwn*, *delwn*, *celwn*, *gnelwn*. Proceeding northwards through Breconshire, base forms with *-s* emerge, and one finds forms such as these for the third person singular imperfect: *gnele/gnese*, *ele/ese*, *dele/dese* in variation (G. E. Jones, 1983: 260–65). Further north still in the Dyfi basin area of mid-Wales, the *l* base forms have been completely supplanted by the *s* forms (see Sommerfelt, 1925: 78–80).

Close central vowel

An extremely important isogloss that occurs in mid-Wales is that demarcating the spread of the close central vowel [ɨ], orthographic *u* as in *du*, "black", or *y* as in *dyn*, "man". The presence/absence of the central vowel is considered to be the feature that most distinguishes northern Welsh from southern Welsh. Its isoglossic route was located in the first instance by Darlington (1902: 14–15), and confirmed (but with slight adjustments) in a later study by Sommerfelt[3] (1925: 133–35). More recent work, however, has uncovered the occurrence of the central vowel in the speech of informants in the Llanwrtyd area of north Breconshire (G. E. Jones, 1983: 28–29), and on the Brecon–Radnorshire border.[4] The details of its occurrence in north Breconshire so closely match those in Sommerfelt's account (see G. E. Jones, 1983: 72–78) that it seems highly unlikely that we are dealing with a 'relic' area in north Breconshire, but rather that the central vowel has a much wider distribution over mid-Wales than was hitherto supposed. It follows, therefore, that the Darlington/Sommerfelt isogloss (shown in this volume, see Chapter 2, Figure 2.2) has been plotted too far north. This evidence from Breconshire is an indication of the crucial place Breconshire occupies in the mid-Wales transition zone.

Lexical evidence

The lexical evidence from Breconshire[5] also sheds a great deal of light on some interesting speech areas. A. R. Thomas (1973) has shown that the boundary of the south-east Wales speech area — one of the major speech areas established in *LGW* (see *LGW*, Figure 5, or this volume, Figure 2.4), and the boundary of East Glamorgan — one of 16 minor speech areas established in *LGW* (see *LGW*, Figure 14) run for part of their route in the Usk Valley and Epynt mountain area of Breconshire. This means that south Breconshire frequently has many lexical items in common with Glamorgan, e.g. *clwydi*, "gate" (*LGW*, Figure 108), *mysgu*, "to untie bootlaces" (*LGW*, Figure 275). It is interesting to note that the northern boundary of some phonological and morphological features common to the Welsh of Glamorgan and south Breconshire also occurs in the Usk Valley/Epynt mountain area (see remarks on *-ws* above, and see G. E. Jones, 1983: 436–38).

The study[6] of the distribution of some lexical items in south-east Breconshire has revealed the existence of a new speech area in this south-eastern corner of Wales which spans south-east Breconshire and north-east Glamorgan. For example, the word for "lightning" in south-east Breconshire is *goleuni*, and P. W. Thomas (1984: 132) has shown that this is also the word in north-east Glamorgan. Another item sharing a similar distribution in both areas is *riciard*, "rickyard" (P. W. Thomas, 1982: 79).

The occurrence of the same lexical items in the north of Breconshire and along its eastern flank especially links the county with the Dyfi basin area of mid-Wales. This area includes parts of the old counties of Merioneth and Montgomery. Examples of such lexical items are *troi*, "to plough" (*LGW*, Figure 64); *ffald*, "sheepfold" (*LGW*, Figure 71); *sangid/siengid*, "to trample" (*LGW*, Figure 117); *hancsiar*, "handkerchief" (*LGW*, Figure 168); and *cratsh*, "cratch" (LGW, Figure 199). As A. R. Thomas (1973) has shown (see *LGW*, p. 80, and G. E. Jones, 1984c: 97 for further examples) the distribution of these items clearly indicates the existence of a speech area that originally extended along the eastern flank of mid-Wales spanning these counties and including Radnorshire.

In this context, three interesting lexical items are *weinws*, "cart-house" (*LGW*, Figure 70), from English "wain-house"; *ffelys*, "outer circle of a wheel" (*LGW*, Figure 204), from English "*felloe, fellys*"; and *troffin*, "roof-gutter" (*LGW*, Figure 92) from English "troughing". These three items are borrowings from English[7] and are peculiar to the Welsh dialects of the border area and are probably quite old (rather than recent) borrowings (see further *LGW*, p. 80). The very proximity of these border dialects to the English/Welsh divide would have made them susceptible to lexical interference from English, and the evidence of parochial returns on language use, referred to above, showed that these border areas had an English-speaking element in the population in the mid-eighteenth century.

Breconshire Welsh does also have many words that are peculiar to it, and to conclude this chapter, we may examine some of these. Examples are *slap (e)ira*, for "sleet" (see G. E. Jones, 1985c: 109–10); *slap* being a borrowing from English meaning "refuse fluids, rinsings"; *sieglyn/jaglyn*, "a small load of hay", also a borrowing, from English "jag" meaning "a small load"; *cede*, "an implement to carry hay to animals"; *llior lla(e)th*, "a milk skimmer"; *cryn(h)oddi*, "to tidy the house" (see G. E. Jones, 1985c: 107); *tes bach (gŵyl) Mihangel*, "an Indian summer"; *twlu dŵr*, "dew falls" (see G. E. Jones, 1985c: 111); *hala dechreunos*, literally "to spend the evening", a term for a social custom of gathering in a neighbour's house to hold a knitting assembly (see G. E. Jones, 1985a: 116–18).

Notes to Chapter 9

1. The distribution of some lexical items do mark the territory of the old Cantref Buellt as a distinct speech area within Breconshire, but these do not correlate exclusively with the Cantref Buellt area, but occur also in areas to the west and north of Cantref Buellt. An example is: Cantref Buellt: *mellt*, "lightning"; remainder of Breconshire: *llyched/goleuni*. Two items which seem to be peculiar to the Cantref Buellt area are *tŷ cobin*, "hayshed" and *poten*, "potato and swede mash". For full details see G. E. Jones & A. Jones (forthcoming a).
2. See Office of Population Censuses and Surveys (1982: 55, Table 42). The population of the District of Brecknock in the 1981 Census was 38,148, and the total number of Welsh speakers was 9,232.
3. This isogloss was drawn on a map by Iorwerth Peate and published in Sommerfelt (1925). Peate also sought to locate the boundary of the distribution of the central vowel and some other dialect features in the Dyfi basin of mid-Wales (Peate, 1925: 21).
4. This evidence is discussed in detail in G. E. Jones (forthcoming).
5. This evidence is presented in detail in G. E. Jones & A. Jones (forthcoming b).
6. See note 5 above.
7. It should be noted that the first element in *weinws* may be an indigenous Welsh word, *gwain*, "wagon". Hence *weinws* may be a hybrid form from Welsh *gwain* and English *house*. See *LGW*, p. 80 and p. 113.

10 Age-related variation in the Welsh dialect of Pwllheli[1]

ANNA E. ROBERTS

Pwllheli is a small, quiet, pleasant seaside town on the Southern side of the Llŷn Peninsula in the old county of Caernarvonshire. Its population of 4,000 is probably trebled during the peak tourist season in summer. Despite this, even during the couple of months of enforced anglicization Welsh is frequently heard spoken in shops and in the famous Wednesday market.

The surrounding area is rural and even to this day it would be possible for an English-speaking person to learn Welsh naturally in this environment and be absorbed into the community. Local inhabitants, however, are well-aware of the fact that "the enemy" is strong and there is an awareness of the fact that the area is one of the last bastions of the Welsh language. However, conflict exists in this respect because it is a financially deprived area; there are no heavy industries and employment is mainly on farms, in shops, hotels or offices and such an area welcomes the financial contribution tourists make during the summer months. Some tourists, also, find the area so attractive that they choose to retire to the area and, indeed, in the 1981 Census it is seen that the ratio of old (65+) to the remainder of the population in Dwyfor is around 1:4. The talented and less-talented youngsters often choose to leave the district to find employment, further impoverishing the region of its native Welsh speakers.

Those youngsters that remain, however, are not unaffected by modern life and the spoken dialects of the younger and older Welsh native speaker, although having much in common, show some divergences, especially in the semantic and grammatical fields. It could be argued that the prevalence of English and American television in the pre-S4C days when there was little opportunity to watch Welsh programmes has had its effect on the young during their formative years and that this is reflected in their spoken dialect. However, these matters do not have a direct bearing on the present essay, but they do serve to provide the reader with the background to what follows.

Initially, I shall look at the dialect of the Pwllheli area from the phonetic point of view. In this respect, the dialect has much in common with the spoken Welsh of Gwynedd as a whole although there are slight, but comparatively insignificant differences, in articulation. Despite the fact that Pwllheli is a rural town, the dialect shows many English influences which are not present to such an extent in the spoken Welsh of some rural areas such as the far point of the Llŷn peninsula. To the layman Gwynedd Welsh is easily distinguished from the dialects of other parts of Wales by the predominance of the /a/ phoneme in the last syllable of words which are orthographically represented by "e" for example [kapal], "chapel", [kerðad], "walk", [goglað], "north" and by the phoneme /i/. Allophones of /i/ are found in many words for example [mi:l, air, oirax, kəmri] viz. "donkey", "gold", "colder", "Wales".

In the dialect of Pwllheli there are 32 phonemes:

/p/, /t/, /k/, /b/, /d/, /g/, /x/, /ð/, /v/, /f/, /ŋ/, /h/, /l/, /ɬ/, /m/, /n/, /r/, /s/, /ʃ/, /θ/, /dʒ/, /tʃ/, /m̥/, /j/, /w/, /a/, /e/, /i/, /o/, /i/, /u/, /ə/.

Of these, a few deserve to be singled out, mainly because they show English influences.

The consonants have much in common with those of other parts of Wales and, in general, have not been singled out for attention. In passing, however, it may be noted that one borrowed consonant is generally absent in the spoken Welsh (and English) of the district and that is /z/ as in the English "zoo", which is borrowed in the dialect as: [su:]. Many "borrowed" English consonants have, by now, become a long-established feature of this dialect, for example /ʃ/ as in [ʃi:t] and [ʃed], [poʃ], [sblaʃ], "sheet, shed, posh, splash". This is not an allophone of /s/ as proved by a pair of borrowed words:

si:t (not often heard), "seat";   ʃi:t, "sheet".

It is also found, however, in native words such as [ʃarad] and [iʃo] where it is orthographically interpreted as "siarad", "to speak", and "eisio", "want". It may be noted, however, that /ʃ/ is found in the ultimate position in borrowed words only, as in [poʃ], [sblaʃ].

Other borrowed phonemes are /dʒ/ and /tʃ/ which occur in borrowed words, now well established:

[dʒaŋgljan], [dʒe:l], [dʒob], [mindʒi],
"to jangle", "jail", "job", "mingy".
[tʃampion], [tʃanʃo], [tʃi:ks], [koitʃ],
"champion", "to chance", "cheek", "coach".

Arising from the use of this second borrowed phoneme, another very interesting phoneme is occasionally heard. It happens because mutations remain a vital and integral part of this dialect under certain circumstances, although the rules of dialectal mutation do not always coincide with the rules found in grammar books. Normally following /ən/ 'my' in the dialect one hears a nasal mutation

[ən nha:d], [ən nhorθ i],
"my father", "my loaf".

Similarly, after /də/ "your" one hears a soft mutation:

[də da:d], [də dorθ di],
"your father", "your loaf".

When borrowed words beginning with the allophone /tʃ/ are used in similar phrases two forms of the word occur at random, viz.

[tʃoklet] "chocolate"	[tʃips] "chips"
[ən tʃoklet i] "my chocolate"	[ən tʃips i] "my chips"
[ən nʒhoklet i]	[ən nʒhips i]
[də tʃoklet di] "your chocolate"	[də tʃips di] "your chips"
[də dʒoklet di]	[də dʒips di]

This /nʒ/ phoneme is never heard under any other circumstances and arises as the direct effect of the Welsh nasal mutation occurring in the borrowed word.

This phoneme /dʒ/ does not mutate, viz.

[ən dʒam i] "my jam";
[də dʒam di] "your jam".

Unless there is a conscious effort to speak with an English accent native Welsh phonemes are retained. Even when speaking English the native Welsh person in this area will often say [egs'beriment], "experiment", or [sgu:l], "school", and if words are borrowed in spoken Welsh then it is rare to hear anglicized forms such as [diskəvrjo], "to discover", and it would be quite usual to hear the phrase [egs'gius mi:], "excuse me", in a Welsh context. In this type of position the sound preceding /s/ has more in common with the phoneme /g/ than the phoneme /k/. It is a partly voiceless, lenis, aspirate sound.

Whilst considering the plosives, it should be noted that unlike some Southern Welsh dialects /d/ when it precedes /j/ at the beginning of a word is not dental alveolar although its point of articulation is slightly further back, for example.

[djaul], "devil";
[dja:ni], "my goodness".

As attention is focused on the fricatives one finds, once more, that this Northern Welsh dialect, in common with other North Walian dialects, always retains the phoneme /x/ at the beginning of words for example

[xwadan] "duck", [xwe:x] "six", [xwi:θ] "left".

The fricative /ð/ is a common phoneme but is only found at the beginning of two words [ðari] "did", and [ðo:i] "yesterday". It is usually retained as the last phoneme of a word but, sometimes, in this dialect, especially amongst older speakers it is omitted at the end of monosyllabic words. Compare [gwe:ð], [gwe:], "team (of horses)". Similarly, the fricative /v/ is omitted at times. An affirmative response to an invitation would yield the answer /do:v/ or /gna:v/ but when the personal pronoun is included the /v/ is lost:

[do: i:], "I shall come";   [gna: i:], "I shall do".

As is the case in other Welsh dialects /h/ has many allophones and a detailed description may be found in Arwyn Watkins (1961:17). In two respects this dialect's use of /h/ is interesting. It is found in phrases including the preceding personal pronoun — (first person singular) — +[p, t, k], for example:

[əŋ ŋha:θ i:] "my cat";   [əm mhurs i:] "my purse"

and also when the pronoun is understood, but omitted [ŋha:θ i di hon], "this is my cat". When the pronoun is omitted [h] has a very weak articulation. In cases where the preceding personal pronoun (third person singular feminine) + vowel or [m, n, r] occurs [h] is usually retained, for example:

[i haval hi], "her apple";   [i mham i], "her mother";
[i hra:u hi], "her spade".

but it can be omitted: [i aval i/j aval i].

Having noted some instances where there may be dialectal variations in the use of the consonant phonemes, attention can now be focused on the vowels. A detailed description of the vowels of the Gwynedd dialect can be found in R. O. Jones (1967) and in general this dialect is not dissimilar. As already mentioned its use of /a/ in the final syllable of words is a North Walian or Gwynedd distinctive feature, for example [kapal, kerðad, goglað, hetar], "chapel, walk, North, iron". The phoneme /e/ is occasionally found in the last unaccented syllable but usually reflects an influence of education and is found in words such as [gramadeg], "grammar"; [ɬəvrgeɬ], "library"; or it occurs in borrowed words such as [' aksɪdent], "accident"; [kompartment], "compartment"; [ko:t kamel], "camel hair coat".

In the last syllable of other borrowed multi-syllabic words the vowel phoneme /ə/ is found, for example [di·səl], "diesel", ['dresmekər], "dressmaker". Another allophone of the same phoneme is retained in monosyllabic words such as [pə:m], "perm"; [tə:m], "term"; [fə:n], "fern" but often one hears [pərm] and [tərm].

A feature which is less distinctive in dialectal terms, but nevertheless interesting, is the use of the allophone [a·]. It occurs in borrowed words which have not been fully established as part of the dialect and retain most of their original features, for example ['ba·rgenjo], "to bargain", and ['pa·ləmed],"parlourmaid". However, other variants of these words occur, viz. [bargeinjo] which is more common and ['palə'me:d]. The phoneme /e·/ is found also in the borrowed words but is not usually variable with /e/, for example

[be·kən], [be·ljo], [eŋge·dʒo], ᶠfe·ljo]
"bacon", "to bail", "to become engaged", "to fail".
The same is true of /i·/, viz. [kompi·tjo], "to compete" and [di·lar] "dealer". The phoneme /i/ varies with /i/ in some monosyllabic borrowed words. Such forms as [pɪl, bɪl, sɪl, tɪp, tɪn] are more common but some vary unconditionally:
[pil, bil, sil, tip, tin].
"pill, bill, sill, tip, tin".
There remains also one native allophone which varies with other phonemes. It is [ø] an allophone of /ə/ and it always occurs before [u]:
køuras, "giant of a woman";   møur, "big".
It varies with /a/ and /o/:
mour, mawr, møur, "big".
It is probably heard more commonly amongst the older generation.

In the preceding paragraphs variable forms have been discussed. They reflect a binary choice system and variables can be used by the same individual and this sometimes depends on the context. However, many of the older generation were taught through the medium of English, and a subconscious effort to produce "educated" speech sometimes gives rise to less common anglicized forms. The individual is able to choose a preferred form under particular circumstances and can use different linguistic codes under differing circumstances. Older native speakers, however, who live further away from the ruro-urban centre such as those living in Llangybi village, showed fewer English influences. The same is true of people living nearer the nucleus but not in daily contact with English influences. The last two groups were also educated through the medium of English, but they have not been influenced to the same extent. To sum up, however, English influences on the phonetic structure of the dialect are not extensive.

The main impact of the dominant English language is on the vocabulary and the semantic interpretation of words, but it has also encroached on the field of Welsh grammar as shall now be seen.

Forming the plural of nouns readily springs to mind as a field of English influence. Most 'new' borrowed words form plurals by adding the suffix[-s], [-is] or [-is], for example

ambarel	ambarels	"umbrella/s"
aksent	aksents	"accent/s"
bandedʒ	bandedʒis	"bandage/s"
ambiulans	ambiulansis	"ambulance/s"
bras	brasis	"brass/es"

However, most recorded categories of plural forms coincide with literary forms, for example, adding a suffix (with or without vowel change)

tre:	trevi	"town/s"
amkan	amkanjon	"intention/s"
botum	botəma	"button/s"
karpad	karpedi	"carpet/s"
kartra	kartrevi	"home/s".

Others drop the last syllable (with or without vowel change):

seran	se:r	"star/s"
moxin	mo:x	"pig/s"
plentin	plant	"child/ren".

Many common words form the plural just by vowel change:

ja:r	jeir	"chicken/s"
tro:id	tra:id	"foot/feet"
tɨ:	tai	"house/s".

One more distinctive dialectal feature is the omission of one syllable or one vowel (with or without vowel change) plus a suffix:

aval	vala	"apple/s"
kalon	klona	"heart/s"
papir	pira	"paper/s"
kena	knavon	"rascal/s"
asan	sena	"rib/s"
kara	kria	"shoelace/s".

A few words form the plural irregularly:

bluiðin	blɔnɔðoð,	"year/s"
ɬa:u	duilo/dilo/deilo, "hand/s".

A few examples were found of variant plural forms. On the whole they reflect the fact that the borrowed English suffixes are productive:

kakan	ke: ks/kena,	"cake/s"
kara'van	kara'vans/karavana,	"caravan/s".

In an exercise to find the prevalence of the English suffixes in a randomly chosen section it was found that they occurred in 35.1% of the nouns. This figure serves as a guideline only to trends.

There are no examples of changes in adjectival forms as a result of English influences (apart from the borrowing of a few adjectives). However, despite this, there is an obvious trend towards uniformity. Plural and feminine forms of the adjective are quite frequently not used. Indeed, in the dialect of the young, it could be said that they are rarely heard. Amongst the older generation, however, forms such as the following occur frequently:

[gwarθag dion], "black cattle";
[kawodið trəmjon], "heavy showers";
[hen go:id møur fərvjon], "tall strong trees".

The same is true of femine forms such as:

['kardigan velan], "yellow cardigan";
[kəmdeiθas gre:], "strong community".

Once more amongst the young an attempt at uniformity is seen in comparison of adjectives. The most common irregular forms are still in common usage:

da:, kəsdal, gueł, gora,   "good", "as good", "better", "best";
ba:x/bɔxan, łiad, łai, łia,   "small", etc.;
dru:g, gweiθad, gwaiθ/gweiθax/gweiθa/, "bad", etc.;
hauð, hausad/hauðad*, hausax, hausa/hauða*, "easy", etc.

These regularized forms (marked by *) were heard amongst the young.

Having noted the above comparison forms it should be stated, however, that the periphrastic style of adjective comparison is gradually overtaking the synthetic method and that it is very frequently heard these days. For example

[ma:n vuł prəsir dɨ merxar de],

"It's busier on a Wednesday, isn't it".

There do not seem to be English influences on the use of the personal pronoun. A dialectal feature (which is common to the whole of Gwynedd) is the use of the independent simple personal pronouns (second person singular) [xdi:] [ə'xdi:] and [xdiθa]. The use of the usual Welsh /ti/ smacks of a certain formality although that would be less formal than the use of the plural form [xi:] with a singular meaning.

The forms of the independent personal pronouns, third personal singular, which follow are another dialectal feature of North Gwynedd:

[vo:, o:, ə'vo:], "he/him";

[vənta, vonta], "him also";

[hiθa], "she herself"

and plural

[nhu:, nu:, ə'nhu:], "they";

[nhuθa], "they also".

On the whole, the use of the personal pronoun does not differ much from its literary use. One frequent use of the simple personal pronoun which does not occur in the literary language is its use in narrative conversation as subject of the defective verb [ðari], for example:

[ðarɨ vi vɨnd wedɨn] "I went afterwards";

[ðarɨ xdi: weld o] "You saw him".

The preceding dependent personal pronouns are regularly used to denote possession. The first person singular has various forms of which [ən, əm, əŋ] are the most common forms, followed by the appropriate nasal mutation or lack of mutation but [və] and [v] are heard:

[ən sbi:tʃ i], "my speech";   [əm mraud i], "my brother";

[əŋ ŋhri:s i], "my shirt".

[v] is common in two phrases only: [ən v amsar i], "in my time" and [v hɨːn], "myself". The form [vɨːn] has also been heard. [və] is a reflection of literary influences. However, amongst the younger generation, children in particular, this pronoun can be omitted

[tɨː vi di hun], "this is my house";
[ən tɨː xdiː ia], "In your house, yes?"

and [tɨː niː], "our house", is common among all speakers.

This pronoun is even more frequently omitted amongst both the old and the young in the genitive use immediately before the verbal noun:

[a hunu n kəwiro vi], "and that one corrected me";
[a dəma vi n gluad vo], "and I heard him".

Note that the nasal mutation has been dropped in the first example but that the soft mutation that would have been there if the pronoun were included has been retained in the second.

The demonstrative pronouns also reflect their literary use apart from the fact that in adjectival use [əma,ma] is far more commonly used than [hun/hon]:

[ən r eglus ma evɨd], "in this church also";
[i r kɨlx ma], "to this district".

The form [naku] is also fairly commonly used and refers to an object which can be pointed at but is some distance away:

[wedi xi vɨnd dros naku], "after you've gone over that".

When reference is made to time [naku/aku/ku] are never used even though the reference may be to a time some distance removed:

[r usnos na], "that week";   [ə durnod na], "that day";
[noson ono], "that night".

Prepositions, once more, reflect much that is true of standard written Welsh. Their declined forms combine with personal pronouns and thus we get forms such as

['arnaxdi/'anaxdi, 'gənaxdi], "on you/with you".

However the root does not always coincide with the literary root.

Examples are:

dros -root	[drosd---]	
heb -root	[hebd---]	
hruŋ-root	[hruŋθ-, hrəŋθ-].	

The preposition [gin] does not follow at all closely the written pattern:

	Singular	Plural
(1)	'gənai/gini	'gənoni/'ginoni/'gənani
(2)	'gənaxdi/ginti	'gənoxi/'ginoxi/'gənaxi
(3)	'gənovo/ginovo	'gəninu/'gininu/'geninu
	gəni/gini	

It combines with the verb [bo:d], "to be" to mean "to have" but it is also common in other phrases such as [bod gora gin], "to like best":

[vresd di gora gənox xi],
"You like the breast meat best of all";
[bo:d ðru:g gin]
"to be sorry";
[ma ðru:g gini ðim i:n ðima ɛn ti eto],
"I'm sorry, not a ha'penny in the house again".

Finally, attention needs to be focused on the verb. The short forms of many verbs both regular and irregular are commonly used but the periphrastic forms occur more frequently. Many forms correspond closely to the standard written forms (bearing in mind that the written "e" often becomes /a/ in this dialect). However, all regular and many irregular verbs form the third person singular present by using root + suffix [-iθ]

agor	agoriθ	"he will open"
endʒojo	endʒoiθ	"he will enjoy"
atab	atebiθ	"he will answer"
ɬnai	ɬneiθ	"he will clean".

The last two also exhibit a vowel change.

One common exception to the above pattern is [medri], "to be able" which often has [medar] as the third person singular present tense form. The form [medriθ] is also fairly common.

[vedar vo:d reit gle:n], "He can be quite nice".

Some forms of verbs are not often found in the dialect. The pluperfect, for example, is not often used. It occurs mainly in a small number of verbs, most of which are irregular in one way or another, such as [hroid], "to give"; [ka:l], "to get"; [mind], "to go"; [duad], "to come"; [gneid], "to do"; [bo:d], "to be", and a defective verb [dəlun] used only in the imperfect and pluperfect:

	Singular	Plural
Imperfect	(1) dəlun	dəlan
	(2) dəlaxd	dəlax
	(3) dəla	dəlan
Pluperfect	(1) dəlsun	dəlsan
	(2) dəlsaxd	dəlsax
	(3) dəlsa	dəlsan

There is very little, if any, difference in the use of these forms but the younger generation tend to use the imperfect versions.

There is one feature of the pluperfect which deserves attention (it is also true of many plural forms of the past tense). The phonemes /s/ and /θ/ vary unconditionally in these forms:

[keisun i/keiθun i:], "I would have it";
[deisa/deiθa vo]:, "he would come";
[gneisun i/gneiθun i]:, I would do".
and past tense (plural)
[deison ni/deiθon ni:], "we came";

As is the case with the pluperfect, the impersonal form of the verb is rarely used. Any use of the present, imperfect or pluperfect forms can be dismissed as untypical of the dialect and the probable result of the influence of literary forms. Amongst the older generation, however, the past tense impersonal form is used quite often:

[kavwid], "was had"; [doud], "was brought"; [kanwid], "was sung"; [troud], "was turned"
but no examples of [bo:d] in its impersonal forms were recorded during the survey.

[mi kanwid hi droion], "it was sung several times;
[aud a vo i fur], "he was taken away".
The only truly common form, however, is [ganwid], "was born":

[ən ər ənis əŋ ŋanwid ia], "Yes, I was born at 'Ynys'";
[ən lo:n berx ganwid vi: te], "I was born in Abererch Road".

This verb is never used in its short form, apart from this.

The subjunctive is uncommon and its only use recorded in the third person singular of [gwneid] – [nelo] and [bo:d] – [bo:]. The first example being more common than the second:

[d os nelo vo ðim bi:d a vi:], "It's got nothing to do with me".

The imperative, on the other hand, is very commonly used in the second person singular and plural as would be expected:

[tewi   taːu teux], "be quiet";
[hroiːd hroː hroux], "give";
[duad   tɨd deux/doux], "come".

In the case of [boːd] the third person singular and plural of the imperative were recorded:

[bəðad/boːd o]   [bəðad/boːd nhuː/nuː]
[mi vəðan niːn sdopjo 'baðati duɨð vəno hi ar oːl paːsg.]
"They would stop, whatever the weather after Easter".

One verb is only found in the second person singular and plural imperative forms [uda] and [udux] and is of very frequent usage, "take this".

Apart from forms already noted, many other common forms are heard in the present and past tenses and they correspond fairly closely to written Welsh, for example:

kana, "I sing";	kanan, "we sing";
kani, "you sing";	kanux, "you sing";
kaniθ, "he/she sings";	kanan, "they sing";
kaniʃ, "I sang";	kanon, "we sang";
kanisd, "you sang";	kanox, "you sang";
kanoð, "he/she sang";	kanon, "they sang".

Note, however, that there is no "affection of vowels". The short imperfect forms are less commonly heard.

The verb [boːd], "to be", has many forms, for example:

Present (1) ədu/duː/ədwi/dwi/əndu, "I am";
         (2) uːt/uti/uɨt tiː/wɨti, "thou (you) are";
         (3) maː/maːɨ/mavo, "he is";
             ədi
             oːis/oːs/
             sɨː/sɨð/s
         (4) ədan/dan/əndan, "we are";
         (5) əndax/ədax/dax, "you are";
         (6) əndɨn/ədɨn/dɨn, "they are".

There are also several forms of the first-person singular past tense:

bɨːʃ/bɨov viː/bɨːm i/bɨom i, "I was"

One feature of the dialect is the use of [ðari] + personal pronoun + infinitive to form the past tense, for example:

[ðari̇ mi weld o], "I saw him";
[ðari̇ o gluad ə niws], "he heard the news".

This structure bears some similarity to the use of [dəma] + personal pronoun for example:

[dəma vi weld o], "I see him", (there's me seeing him).

The use of [dəma], however, is dramatic quite often and is used in a narrator's dialect to create excitement or tension whereas [ðari] has no dramatic overtones under usual circumstances although if special stress is placed on it it can create a sense of excitement.

Forms of [gneid] "to do" are often used for the same purpose by the younger generation, for example

[na:θ o m eni̇ł], "he didn't win".

Having discussed a few verbal forms, it is appropriate to look briefly at the use of short and periphrastic forms. Are these forms interchangeable? In general, the answer is "no".

Short forms of irregular verbs are possibly in commoner usage than those of regular verbs. The sentences that follow are three hypothetical forms which can be studied as examples here:

(1) [eiθ o əno i weld o reit amal xi];
(2) [vi:ð o n mind əno i weld o reit amal xi];
(3) [ma vo n mind əno i weld o reit amal xi].

These three sentences could be translated as follows:

(1) He will go to see him quite often, you know;
(2) He does go to see him quite often, you know;
(3) He goes to see him quite often, you know.

Here it seems that the short form of the present tense is used to convey the future. This is often, but not invariably true:

[wela i xi heno], "I'll see you tonight";
[o, wela i:], "Oh!, I see".

If we look at the imperfect and quote three hypothetically possible forms one realizes that the semantic differences are barely perceptible:

(1) [a:i o əno i weld o reit amal xi];
(2) [vəða vo n mind əno. . .] etc.;
(3) [oið o n mind əno. . .] etc.

These three sentences could be translated as follows:
(1) He used to go there quite often to see him, you know;
(2) He used to go there etc.;
(3) He used to go there etc.

The sense of the habitual is possibly more implicit in the second example but (2) or (3) could vary unconditionally. These would be the commoner forms. This seems to suggest that short forms are uncommon, but in the speech of older people, in particular, the short forms of the past tense are often heard:

[a wedyn veðj a noð kərnol ən do];
"And then Colonel took possession of course".
[vðəlon basa goɫi o adag hono es blənəðoð.];
"They thought that they would lose him at that time years ago".

and younger people also use some forms frequently, for example

[eʃi əno], "I went there";
[weloð o hi a hredag], "he saw her and ran".

But whereas the older generation says [wrandawiθ o ðim], "he won't listen", the younger generally use the periphrastic verb [neiθ o ðim gwrando], the old say [be 'aluni o?], "what shall we call him?"; the young, however, ask [be na:n ni alu vo?].

Throughout this chapter constant reference has been made to differences between the spoken dialect of the old and the young. In fact, it is not simply a matter of age. Many other social and environmental influences prevail, for example, social standing, geographical location (urban or rural), education, context of conversation and so forth. All this should be borne in mind, but having conceded that other factors are relevant it is still correct to state that many differences exist between the dialects of young and old.

One tendency is for the accent in borrowed words to reflect that found in English in the dialect of the young and middle aged, for example:

Old	Young	
marma'le:d	'marmaled	"marmalade"
maro'bo:n	'marobon	"marrowbone"
seli'bretjo	'selibretjo	"to celebrate"
opə'retjo	'opəretjo	"to operate".

However, many older people as time goes by also adopt this English stress pattern.

Similarly, those of the older generation who do not follow English patterns of accentuation would also pronounce borrowed words differently:

Old	Young	
butlar	bətlər	"butler"
sentans	sentəns	"sentence"
oke:ʃons	oke·ʃəns	"occasions"

However, words in common borrowed usage such as [opəre·ʃon], "operation" and [tʃe·rman], "chairman" are used by most speakers of the dialect in their more Welsh form. Other words such as [be·kən], "bacon"; and [pulo·vər], "pullover", are never, or hardly ever, pronounced with [a] instead of [ə].

Another very important part of the dialect are the mutations. The nasal and aspirate mutations are still used but less frequently and some uncertainty exists as to their "correct" usage at times. In the written language [ən], "in" is followed by a nasal mutation when that is appropriate. However, it is infrequently heard in this context in this dialect:

[ən baŋgor], "in Bangor";
[əm barti], "in the tannery";
[əm buɬeli], "in Pwllheli";
[ən dop r a:ɬd], "at the top of the hill";
[əŋ gənarvon], "in Caernarfon".

Note that in some instances it has been replaced by the soft mutation.

The nasal mutation, however, is often heard after [ən], "my":

[ən əŋ ŋhoisa], "in my legs";   [ən nhaid i], "my grandfather".

But often the pronoun is omitted, especially by the younger speakers and then the mutation is also omitted as it is a different construction:

[ki: vi: di hun], "this is my dog".

The aspirate mutation is not heard very often. There are set phrases where it is heard:

[kar a xefil], "horse and cart";   [pen a xunfon], "head and tail".

but often [a], "and", is followed by the root consonant:

[kar a kefil], "horse and cart";   [ki: a ka:θ], "dog and cat".

In some phrases such as [kin salad a xi:], "as sick as a dog", the mutation is used. However, nowadays the use of [a] "as", has become infrequent and has been replaced by [va:θ a] and frequently the mutation is omitted.

[oð o n wan va:θ a ka:θ], "He was as weak as a cat;
[uti vaθ a knonyn], "You're (wriggling) like a worm".

The soft mutation remains an integral part of this dialect. Examples of its usage in borrowed words have already been quoted in this chapter. Spoken Welsh devoid of soft mutations sounds alien to the native ear. However, some examples such as [ə tent], "the tent", do not necessarily reflect a missing mutation for the gender of some borrowed words is uncertain. A common example is [ə tre:n], "train", which can be either masculine or feminine but is usually feminine in this particular dialect. A Welsh word the gender of which is often unclear is [ə ku:x], "boat". Many children talk of [ə gu:x] (feminine) whereas older people talk of [ə ku:x] (masculine).

In one structure, however, when [ən] is used adverbially or as a verb complement, the soft mutation is not used when English adjectives are used:

[ən doudi], "doudy";
[mai̯ o n kru:d], "he's crude";
[ma hunu n 'kwalifeid], "he's qualified".

English influences quoted in this article have not demonstrated any major impact of English on the structures of the language and indeed most structures remain unscathed, but instances where English patterns seems to be slowly superseding the Welsh patterns do occur. The first instance occurs in structures which include a borrowed English verb which usually has a preposition or adverb to follow in English:

[adai̯ xi garjo mla:n], "I'll let you carry on";
[manu n kaʃo meun], "they're cashing in";
[ag mið ari̯ əm dipθi̯·rja dori aɬan ən ə kamp], "and an outbreak of diphtheria occurred in the camp".

The second instance is not at all common in the spoken dialect of middle aged and older people but it is on the increase amongst the younger generation. It imitates the English structure "what is he like":

[be di o vel?], "What's he like?".

Other prepositions are used finally:

[ɬe ti n mind i?], "where are you going to?".

These structures are in common usage amongst most Welsh-speaking children throughout Gwynedd.

Finally, instances where the English word order is followed have been heard when a borrowed English adverb of degree qualifies another adjective but this use is not common:

[manu n breitjax broun], "they're a brighter brown";
[ge:ʃ i go:t evo sip breit gla:s], "I got a coat with a bright blue zip".

The borrowing in the field of vocabulary is so extensive that it can only be briefly discussed. One would expect borrowing to reflect new inventions and processes but many words are borrowed unnecessarily. The young will often use an English word when the older generation use a native word. The difference is seen most clearly when one compares words used by the older generation in the rural community and those used by the urban young:

Old	Young	
kregin	ʃels	"shells"
xwibjani	wislo	"to whistle"
xwiljo	sərtʃo	"to search"
driŋo	kleimjo	"to climb"
neidjo	dʒəmpjo	"to jump"
tuad/tuod	sand	"sand"
la'mo:r	bi:tʃ	"beach".

Another gap between generations arises because times change, there are new methods of farming, old crafts disappear. The following are some such words:

[grudan], "connect chain on a cart";   [hraun], "horse hair"; [hresal], "hay-rack"; [łəmri], "flummery"; [radał], "bakestone/ griddle";   [sbondjo], "to play game with buttons".

Other words are lost for no obvious reasons:

[folog], "a silly girl/woman"; [hrumos], "cramp";   [palat. . .], "a giant of a . . .".

Many of these words would probably not be part of the passive vocabulary of the younger nor even the middle-aged population. It is interesting to note how forms borrowed from English previously have now been borrowed in more modern forms by the younger generation:

Old	*Young*	
drek∫un	a'dres	"address"
seŋal	siŋgəl	"single"
sgeilad	sgeileit	"sky-light"
sinsir	dʒindʒir	"ginger"

A parallel but less common trait is the tendency for old and young to use different Welsh words to convey the same meaning:

Old	*Young*	
privjo	təvi	"grow (of a child)"
sgrivan	sgweni	"handwriting"

Differences in vocabulary, however, as would be expected, occur not only between younger and older age groups but also between those who have had higher education (and this would include those who have attended extra-mural university classes) and those who left school early.

Ordinary education	*Higher education*	
kopio	eveləxi,	"to copy"
kəsgodi	ɫexi,	"to hide"
o:il	oleu,	"oil"
prəvaid ba:x	prəvetax,	"flies"

The people who use the words in the second column belong to a very small group who possess language awareness. Some realize that the words they use can create an impression, others wish to speak "pure" Welsh. Some use such words always, others use them under particular circumstances and can switch from one mode to another, depending on which is acceptable to the company they are in at any one time.

Another distinctive feature is the lack of idiomatic expressions in the spoken dialect of the young. The following are taken from the spoken dialect of older people.

[na: hi m bid a hi: wir],
"she didn't want to have anything to do with her, indeed";
[mai n duad vuru r sil],
"she's coming at the weekend".

It is possible, but I have no scientific evidence to corroborate this, that younger people as they grow older change their dialectal pattern to a certain extent, and their vocabulary in particular. Even ideolects are not static and trends as people grow older need not always reflect the English influences which are marked during youth. Occupation, social status and so forth can change a person's manner of speech.

English encroachment on phonology and structure is probably occur-
ing very slowly as time goes by but English influences on vocabulary has
gathered increased momentum in recent years. It could be argued that
the second World War, education, increased population mobility, the
prevalence of radio and television and probably all four have given rise
to this. There is no doubt that both old and young borrow from English
in their spoken dialect but younger speakers borrow more extensively.
These are early days yet to look for a stemming of the tide as a result of
S4C (with increased hours of Welsh viewing) and Welsh medium education
in schools. In Gwynedd, and Dwyfor in particular, District and County
Councils also are consciously promoting use of Welsh and this could have
an effect. On the other hand, the non-conformist chapels and Sunday
Schools are on the wane and these have long been a source of life to the
Welsh language. However, unless social conditions change drastically the
demise of this dialect is unlikely within the foreseeable future.

Notes to Chapter 10

1. This chapter is based on research reported in Roberts (1973).

Part IV:
Non-Geographical Varieties
of Welsh

11 Literary Welsh

DAFYDD GLYN JONES

A historical sketch[1]

A language of tradition

Since it came into existence, some 14 centuries ago, Welsh has been a language of literature. It has not, for the entirety of this long period, been a language of law and government, and therefore of formal education and the professions. These two facts have between them determined the character of modern literary Welsh, its relationship with all other varieties of Welsh, and attitudes towards it on the part both of those who are equipped and inclined to use it and of those who are not.

Generalization about the language of the earliest Welsh literature, the poetry of Taliesin and Aneirin, is inhibited by the fact that the manuscripts in which it has been preserved are no earlier than the thirteenth century. During the centuries of transmission between the late sixth, when the authors are believed to have lived, and the ninth, thought to be the date of the first committal to writing, it is most likely that the language, like the content, would have undergone changes. Modern scholars, noting in the poetry linguistic features older than what is believed to have been the Welsh of the ninth century, have not been unanimous as to the conclusion that should be drawn. Where some have seen genuine antiquity, others have seen archaism, an aesthetic device. Whichever it be, the accurate transmission of old linguistic forms or else their affectation for an artistic end, the practical result is much the same. The formation of Welsh out of the wreck of the old Brythonic or British language appears to have been a rapid process, completed, some believe, within the span of two generations in the mid-sixth century. Almost as striking is the fact of its settling down, within three centuries at the most of its dramatic birth, to become one of the most conservative languages in Europe. Whatever the inherent features may have been which inclined it thus, features of the language itself or of the historical situation, the social life and the material conditions by which it was governed, we may fairly safely assume that they were reinforced by the highly traditional concept of their own function which was accepted by the early poets, a concept traceable through Celtic to Indo-European precedents. The function was political, ritual and in part magical, to maintain the identity and the morale of the realm by praising its king, and through eulogy of the living and elegy of the dead to extol the virtues believed necessary to the realm's survival. This traditional rôle seemed to demand with it traditional forms and a traditional language. Thus was established the conservatism in the literary medium, characterizing at least a 1000 years of prose and verse, which makes it possible for a Welsh reader of today to recognize the language even of the earliest surviving literature as unmistakably his own. All introductions to the work of the *Cynfeirdd* ("The Earliest Poets"), Taliesin, Aneirin and their successors up to the eleventh century, including the unknown authors of the "Llywarch Hen" and "Heledd" sagas, quote famous lines and stanzas which a modern literate Welsh speaker can understand and appreciate. They are, of course, a selection from a body of verse the greater part of which is not accessible except with the assistance of scholarly comment, and which even then retains many obscurities; but that such a selection should have been at all possible is itself something remarkable. Add a line here, modernize a word there, and stanzas from the Heledd cycle, believed to have been composed around 850, can still make a pop-song for today.

As we reach the Middle Ages it becomes possible to generalize with less risk about the characteristics of literary Welsh. In the twelfth and thirteenth centuries we can see two distinct varieties of it. One of them belongs to the work of the court poets, *Beirdd y Tywysogion*, "The Poets of the Princes", alternatively known as *Y Gogynfeirdd*, "The Poets Next-to-the-earliest". In inheriting the function of the *Cynfeirdd* and their status in society, they not only repeated their themes, re-worked their imagery and invoked their names, they also re-utilized their language. This time there can be no doubt, it is deliberate archaism in vocabulary and syntax, taken up in re-assertion of a traditional loyalty. It combines with elaborate verse forms to produce a poetry which is formal and elevated, distanced from common life, addressing itself to a select aristocratic audience. Something of a contrast is provided by the language of the prose literature which has been preserved from the mediaeval period, the narrative prose of the Mabinogi and romances, the legal, historical and religious texts, and the translations into Welsh of French and Latin prose works. In such a large and varied collection of writing we naturally encounter a diversity of manner. Even when attention is confined to the 11 original Welsh imaginative tales (the *Mabinogion* as they are often referred to for convenience) the contrasts are evident: the directness of *Owain*, in which the formulae of oral narration are clearly discernible; the superabundance of descriptive detail in *Breuddwyd Rhonabwy*, and the even more rhetorical profusion of compound epithets in *Geraint, Peredur* and famous passages of *Culhwch ac Olwen*; the restraint of the description and the naturalism of the dialogue in the Four Branches of the Mabinogi. It is in the last named, and especially in the direct speech quoted, that we find the clearest contrast to the language of the *Gogynfeirdd* and the best intimation of what the spoken Welsh of the period may have been like. But this, it must be stressed, is an extreme. The mediaeval prose tales, no less than the contemporary poetry, are literary and very often consciously so, displaying special resources and delighting in their effect. We should remember also that we are still in a period when a great deal of recorded literature, poetry no less than prose, is a transcription of something composed in the head and for the ear; literary language is still a special kind of spoken language.

Following the loss of political independence in 1282 and the replacement of the Princes as patrons of the bards by another social class, *Yr Uchelwyr*, "The Nobility", the stylistic extremes of the *Gogynfeirdd* were gradually abandoned. But Dafydd ap Gwilym (?1320–70), regarded as the herald of the new period, is still a difficult poet, as are several of those who followed him between the fourteenth and the sixteenth century. Welsh poetry remained a learned art, allusive and tradition-conscious, using complex forms whose rules became increasingly regularized until they were codified in the mid-fifteenth century into the system which includes *cynghanedd* and the "24 metres", the only surviving system of Welsh laws. Correspondingly the language remained at heart conservative, although in one respect, that of word-borrowing from English, some of the late mediaeval bards showed a lack of compunction which a modern writer of Welsh would not dream of emulating. They could afford it. Welsh was the only language they knew well; it served all their everyday needs; it was not prohibited from any sphere of secular life. In the world of *Beirdd yr Uchelwyr*, borrowing served the ideal of *amlder Cymraeg*, "amplitude of Welsh", listed in the bardic grammar as a requirement of good poetry. Solicitude for his language was something which was expected of the professional poet, part of the attitude of mind which he would develop during his long apprenticeship to enter his profession; solicitude not in the sense of fear for its survival but in the sense of reverence for a medium which he knew to be somewhat set apart from ordinary language, developed and refined since time immemorial for a special function, and still requiring to be studied, learnt and cultivated.

Change and continuity

The social and political revolution of the sixteenth century brought great changes to the world of Welsh literature. The poetic tradition went into a gradual decline, from which it was not to recover fully till our own century. But there was also a continuity, in that the language of the poets, together with some of their learning, came to be adopted by a succession of prose writers who were inspired by the ideals of Renaissance humanism and driven to take one side or the other in the controversies of the Reformation. By becoming the medium of the Welsh Bible, the language of the bardic tradition was retained as the basis of all literary Welsh up to the present day. The great scholars who were involved in the provision of the scriptures in Welsh — William Salesbury who translated the New Testament (1567), William Morgan who translated the entire Bible (1588) and John Davies, believed to be chiefly responsible for the revised edition of Morgan's translation (1620) — were men who had entered with enthusiasm into the New Learning, but who were also intimately familiar with the old native culture and had apparently had access to some knowledge which was supposed to be the preserve of the bards. Others among the Welsh humanists show, in varying degrees, the same combination of interests — grammarians like Siôn Dafydd Rhys and Gruffudd Robert, antiquaries like Humphrey Llwyd, David Powel, Thomas Wiliems and Robert Vaughan, translators like Huw Lewys, Edmwnd Prys and William Midleton. Their introductions and dedicatory epistles strike a new note of urgency as they expound upon the problems faced by an old culture in a new predicament, and some of their phraseology is peculiar to the age: yet they express some traditional concerns. *Mawrhau, coledd, cynnal, ymgeleddu, urddo, trwsio, cyweirio, harddu, perffeithio, diwallu,* ("to extol, cherish, uphold, succour, ordain, mend, repair, beautify, perfect, replenish") are all verbs which figure in their exhortations, the object in all cases being the Welsh language itself. The words of the young William Salesbury (1546: 5), in the introduction to his first book, which is also one of the earliest printed books in Welsh, are famous and often quoted:

> "Do you suppose that there is no need for fitter words, and a greater variety of phrase, to set out learning, and to discourse of doctrine and science, than that which you use in your daily converse, buying and selling, eating and drinking? If that is what you suppose, you are deceived. And you may take this by way of a warning from me: unless you safeguard and repair and perfect the language before the present generation is out, the work will be done too late."

The urgency is that of the Renaissance scholar eager to cultivate language for its own sake as a prime invention and characteristic of man; it is at the same time the urgency of a Welsh Protestant earnestly desiring the spiritual enlightenment of his fellow-countrymen. In all that, Salesbury voices the concerns of his age. But he also speaks for the Welsh tradition. The immediate purpose of "repairing and perfecting" the language, for him, was to make it a suitable medium for encompassing the New Learning in its diverse forms: but the activity itself was one in which the poets had traditionally engaged, as the humanists readily acknowledged in references to them as *penseiri yr iaith*, "the architects of the language", and *vetustae linguae custodes*. One of the methods recommended by the humanists, the large-scale coining of new terms, to which the grammatical analysis of prefixes and suffixes was ancillary, was nothing new to a tradition in which the creation of new compounds had been the delight of generations. The humanist interest in lexicography has, in the Welsh context, a precedent in the bardic practice of keeping word-lists which were to be memorized. The desire to elevate the literary language above the level of "buying and selling, eating and drinking" is one which the poets traditionally would have understood and shared; the language of the *Gogynfeirdd* is but one extreme example.

The Renaissance coincided with the incorporation of Wales in the realm of England, and by the same act the proscription of Welsh as a language of the state. The Welsh humanists, as did all of their class, heartily endorsed the first of these developments, and are not known to have opposed the second. But it is hard not to believe that the intensified desire to protect, uplift and upgrade the literary medium was not in some way compensatory for the demoting of the Welsh language in the secular and political sphere. As in earlier crises, the language itself, and especially the literary language with its centuries of tradition, was recognized as the symbol of continuity and carrier of the inheritance.

One of the problems brought by the new age, by the coming of the printing-press in particular, was the need to standardize the spelling of Welsh, as of other languages. Nearly all the Welsh humanists had their own proposals regarding orthography, the best known and most controversial being those which were put into operation by William Salesbury in the New Testament and Prayer Book of 1567. The idea was that Welsh should be made as similar as was possible to Latin in its printed appearance. Forms like *popul, tempor, descen, eccles* (still meant to be pronounced *pobl, tymor, disgyn, eglwys*) were designed to show derivations from Latin, real and imagined. To a fellow-Protestant and translator, Maurice Kyffin, the end product was something "so stilted and so foreign that the ear of a true Welshman could not bear to listen". The word "listen" suggests a misunderstanding of Salesbury's purpose; but Salesbury should probably have known better than to expect people to write one thing and say another in a language which had no tradition of relating orthography to derivation. Morgan in his 1588 Bible had the good sense to drop Salesbury's Latinized spelling, while profiting greatly from the example of the sound and traditional Welsh which lay underneath. John Davies, for his part, was a little more traditionalist than was Morgan in his ideas on orthography and grammar generally, and the influence of the 1620 Bible is believed, if anything, to have strengthened the conservatism of literary Welsh.

Counter to the long tradition of wishing to exalt and embellish the language itself, and of regarding it as rather more than a means of communication, historians of Welsh literature have been aware of another tradition, observable certainly since the Reformation and traceable over several generations, one of caring less for the medium than for the message. Authors, especially of prose works, will admit to being somewhat daunted by the antiquity and the prestige of the literary language, and will adopt a posture of either forestalling or defying criticism. "I know I can't write Welsh as it ought to be written, but here goes" is an attitude encountered in prefaces four centuries ago, and likewise today; alternatively, a personal decision will be announced, of having adopted the everyday language, complete with borrowings and vulgarisms, in order to be immediately accessible to the ordinary uneducated reader, as in Gruffudd Robert's preface to the Catholic tract *Y Drych Cristianogawl* (1585). Maurice Kyffin, an author whom none would regard as deficient in resources or skill, remarked in his preface to *Deffiniad Ffydd Eglwys Loegr* (1595) that "the hungry will have his food from a wooden bowl no less readily than from a silver dish", expressing a Protestant humanist emphasis somewhat different from that of Salesbury, and supplying a watchword for a succession of authors and translators who between the sixteenth century and the nineteenth wrote in Welsh first and foremost at the prompting of reformist or evangelical zeal. This too has been an honourable tradition, including as it does the homely exhortatory verses of Rhys Pritchard (*"Yr Hen Ficer"*) and the hymns and prose-writings of William Williams, Pantycelyn. Some commentators have regretted that this tradition did not prevail over the other one. Without going all the way with such a view, it is possible to accept that the desire to uplift and embellish the language did, in conjunction with other factors, play a part in producing one or two unfortunate results. Chief among these was the

strange and sad corruption of the written language which began in the
late eighteenth century and came to a head in the mid-Victorian era.

Damage and repair

A feature of the Welsh literary life of the eighteenth century was
the re-adoption of some Renaissance ambitions which had remained unful-
filled. One of these was the dream of an epic poem which would establish
the reputation of Welsh among the languages of the world. It was this
dream which impelled the young Goronwy Owen, setting out to write
Cywydd y Farn Fawr (a poem of the Great Judgement), an experiment
in creating an idiom for the Welsh epic, to go turfing out of dictionaries
words which were already ancient when used by the *Gogynfeirdd* six
centuries earlier. Goronwy endowed the ambition and the example to
another generation, and unfortunately to writers whose sensibility did not
match his own. One of the consequences was the blown-up, unnatural
language found in so much nineteenth century Welsh literature, prose no
less than verse. There were other contributory factors. One was the
mesmerism exercised by the English language, the widely held assumption
that the way to "elevate" Welsh was to arrange its words according to the
patterns of English. Another factor was the influence of pseudo-scholar-
ship. Speculation about the origin and nature of language was a preoccu-
pation of the late eighteenth century, and Wales, lacking the institutions
to foster professional scholarship, was for a time defenceless against some
of the weird notions to which it gave rise. William Owen Pughe
(1759–1835) was a London Welshman of undisputed patriotism and
unflagging diligence. To provide a model of how the Welsh epic might
be written he published in 1819 a translation of *Paradise Lost* into an
extraordinary kind of Welsh which he had invented himself, and had first
presented to the world in his Grammar and Dictionary of 1803. The
ingredients were first the syntax of English and secondly a notion, not
uncommon in the period, that all words could be divided into elements
which had fixed meanings. There were individuals who objected to Pughe's
Welsh as soon as it appeared, but on the whole nineteenth century Wales
was more tolerant of his particular kind of nonsense than Elizabethan
Wales had been of Salesbury's. His influence permeated Welsh writing
for two or three generations after his death, although there were some
who managed fairly well to escape it. By the middle years of the Victorian
era literary Welsh had deteriorated to its worst condition ever.

In the meantime there had been great strides in genuine linguistic scholarship. Continental scholars had come to know a good deal about the development of Welsh, its place in the Celtic group of languages and the relationship of that group to others in the Indo-European family. In due course Wales came to benefit. By the last two decades of the nineteenth century there were persons equipped and willing to tell the Welsh literary public that what had been accepted as Welsh for some three quarters of a century was not Welsh at all. Two of them were especially influential. Robert Ambrose Jones or Emrys ap Iwan (1848–1906) was a Calvinistic Methodist minister in the old county of Denbigh, an author of satire and polemical essays, and one of the main founders of modern Welsh political nationalism. John Morris-Jones (1864–1929) was the first Professor of Welsh Language and Literature at the University College of North Wales, Bangor. There were dissimilarities between them. Emrys ap Iwan had no ear for poetry; his recommended models of good Welsh were taken from a succession of prose writers from the Reformation to the Methodist Revival. John Morris-Jones was a poet himself, and appealed always to the authority of the bardic tradition in its classical period, the late Middle Ages. Emrys ap Iwan, although he had received the good formal education which his denomination provided for ministerial candidates, was largely self-taught in Welsh language and literature; this may be reflected in the fact that he was both more pedantic and more innovative than Morris-Jones in some of his proposals. Yet in their basic commitment these two men were very similar: to rid Welsh writing of anglicisms, Pugheisms and the turgidity which characterized Victorian prose was, to both of them alike, part of a wider crusade, to educate their generation in taste and to restore the Welsh-speaker's self-respect. It is interesting that in their search for the best possible models, both of them refuse to be mesmerized even by the prestige of the 1620 Bible. Emrys cites Edward James, whose translation of the Tudor *Homilies* was published in 1606, as the best writer of Welsh prose in the post-Reformation period, better if anything than William Morgan himself; Morris-Jones is equally uninhibited when he suggests that some of the mediaeval translations of Scripture are preferable in some respects to the great Renaissance Bible, being closer to common speech.

Both of them had important things to say on the relationship between spoken and written Welsh. Both of them have been appealed to by proponents of *Cymraeg Byw* and by its opponents; it is not impossible to understand why, because there appears to be something of the same contradiction in their views. At times, the two of them admit to finding the difference between written and spoken forms a bit of a problem. In a satire entitled *Breuddwyd Pabydd wrth ei Ewyllys*, "The Wishful Dream of a Papist", published in 1890–92, Emrys had demonstrated some of his ideas as to how the gap might be narrowed, and also on the related but slightly different matter of how spoken forms might be represented in print; Morris-Jones admitted that he liked the suggestions, although he was reluctant to undertake the same kind of experiment himself. He also wrote around the same time:

> "As linguistic knowledge becomes more widespread. . . our literary language will slowly alter to meet our spoken language; and then an educated Welshman will be as ashamed of speaking a dialect as he is of speaking the literary language today. That is our hope. . . for if the old Welsh language is to live, it must become one language — the same in speech as in writing." (p. 68)

The words occur in a long entry which he wrote for the second edition of the Welsh encyclopaedia, *Y Gwyddoniadur Cymreig* (1891). He was then 27 years of age and had served a year in the newly-created lectureship in Welsh Language and Literature at Bangor. The article contains the embryonic form of the authoritative *Welsh Grammar, Historial and Comparative* which he was to complete in 1913, and contains also an outline of the programme to whose fulfilment he was to devote the rest of his life. But it is significant that the one part of this programme which was quietly dropped was the idea that the diverse forms of Welsh could and should be made into "one language"; this was to occupy him less and less as the years went by, and as the work of describing the subtleties of classical literary Welsh engaged him more and more. His grammar of 1913 is essentially a description of the literary language as exemplified in poetry up to the sixteenth century. His eisteddfod adjudications are packed with advice on what is correct, that is to say natural, in the traditional written language, and with exhortations that this was a special kind of language to be learnt and mastered, and not tinkered with. Although he lays great stress on the areas in which contemporary spoken usage and the traditional literary language agree (against what was supposed by the Victorians to be literary Welsh), he saw clearly that there were areas in which they did not agree, and in the work of his maturity he never tried to force them into agreement. The same is true of Emrys ap Iwan who, though he may have thought it desirable to bridge the gap between written and spoken language, stressed repeatedly that acquiring mastery of written Welsh was something essentially different from learning at one's mother's knee, that literary language always possesses special resources which are acquired partly through a study of grammar and partly through immersement in the classics. It is, he also insists, no small labour, for Welsh is "a difficult and subtle language"; but the reward is great: "indeed, those who observe most strictly the rules of the Welsh language are also those who write most freely, and they are the ones who write most unlike one another".

The contradiction which we mentioned may be resolved, at least partially, if we remember that when Emrys and Morris-Jones spoke of the literary language as being "too artificial", "too removed from common usage", it was the Victorian literary language, Pughe's concoction, that they were referring to — though admittedly not in all cases. It was certainly what Morris-Jones had in mind when he quoted approvingly in the encyclopaedia article of 1891 the words of Henry Sweet (1884: 484):

> "It is greatly to be wisht that educated Welshmen would cultivate the genuine spoken language, insted of the artificial jargon of the newspapers and reflect that the superiority of such a work as the *Bardd Cwsc* consists precisely in its style being founded (as shewn by the numerous English words) on the everyday speech of the period."

It cannot be reiterated too often, Emrys ap Iwan and John Morris-Jones were essentially modern and scientific linguists in that they accepted the primacy of speech and appealed to custom and instinct rather than to logic. The standard, as Morris-Jones put it, was "what an intelligent, unassuming Welshman would say".

Their ideas did not meet with immediate acceptance. Those of Morris-Jones, especially, aroused much hostility among the quite numerous class of self-educated writers to whom Victorian Welsh had become the natural thing. A rival idiom, based partly on classical usage and partly on speech, was something new and strange in the 1890s. It was nicknamed *Cymraeg Rhydychen*, "Oxford Welsh", because Morris-Jones was one of a circle of Oxford graduates who had come under the influence of Sir John Rhŷs and had created a forum for discussing their ideas in *Cymdeithas Dafydd ap Gwilym*, the Welsh society founded at Oxford University in 1886. Another member of this circle, a close associate of John Morris-Jones, was perhaps more influential than anyone else in promoting "Oxford Welsh". He is Owen Morgan Edwards (1858–1920), who as essayist and editor of several periodicals, gave wide currency to the new idiom and encouraged its use. His publications, and especially the widely influential *Cymru* (a monthly known as "*Y Cymru Coch*" from its red cover) were bought and read by the very section of the literary community that was initially most opposed to Oxford Welsh. His intervention was crucial and decisive, and he worked primarily by example. Morris-Jones relied more on exhortation, using three main media (and I believe I am listing them in ascending order of importance): his published articles, his lectures as Professor of Welsh, and his adjudications in the National Eisteddfod. The last contribution of his career (if one excepts the posthumous *Welsh Syntax: An Unfinished Draft*, 1931) was to draw up in 1928 the report of a commission on Welsh orthography. *"Pwnc yr Orgraff"*, "The Matter of Orthography", had been part of the controversy over Oxford Welsh; it had been a contentious topic for generations, and is still potentially so. That is part of the price that has to be paid for having a near-phonetic language. Because Welsh spelling is on the whole so consistent, small inconsistencies and ambiguities in matters such as the doubling of *n* or *r*, the indication of long vowels and of stress accents, and the different sounds which can be represented by the symbol *y*, are known to have sent Welshmen into convulsions. Englishmen would not understand what the fuss was about. But Morris-Jones's recommendations cleared up many of the difficulties, and have served us well for half a century. By his death in 1929 the mission he had outlined in 1891 was effectively completed; literary Welsh was more or less as he wanted it to be. "Oxford Welsh" is the language of the 20th century Welsh classics, prose and verse.

Literary Welsh is probably used today for a wider variety of purposes than ever before, and several factors account for this: an increase, since the 1950s, in the use of Welsh as a medium of secular education; a diversification in the range of Welsh books published; steps taken towards official recognition of the language; and the establishment of Welsh radio and television channels. These developments have been belated, and are still restricted in scope and effect. Whether they have come in time to stem the tide still running strongly against the Welsh language, none can say; and in themselves they are insufficient. The situation of Welsh today is far more perilous than when Emrys ap Iwan, John Morris-Jones and O. M. Edwards addressed themselves to its problems: the disappearance of monolingual speakers has altered its position radically and essentially. As recently as 60 years ago it was possible to appeal to the authority of the spoken language in order to eradicate some of the corruptions which had affected the literary medium. Because of the pervading influence of English, this is no longer possible. The literary language has to serve as the only standard of correctness. In the history of Welsh, this is an unprecedented situation, and not at all a desirable one.

Some grammatical features

What other kinds of Welsh?

Literary Welsh as opposed to what? How many kinds of Welsh are there and what shall we call them? We cannot omit the questions, although they will have been posed in all other contributions to this book.

It has long been recognized that the simple contrasting of the "literary" and the "colloquial" is insufficient and misleading, more so perhaps in the case of Welsh than of many languages, because of the strategic importance of a common standard spoken form, which bridges some of the extremes and is understood and accepted in all the regions. Its establishment as a distinct dialect came with the religious awakening of the 18th century; it became the language of the pulpit and of the institutional religious life throughout Wales; in the secular sphere it became the medium of public address and formal discussion, and with the coming of radio communication it was naturally adopted as the language of announcements and news bulletins. Although Emrys ap Iwan, writing on "The Preacher's Welsh" in 1893, could point to several things in it that he wanted to correct, this public and semi-official spoken language must have proved fairly resistant to the corruptions which afflicted literary Welsh in the 19th century. It was, after all, half-way to every-day speech. Saunders Lewis (1968: 6) commented:

> "The truth of the matter is that every monoglot Welsh-speaker, up to 1914 and in some degree up to 1938, was a bilingual person. He had the language of his locality, the language of the street and the quarry and the pit and the rugby field and the shop. He also had the language of the *seiat* and the prayer meeting and the meeting of brethren and the literary meeting. . . And the ordinary Welsh-speaker, whether a deacon or a member of the Sunday School or of the *Seiat Bwnc*, never got them confused. He knew which language to use wherever he might be."

It is probably true to say that with the decline of religion, knowledge of the common spoken language has become more passive; this has been compensated for in part by the wide currency it has been given on radio and television. (The word "common" I have included purposefully, because there is also a standard form, a correct and natural form, of any local dialect. And there are, for that matter, sub-standard forms of the common public language: *Beth All Rhieni ei Wneud am Gyffuriau?*, "What

Can Parents Do about Drugs?" is the title of a pamphlet currently available, we are told, from any doctor's surgery, any chemist's shop, or the Information Department of the Welsh Office.) The main fact to be established about common standard spoken Welsh is that it is not used everywhere and on all occasions. R. M. Jones (1979) has emphasized that it is "contextual". Ifor Williams (1946) called it *"Cymraeg dydd Sul"*, "Sunday Welsh".

Thus we already have three categories: the literary language, the common standard spoken language and the local dialects. Greater refinement is possible. Megan E. Roberts and R. M. Jones (1974) propose that Welsh be viewed as having three main "levels" (literary language, standard speech and local dialect), each with a variety of 'registers' within it, and each also having two 'modes of expression' (the spoken and the written). The logic of this three-dimensional model is not difficult to discern. The dialogue in the stories of Islwyn Williams, the plays of W. S. Jones or Caradog Prichard's novel *Un Nos Ola Leuad* is local and informal in the extreme, but it is part of literature; here therefore we have written colloquial Welsh, or very informal literary Welsh, which amounts to the same thing. The language of a personal letter, meant for the eye, is likely to be less formal than the language of a news bulletin, meant for the ear. In view of this, another distinction which I have found most useful, and on which I shall be relying heavily in the pages that follow, is the one consistently maintained by R. M. Jones & A. R. Thomas (1977), between the *formal* on the one hand (it may be the formal written or the formal spoken) and, on the other, *informal or spontaneous spoken Welsh*. But then, as we all know, informal spoken Welsh is not a uniform thing, because there are so many local variants of it. Modern authorities, for example, A. R. Thomas (1973), recognize some six main dialects (north-western, north-eastern, west midland, east midland, south-western, south-eastern — each with sub-divisions). But if we followed John Morris-Jones (1891) in relating the division to the traditional provinces of Gwynedd, Powys, Dyfed, Glamorgan and Gwent, we would not go far wrong.[1]

Some areas of difference

Our survey will be impressionistic, but will try to indicate the differences that are most marked. In this sub-section we shall consider five areas: the main sound differences; initial mutations; the prefixed genitive pronouns; the inflected prepositions; and a selection of verb forms.

Sound differences

It is a clear rule that formal Welsh retains, in final unstressed syllables, certain diphthongs which in spontaneous speech are reduced to single vowels. *Ae* as in *trafodaeth* becomes *e* throughout Powys and the south-west (*trafodeth*), and *a* in Gwynedd and in some south-eastern dialects (*trafodath*). *Ai* in the same position (*tamaid*) may become *e* in Powys and Dyfed (*tamed*) and *a* in parts of Gwent and Glamorgan (*tamad*). In Gwynedd its behaviour is more complex. Frequently enough it is *a*, with no doubt at all: *tamad, aetha, bydda, dima, petasa, twrna, boliad, cowlad, cwpanad, diawlad, sachad, cïadd, anifal, cesal, adan, celan, cadar, genwar*; but in many common cases there is free variation (yes, in spontaneous speech) between *ai* and *a*: *lifrai, lifra*; *bleiddiaid, bleiddiad*; *cwsmeriaid, cwsmeriad*; *Cymreigaidd, Cymreigadd*; *dwyrain, dwyran*; *araith, arath*; *cyfraith, cyfrath*. Quite frequently, where variation is possible, the *ai* is commoner: *defaid, defad*; *enaid, enad*; *tanbaid, tanbad*; *poblogaidd, poblogadd*; *hafaidd, hafadd*; *pedair, pedar*; *perffaith, perffath*. But then, sure as anything, there are cases where *ai* is regularly retained, as in the literary language: *cyfaill, damwain, arwain, henaint, rhywfaint, cwrtais, dyfais, gobaith*. It is not easy to summarize a rule determining where *ai* should be kept, but the tendency is strong:

(i) where the final syllable is a noun in its own right, as in *adlais, addoldai, ymgais, pwyslais, adwaith, arwyddair* (yet *uniath, llediath* are obvious exceptions, as are all compounds of *-rag* < *-wraig*, for example *gweithrag*);

(ii) where the word is not so common in its occurrence, tending to belong to the upper registers of speech, as in *anghenraid, academaidd, afreolaidd, nefolaidd, cofadail*;

(iii) where instinct warns that *a* would lead to ambiguity, and especially so in plurals which have a singular in *-ad* (*beirniad, hynafiad, llafariad*) or in *-an* (*cyfan*); where there is no danger of ambiguity there is free variation: *blaenoriaid, blaenoriad*; *cwsmeriaid, cwsmeriad*; *doctoriaid, doctoriad*. In some northern dialects the literary and formal *ai* may be reduced to *i*, sometimes where there is danger of ambiguity (*bychin, cyfin, llygid*), and sometimes where there is none (*cymint, erill*). A case that must be considered separately is that of *-aid* and *-aist* in the first and second singular verb endings of the past tense; they are usually *-is(h)*, *-ist* in Gwynedd, with the exception of Ardudwy (the northern half of the old county of Merioneth) where they are *-as(h)*, *-ast*, as in a group of south-eastern dialects. (We might therefore be misled by John Morris-

Jones where he states (1891: 67): "*ai* in a final unstressed syllable remains *ai* in Gwynedd (*enaid*)". Neither was Emrys ap Iwan presenting the whole truth when, in the transcription of an imagined lecture by a northern speaker which forms part of *Breuddwyd Pabydd Wrth ei Ewyllys*, he turned every unstressed final *ai* into an *a*, except in the plural ending *-iaid* which he rendered as *-ied*.) Literary and formal spoken Welsh retains, again in a final unstressed syllable, the *au* which Gwynedd, agreeing with some Gwent-Glamorgan dialects, reduces to an *a*, as in *minna, ynta, fala, tena*; throughout Powys and Dyfed it is *e*.

Retention of a final unstressed *wy* is a feature shared by the literary language, formal speech and southern dialects; towards the north there is a moderate tendency to reduce to *w*, as in *abwd, annwd, nodwdd, morthwl, achwn, morwn, olwn*. But once more there is agreement between the literary and the northern to retain the diphthongs *ae* and *oe* in monosyllables. *Traed, coed* are the literary and northern versions, corresponding to the standard southern *trâd, côd*; this mutation does occur in one very localized northern dialect, that of Caernarfon town, but most northern speakers would say that it is sub-standard — something which they probably would not say of vowels with very similar values heard in southern speech.

Coming to mutations of individual vowels, we find that the literary language and formal speech agree with Dyfed–Powys in keeping *e* in the final unstressed syllable (*bore, cyfle, ateb, oeddech, agored, cerdded, lleted, carreg, capel, ambell, aber, potes, geneth*). This becomes *a* in Gwynedd and parts of the south-east, but not without exception. We do not have *bywydag, *Testamant, *caethfarch — the same constraints seem to operate as with the change from *ai* to *a*.

Two other important sound changes involve the retention or loss of a consonant. The literary language is inclined to retain a final *f* which spontaneous speech has a tendency to drop, as in *cynhaeaf, cyntaf, nesaf, dioddef, haf*, and in *caf* and all first-person singular "present" tense endings. But there are exceptions either way: *tre, adre, hendre, pentre* may be chosen in writing or in formal speech; spontaneous speech may well keep the *f* in the first-person singular verb when not followed by an affixed pronoun: *fyddi di yno? byddaf*, "will you be there? yes I will", and again in the first-person inflected preposition whenever that is not followed by the pronoun: *mi ges fy ngwynt ataf*, "I got my breath back"; *mi rois fy nghôt amdanaf*, "I put my coat on". Finally, the modern formal written language holds tenaciously to the final *t* in the third-person plural of verbs and of inflected prepositions, which is omitted by all dialects and by formal speech except when reading (*gwnânt:gwnân, ynddynt:ynddyn*).

Initial mutation

A book of Welsh grammar will list some 40 rules governing initial consonantal mutation. The fact that today all of them can be broken, and are broken with increasing frequency, is an indicator of the condition to which the Welsh language has been brought. The Welsh-speaker's built-in grammar, the programme which enables him to say what he wants to say without hesitation or ambiguity, is being interfered with and impaired in a way which a monolingual or near-monolingual of 50 years ago, and likewise a monoglot speaker of English or any other language, would find almost impossible to understand. *Pobl mawr, yn brysur mynd, un tref, y brenhines* are all offensive enough to the eye and ear of someone who is used to the traditional mutation: but there is also a more serious type of mutation error which can reduce a statement to nonsense or reverse its intended meaning. I have experienced difficulty in explaining to classes that there is a difference, and something rather more than a shade of difference, between *plismon a drawodd glöwr*, "it was a policeman whom a miner struck", and *plismon a drawodd löwr*, "it was a policeman who struck a miner". Having said all that, it must be recorded that, as things stand, most Welsh-speakers mutate as they have always done, and that the rules of mutation are still essentially the same in the written language and in the dialects. In very few cases can spoken Welsh, local or common, be said to have developed a system different from that of the standard literary language. (See also this volume, Chapters 7 and 20).

The best known of such instances, and the only one with a fairly wide geographical distribution, is the development of a soft mutation of /b, k, p, t/ after the preposition *yn*, "in", where literary Welsh retains a nasal mutation only: *yn Fangor, yn Gaerdydd, yn Bwllheli, yn Dregarth*. It is as if the mutation following the predicative *yn* has become adopted after the preposition *yn*. The standard *ym Mangor* etc. has not been entirely ousted, even in spontaneous speech; and in this matter standard spoken Welsh sides strongly with the literary practice. The softening of /d/ to /ð/ after *yn*, for example *yn Ddeiniolen*, sounds distinctively low; as an alternative to the formal and literary nasalization, retaining the radical /d/ is the respectable choice. And in the same position /g/ is never softened away; it is either the nasal as in the literary language or a reversion to the radical: *yn Garndolbenmaen, yn Glanaman*. All other departures from the literary practice are either very localized, like the soft mutation which occurs in one dialect of eastern Dyfed after the genitive *yn*, "my" — *yn fam i*, "my mother"; or else not regular enough in any dialect to establish a rule, for example, the soft mutations now occurring with some frequency after *os*, "if", and *pryd*, "when" — *os ddaw, pryd ddaw*.

Beyond that, all we can safely say is that spontaneous spoken Welsh is a little more willing than is the literary language to forego mutation, and that the standard spoken language stands somewhere in between. A rule given in several grammar books states that there is nasalization in *blwydd, blynedd, diwrnod* and *dyn* after the numerals *pump, saith, wyth, deg, pymtheg, ugain, cant*. In *pum mlwydd, pum mlynedd* etc., speech agrees; but when *pum niwrnod* is replaced in speech by *pum diwrnod*, one does not feel that there is anything much wrong. Nasalization of *dyn* — *pum nyn, ugain nyn, can nyn* — is now almost too posh to be true. The spirant mutation after the conjunction *a*, "and", is occasionally dropped in speech, especially if the word following the *a* is an obvious loan word or not so common in Welsh — hearing *India a Pacistan*, we are not aware of any great transgression. Soft mutation after *saith* and *wyth* is no longer as regular as traditional grammars might lead us to believe, but the relaxation of the rule, allowing *saith cant, wyth pabell*, is almost as common in writing as in speech. Two instances where the rule of soft mutation is more readily overlooked in speech than in writing are:

(i) the initial consonant of a noun opening an adverbial phrase, as in *mi es yno dydd Llun* (rather than . . .*ddydd Llun*); and

(ii) the initial consonant of a noun or verb-noun occurring as a genitive after a feminine noun: *siop pob peth, cyllell torri ewinedd*.

In both cases it must be stressed that the mutation has by no means been lost in speech, and that the tendency towards relaxation is also seen in writing.

Prefixed genitive pronouns

Here we have a high proportion of clear and obvious differences within a small compass. Table 11.1 will show what we mean. It will be noticed that only in the second-person singular do formal literary Welsh and spontaneous spoken Welsh agree entirely. *Fy* occurs in spontaneous

Table 11.1

	Literary	Spoken
Singular	(1) *fy*	*fy, y, yn*
	(2) *dy*	*dy*
	(3) *ei*	*i*
Plural	(1) *ein*	*yn*
	(2) *eich*	*ych*
	(3) *eu*	*i*

Literary stands for formal literary Welsh.   *Spoken* stands for spontaneous spoken.

speech before *hun*, *hunan* and also in phrases such as *yn fy myw*, *yn f unfan*, *yn f ymyl*; otherwise it is *y* (before a consonant) as in *y nhŷ fi*, or *yn* (before a vowel) as in *yn esgid i*. The weight of tradition is strongly in favour of the spoken forms *i* (singular and plural), *yn* and *ych*. While the plural *eu* is a genuinely old literary form, *ei*, *ein*, *eich* are Renaissance Latinisms based on a false etymology. It is worth noting that John Morris-Jones, after he had recounted the dubious history of these three forms, held his hand and did not recommend restoration of the old spelling: he accepted *ei* in writing because it was distinguishable from the preposition *i*, and *ein* because it could not be confused with the preposition *yn*. At the same time he urged that they be pronounced *i*, *yn*, *ych*. This became an orthodoxy, largely unchallenged until T. Arwyn Watkins (1968) pertinently asked how many of us begin the Lord's Prayer "*Yn tad, yr hwn wyt yn y Nefoedd*". Common standard spoken Welsh varies in its choices. In a lecture or sermon, or in an impromptu public announcement, *i*, *yn*, *ych* are what we are most likely to hear; *ei*, *ein*, *eich* are not unnatural in a news bulletin or a radio announcement, and in a public reading or recitation of a set piece they are the most likely choice. To an outsider it may sound impossibly complex: to a practised Welsh-speaker it is not. He does what comes naturally, and will continue to do so until that is rendered impossible by the pressure of English.

Inflected prepositions

Reference has already been made to the loss in speech of final /f/ in the first-person singular and of final /t/ in the third-person plural. This, together with the final /n/ for /m/ in the first-person plural, is the sum of the difference in one group of inflected prepositions (See Table 11.2). *Am* (with the stem *amdan-*), *at*, *dan* agree. *O* also agrees in principle

TABLE 11.2

		Literary	Spoken
Singular	(1)	*arnaf*	*arna*
	(2)	*arnat*	*arnat*
	(3)	*arno* (*m.*)	*arno*
		arni (*f.*)	*arni*
Plural	(1)	*arnom*	*arnon*
	(2)	*arnoch*	*arnoch*
	(3)	*arnynt*	*arnyn*

TABLE 11.3

		Literary	Spoken
Singular	(1)	*trosof*	*trosta, troso*
	(2)	*trosot*	*trostat, trostot*
	(3)	*trosto* (*m.*)	*trosto*
		trosti (*f.*)	*trosti*
Plural	(1)	*trosom*	*trostan, troston*
	(2)	*trosoch*	*trostach, trostoch*
	(3)	*trostynt*	*trostyn*

(*ohonof, ohono*, etc.), with the difference that in northern dialects there
is a replacement of the final /o/ by /a/ in the first- and second-person
singular and plural (*ohona i, ohonat ti, ohonan ni, ohonach chi*) corresponding, as it were, to an extension of /o/ to first- and second-person
singular in southern dialects (*arno i, arnot ti*). A second group of declen-
sions, that which includes *rhag, rhwng, heb, yn, tros, trwy*, shows more
radical differences. *Tros* (See Table 11.3) will illustrate. The literary third-
person stem is adopted in speech for all persons; compare *hebdda i,
trwydda i* etc. The alternatives occurring in *rhwng — rhyngdda i, rhyngddo
i, rhynddo i, rhynto i —* are likewise varieties of the third-person stem.
A third declension, common to *gan* and *wrth*, shows yet another pattern
in speech (See Table 11.4). A common form *gen* is acceptable in both
speech and writing for the first- and second-person singular (*gen i, gen
ti*), but cannot be used without the affixed pronoun; in some northern
dialects it occurs as *gin*. An extension of the *gandd-* stem to the first- and
second-person plural is often heard in quite respectable circles (*ganddom,
ganddoch*) but is really an artificial creation. A development now observable in spontaneous speech, north and south, is the replacement of the

TABLE 11.4

		Literary	Spoken
Singular	(1)	*gennyf; gen*	*gynna, genna, gynno; gen, gin*
	(2)	*gennyt; gen*	*gynnat; gen, gin*
	(3)	*ganddo (m)*	*gynno, genno*
		ganddi (f)	*gynni, genni*
Plural	(1)	*gennym*	*gynnon, gennon*
	(2)	*gennych*	*gynnoch, gennoch*
	(3)	*ganddynt*	*gynnyn, gennyn*

whole declension by the all-purpose *gynno* or *genno* (*gynno fi, gynno chdi, genno nhw* etc.); we would probably classify it as sub-standard, but it is a natural enough development.

Verb forms

Here again we can begin by noting a familiar pattern: in the so-called "present" tense literary Welsh retains the final /f/ in the first-person singular (*canaf*), very rare in the informal spoken language; and retains also the final /t/ in the third-person plural of all tenses (*canant, canent, canasant*), long ago dropped in all speech, formal and spontaneous, but re-entrenched in writing since the sixteenth century. The literary language also retains an affection in second person forms, singular and plural, which speech tends to forgo (*ceni, cenwch* as opposed to *cani, canwch*): it was most interesting that when the 1975 New Testament took a chance on *carwch eich gelynion* (for "love your enemies"), readers were uneasy. While third-person singular "present" tense endings in *-iff* and *-ith* are very common in spontaneous speech, and have been for a long time, the literary language still shows a strong preference for the bare stem third-person forms, unaffected as in *câr, gall, chwardd, gwêl*, or with affection or other vowel mutation as in *saif, geilw, ceidw, etyb, cyll, paid, ŷf* etc. Some of the stem, affected and mutated forms are alive enough in speech, occurring as alternatives to *-iff, -ith* forms (*geill, gallith; pery, parith; gwêl, gwelith; rhydd, rhoith; tyr, torrith; cyfyd, codith; myn(n), mynnith;dyfyd, deudith* or *dwedith*); even today preference for certain *-ith* forms, for example *medrith* for *medr*, indicates sub-standard Welsh. On the other hand there are some of the affected or mutated forms — *geilw, ceidw, lleinw, etyb, egyr, gesyd, enfyn, gedy, paid, naid, baidd, prawf, glŷn* — which must now be regarded as highly literary choices. In the past and imperfect tenses, literary Welsh retains a final /m/ in the first person plural, which is invariably /n/ in spontaneous speech (*aethom*: *aethon*). In the three plural persons of the past tense, spontaneous speech invariably drops the medial /a/, and some dialects drop the /s/, both of which are retained in the literary forms (*canasom*: *can(s)on*, *canasoch*: *can(s)och*, *canasant*: *can(s)on*). In second-person singular imperatives, the literary language keeps to a range of traditional stems or affected forms such as *cân*, *cadw*, *cwyd*, *aros*, *paid*, *ŷf*; in the dialects there has become established a range of forms with -*a* endings (*cana*, *cadwa*, *arhosa*, *peidia*, *yfa*) which, without having superseded all the traditional forms, are available as alternatives to them; it is equally true that, in certain verbs, choice of stem forms (*byt* rather than *byta*, *isht* rather than *ishte*) is a feature of dialect, not of literary usage.

The verbs *af*, *caf* and *gwnaf* have, in the dialects, adopted a number of past-tense forms strikingly different from those of the literary language. The first- and second-person singular forms *es*, *ces*, *gwnes* and *est*, *cest*, *gwnest* have gained partial acceptance in literature; *euthum*, *deuthum*, *gwneuthum* and *aethost*, *daethost*, *gwnaethost* might well have been superseded were it not for a fairly conscious rearguard action in their favour during this century; this is not so true of *cefais*, *cefaist*.

Writers' instinct has been more resistant to the past plurals of which there is a wide choice in the dialects: for example for *cawsom* there occur *cafon*, *ceson*, *ceuson*, *ceuthon*. A feature of this category of verbs is the tendency to adopt a common past tense form for all persons, with regional variation: the north-western *euso*, *geuso*, *gafo*, *gatho*, *gneutho* which are still distinctly low, and the southern *eso* or *etho*, *ceso*, *netho* which can well pass as standard local speech, although not accepted in literature. It is a development which appears to parallel the adoption of the all-purpose *gynno* as a preposition. Yet another feature of the same category, strictly confined to southern speech, is the adoption of stems in -*el*-, as though salvaged from the subjunctive *gwnelwn* etc., in the imperfect used with a conditional sense — *elen*, *celen*, *gnelen* etc.

Bod, "to be", is a world of its own, as are its counterparts in other languages. The paradigms in Table 11.5 may give some indication of how far the dialects differ from the standard literary forms. The second-person singular *wyt* is the only form common to literary Welsh and to all the dialects. *Ydwyt* in speech is almost impossible. In the past tense (See Table 11.6) the main differences are in the first- and third-person singular forms; and *bûm*, *bu* are not unfamiliar in spontaneous speech. Verbs generally agreeing with *bod* (*adnabod*, *darganfod* etc.), where they have a past tense, have spoken forms in which 'regular' verb endings are

TABLE 11.5 *Present tense*

		Literary	Spoken
Singular	(1)	*wyf; ydwyf*	*w; ydw*
	(2)	*wyt; ydwyt*	*wyt*
	(3)	*yw; ydyw*	*yw* (S only); *ydi*
Plural	(1)	*ŷm; ydym*	*ŷn* (S only); *ydyn, yden, ydan*
	(2)	*ych; ydych*	*ŷch* (S only); *ydech, ydach*
	(3)	*ŷnt; ydynt*	*ŷn* (S only); *ydyn, yden, ydan*

Note: The adoption of *o-* stem, giving *odw*, and the hardening of the /d/, giving *otw*, provides a further variation in a group of south-eastern dialects.

TABLE 11.6 *Past tense*

		Literary	Spoken
Singular	(1)	*bûm*	*bues, buis, buo, buom*
	(2)	*buost*	*buest, buost*
	(3)	*bu*	*buo, buodd*
Plural	(1)	*buom*	*buon*
	(2)	*buoch*	*buoch*
	(3)	*buont*	*buon*

adopted with a *-bydd-* or *-fydd-* stem (*adnabyddais, darganfyddodd* etc.); common though they are in speech, a writer familiar with the tradition of written Welsh will not use them. In the imperfect tense (See Table 11.7) the divergence is small. The only literary form which has no counterpart in spontaneous speech is *ydoedd*. In the iterative imperfect (*byddwn, byddet* etc.) the forms are the same except for the regular *byddem: bydden* difference in the first-person plural, and again the loss of final /t/ in the third-person plural *bydden*. In the future and iterative present (*byddaf, byddi* etc.) the paradigms are exactly the same. In the pluperfect (which occasionally in writing and often in speech deputizes for the imperfect conditional), the forms are the same except for the usual vowel changes summarized above, and the omission of /u/ from the stem, giving *baswn, baset* or *basat, base* or *basa* etc.

We need in Welsh something comparable to the French *Dictionnaire de 8,000 verbes. . . conjugés*, listing side by side the literary paradigms

TABLE 11.7   *Imperfect tense*

		Literary	Spoken
Singular	(1)	*oeddwn*	*oeddwn, ôn, oen, own*
	(2)	*oeddit, oeddet*	*oeddet ', oeddat*
	(3)	*oedd; ydoedd*	*oedd, ôdd*
Plural	(1)	*oeddem*	*oedden, oeddan*
	(2)	*oeddech*	*oeddech, oeddach*
	(3)	*oeddynt*	*oedden, oeddan*

and all the localized spoken variations, making room for *cath, jenges, llneuish, cymodd, gadlonwch*, alongside *cafodd, dihengais, glanheais, cymerodd, gadewch lonydd*, and illustrating the whole spectrum from the suspect *doswch* (a plural imperative formed by adding a plural ending to the singular imperative), through the virtuous *egyr*, to the preposterous *diylch*. Such a handbook would note, for example: those verbs which, at least in some dialects, take their stems directly from the verb–nouns, producing forms not accepted in the literary language — *chwerthis, tarodd*, rather than *chwerddais, trawodd*; verbs which are highly defective in literary Welsh but are fully conjugated in speech (*mi fywith, mi farwodd* etc. occur naturally, at least in some northern dialects, whereas in literary Welsh they are reduced to hardly more than the verb–nouns); and verbs which are slightly less defective in the literary language than in spontaneous speech, for example *piau*, whose third-person singular past tense, *pioedd*, is confined to a highly literary register.

How wide a gap?

Enough will have been said to indicate that in certain important areas the differences are clear and substantial: the conditions of its existence have created within the Welsh language a range of variation the like of which English, for all its world-wide distribution, has never known. Yet it may be pertinent at this stage to remind ourselves of two things: first that several of the examples listed in the previous sub-section represented extremes which the common standard spoken language is often able to bridge; and secondly that even when dealing with the two extremes, the formal literary and the spontaneous spoken, it is possible to make too much of the difference.

That it is based on an over-simplified contrast between the "living" (equated with informal speech) and the "dead" (equated with the literary) is one of the criticisms which have been levelled at the *Cymraeg Byw* ("Living Welsh") movement, and the error is usually traced by the critics to two sources: the radio lecture *Cymraeg Byw*, delivered by Ifor Williams in 1960, and a lecture on *Yr Iaith Lafar a Llenyddiaeth*, "The Spoken Language and Literature", given to the Welsh Academy by Griffith John Williams shortly before his death in 1963. As it happened the lectures were in each case a final pronouncement on the condition of the Welsh language by a distinguished academic who had spent a lifetime in its study. They were expressing a traditional concern among users of Welsh, and among its well-wishers over many generations, that by its conservatism the literary language had distanced itself from Welsh as understood by the ordinary user. Evidence of this concern is plentiful in the introductions to sixteenth and seventeenth century prose works, and we have observed that John Morris-Jones and Emrys ap Iwan shared it to some extent. But the two pronouncements of the early 1960s were somehow more pointed than any earlier ones had been, and the age was also receptive. Some of their suggestions were taken up by a panel of educationists and developed into a programme of language reform. As other chapters in this book will no doubt be mentioning, the outcome has become a matter of disagreement at least as heated as the turn of the century debate over orthography. Eurys Rolant (1984) finds in the recommendations of *Cymraeg Byw* "a new prescriptivism", based on inaccurate description and arbitrary judgements. Ceinwen H. Thomas (1979), arguing from a similar standpoint, sees in them "the coining of a new, spurious dialect".

As it would be unsporting not to take a side, I am prepared to say that I find much to agree with in the traditionalist case against *Cymraeg Byw*. Some of the objections made by Ceinwen H. Thomas (1979), reviewing the second-language textbook *Cymraeg Cyfoes* (1975), I would find extremely difficult to refute, as when the book assumes that the conjunctive and re-duplicative pronouns are not common enough in colloquial Welsh to require that the learner be introduced to them: they have, of course, spoken forms which are a little different from the literary forms (e.g. *finna*, *nhwtha* rather than *finnau*, *hwythau*; *y fi*, *y nhw* rather than *myfi*, *hwynthwy*), but half an hour spent in any Welsh-speaking community, north or south, will confirm that they are very much alive in every-day speech. Similarly, there is the matter of noun–adjective concord: it is true that spontaneous speech tends to use the feminine and plural of adjectives less often, and true for that matter that the literary language began to forego this concord six centuries ago; but the process is far from being complete. Again with the adjectives, it is certainly true that speech, spontaneous and formal, often opts for the analytical method of compari-

son, that is placing *mor, mwy, mwya* before the positive form (*mor fawr,
mwy ffeind, mwya caled*), but to say that the concise or morphological
forms (*cymaint, ffeindiach, cleta*) are "hardly ever heard" can be very
misleading. If the adjective is not so common, or a polysyllable, the
analytical method tends to be chosen, even in literature; but again there
are exceptions. With some monosyllable adjectives, speech tends to choose
the analytical form for the equative degree (*mor las, mor oer, mor drwm*),
but for the comparative and superlative degrees it almost invariably
chooses the morphological form (*glasach, oerach, trymach*; *glasa, oera,
tryma*). Speech may have its own form, for example *hirach*, "longer",
anoddach, "more difficult", as alternatives to the literary *hwy, anos*: but
this does not alter the principle. In spontaneous spoken Welsh we often
rely on intonation to produce an emphasis in a question, for example "*i'r
dre 'rwyt ti'n mynd?*" ("is it to town you're going?"), "*ti sy 'na?*" ("is that
you?"), and are therefore able to dispense with the interrogative particle
ai, which opens an emphatic question in both the literary language and
formal speech. But it is incorrect to say that the *ai* has disappeared from
conversational Welsh; it is to be heard if anything more often in an
indirect question, for example, "*wn i ddim ai fo wnaeth*" ("I don't know
whether it was he who did it"). It is often supplanted by the incorrect *os
mai*, but that is a different matter. We read that the preposition *â* is not
heard in conversational Welsh after *peidio*, that *paid mynd, peidiwch
gofidio* alone are natural. Half the truth, perhaps, of southern dialects;
but scores of thousands of northern speakers would reply "*paid â malu*".
Again, southern dialects provide the grounds for a claim that a medial
/s/ is no longer heard in past tense forms of the verb, that *gwelon, clywoch*
are what we will hear. These forms may be spreading gradually from the
south to the north, and a head-count might well reveal that they are the
forms now used by a majority of Welsh-speakers. One cannot therefore
object to their selection as the forms which learners are initially taught.
But it is something quite other to say that *mi welson ni, chlywsoch chi
ddim* never occur. We travel further into the realm of fantasy when we
read that the initial aspirate /h/ is not heard after *i*, "her"; *yn*, "our" and
i, "their". *I ochor hi? Yn arfer ni? I eglwys nhw?* Always? As Ceinwen
Thomas notes (1979), it is evident that the description is based on a group
of Glamorgan and eastern Dyfed dialects which do not sound an initial /
h/ in any case. And so on. Having considered these instances, and there
are others of like kind, it is hard to disagree with the conclusion (C. H.
Thomas, 1979: 118) that the end result will not be a narrowing of the gap
between the literary and the spoken, but its widening into a chasm that
can never be closed.

The reader may now accuse me of a base electicism when, having agreed so far with the traditionalist critics of *Cymraeg Byw*, I refer again approvingly to a suggestion which comes from what is regarded as the opposite quarter. The three-dimensional model proposed by Roberts & Jones (1974) has the virtue of enabling us to see all the varieties of Welsh, from the most pedestrian to the most elevated, as belonging essentially to one *continuum*; it therefore offers, to my mind, the best alternative yet to the naïve counter-opposition of the colloquial and the literary, the living and the dead. Although a case could be made for the description "dead" as shorthand for what the grammars call "not productive in speech", it becomes inapposite when applied to any form, however rare or archaic, which occurs anywhere within the *continuum* which is the language as used today. To give an example, it is not every day that we would want to use the construction which places the preposition *o* after the verb–noun in a noun or adverbial clause, as in *gwn fynd ohono*, "I know that he has gone", *wedi mynd ohono*, "after he had gone"; but there is a time and a place for it. It belongs to a fairly high register of the formal literary language, as do also the following: the possessive pronouns *eiddof*, "mine", *eiddot*, "thine" etc., corresponding to the more familiar *f'un i*, *dy un di* etc.; the relative clause without an antecedent, as in *a fynno ddeall, darllened*, "he who wishes to understand, let him read", which spontaneous speech uses only in set phrases, essentially quotations; the use of a conjunctive pronoun in apposition with a noun, translateable as "for his part" etc., as in *fy nhad yntau, y frenhines hithau*; the placing of a pronoun other than *mi* in front of the verb, as in *ti wyddost, hi aeth* etc., a feature shared by highly literary language and one or two south-eastern dialects.

In spontaneous speech only a handful of adjectives (*annwyl, gwir, hen, unig, prif*) are placed in their positive degree before a noun; literary practice extends the principle to other adjectives, mainly as a device of poetry, but occasionally also in prose for rhetorical effect. *Im, it*, monosyllable forms of the inflected preposition *i*, are again high and poetical, belonging to the same band as "ere", "nigh" and "quoth" in English, but still not obsolete in the same way; reading the works of R. Williams Parry, we do not find anything unnatural in "*Ond hynny nid yw ofid im*".

The experienced user of Welsh will know which literary forms and constructions still meet a need, and which ones are so archaic or so elevated as to make their use something of a risk. At one end of the spectrum are literary forms so mild that we have to remind ourselves that we do not use them very often in spontaneous speech: the plural ending *- wyr*, very frequently, but not invariably, replaced in speech by *-wrs*, as in *chwarelwrs*, *pregethwrs*; the adjectival ending *-ig*, so useful in writing and in formal speech to distinguish between *Cymraeg* (Welsh in language) and *Cymreig* (Welsh in other respects), *Saesneg* and *Seisnig* etc.; the independent pronoun *mi* in any position except after the preposition *i*; and the affixed genitive pronoun *'w* occurring after *i*, and now largely replaced in spontaneous speech by an *'i* which is subsumed by the preposition, giving *i fam*, "to his mother". These four features occur regularly in formal speech, which may be one reason why we do not feel that they are particularly literary. At the other end there are forms which today have a very restricted use, and would advisably be confined to poetry, although some of them will be encountered in the mandarin prose language cultivated by some writers in the inter-war years, in an uprush of enthusiasm for literary Welsh as re-established and refurbished by Morris-Jones: *e ddaw* as opposed to *fe ddaw*, and the form *o* instead of *os*, "if", as in *o mynnwch wybod*; the omission of the predicative *yn* after a copula, as in *wyt ŵr*, "you are a man", *buost ddoeth*, "you were wise"; and the occasional extra-posh mutation such as the one in the last line of the play *Gwaed yr Uchelwyr*, "*rhaid i chi sgrifennu at Ito*". Use of the equative degree of the adjective either in an exclamation (*hardded oedd!*) or in a noun clause (*rhyfeddais wyched oedd*) can be placed a little down the scale, just about acceptable in modern literary prose. It is but a small alteration to choose *ni*, *nid*, *nis* as a negative relative pronoun, replacing the *na*, *nad*, *nas* of the ordinary registers, but it has an unmistakeable effect, and is sometimes felt to earn its place by the note of heroism or reverence it produces, as in the titles *Peth Nis Lleddir* and *Y Porth Nid â'n Angof*. The construction placing *oll* in apposition with a noun (*y dynion oll* rather than *y dynion i gyd*), and the choice of *oni(d)* in preference to the *os na(d)* of every-day speech, are both common to the formal literary language and to formal speech; in the right contexts, they do not sound unnatural.

Even the formal literary language, when we have separated it from the informal literary language of dialogue, monologue and character narration, is seen to have categories and sub-divisions within it, overlapping but distinct. It includes what R. M. Jones (1985a, b) calls "the academic register", which it shares in common with the formal spoken language. It includes also the poetic register. Whether we like to admit it or not, the survival of a distinct poetic language is a fact of Welsh literary history up to the present day. We have made a habit of saying that, since the 1930s and following the example of T. H. Parry-Williams, D. Gwenallt Jones and the later work of R. Williams Parry, the idiom of Welsh verse has moved closer to that of every-day speech. It is true in a sense. The belief tenaciously held by John Morris-Jones, that poetry can only be composed in a select diction which excludes certain every-day usages, has long ago been abandoned, if indeed it was ever fully shared by any of Morris-Jones's own contemporaries. What is however true is that there are still certain recognizable usages which by common consent are confined to poetry. In every-day speech, in narrative or discursive prose, in any utilitarian context, they would sound ridiculous, but they are appropriate and functional as part of a poetic code which the Welsh reader understands and respects.

Biblical Welsh is another sub-category within the literary language, clearly identifiable in that the Welsh Bible, like the English one, is the only 400 year-old book still in regular use, but perhaps a little less distinct than Biblical English is from the secular literary idiom; the reasons for this are the influence that Morgan's Bible has had on literary style generally, and the fact that so much of the institutional life conducted in Welsh, up to the 1940s, arose from religion or was connected with it in one way or another. Although we are now witnessing the passing of the last generation of those who could apply a Biblical allusion and a Biblical turn of phrase to any situation in every-day life, whether grave or comic, the idiom of Morgan's Bible will continue to have a place in the consciousness of Welsh readers for some years yet. This is the reason why the Welsh Academy's new English–Welsh dictionary, when it appears, will be seen to retain Morgan's wording when translating well-known Biblical phrases, although they may have been rendered anew in the 1975 New Testament. Comparison between the old version and the new of any chapter in the New Testament would quickly demonstrate the character of what we have traditionally regarded as Biblical Welsh. The "Biblical" is what has disappeared. Small indications are the general avoidance of the subjunctive (*pan wnelych elusen* has become *pan fyddi'n rhoi elusen*), the replacement of the conjunctions *canys* and *eithr* by the more modern-sounding *oblegid* and *ond*, the abandoning of the pronouns *efe* and *hwynt* for *ef* and *hwy*, and the modernization of certain verb and noun forms (*clybu*, *cymerth*, *ymado*, *myned*, *dwfr* have become *clywodd*, *cymerodd*, *ymadael*, *mynd*, *dŵr*). The use of verb tenses is brought into line with the spoken practice, periphrastic forms being preferred for the true present, the imperfect and the pluperfect. There are also three or four important syntactical changes. The old *subject* + *verb* + (*object*) word order, the abnormal sentence as it is known (*angylion a ddaethant*), is found to have been regularly replaced by the normal sentence construction (*daeth angylion*). The use of a demonstrative pronoun in apposition with the antecedent of a relative clause, as in *Simon, yr hwn a elwid Pedr*, is discontinued, giving *Simon, a elwid Pedr*. In an oblique relative clause governed by a preposition, the construction which is standard in speech and in modern literary prose, *y byd yr ydym yn sôn amdano*, replaces *y byd. . . am yr hwn yr ydym yn llefaru* which is used very often in the old translation. Verb–subject concord in a positive relative clause with a plural subject, *y brodyr a ddaethant o Facedonia*, has given way to the non-agreement which is the rule of speech and of modern writing, *y brodyr a ddaeth o Facedonia*. The absolute phrase introduced by a conjunction, *a hi eto'n dywyll* is generally dispensed with in favour of an adverbial phrase or clause, *tra oedd hi eto'n dywyll*, exception being made of some cases where it is natural in modern Welsh, for example, *a thi dy hun heb weld y trawst sydd yn dy lygad di*.

Colloquial or simply wrong?

There is one other thing which we must briefly deal and dispense with if we are to approach a definition of literary Welsh. We sometimes see quoted as examples of the "spoken" as opposed to the "literary" or the "formal" forms which we should, to my mind, continue to regard as corruptions, whether they occur in speech or in writing. Opinions will of course vary regarding what should be placed in this category. Even some of the most modern Welsh grammars describe some things as sub-standard because they offend the instinct of any natural Welsh speaker. For example, R. M. Jones & A. R. Thomas (1977) reject *syniad fi oedd o*, "it was my idea", and strike a prescriptive note by referring to its "disturbingly high frequency in the speech of young children". "*Dydy John heb gyrraedd*", "John has not arrived" is with all justification classified as unacceptable. For my own part I would not share the book's tolerance of *dwi'n edrych ar*, "(which) I'm looking at", and *y dre mae Mair yn cerdded i*, "the town to which Mair is walking", with the preposition uninflected in both instances; or of *dwi'n dadlau efo*, "(which) I'm arguing with", with the pronoun omitted after *efo*. I would also continue to regard as basically wrong in Welsh the postponement of the preposition, whether inflected or not, in a pronominal question governed by a preposition: *be 'dach chi'n sôn am(dano)?*, "what are you talking about?". And if ever anything was sub-standard Welsh, surely it is the omission of a particle (*mai, na, taw*) introducing the noun clause in *mae Mair yn gwybod John oedd yn chwerthin*, "Mair knows (that) it was John who was laughing".

It is correctly recorded that there is a tendency to omit the particle in *mae'n ymddangos bydd John yn gweithio*, "it appears (that) John will be working"; when the noun clause has a future reference the loss of the particle is not a painful one. But *mae'n ymddangos 'roedd John yn gweithio*, "it appears (that) John was working", judged acceptable on p. 216, looks very dubious to me. It is no doubt correctly recorded (p. 352), in discussing the interrogative particle in an indirect question, "indeed *os*, "if", is the typical choice in spontaneous speech": this may well be, by now, the choice of a majority of Welsh speakers. But rather than rely on an all-Wales head-count I should still prefer to take a cue from those speakers to whom *gofyn iddo fo ydi o'n dwad, wn i ddim fydd hi yno, 'rydw i'n ama fydd gen i amsar* is what comes naturally, with the mutation, where necessary, showing the effect of *a*, the correct interrogative particle. True enough, "the ear of a true Welshman" cannot be referred to today with the same certainty as when Maurice Kyffin used the phrase. Now that the monolingual Welsh speakers have gone, we have to fall back on the temporary authority of the literary language and the uncertain instinct of bilinguals. Under pressure, each one of us might have to admit that by "the ear of a true Welshman" he means "my own ear". This is merely to record the difficulty. I am also aware that the factors of age and background are omissions from this article. A careful diachronic study encompassing the last 40 years and taking education and social class into consideration might well require several of my observations to be qualified. The 1960s, in which there coincided the universal invasion of television with the passing of the last generation reared in a wholly Welsh-speaking environment, must be seen as a major watershed.

Likes and dislikes

It has been suggested earlier, echoing other commentators, that the danger in *Cymraeg Byw*, and in grammars inspired by it, is to carry weight-watching to extremes, ending up with an impression that colloquial Welsh is more starved of resources than it actually is. Without recanting anything that has been said, it must now be recognized that spoken Welsh is no exception to the general tendency of spoken language to select, to simplify and to make do on less. The resources of the verb will illustrate the case well. Welsh has a subjunctive, characterizing the upper registers of the written language, and sometimes used with a little ostentation; we rarely encounter it in speech, formal or informal, outside set phrases such as *da boch chi, fel fynnoch chi, y calla dawo, doed a ddelo*. Both the third-person imperative, for example *aed*, "let him go", *safed*, "let him stand", and the impersonal imperative, for example *eler*, "let there be a going", *gwrandawer*, "let there be a listening", are found useful in the formal language, written and spoken, but spontaneous speech now dispenses largely with the former and almost completely with the latter, again with the exception of set phrases. The impersonal conveying a passive is a prominent and hard-working constituent in literary Welsh, with the formal spoken language agreeing strongly, as any news bulletin will exemplify. In spontaneous speech the "present" forms (*-ir*) have become rather rare; on the other hand past and conditional imperfect forms (*-wyd, -id*) do occur with some frequency, indeed some verbs, at least in some dialects, have a spoken past impersonal slightly different from the usual literary form, for example *awd, rhowd* corresponding to *aed* or *aethpwyd, rhoed* or *rhoddwyd*. But, in the main, spontaneous speech will either convey the passive by an analytical method: *mae e'n cael ei gadw* rather than *cedwir ef*, "it is kept"; or else avoid the passive: *maen nhw'n dweud*, "they say", instead of *dywedir*, "it is said". The morphological pluperfect of the verb (*-aswn* etc.) is now a highly literary feature, useful but not to be overdone even in literature; formal speech tends to avoid it, preferring the analytical form, and informal speech avoids it almost completely, the only exceptions being:

(i) *baswn* (etc.) and *dylswn* (etc.) which are not always pluperfect in meaning, used often as replacements for the imperfect conditional;

(ii) an occasional occurrence in an area of the south-west, always with a conditional meaning, for example *gnelsen*, "I would have done".

It is possible in principle to make any Welsh verb a reflexive by prefixing *ym-*. But only the formal language, written and spoken, avails itself regularly of this facility; informal speech again opts for the analytical method, using *fy hun, dy hun* etc. as objects of the verb. Even what would appear to be exceptions in informal speech are not really exceptions. *Ymolchi*, "to wash", can be a transitive verb as well as a reflexive: *y fam yn molchi'r babi*, "the mother washing the baby"; so can *mystyn*, a derivative of *ymestyn*, "to reach or stretch". The reflexive force has been lost in *ymadael*, "to depart", *ymdopi*, "to manage, and *myllio*, from *ymhyllio*, "to rave". *Ymweld*, "to visit", *ymladd*, "to fight", are reciprocative rather than reflexive.

Vocabulary is another obvious area of difference. Because its range of uses is wider, encompassing abstractions and specialized fields, the vocabulary of any formal language, written or spoken, will be ampler than that of its informal counterpart. Moreover, in a situation of unequal and unstable bilingualism, the literary vocabulary of the weaker language is likely to be "purer" than its spoken vocabulary, tolerating fewer unassimilated borrowings. Welsh conforms with both of these general rules. In theory, any English verb can be made into a Welsh one by adding *-(i)o*, *-(i)an* (*enjoio, warnio, riteirio, alowio, atacio* etc.) or a personal ending. But the literary language is wary of accepting these easy coinages, preferring on the whole stems which look more indigenous. In *Geiriadur Prifysgol Cymru* examples abound of lightly touched-up borrowings, introduced by someone or other and used once or twice in a literary context before being laid aside and forgotten: the literary language, by the operation of some instinct, rejects them by the hundred.

With the exception of this broad category, it would be unsafe to maintain that any individual word is unacceptable in literary Welsh. It is the informal spoken language which is stubborn and choosy. The ready admittance of regional dialect words has been a characteristic of Welsh literary prose over the last 100 years, most evident in narrative fiction, but observable also in essays and memoirs. After all, the material has so often been drawn from the life of ordinary Welshmen in clearly defined localities. In novels and stories, some overspill of character speech into the narrative passages is frequently to be seen. No doubt, if we looked hard, we could find some words, especially in strong or eccentric dialects such as those of the old Pembrokeshire or Caernarfon town, that have never been used in literature outside dialogue or character speech. But generally speaking the modern literary language has been highly receptive to colloquial words and phrases, and in some notable cases has put them on special display. Here it must be stressed that we are talking about the written literary language; formal speech is more reserved.

Alongside a list of local colloquial forms which have been readily accepted by the literary language, we could in no time at all draw up a sizeable list of standard Welsh words which spontaneous speech in all localities is reluctant to take up. They are not abstract or specialized terms in any way. In a monolingual society they would be every-day words; it is the condition of transitional bilingualism which relegates them to the literary and formal spoken language, dependent on the conscience of the educated for their survival. The list would include not only nineteenth and twentieth century coinages such as *heddlu, trydan, hofrennydd, darlledu,* but also old and established words such as *llen, blwch, athro, grawnwin, defnyddio.* The ordinary Welsh speaker will have a passive knowledge of this vocabulary. He may sometimes refer to it dismissively as "*Cymraeg mawr*", "big Welsh", especially if his attitude is for some reason hostile to the social groups who make most use of it; just as often, oftener perhaps, he will refer to it deferentially as *"Cymraeg da"*, "good Welsh"; and without any doubt this is the vocabulary he prefers to see in print. But in informal talk he will choose the more anglicized counterpart in each case — *polîs, letrig, helicoptar, brôdcastio, cyrtan, titshiar, grêps, iwsio*. There is probably a degree of regional variation in this matter. Am I correct that *stafell, swyddfa* are more acceptable in the south?

As with vocabulary, so also in morphology and syntax, the tendency is the same. It is the spontaneous spoken language that is selective and stubborn. Literary language, although in a sense it is the more conservative of the two, always has more "give" in it, because conscious choice has played some part in its making. To extend a comparison offered by Ifor Williams, spoken language may indeed be viewed as a flowing river, in contrast with the still lake of literary language; altering the outline of the lake may take some doing, but to divert the course of the river will take considerably more. What it amounts to is that speech is primary; it is the spoken language that does the pushing — with the additional factor in this case that spoken Welsh is being pushed hard from behind by another language. Ideally, our definition of literary Welsh, or of any literary language, should include first a list of all those features that are obligatory in it, but not in the spoken form; and secondly and more important still a list of what is obligatory in speech but optional in writing. In the remaining paragraphs we shall attempt a rough summary of what such a description might contain.

In extending our list of the likes and dislikes of literary Welsh, we may usefully note some cases in which literary usage is supported by some local dialects against others. We are traditionally taught, and on some good evidence, that the foundations of the Welsh prose tradition were laid in the south; that the bardic tradition was stronger in the north; and that there was an influx of northern usages into prose during the Renaissance, mainly because some confirmed northerners had their way with the Welsh Bible. We will content ourselves with a few examples, not in any particular order and not revealing any clear pattern, of where literary Welsh stands in relation to the two main dialect groups. First, and briefly, the lexical aspect. There is a common assumption that the literary language favours a northern vocabulary, and some of the old favourites which spring to mind do suggest that this may be so, for example *bwrdd*, "table"; *ceg*, "mouth"; *gorffen*, "to finish"; *cetyn*, "pipe", *cwyno*, "to complain", *disgwyl*, "to wait"; *edrych*, "to look"; *mellten*, "lightning"; *allan*, "out"; *i ffwrdd*, "away"; *i fyny*, "up" against *bord, pen, cwpla, pib*,

achwyn, erfyn, dishgwl, llucheden, mas, bant, lan; but there are examples
of preference for the southern word or form, for example *gyda*, "with";
nawr, "now"; *allwedd*, "key"; *dant*, "tooth" against *efo, rwan, goriad,
daint*. Often the literary language has no particular preference, finding
llwynog and *cadno*, "fox", *deffro* and *dihuno*, "to awaken", *barrug* and
llwydrew, "hoar frost", all acceptable; sometimes it may go for a neutral
choice, *wylo* rather than *crïo* or *llefen*, "to cry", *llaid* rather than *mwd* or
llacs, "mud". There is somewhere a statistical answer to the whole question; a computer could give it in next to no time if we spent 12 years in
feeding it with the information.

Two distinctive phonological features which literary Welsh shares
with northern dialects are, first the retention of the initial /ch/ in *chwaer,
chwith* etc., where the south would say *whâr, whith*; and secondly the
inclusion of a consonantal /i/ in a range of verb, noun and adjectival
endings, for example *peintio, gweithiodd, mawrion, pigiad* against *peinto,
gwithodd, mowron, pigad*. Gender might be another field of study; for
example literary use concurs with the northern in making *cinio*, "dinner",
cyflog, "wage", *munud*, "minute", masculine, and with the southern in
making *rhyfel*, "war", masculine; *breuddwyd*, "dream", in the literary
language may vary, sometimes masculine as it is most often in the north,
sometimes feminine as in the south. The southern second-person singular
pronoun *fe, e* is freely accepted in literature as an alternative to the more
strictly literary *ef*, while the northern *fo, o* is generally confined to speech.
Literary Welsh chooses to retain *i mi*, as does standard northern speech,
rather than mutate to *i fi*, which is southern practice; one southern author,
D. J. Williams, has insisted on following the practice of his own dialect
in this small matter, outside dialogue and character speech. But *bach* is
mutated after a feminine noun, as in the south. The choice of *gan* rather
than *gyda* to indicate possession — *mae gen i* rather than *mae gyda fi*, "I
have" — is common to literary and northern usage, as is the choice of
the order *mae gen i dŷ* rather than *mae tŷ gen i*, "I have a house"; but in
its reluctance to adopt *efo*, "with", the literary language sides with the
south. It tends to reject the southern *mynte*, "he/she said", choosing
meddai, which is common to north and south, otherwise *ebe* which has
become rare in spontaneous speech except in the occasional northern
form *ebra* which in turn is related to the archaic and highly literary *ebr*.

Northern spontaneous speech will not use *hunan* after a singular
pronoun, always choosing *fy hun*, "myself" etc.; literary Welsh accepts
both. The use of *hwn, hon, hyn* as demonstrative adjectives is again
literary and southern, contrasting with the northern adoption of the all-
purpose *yma*, as in *y dyn yma* "this man", where a southerner would be

more prepared to say *y dyn hwn*. In northern speech *hwn, hon, hyn* occur only as demonstrative pronouns, for example *hon ydi hi*, "it's this one"; *hyn ydw i'n ddeud*, "this is what I'm saying". On the other hand *hwnnw, honno* occur adjectivally in north and south as in the literary language, although frequently curtailed to *'nw, 'no; hynny* as a plural demonstrative adjective is common to the literary and the southern, sometimes curtailed to *'ny* in southern speech: its replacement by the pronoun *rheini* tends now to be confined to northern speech. Following persistent exhortation by John Morris-Jones, this century has witnessed the restoration to the literary language and to formal speech of the verbial particle *yr, 'r* in a mixed sentence such as *cerdded yr oeddwn i* (literally "it was walking that I was doing", or good Wenglish "walking I was"), and this is also by and large southern practice. Northern informal speech tends, and perhaps increasingly, to omit it, giving *cerdded oeddwn i* as if in imitation of the copula sentence with noun or adjective predicate, *athro oeddwn i*, "I was a teacher"; *prysur oeddwn i*, "I was busy". The literary language also agrees with the south against some northern dialects in insisting on an article when the noun is definite.

It is not true of all dialects that absence of an article makes a noun indefinite. *I tŷ*, "into the house"; *yn lôn*, "in *the* road"; *deud wrth plisman*, "to tell *the* policeman"; *ma dyn glo'n dwad*, "*the* coalman's coming"; *dos trw cefn*, "go through *the* back", are all regular, if a little short of standard, in Gwynedd. The article could be included in all these examples, but somehow it is not felt to be necessary, any more than in Latin, or in an English newspaper headline, to convey that the noun is definite; it is as though the context, in each case, allows the common noun to assume the character of a proper noun. Here and there in the dialects there occur a number of verb–noun endings which the literary language will not touch: it agrees with the north in rejecting *dringad, treial, galler* (for *dringo, treio, gallu*) which have a limited distribution in the south; and with the south in rejecting *rhoid, taflyd, cuddiad* (for *rhoi, tafflu, cuddio*), heard over a wide area of the north.

Chdi, instead of *ti*, the second-person singular pronoun, occurs regularly, though not in all positions, in most nothern dialects. The moment I say *i chdi*, "to you", which I do say fairly often, I am aware of departing from a standard; *gen chdi* is definitely sub-standard; and *dy dŷ chdi, *mi welist chdi are impossible. The rule in the dialects where it occurs would appear to be that *chdi* is unacceptable as a supplementative pronoun, except following a non-inflecting preposition (*â, efo, fel, heb-law*), and also in some interesting cases where the preposition has dropped the traditional second-person ending in order to accommodate *chdi*, for example *ata chdi*, *drosda chdi*, and has then by a process of regression developed into a new inflected form which can be used without the pronoun: *atachd*, *drosdachd*. As a substantive pronoun *chdi* is perfectly acceptable. Yet — and this is what matters to us now — I am fairly sure that it has never been used in literature outside character speech. It would be impossible to prove that there is anything wrong with it. But the writing hand refuses to write it. The literary language is almost as intransigent in its rejection of the second-person "present" verb endings *-iff*, *-ith*. Every-one knows how common they are in all dialects, but ever since John Davies remarked in 1621 *"numquam since indignatione audio"* (yes, *audio*), written Welsh has become increasingly resistant to them. They may occur in a lecture or public address, but hardly in a news bulletin; the preacher might use them occasionally during his sermon, but most probably not in his prayer. Argue as one will, there is an instinct at work, this time almost as binding as the instinct governing spontaneous speech. In a not dissimilar way literary Welsh came to reject the third-person singular past tense ending *-ws*, common though it is in southern speech, and although it is so close to the *-wys*, *-as* and *-es*, which were once standard in literature. A thumbs-down by John Davies may again have been decisive.

We have already recorded that the spontaneous spoken first-person plural past tense ending, north and south, is *-on* without exception; *-on* and *-om* vary in formal speech; but the hand of its own accord writes *-om*, and no good will come of trying to force it. The literary language still chokes on the "new" (now not-so-new) numerals, *un deg un* etc., except in certain restricted contexts. Most of us who write Welsh will probably admit a certain ambivalence in our attitude towards these. It would be useless for me to deny having written *cant tri deg wyth o bunnoedd*, "a hundred and thirty eight pounds", or to promise never to do so again. But in any kind of literary composition, that hand, I am sure, would write *cant a deunaw ar hugain*. And for some reason or other they have never developed a system of ordinals to accompany them, in speech or in writing. Trying to force **un deg unfed* would lead only to disaster. The rejection of *rheini*, "those", as an adjective is an example of the literary language having become stricter in the course of the present century, following the re-establishment of traditional standards during its first quarter. Another example is the now regular inclusion of the relative pronoun *a*. The dialects omit it freely, as did many writers up to the 1920s. *Yr olygfa welir*, "the view that is seen"; *bryn fu'n ynys unwaith*, "a hill which was once an island"; *y pethau hoffai ef*, "the things he liked"; *yr argraff gyntaf wnaethant arnaf*, "the first impression they made on me", are all examples from the works of O. M. Edwards. With the completion of Morris-Jones's description of the literary language, the *a* was restored and its place is now secure. All formal Welsh is insistent on retaining *nid* at the opening of a negative inverted sentence or constituent, rather than the southern *nage* or the *d(d)im* which occurs as an alternative in the north: *nid John wnaeth*, "it wasn't John that did it". *Ddim John wnaeth* is common, and becoming commoner, in my dialect, but a better class of speaker will still say *nid*. *Mai* is still the literary and formal choice for opening an inverted noun clause, for example *'rwy'n credu mai dyna'r gwir*, for "I believe that to be the truth", sometimes allowing as an alternative the southern *taw*, never the northern *na* which has become common alongside *ma'*. For "her mother", dialects over a wide area will say "*i mham*"; likewise *i mhath hi*, "her type"; *i mhalu nhw*, "breaking them". In the early years of this century writers wrote the /h/ (*ei nherth cenedlaethol* — O.M.E.), but John Morris-Jones decreed against it, and it remains banned. There is nothing wrong with it. One day I might just try to force that hand. . .

But if formal language can be stubborn, spontaneous spoken language is by its nature more stubborn. A few examples will illustrate. Literary Welsh will tolerate the epenthetic vowel in *pobol, ochor, llwybyr, cwbwl*; John Morris-Jones (1890) could find no objection to writing it "when we feel the urge", and in speaking, even on the most formal occasions, we nearly always sound it. It is, on the other hand, almost impossible to imagine the informal spoken language accepting *pobl, ochr* etc. There is no indication that every-day speech will re-accept *chwi*; but *chi* is being admitted gradually into the literary language, without too much protesting. For negative commands, literary language uses *peidio* + *â*/*ag* + *verb–noun* freely: *peidiwch ag ofni*, "do not fear"; spontaneous speech will no longer admit *na*/*nac* + *verb*, *nac ofnwch*, except possibly in the occasional set phrase, for example *na phoener*, "not to worry". *Nhw* can occur in poetry and in formal speech without raising an eyebrow, but informal speech will no longer have *hwy*, let alone *hwynt*. The infixed pronouns *'th, -s*, as in *i'th dŷ*, "to your house" and *nis gwelais*, "I did not see him/her/it", are clear markers of formal literary language; spontaneous speech will not use them, and it also replaces the first person *'m* with *'n*: *i'n ardal i*, not *i'm hardal i*, "to my locality". *Mae dyn* in the literary language can mean either "there is a man" or "man is"; the context would have to show which was meant. The ambiguity is removed at a stroke in *mae yna ddyn*, which can only mean "there is a man"; the adverb thus placed makes up for the absence of an indefinite article. Literary Welsh avails itself of this useful device occasionally, not always: some authorities disapprove of it. Speech, again stricter, will always include 'na or yna if the sense demands it.

We have already referred to the final /t/ in gwelant, iddynt. Broadly speaking, the choice is either mi welan nhw or gwelant (hwy), fe welant (hwy). Mi welan nhw may be heard in high formal speech, and circumstances can be imagined where it might occur in literary prose or verse without causing any offence. Strength of feeling may suddenly impel one to write a colloquial form, changing back, when the blood has cooled, to a more formal register without being aware of any great inconsistency. But it is hard to imagine informal speech over re-accepting gwelant, ynddynt. This will be an old chestnut to all who have studied some of the history of the Welsh language. We have all dutifully learnt that the /t/ vanished from speech a 1000 years ago, and that gwelan, ynddyn were common in writing up to the translation of the Bible. One thing is however certain, if its restoration by John Davies was a mistake, it would be absurd to try and exclude it from the literary language today. Three and a half centuries are longer than anyone can remember, and longer than most people can conceive of. The choice is clear between, on the one hand, ânt a gwelant, ynddynt and on the other mi ân ac mi welan(-nhw), ynddyn-nhw, As John Morris-Jones (1913) recorded, ân and gwelan (the spoken form of the verb, but without the pre-verbial particle) and ynddyn (the spoken form of the preposition without a pronoun after it) have a restricted literary use in poetry.

The heart of the matter

We come finally to three features in which literary and spoken Welsh differ essentially and systematically from each other: the use of pre-verbial particles, the use of affixed or supplementative pronouns, and the use of the verb tenses. In each case the spoken language is the less tolerant of alternatives; an ideal definition of literary Welsh would centre on its relative flexibility in these three matters.

Pre-verbial particles

A general impression is that the spoken language is generous with the affirmative mi, fe and sparing with both the negative ni, nid and the interrogative a, ai; the written language is the other way round, but all in all more tolerant. The modern literary language can accept wn i ddim, "I don't know"; 'does dim amser, "there is no time"; welodd hi mohono, "she did not see him/it", happily enough alongside *ni wn, nid oes amser, ni welodd hi mohono*; but with a very small number of localized exceptions the spoken language, formal no less than informal, is very reluctant to negate by the second method. With the interrogative *a* both variants of Welsh show perhaps a little more flexibility, but on the whole the literary language is more prepared to omit it than is the spoken language to restore it. Its omission from second-person address is very common in writing: *glywaist ti?*, "did you hear?"; *gredwch chi?*, "will you believe?" etc. As for the affirmative particles, a rule determining when they should be used in the literary language is not easy to define. *Fe* or *mi* would certainly be used in a case like this: *gwadai iddo erioed fod yn aelod, ond fe fu*, "he denied ever having been a member, but he was". Apart from this, the consideration is perhaps more stylistic than grammatical; emphasis sometimes requires a particle, taste prohibits a too frequent use. Having got along for several sentences without using the particle, we may suddenly feel that one is needed for the sake of rhythm or emphasis:

Canodd y cloc larwm am saith o'r gloch, a chodais innau ar f'union. Bwyteais frecwast yn gyflym a chychwyn i'r orsaf mewn da bryd, debygwn i. Ond mi gollais y trên.

"The alarm clock rang at seven o'clock, and I got up immediately. I ate breakfast quickly and set off for the station in good time, as I thought. But I missed the train."

The *mi* somehow earns its place; on the other hand it would be hard to prove that its omission would alter the meaning.

In spontaneous speech there is not the same liberty to omit the particle. With a small number of standard exceptions (in a reply to a question, in a command, and where the verb is the third-person singular present of *bod*) the majority of local dialects always include one of the particles (*fe* in the south, *mi* in the north) before a verb, or else show its influence by mutation, as in *welis-i dy dad bora 'ma*, "I saw your father this morning"; *godes-i am saith heddi*, "I got up at seven today", without thereby creating any emphasis. Sometimes the north will have an additional *mi* before *'rydw, 'roedd, 'roeddech* etc., where there is already a pre-verbial of a kind. To produce an emphasis in these dialects, we must rely on intonation. The one important exception to all this is the group of dialects in Glamorgan and eastern Dyfed which regularly omit the pre-verbial and the mutation which would have shown its effect, while at the same time including an affixed pronoun, thus differing from all the other dialects and differing also from the literary language in that the pronoun is quite unemphasized: *ces i wobr*, "I had a prize": *gwedodd e 'tho i*, "he told me"; *gwelon ni fe*, "we saw him/it". As the areas where this construction occurs are highly populated, this may well be the choice of a majority of Welsh speakers; but there are wide areas where it does not occur. It also misses, as the literary language does, a certain precision which the inclusion of the particle may achieve. The literary *gwelodd hi* has an essential ambiguity which only the context can remove; it can mean "she/it saw", or else "he/she/it saw her/it". The dialects which use a pre-verbial resolve the difficulty immediately by the clear difference between *mi welodd hi* (which can only mean "she/it saw") and *mi gwelodd hi* (which can only mean "he/she/it saw her/it").

Affixed pronouns

These have two uses:

(i) after personal forms of verbs and prepositions, as in *dywedaf i*, "I am saying"; *gennyt ti*, "from you" or "in your possession";
(ii) to supplement another pronoun, prefixed or infixed, as in *dy gar di*, "your car"; *o'ch gwlad chi*, "from your country".

The practice in the written literary language is to include them only for semantic and stylistic reasons. This includes the emphatic use: *mae fy nghar i'n well na dy gar di*, "my car is better than yours", where **mae fy nghar yn well na dy gar* would be wrong, as in speech; and also some non-emphatic uses, occasionally for the sake of rhythm, and more importantly to avoid ambiguity with a third-person singular pronoun: it may be necessary to distinguish between *fe'i gwelodd ef*, "he/she/it saw him/it", and *fe'i gwelodd hi* "he/she/it saw her/it". All the dialects, on the other hand, use the affixed pronouns freely with no emphasis at all, emphasis where required being produced by intonation. In order that the non-emphatic or atonal use be shown in writing, for example in the dialogue of plays and novels, both John Morris-Jones (1891) and Ifor Williams (1926) proposed hyphenization, for example *mi welais-i, wrthat-ti, ych tŷ-chi*; this good suggestion has been generally welcomed, but few writers ever remember to use it. The same practice might well be adopted in prose discourse outside character speech, as a correct and legitimate way of bringing writing nearer to the spoken language, but no-one that I know of has tried it; the literary language will only take so much, and generally finds the affixed pronoun unnecessary except for emphasis. Therefore *a gaf i fenthyg dy gar?*, "may I borrow your car?" can be acceptable on paper, and likewise *a gaf i fenthyg dy gar di?* But in speech only (*a*) *ga i ffenthyg dy gar di?* would be correct. That is the general rule, the affixed pronoun usually though not necessarily omitted in the written language; and speech, stricter as always, insistent on including it except in certain cases which are not all easily defined. One of these exceptions presents no difficulty: it has long been accepted that speech omits the affixed pronoun when it refers back to an antecedent which is the subject of the sentence. *Mi es i'n chwys drosta*, "I began to sweat all over", but *mi ddaeth rhyw deimlad drosta-i*, "a feeling came over me"; *'rydw i wedi colli'n llyfr*, "I have lost my book", but *'rwyt ti wedi colli'n llyfr-i*, "you have lost my book", that is **mi ddaeth rhyw deimlad drosta*, **'rwyt ti wedi colli'n llyfr* are incorrect in all speech (all writers of dialogue take note). E. I. Rowlands (1981) has refined upon this rule, indeed has corrected it, with the suggestion that the regular spoken practice is *not to use an affixed pronoun (or, to use his preferred term, a supplementative pronoun) in referring back to any antecedent which is not genitive*, and he gives the examples: *mi welis-i'r dyn yn ei dŷ*, "I saw the man in his [own] house"; *ma gen y dyn ei syniada*, "the man has his ideas"; *but ma llyfra'r dyn yn ei dŷ-o*, "the man's books are in his house". And there the difference is clearly seen: *mae llyfrau'r dyn yn ei dŷ* would be all right in the literary language.

Another well-established rule is that speech and writing agree to omit the first- and second-person affixed pronoun, except for emphasis, after 'names of near relations' (Morris-Jones, 1931: 84). A near relation is not necessarily a blood relation, but the rule would appear to be stronger where there is a blood relationship: *mi welais i dy dad*, "I saw your father"; *mae hi'n cofio'ch mam*, "she remembers your mother"; never . . .*dy dad di, . . .'ch mam chi* unless for the sake of emphasis; but in *mi rhois-i o i dy bartnar(-di)*, I gave it to your mate"; *maen-nhw'n nabod ych mistar(-chi)*, "they know your boss" — there is more room for choice. But there is yet another context in which speech omits the affixed pronoun. It is unmistakeable, but not so easy to define. *Mi brynes fuwch*, "I bought a cow"; *mi cei o am bunt*, "you can have it for a pound"; *wel mi fwriodd*, "well it rained"; *mi fasat, basat*, "you would, wouldn't you"; *fe arhosodd wythnos*, "he/she/it stayed a week"; *mi wellith*, "he/she/it will get better"; *mi gwelwn o'n dwad*, "I could see him/it coming"; *fe glywsoch be ddigwyddodd*, "you heard what happened"; *mi enilli*, "you'll win"; *mi welet wahaniaeth*, "you'd see a difference"; *fe fyddwch yno cyn nos*, "you'll be there before nightfall"; *mi ddwedson be oedd yn bod*, "we said what the matter was"; *mi wyddost am Wil*, "you know what Wil is like"; *mi ddysgwch*, "you'll learn". Would anyone want to deny that these occur in spontaneous speech? They would seem to be limited to the dialects which regularly use a pre-verbal, and most common perhaps in the dialects which choose *mi* rather than *fe*, that is northern and central ones. The best writers of dialogue are sensitive to this subtlety, and indiscriminate inclusion of the affixed pronoun is clearly wrong. But what is the rule? It is difficult to see that it has anything to do with person or tense, although there seems to be some weakening of the rule with the first singular person future: *mi ddo-i*, rather than *mi ddo(f)* would be the natural choice to convey "I'll come". All that can safely be said is that an instinct rejects the pronoun when there is any danger that it might divert attention from the verb, or weaken the force of the verb in any way. This is certainly suggested by those cases where two verbs are contrasted. A good, natural Welsh speaker will not weaken the second verb with a pronoun: *welis-i rioed mo Lloyd George, ond mi clywis-o ddwywaith*, "I never saw Ll.G. but I heard him twice"; *nid i fenthyg o wnaeth-hi, mi dwynodd o*, "she didn't borrow it, she stole it"; *criö wir, mi sgrechiodd*, "cried indeed, he/she screeched"; *pan weli-di, mi goeli*, "when you see, you'll believe". However light or enclitic, the pronoun must earn its place. We are however, even in this latter case, dealing with an exception, allowed by the spoken language to its own rule of generally including the affixed pronoun, a rule which is different from that of the written literary language, and more binding. (It will also be noticed that all the illustrations were positive statements. In a question, for example *brynes i fuwch?*, and in a negative statement, for example *phrynes i ddim buwch*, speech makes the pronoun obligatory.)

Verb tenses

In spontaneous spoken Welsh the use of concise or morphological forms is very restricted, an obvious and important example of the preference in speech for the analytical method. It has long been recognized that the concise forms labelled "present" in traditional grammars, with very few exceptions, refer to the future. *Mi a-i adra, fe gei dithe wobr, mi gollith-hi'r trên, fe weliff e wahanieth, mi beintiwn-ni'r tŷ, mi newidiwch-chi'ch meddwl, fe gychwynan-nhw*: they are all future, as any Welsh speaker would confirm, if pressed ("I'll go home", "you too will get a prize", "she'll miss the train", "he'll see a difference", "we'll paint the house", "you'll change your mind", "they will start"). John Morris-Jones (1913) declared that only *bod*, "to be", *gwybod*, "to know" and *adnabod*, "to know or recognize", have a true present meaning in their concise forms, even in the literary language. Stephen J. Williams (1959) admits a few more verbs to the same company — *gweld*, "to see"; *clywed*, "to hear"; *credu*, "to believe"; *tybied*, "to suppose"; *gallu*, "to be able", and *medru* (also "to be able"). One can understand why: the action involved is in each case such as to make the present a continuous one, not a simple present. Perhaps we could extend the licence a little further and suggest that, in the literary language, any verb may be used in its concise 'present' form to convey the present provided it has a hint of the continuous about it. *Saif yr hen fwthyn o hyd*, "the old cottage still stands"; *erys y broblem*, "the problem remains"; *dymunaf wybod y gwir*, "I wish to know the truth", do not sound incorrect, because a combination of present and future, that is a continuous present, is implied in each case. In the spontaneous spoken language it is different. Here the basic rule holds, allowing far fewer exceptions, that a true present can be conveyed only through the periphrastic method: *'rydw i'n mynd* , "I go". Imagine a piece of narrative using a historic present, something like this:

> "*Mae'r drws yn agor a daw dyn i mewn. Saif am funud, gan edrych o'i gwmpas. Yna cerdda ar draws yr ystafell at y silffoedd llyfrau. Cydia yn un o'r llyfrau a dechrau troi'r dalennau. Wrth iddo wneud hynny fe syrthia darn o bapur rhydd i'r llawr.*"
> "The door opens and a man comes in. He stands for a moment, looking around him. Then he walks across the room to the book-shelves. He picks up one of the books and begins to turn the pages. As he does this a loose sheet of paper falls to the floor."

There is no great difficulty in accepting the forms *saif, cerdda, cydia, syrthia* as having a present reference. So long as these literary forms are retained the issue of the tense is fudged. But the replacement of any of them by the spontaneous spoken form in *-ith* would immediately give the game away.

The behaviour of the imperfect is very similar. Only in the literary language do the concise forms labelled "imperfect" (*-wn, -it, -ai* etc.) unfailingly convey what Jones & Thomas (1977) call "a durative activity in past time". *Mi awn i, fe gaet ti, fe safe fe, mi glywa hitha* in all speech would convey, according to the context, one from a number of volitional, predictive and conditional meanings. Jones & Thomas (1977: 89f) separate four of them. To convey a true imperfect in speech we would need to say *'roeddwn i'n mynd* (or *byddwn i'n mynd*, if that be the intended meaning), *'roeddet ti'n cael, 'roedd e'n sefyll, 'roedd hitha'n clwad* etc. In the literary language, *cerddwn* and *yr oeddwn yn cerdded* can be synonymous; they do not have to, but they can. In the spoken language they cannot. In the early days of *Cymraeg Byw* writers frequently overlooked this fact, and wrote sentences such as *fe safe-fe pan ddois-i i mewn* (meant to convey "he was standing when I came in"). It was assumed that throwing in a pre-verbial or an affixed pronoun or both, and replacing *-ai* with a colloquial ending, would automatically give a spoken imperfect.

We have already noted that the concise pluperfect does not occur in speech with any indicative force. There can be no objection to such a use in literature. Of the four tense paradigms in Welsh, only the past (*-ais, -aist, -odd* etc.) can be used in speech to convey exactly the same thing as it would in writing. Even then there is a tendency in spoken narrative to avoid repetition of the concise past tense, sometimes by using a verb–noun instead of a verb, sometimes by adopting the construction *dyma + subject + yn + verb–noun*.

> "*Trodd yr allwedd, llwyddodd i agor y drws, a chamodd i mewn i'r ystafell. Ar ôl cymryd dau gam baglodd ar draws rhywbeth. Safodd am funud i ystyried. Yna ymbalfalodd am y golau.*"
> "He turned the key, managed to open the door, and stepped into the room. After taking two steps he tripped over something. He stood for a moment to think. Then he fumbled for the light."

The sequence of past forms is natural and acceptable enough in this literary narrative. Speech would want more variation, something like this, though not necessarily this:

> "*Dyma fe'n troi'r allwedd, a llwyddo i agor y drws, a chamu i mewn i'r ystafell. Ar ôl cymryd dau gam fe faglodd ar draws rhywbeth.*
> "*Dyma fe'n sefyll am funud i ystyried. Wedyn ymbalfalu am y golau*".

This spoken narrative put into writing can soon become tedious; the repetition of *-odd* is, if anything, easier on the reader's ear. Speech and writing are different. What is more, the variation between *dyma. . .* and *fe + verb* in the spoken version is not completely arbitrary; there may well be a grammatical rule at work, as well as stylistic considerations. *Dyma. . .* and *fe + verb* can convey slightly different shades of the past tense, both of which are adequately covered in the literary language by *-odd*. Again, speech is stricter.

If the spoken language is, in this important matter, more precise, more consistent, surer of its own mind, should the written language try to follow? Eurys Rolant (1984) has proposed that it should: that henceforth in writing (allowing the poet his traditional licence to differ) we should adopt the verb system of the spoken language, writing down the periphrastic forms each time a true present, imperfect or pluperfect indicative is meant. All writers of Welsh would do well to consider the proposal, and also the warning which follows — that beyond this very little can be done by conscious resolve to bring written and spoken Welsh closer together. Developments over many generations have made them what they are, each with its own correctness. And the common standard spoken language is itself a work of consensus, not of legislation. Attempts to create a new common language by prescription can lead only to disaster, and the urge to do so seems to have behind it an assumption that there is something wrong with the Welsh language itself. Is that in its turn anything other than a new variant of the old self-accusation syndrome which has cramped the Welshman's style throughout his known history? To blame himself when he should be blaming his circumstances, to change the language instead of changing the conditions underlying its existence — they are not conscious choices to the modern committed Welsh speaker; but the temptation, itself the product of circumstances, is always there. "Leave your language alone", urges the American title of a modern introduction to linguistics (Hall Jnr, 1950). Welsh speakers would do well to heed the injunction, while remembering in all cases to append another one: ". . .and change the world".

Notes to Chapter 11

1. For a recent assessment, see Thorne (1984).

Further reading

(a) A few items in English on individuals and periods mentioned in the section "A historical sketch":

GREENE, DAVID 1971, Linguistic considerations in the dating of early Welsh verse, *Studia Celtica*, VI, 1–11.
JACKSON, KENNETH H. 1969, *The Gododdin. The Oldest Scottish Poem*. Edinburgh: Edinburgh University Press.
JONES, R. BRINLEY 1970, *The Old British Tongue. The Vernacular in Wales 1540–1640*. Cardiff: Avalon Books.
LEWIS, SAUNDERS 1924, A School of Welsh Augustans. Wrexham: Hughes & Son, London: Simpkin, Marshall, Hamilton, Kent & Co.
—— 1947, The essence of Welsh literature, *Wales*, VII, 337–41. Also in A. R. JONES & G. THOMAS (eds) (1973), *Presenting Saunders Lewis*. Cardiff: University of Wales Press.
—— 1969, The Tradition of Taliesin, *Transactions of the Honourable Society of Cymmrodorion, 1968 Part II*, 293–99. Also in A. R. JONES & G.THOMAS (eds) (1973), *Presenting Saunders Lewis*. Cardiff: University of Wales Press.
PARRY, THOMAS 1958, *John Morris-Jones 1864–1929*. Cardiff: University of Wales Press.
THOMAS, ISAAC 1967, *William Salesbury a'i Destament: William Salesbury and his Testament*. Cardiff: University of Wales Press.

WILLIAMS, GLANMOR 1967, *Welsh Reformation Essays*. Cardiff: University of Wales Press.
WILLIAMS, IFOR 1944, *Lectures on Early Welsh Poetry*. Dublin: Dublin Institute for Advanced Studies.

The following titles in the "Writers of Wales" Series, University of Wales Press, Cardiff, will be found useful:

BROMWICH, RACHEL 1974, *Dafydd ap Gwilym*.
HUGHES, GLYN TEGAI 1983, *Williams Pantycelyn*.
JAMES, ALLAN 1987, *John Morris-Jones*.
JARVIS, BRANWEN 1986, *Goronwy Owen*.
LLOYD, D. MYRDDIN 1979, *Emrys ap Iwan*.
MAC CANA, PROINSIAS 1977, *The Mabinogi*.
WILLIAMS, J. E. CAERWYN 1978, *The Poets of the Princes*.

(b)   A reader of Welsh can follow the discussion on "spoken and written language" in these contributions. They have been divided into two groups so as to suggest the broad lines of the debate, but it is not suggested that either of the two lists represents a cohesive party.

(i)   JONES, BEDWYR LEWIS 1966, Y llenor a'i iaith, *Taliesin*, 13, 29–39.
       JONES, R. M. 1985a, Cymraeg llenyddol llafar, *Y Traethodydd*, CXL, 146–61.
       —— 1985b, Cyweiriau'r iaith lenyddol, *Barddas*, 92–93, 23–24.
       LEWIS, HENRY 1931, *Datblygiad yr Iaith Gymraeg*. Cardiff: University of Wales Press.
       LLYWELYN-WILLIAMS, ALUN 1948, Arddull lafar, *Transactions of the Honourable Society of Cymmrodorion 1948*, 92–104.
       WILLIAMS, GRIFFITH JOHN 1967, Yr iaith lafar a llenyddiaeth, *Taliesin*, 15, 18–29.
       WILLIAMS, IFOR 1926, Rhagair, *Tŷ Dol (Henrik Ibsen)*. Bangor: Evan Thomas, iii–vi.
       —— 1944, Cymraeg llwyfan, *Meddwn I*. Llandybie: Llyfrau'r Dryw, 54–56.
       —— 1960, *Cymraeg Byw. Darlith Flynyddol y B.B.C. yng Nghymru*. London: B.B.C.
       —— 1968, Cymraeg y pulpud, *Meddai Syr Ifor*. Caernarfon: Llyfrau'r M.C. 15–25.
       WILLIAMS, STEPHEN J. 1942, Y gymraeg a'r dyfodol. *Transactions of the Honourable Society of Cymmrodorion 1942*, 148–57.
(ii)   LEWIS, SAUNDERS 1968, Rhagair, *Problemau Prifysgol*. Llandybie: Llygrau'r Dryw. 5–9.
       ROLANT, EURYS 1984, Cymraeg iach, *Y Traethodydd*, CXXXIX, 78–92.
       THOMAS, CEINWEN H. (1967), Review of *Cymraeg Byw, Rhif 2*, *Llên Cymru*, IX, 242–49.
       —— 1974/9, Y tafodieithegydd a 'Chymraeg Cyfoes', *Llên Cymru*, XIII, 113–52.
       WATKINS, T. ARWYN 1968, Llafar llenyddol Cymraeg. In T. JONES (ed.), *Astudiaethau Amrywiol a Gyflwynir i Syr Thomas Parry-Williams*. Cardiff: University of Wales Press, 122–36.

(c)   A number of articles by T. J. Morgan, taken together, provide an invaluable
introduction to Welsh stylistics:

MORGAN, T. J. 1937, Llawlyfr iaith ac arddull, *Y Llenor*, XVI, 135–55.

——— 1947, Arddull yr awdl a'r cywydd, *Transactions of the Honourable
Society of Cymmrodorion 946–47*, 276–313.

——— 1948, Rhyddiaith Gymraeg: rhagarweiniad, *Transactions of the Honourable Society of Cymmrodorion 1948*, 184–252. Also in (1951) *Ysgrifau
Llenyddol*. London: Griffiths, 130–202.

——— 1965–66, Y cywiriadur, *Y Genhinen*, XVI, 30–39.

——— 1967, Fel a'r Fel, *Y Genhinen*, XVII, 118–25.

——— 1967, Yr adnoddau llenyddol. In I FOSTER (ed.), *Cyfrol Deyrnged
Syr Thomas Parry-Williams*. Llandysul: Gwasg Gomer for the National
Eisteddfod Court, 49–72.

——— 1970, Cymraeg naturiol gywir. In J. E. CAERWYN WILLIAMS (ed.),
Ysgrifau Beirniadol, V. Denbigh: Gwasg Gee, 254–75.

——— 1976, Safonau ysgrifennu rhyddiaith. In G. BOWEN (ed.), *Y Traddodiad
Rhyddiaith yn yr Ugeinfed Ganrif*. Llandysul: Gwasg Gomer, 348–67.

12 Official Welsh

BERWYN PRYS JONES

Official language is the offspring of bureaucracy. Its characteristics are conservatism, a lack of wit and spirit and, at times, a verbosity which strangles the meaning of what it attempts to convey. It is simply, or supposedly, a cool purveyor of facts and a dispassionate exponent of argument. It is, in short, language shorn of all the entertainment, drama and life of which language and literature are capable. Official language is the least living of all the children of speech.

Yet we must have it and are inevitably drawn into it by one means or another. No coherent society with pretensions to civilization has yet been able to survive for very long without it or, for that matter, with it. Any framework of laws which seeks to avoid becoming a laughing stock or ultimately repressive, has to be couched in classically phrased language in a manner which commands respect.

The Laws of Hammurabi, preserved in the Louvre in Paris, provide a striking example of such "official" language being used to perpetuate a code of rules by which an organized society may, or should, abide. Present-day English law, complex and occasionally impenetrable though it may be, is only an elaborate amplification of such material, sanctified by tradition and solemnly altered only after considerable thought and lengthy debate. And the language in which it is expressed remains relatively static.

The Laws of Hywel Dda, as the corpus of early Welsh law is known, provides us with our only example of early official language in Welsh. That they were skilfully compiled is evident from the late Sir Thomas Parry's description of them in his *Hanes Llenyddiaeth Gymraeg* (1944), translated into English by Sir Idris Bell:

"...in the Middle Ages... in Ireland especially, and to a less extent in Wales, ... the possibilities of prose as a tool in the hand of an artist were recognised. When this happened is unknown, but it is clear that the Welsh language, as regards construction and vocabulary, was adapted for the performance of really difficult tasks as early as the tenth century. . . .The Laws prove two things not without importance in this connection. First of all, that the Welsh language contained an abundance of words and technical terms with definite and exact meanings. . . .here in the Laws we find words used with exact precision by minds anxious to set forth every proposition with complete clearness. The lawyers carefully considered every rule, discussed it no doubt, and fully understood it, after which they clothed it in words so that others should see it as clearly as themselves. The language possessed all the resources, both words and constructions, which they required to express a law with unambiguous precision. In a word, Welsh was an instrument adapted to the reason and the understanding. . . Here are lawyers whose skill is directed not to administering the law (there were judges for that), but to writing it, to giving it permanence in words, to ordering words and sentences in such a way that what was stated should be quite clear." (Parry, 1955: 67–68).

However, the Laws of Hywel Dda cannot provide us with a basis for a 'genre' of language which could conceivably serve to satisfy the requirements of an official language today. They are, after all, over a 1000 years old, with roots going back much further. Formulated at an early period in the development of the Welsh language, their vocabulary and syntax now appear antiquated since they applied to, and now in a curious way reflect, an era of which few but erudite scholars are aware — the era of an independent Wales.

The loss of Welsh independence in 1282 brought an end to the development of Welsh as an official language. Latin had long been enduring a painful decline into that most dead of all languages, an official language, the lingua franca of kings, diplomats and prelates. It did not, however, face the sudden shame of being made officially unofficial by a monarch who may have spoken it as a first language. The Act of Union remains to this day a slur on the Welsh language — it was made an outcast in its own land, a leper where it had once held sway.

This loss of status was a profound blow. It undermined the Welsh people's total confidence in the language they spoke, the thoughts they expressed, the emotions they felt. Now, there was a higher authority, a language for the most part beyond their grasp, spoken by an alien people who would not fail, even if unconsciously, to exploit their language for their own purposes. The Welsh were obliged to live in that uncomfortable position — at a disadvantage.

Yet the irony of the situation is a compelling one. The Welsh, deprived of their own official language, the deadest form of language, were gradually persuaded to lose faith in their own living tongue and to aspire to a medium of communication practised in a hitherto foreign land. The loss of the dead official language foreshadowed, and was meant to foreshadow, the death of the living language itself.

Irish, Gaelic and Breton joined Welsh in this abject condition. Accorded little if any official status, they were despised by the overlords and their retainers and subjected to a gradual whittling away of their innate authority as languages it was seemly and advantageous to speak. The claim that Irish was a language fit only for dogs to speak did nothing for Irish self-esteem! The genius of their race, expressed in their own language, was trampled upon by a speaker whose casual arrogance (and there is no arrogance worse than casual arrogance) still echoes painfully down the centuries. It is, of course, part of the linguistic armoury of the overbearing and the snob to despise the language, customs and religion of a subject race. Language is commonly accorded the status of a "patois", a "vernacular", and any number of other disparaging words and expressions, as a good thesaurus will show.

All this is history. But it is nevertheless pertinent for it shows that the way language is used generates attitudes and prejudices that ultimately affect the fate of that — or another — language. That one language may destroy another is unremarkable because the speakers of language have been doing it to one another since time immemorial.

If the existence of a "dead" (or even deadening or deadly!) official language is in many respects vital to the well-being of the language concerned, it may follow that the elevation of a hitherto despised language to official status may lead to a diminution of prejudice and relaxation of hostility, and even to a realization that what was once disregarded or mocked does actually possess its own merits. Official status confers dignity, even style, just as awarding honours to those who once transgressed the accepted code of honour indicates imminent rehabilitation.

The rehabilitation — some might say the token rehabilitation — of Welsh in this sense may well derive from the 1967 Welsh Language Act, based on the recommendations of the Hughes Parry Report on the Legal Status of the Welsh Language which was published in October 1965.[1] A document couched in official terms thus led in due course to the production of a short document, an Act of Parliament, couched in even more terse official prose, designed to free a living language from the deadening weight of being an unofficial tongue! Such contradictions are, naturally, par for the course for a bureaucracy.

The Act, all two and a half pages of it, begins ponderously,

"Whereas it is proper that the Welsh language should be freely used by those who so desire in the hearing of legal proceedings in Wales and Monmouthshire; that further provision be made for the use of that language, with like effect as in English, in the conduct of other official or public business there."[2]

But it is Clauses 2(1) and 3 that opened the door to a new era. Ministers "may by order prescribe a version of (any) document or words in Welsh" and "anything done in Welsh in a version authorised by Section 2 of this Act shall have the like effect as if done in English". (Welsh Language Act 1967: 1–2). Excommunication lapses; bring in the penitent!

The Act was essentially the creation of the Welsh Office, on the one hand, and, on the other, of the increasing political agitation which had encouraged the Government of the day to establish the Hughes Parry Committee in the first place. And, having created this child, pale and sickly though it looked to some people at the time, and even paler and sicklier it may appear to many today, it was found that its influence could be limited, and even contained, but not ignored. The language, having languished for almost eight centuries outside the gates of government, despised and, at best, ignored, suddenly found itself to be a factor — yet another factor — to be taken into account in the endless bureaucratic decision-making processes which have provided the raw material for several well-known comedy series! Welsh had, at last, gained access to the corridors of power and its transformation into an official language had begun.

Granting official status is of no use unless that status is immediately apparent. Demonstrable signs of activity were required. Bureaucracy cannot survive without documents. Documents must be provided in Welsh. There are too many of them. What shall we do? We need a policy. Which documents have to be translated into Welsh? Which documents is there pressure for?

The main criteria were provided by the Hughes Parry Report itself — demand, expediency and expense (para. 191) with the coda "as well as prestige" omitted but not ignored. It was also accepted that correspondence received by government departments in Welsh would be replied to in Welsh.

A limited amount of translation work had already been done by staff at the Information Division of the Welsh Office, but the Hughes Parry Report recommended the establishment of a small panel of translators as the most satisfactory way of ensuring accurate, uniform and appropriate translations. The panel would be part of, or associated with, the Welsh Office itself.

Two decisions were taken, to appoint a full-time professional translator and to appoint a translation panel of experts in language, law, history and other fields to provide advice and guidance. The first translator was appointed in 1967 and was immediately deluged with work. Most divisions within the Welsh Office, not to mention other government departments, had a whole host of documents which required translation.

A policy for the type of language to be used was quickly decided. Bureaucratic language being what it is, it was almost inevitable that standard literary Welsh would serve as the basis for all official translations unless the particular context, such as a slogan or dialogue, demanded a more colloquial turn of phrase.

This immediately created problems. Welsh speakers were not accustomed to official documents in Welsh. Indeed, the English versions still retained an air of official authority superior to the Welsh ones, so despite the principle of equal validity enshrined in the Welsh Language Act, the Welsh speaker still had problems of status to confront. It was also patently obvious that the new Welsh-language documents were translations constrained by an English straitjacket and therefore, somehow, second-hand. The classical nature of the Welsh used formed another barrier: it was "proper" Welsh, "perfect" Welsh, even "textbook" Welsh, the kind of "pulpit" Welsh many people could understand but were not proficient in its use. The complaint "my Welsh isn't good enough" echoed throughout the land.

A further, equally frustrating, factor was the apparent reluctance of certain bodies, even governmental institutions and government-funded agencies, to provide Welsh versions of their documents and to accommodate the requirements of those who wished to use Welsh, even where assistance was available. The absence of any Welsh-language material (by design or through indifference) strongly suggested that Welsh was still second-class despite the passing of an Act of Parliament. And the apparent unavailability of documents in Welsh, backed by a casually indifferent, if not downright hostile, attitude on the part of some sections of officialdom compounded the difficulties faced by Welsh speakers who made diligent efforts to obtain the new forms.

It cannot be denied that the classical form of the language did prove to be something of a barrier. Even so, it is difficult to see how any other form could have been used. Unless the translators wrote colloquially (and the plethora of forms for "I am" in ordinary spoken Welsh — *rydw i, dwi, wi, rwy'* — indicates the difficulty of adopting a consistent style by members of a translation unit who could be drawn from all over Wales), there was only one other choice, *Cymraeg Byw* (Living Welsh), a standardized form of the spoken language drawn up by a panel of experts. *Cymraeg Byw* was not, however, meant to supplant classic literary Welsh but to provide, for *learners* of Welsh, a bridge into the spoken language, making it easier for them to converse naturally with native speakers and, of equal importance, for native speakers to converse with them without adopting the classical language so inappropriate in an intimate situation.[3]

The matter of register and style led to the rejection of *Cymraeg Byw* as a tool to be used in official documents. It would perhaps, be suited to straightforward forms, but simple forms, despite the recent and welcome pressure for simpler English, remain in a minority. A Government report in English which contained forms such as "won't", "shouldn't" and "shan't" would rightly be looked at askance and so would the translations of documents which used the forms of *Cymraeg Byw*. The proponents of *Cymraeg Byw* in such situations argue that Welsh-language documents would be more easily understood by the average person, and in this they have a point. However, the clash of language registers involved would compel the translator to decide where *Cymraeg Byw* should or should not be used. A legal document full of weighty phrases and subordinate clauses, qualifications and restrictions could hardly be translated using the forms of *Cymraeg Byw*, unless the English document was first subject to thorough simplification.

It is, of course, a moot point whether official documents need to be so official in tone and character. Yet it is difficult to imagine an official exchange of correspondence between, say, a Minister and Opposition MPS, being conducted in such a matey style as to warrant the use of *Cymraeg Byw*.

The use of classical Welsh in translations of documents is therefore dictated by the formal and official situations from which they arise. But even classical Welsh is not a frozen structure, immune to all change, any more than classical English can be. Tone and style in both languages have changed with the passage of the centuries. The twentieth century has seen a radical departure from the overblown and pretentious Welsh of the nineteenth century (which aped that of the worst English of the time), thanks mainly to the highly talented body of twentieth century Welsh scholars who have gradually but persistently extended the boundaries of the Welsh language. This they did by combining an investigation into issues and subjects where Welsh had not hitherto ventured and an exploitation of all the resources classical Welsh had to offer. An excellent precedent was set by Sir T. H. Parry-Williams, a Professor of Welsh at the University College of Wales, Aberystwyth, who combined a remarkable knowledge of his native language with an interest in medicine, psychology and other sciences to produce innovative essays using classical Welsh and skilfully chosen colloquial and idiomatic expressions to push back the frontiers of classical expression.

The first official translators appointed by the Welsh Office sought to exploit this rich vein of classical Welsh because no comparable source of spoken Welsh was available. Their work has to be understood equally well in all parts of Wales, and acknowledged and respected as the classical language in its new, official form. They were not alone in this respect, of course, since the media, especially the news service, had been down this road before. The formality of English-language news presentation was, rightly or wrongly, reflected in the formality of the Welsh-language news bulletins, giving rise to the concept of "BBC Welsh"; later, in the wake of the production of a multiplicity of Welsh-language forms, extended rather more perceptively to "Whitehall Welsh".

Having thus set the tone, the Welsh Office translators, aided by their advisory Translation Panel and by feedback from Welsh-speaking officials in the various departments, faced the problem of terminology. For a language so recently thrust into the complexities of the twentieth century, Welsh was not so ill-prepared as one might imagine. The Board of Celtic Studies, established by the University of Wales, had already pioneered the basic principles of formulating terminology in Welsh by amalgamating at least three different approaches: direct borrowing where the words presented few orthographical problems, the creation of new words using well-established roots and terminations, and the resuscitation of old words which were capable of taking on a more "technological" significance. In 1965, the Hughes Parry Report had been able to name 11 such lists, covering areas such as education, history, geography, cookery, technical subjects, physics and mathematics and so on, and had advocated the preparation of lists in law and administration — which were soon forthcoming. Although these lists were meant primarily to cater for the increasing demand for Welsh-medium education in schools, colleges and university colleges, they were also of great value to the early translators in that they provided a standard currency of agreed terms for both the academic and administrative worlds. This was vital. To have had two widely divergent lists of Welsh equivalents for technical terms would have been self-defeating.

Although the Hughes Parry Report emphasized the importance it attached to entrusting the responsibility for selecting and coining suitable Welsh terms to a single body such as the Board of Celtic Studies, this has not exactly proved to be the case in practice. A list of Welsh legal terms was prepared by Robyn Lewis (1972), a Pwllheli solicitor, a list of library terms by the Welsh College of Librarianship (Coleg Llyfrgellwyr Cymru, 1978) and a list of archival terms by the Gwynedd Archive Service (A. E. Williams, 1986), while the Welsh Joint Education Committee has largely taken over the role of providing schools with lists of Welsh terms for use in secondary education and examinations.[4]

To quite a large extent, this has freed translators, the main purveyors of official Welsh, from the burden of having to create terminology. In my 12 years as a Welsh Office translator, I can remember few occasions when we have been called upon to invent new Welsh words. Others, better qualified than ourselves, have usually come forward with various alternatives.

Some, seeking "purer" Welsh words to replace direct borrowings from English, have sought to create new words even where the borrowing has already made itself a comfortable home, but the steamroller of language has usually obliterated them. Some new words will live, some will die, just as in English. The lack of a Welsh equivalent for "juggernaut" is no longer a serious matter because the word has, for the moment at any rate, passed out of fashion. Similar fads may pass by without Welsh necessarily having a word for them all. Longer-term words, such as "sexism", may pose something of a problem, but creating a Welsh equivalent such as "rhywiaeth", robs the concept of many of the distinctly condemnatory connotations it has in English. For a gender-based language such as Welsh, this may be no bad thing.

Official Welsh is, of necessity, something of a hybrid. Much of it is the result of the translation of material originally composed in English. No amount of painstaking translation will quite eradicate the Englishness of thought and concept which underlie it. The roots of this recent plant are so firmly embedded in the English original that its colouring, texture and smell strike the average Welsh speaker (if such a creature exists) as more than slightly unnatural. Bureaucratic English, given as it is to tortuous phraseology, numerous subordinate clauses and a grammatical structure which often leaves its main thrust to the end of the sentence, is, when translated into a language which prefers its emphasis to come first, a heavy and cumbersome affair with plenty of opportunity for the meaning to get lost along the way. English can glide along quite happily without its past participles being specifically nailed to a time or tense; Welsh can not. Welsh requires precision in these matters, and that precision demands an extra subordinate clause which, added to all the other subordinate clauses, may further confound confusion.

Some of the main strengths of Welsh — its ability to denote emphasis by altering the sentence order, its use of the infinitive (or, more strictly, the verb–noun), the ease and simplicity of explaining "why" or "because" using the word *gan*, and the highly idiomatic use of the prepositions *i*, *o* and *wrth* appear less commonly in translated Welsh because the concepts underlying them do not spring so readily to mind in English. Something of the life of the language is lost.

Welsh, if I may generalize, is happier with shorter sentences. They pack their punches and go. Long elegant sentences can become an acquired taste, their construction almost a work of art, but it remains difficult to rid them of the impression that they have been constructed artificially, using an expertise acquired from a foreign language. Whether this is, as some would claim, a matter of laziness, is another moot point!

Some have argued that it is necessary to cut through the whole mass of English verbiage in the translation of official documents so that readers can understand the gist of the text expressed more naturally in their native language. Such a position has its attractions. Simplification is always enticing and may sometimes be justifiable, but does it do justice to, and convey the possibly important nuances of, the original? In an age in which rules and regulations abound, we have little choice but to translate to the letter.

However stiff and formal official translated Welsh may appear to some, even, at times, to those who produce it, there is another kind of official Welsh produced, this time, by experts in fields outside the language itself, who have been taught or trained through the medium of English. (The products of the Welsh-medium education now provided at secondary and college levels are only just beginning to filter through into positions of influence, and it is therefore too early to predict how they will react.) The whole tone of the official Welsh of such professionals is more closely allied to their spoken Welsh but the influence, the insidiously pervasive influence of English, is clearly apparent. Their grasp of Welsh grammar may be shaky, but as long as the basic English-based meaning is not too unclear, their official Welsh will do. Mutations may come and go somewhat at random, their control of the *a/y* (who/which/that) relative particle may involve the omission of both, and their weak grasp of the respective boundaries between *cael*, "to have", and *derbyn*, "to receive", *nifer* and *rhif*, "number" and "actual number", *gwerthfawrogi*, "to appreciate", and *sylweddoli*, "to realize" — all of which are coloured by the corresponding usage in English — betrays the essential Englishness of their thought patterns.

Is this inevitable? Yes, it probably is unless the system is changed. Until documents are prepared in straightforward Welsh and translated into equally lucid English, or even vice versa, official Welsh will continue to be the rather oddly unnatural, slightly discordant, slightly strangulated and peculiar creature it has now become. But if its development brings with it an increased respect and an increasing self-respect, I am sure we can easily learn to live with official Welsh, whatever its faults.

Notes to Chapter 12

1. *Legal Status of the Welsh Language*, Report of the Committee under the chairmansip of Sir David Hughes Parry, QC, LID, DCL, 1963–65. London: HMSO, Cmnd. 2785. Its terms of reference were: "To clarify the status of the Welsh language and to consider whether any changes in the law might be made".

2. The Welsh Language Act "An Act to make further provision with respect to the Welsh language and references in Acts of Parliament to Wales". [27 July 1967].

3. See *Cymraeg Byw Rhifyn 3* (Welsh Joint Education Committee: Cowbridge, 1970). This point is made explicitly in the article on the General Principles of Cymraeg Byw by T. J. Rhys Jones (1970: 6–12).

4. These include: Music (1978), Home and Family (1985), Geography (1981), Classics (1983), Religious Studies (1982), Physics and Mathematics (1983), Needlework, Embroidery Sewing and Laundrywork (1984). Other lists are in course of preparation.

13 Broadcast Welsh

MARTIN J. BALL, TWELI GRIFFITHS and GLYN E. JONES

Introduction

The subject of broadcasting and the Welsh language is potentially a vast one, deserving a book in its own right perhaps. Here, in this chapter, we can only hope to scratch the surface of the topic, and because of the nature of this book we have taken an overtly linguistic approach, rather than a political or cultural one. Nevertheless, before we concentrate on certain linguistic aspects of broadcast Welsh, it is profitable to look briefly at the background to the use of Welsh in the broadcasting media.

In a minority language situation it is important for the survival of the minority language in the present day that it has access to the broadcasting media. There are perhaps two main reasons for this. Firstly, as radio and television are so pervasive in modern life, if only the majority language is heard from the electronic boxes in the corner, there is little incentive to switch to the use of the other language. This is particularly important in the case of the exposure of children to the minority language in the home when they are young. Secondly, and probably more importantly, is the status given to a language that is used in broadcasting. Promoters of the Welsh language have long been used to confronting the problem of the greater status accorded to English by many Welsh speakers, particularly children. English is the language of most aspects of modern culture, and its overwhelming use on the broadcasting media is one way of reinforcing this notion.

Therefore, the promotion of Welsh on radio and television serves two purposes in the campaign to preserve and promote Welsh: it guarantees that Welsh-speaking homes need not turn to English to get their entertainment, and it raises the status of Welsh to that of a language "at home" in the modern world of television, pop music, etc.

However, the use of Welsh on radio and television had a slow start. For example, A. D. Rees (1979) in Table 13.1 notes the figures for the hours of Welsh broadcast on radio and on BBC and Independent television

TABLE 13.1   *Weekly broadcasting hours in Welsh: 1959–72*

	1959–60	*1966–67*	*1971–72*
Radio	9.6	12.4	15.1
TV	6.8	11.6	12.7
Totals	16.4	24.0	27.8

between 1959 and 1972. Apart from the fact that these figures were pathetically small, and the growth very slow, they did not bear any relation to the proportion of Welsh speakers during this period. For example, comparing the Welsh to English hours broadcast on both radio and television in Wales in 1972, we find that only about 4.2% was in Welsh when the Welsh-speaking population was just under 20%.

These figures show that radio was always in advance when it came to broadcasting Welsh, and so it continued. Throughout the 1970s discussion continued about the possibility of creating a Welsh-language radio network and television channel. Due to costs, the radio network was the first off the ground. *Radio Cymru* was launched in 1977 on VHF, and to begin with broadcast for restricted hours, but these have increased to about 60 hours a week. On a week day radio in Welsh may be heard from 6.30 in the morning through till 6.00 at night.

This is not the place to chronicle in detail the long, and at times desperate, campaign to bring the long-promised Welsh television channel into being. However, this step has long been seen as vital by language planners for the long-term survival of Welsh, because of the immense influence wielded by television in modern society. After the promise that the new fourth television channel in Wales would be devoted to a Welsh language service was broken soon after the change of government in 1979, a campaign of civil disobedience was launched in Wales that in the long run resulted in a change of heart by the British government. The Welsh television channel — *Sianel Pedwar Cymru* — was launched in 1982. At first it broadcast about 22 hours a week, but this has now increased to 26, the remaining hours being taken up with showing the English language programmes of the English Channel Four. The Welsh language programmes are scheduled to be shown at children's viewing times, and at peak evening viewing times.

This brief background sketch has shown that Welsh on radio and television in any significant amount is a recent phenomenon. The linguistic implications for such a development are enormous. Will there emerge any

new standardization along the lines of BBC English? Will the use of
Welsh on the media help disseminate technical Welsh vocabulary to a
wider audience? How should the media cope with English names and
expressions on news programmes, or interviews in English? How well
do the broadcasters themselves reflect usages within the Welsh speech
community? These are all questions that need to be addressed by the
sociolinguist interested in broadcast language. In this chapter we only
have the space to examine a couple of such problems: one in the area of
radio, the other in the area of television.   ·

Radio[1]

The increase in the use of Welsh on the broadcasting media has led
to a certain amount of reaction by language purists (see Milroy & Milroy,
1985a, for a discussion of the complaint tradition with regard to language
use). These are people who believe that linguistic change and variation
are in fact aspects of a "corruption" of the language concerned from a
previous state of perfection to a contemporary one of loss of standards.
Complaints vary, and may be concerned with pronunciation, syntax, semantics or lexis, but one thing they have in common is that a large proportion of them are aimed at the broadcasting media. This is of course
hardly surprising due to the high profile that broadcast language has in
contemporary society. It could be argued that the growth in complaints
about the use of Welsh on radio and television is a mark of the success
of the language! However, in terms of the level of acceptance that *Radio
Cymru* will achieve in the Welsh speech communities, it could also be
argued that unless this medium reflects the patterns of stylistic and regional
usages of those communities, the network may well be envisaged as an
outside body imposed upon them by an educated élite. As such, the
service will not be accepted, and will not provide a much-needed bolstering
of the confidence of Welsh speakers in their particular patterns of language
use.

This section presents a preliminary study of the use of a small set
of linguistic variables (see Chapter 3 for a definition of this term) in
different types of radio programme from the *Radio Cymru* network, to
see whether variation does correlate with style as it does in the community.

The use of broadcast material in studies of linguistic variation was
suggested by Labov (1972a), who noted that casual styles of speech might
be collected from interviewees taking part in an unscheduled interview as

eye-witnesses to some dramatic event. More recently researchers have begun to use broadcast material as part of investigations into stylistic differences. Bell's (1982) study investigated a single type of broadcaster's speech (that of newscasters) in New Zealand, and reported that their use of linguistic variables correlated with the type of audience that was assumed to be listening. Taking a rather different line, Morin & Kaye (1982) used different types of TV and radio broadcasts (in terms of degree of formality) to investigate stylistic variation in the use of liaison in French. They found that the use of "elevated liaison" increased on the more formal programmes.

This section attempts to undertake a more rigorous application of this latter technique to Welsh. Two aspects of Welsh that have been investigated elsewhere in studies of Welsh speech communities (see Ball, 1984b; 1985b; and this volume, Chapter 7) were chosen, and their usage examined in different radio broadcasts. The previous studies which used more traditional methods of stylistic analysis, would provide information against which to check the results from the study of radio usage.

In looking at types of broadcast material, an obvious first distinction is between the use or otherwise of a script; in other words whether or not the material was based on written or spontaneous forms. It was expected that any programme based on a written script should show a greater degree of formality than programmes utilizing spontaneous speech, whether or not the latter approached a fully casual style.

Script-based programmes can be further divided between those that are read as if written, and those that are read as if spontaneous. A stylistic difference should be expected between programmes in these categories. Spontaneous speech programmes would seem to be divisible into different degrees of formality largely in terms of their subject matter.

It was believed, then, that different degrees of formality should be obtained in different programmes, and the linguistic background of speakers could be regulated to some extent by attempting to ensure that the speakers were all of one basic dialect area and social status. It was not expected that fully casual speech would be found, due to the naturally formalizing effect of the radio studio, nor was it thought possible to control the regional and social class variables very closely. These points must be borne in mind, therefore, when evaluating the usefulness of this technique.

The study

For this study it was decided to choose only one programme from each of the categories mentioned above, by way of an initial investigation into the use of this technique:

(1) written: read as if written;
(2) written: read as if spontaneous;
(3) spontaneous.

The programmes were chosen from the standard broadcasts of *Radio Cymru*. The three items were: the mid-day newscast, a Sunday morning broadcast of a religious service (the sermon here fitted into Category 2 above), and a daily programme of music, interviews and information perhaps best classified as general entertainment. It was expected that the first two would be of a fairly formal nature — and the news, being read directly, would be the most formal. The general entertainment programme, partly owing to the personality of the presenter, appeared superficially at least to be much more informal. All the speakers recorded were from South Wales, and most appeared to have a background that may be characterized as "educated Welsh".

The linguistic variables chosen were:

(1) The nasal mutation after *yn*, "in": This is shown as NM. The variants possible here are the operation of the nasal mutation (standard usage); the substitution of the soft mutation for the nasal mutation; and the substitution of no mutation for the nasal mutation. (See Chapter 7 for further details of these mutations.)
(2) The aspirate or spirant mutation. This is shown as AM. The variants possible here are the operation of the aspirate mutation (standard usage); and the substitution of no mutation for the aspirate mutation. In the single case of verbs following the negative particles *ni*, *na*, the soft mutation may be used instead of the aspirate mutation.
(3) Personal pronouns. These fall into three main types, each having two variant pronunciations:

   (i)   *fy*: [və] – [ən], "my";
   (ii) *ei*/*eu*: [əi] – [i], "his, her"/"their";
   (iii) *ein*, *eich*: [əin, əix] – [ən, əx], "our", "your".

The distinction between standard and non-standard is not so clear here: the left-hand variants have more the status of spelling pronunciations, with the right-hand variants acceptable in standard pronunciation. Many accounts of the pronouns (for example, S. J. Williams, 1959) state that the right-hand variants are the only ones found in "natural" speech. This, however, over-simplifies the role of written *versus* spontaneous context in determining which form is used.

The variables were chosen on the evidence of previous studies, especially the dialect studies referenced in Chapter 2, and the research described in Ball (1984b; 1985b and this volume, Chapter 7).

More details of the radio broadcasts will now be given. The news bulletin was short, but surprisingly, perhaps, contained several examples of AM and NM. Unfortunately, few examples of pronouns occurred, and due to the nature of the broadcast, those that did were all of type (ii). It was characterized by the use of other linguistic variants, both grammatical and phonological, that have been noted elsewhere as formal usages (e.g. B. Thomas, 1980). Those usages included on the phonological level the use of [ai] as the usual plural suffix instead of the more informal [ɛ] or [a], and on the grammatical level by the use of the interrogative particle *a*, and impersonal verbs.

The religious broadcast (*Oedfa'r Bore*) was transmitted from Bethania Chapel, Treforus (Morriston), which is a Welsh Presbyterian chapel. In counting examples of the variables, hymns and readings were ignored, and only the sermon and a "free" prayer were included. The sermon was spoken by the minister and was of especial interest as it appeared to include instances of deliberate style-switching. The story of the sermon concerned a father and his two sons, and when these characters were "speaking", the usage of certain phonological variables changed to less formal variants (e.g. the monophthongization of [ɔɪ]→[oː]. However, many other variables remained at the formal end of the spectrum. It is worth noting that the two occasions when the AM was realized as no mutation in this broadcast were not found in this quasi-informal part of the sermon, but rather in comments linking various parts of the sermon. It should also be noted that pronoun usage differed considerably between the sermon and the prayer, which was not the case with the other variables. The sermon part of the broadcast contained many fewer spelling pronunciations of pronouns.

The last programme, *Stondin Ddyddiol* was presented by Sulwyn Thomas from the Swansea studios of *Radio Cymru*. The programme is interspersed with music and interviews, these latter being of an informal nature. In all, five people including the presenter featured in the programme. Other phonological and grammatical variables suggested that most of the speakers were using a fairly informal style. It should be noted that most of the examples of standard usage of AM were from the presenter, nevertheless even he was not consistent in this.

Results

In listening to the tape-recordings of these programmes it soon became clear that NM was being used with the nasal mutation realized nearly all the time. Most of the examples were with place names, though a few examples with common nouns did occur in *Stondin Ddyddiol* and the news. One example only was found with non-standard usage: the nasal mutation was replaced by the soft mutation with a place name (*ym Brydain*, "in Britain", instead of *ym Mhrydain*) by one of the speakers on *Stondin Ddyddiol*. For these reasons no figures are given for NM in the tables below. This overwhelming standard use of NM goes against the community norms reported in Chapter 7 of this collection. There it was noted that average standard use of NM across all styles was only 37%. However, this variable did show considerable style-shifting, and with certain groups of speakers scores of over 60% standard variant use were recorded. It can also be noted that tests of speakers' awareness of which words should take which mutations, the use of NM after *yn* is generally well known, which is not the case with most AM triggers (Ball, 1985a). This all suggests that both the type of speaker found in the broadcasts, and the formalizing effect of broadcasting have conspired to produce figures higher than that in a cross-section of normal speech.

Table 13.2 below shows the patterns of usage of AM in the three broadcasts, and Table 13.3 shows the patterns of usage of the three pronoun types.

TABLE 13.2 AM *usage: % of standard forms*

	AM: aspirate mutation	AM: no mutation	% standard
News	a × 1; tri × 2; â × 2; ei × 1.		100%
Oedfa	a × 6; gyda × 1; na × 1.	a × 2	80%
Stondin	a × 3; chwe × 1; na(neg) × 1.	a × 5; â × 3; gyda × 1; na × 2.	31%

TABLE 13.3   *Pronoun usage: percentage of non-spelling pronunciations*

	News	Oedfa	Stondin
Type (i) scores			
spelling – non-spelling	—	1–9	0–4
% non-spelling	—	90%	100%
Type (ii) scores			
spelling – non-spelling	4–5	2–30	0–11
% non-spelling	55%	94%	100%
Type (iii) scores			
spelling – non-spelling	—	16–6	0–11
% non-spelling	—	29%	100%
Total % non-spelling	55%	70%	100%

Both tables clearly show stylistic variation in all the variables (except NM), between the three types of broadcast. It is clear that the variables are not of exactly the same nature in that the retention of the standard variant of AM has more status than the "spelling pronunciations" of the personal pronouns. However, a similar stylistic shift is observable. The low figure in Table 13.3 for type (iii) in *Oedfa'r Bore* is due to the high occurrence of *ein* with the spelling pronunciation in the prayer.

These results showing stylistic variation can be compared with results from the wider studies already referred to. Table 13.4 shows the use of AM in four separate styles (described in Chapter 7) compared with figures obtained from the radio programmes. Although the figures are not identical (neither of course are the styles, though they are broadly comparable), the same trend is obviously present, and as we have already noted, completely casual speech is not to be expected from the broadcasts.

TABLE 13.4   AM *usage: percentage of standard forms*

Previous study	(%)	*Present study*	(%)
Casual style:	0	——	—
Reporter's test:	48	*Stondin*:	31
Interview style:	66	*Oedfa*:	80
Sentence list:	94	News:	100

It is also useful to compare the pronoun usages of the radio broadcasts and the main study. Full details of this are given in Ball (1985b), and

TABLE 13.5   *Pronoun usage: percentage of non-spelling pronunciations*

Previous study	(%)	Present study	(%)
Sentence list:	53	News:	55
Prose:	60	*Oedfa:*	70
Reporter's test:	97	*Stondin:*	100

Table 13.5 presents a comparison of the results of the two studies, though for ease of presentation, the three types of pronouns are not distinguished, and the percentages given are for all three types together.

These figures show an even greater correspondence than those for AM, and confirm a clear stylistic cline in terms of the linguistic variables, paralleling the stylistic cline of formality of the radio programmes. From this we can deduce that, in terms of all these variables with the exception of NM, the broadcasters are following community norms. The evidence presented here, then, suggests that radio Welsh is not, as some would claim, an externally imposed variety that native speakers cannot understand; nor, as others would charge, is it guilty of promoting "corrupt" or "bad" Welsh. Just as spoken Welsh varies according to style, so does radio Welsh, and reflects the usages of the speech community to a remarkable extent in the above examples.

Television

In this examination of the Welsh television channel, *Sianel Pedwar Cymru* (S4C), we will be taking a different tack from the first part of this chapter: we will be looking at the use of English. This may seem a strange thing to do in a book on the use of Welsh, but the inauguration of the new service in 1982 raised very important questions about how far the two languages should co-exist.

Linguistic purism and the use of Welsh and English on S4C[2]

Sianel Pedwar Cymru (S4C) has screened a great variety of programmes over the last four years, and of particular interest to this section is its light entertainment programmes, which have included an ambitious glossy 'soap opera' entitled *Dinas*. This programme (and to a lesser extent, a few others) initially invoked a great deal of criticism, mainly in the Welsh language press. The criticism was levelled at the quality of the Welsh used, and in particular at the instances of lexical borrowing from English and at code-switching (i.e. switching from one language to the other). Some of these criticisms are quoted below in translation (translations by G. E. Jones):[3]

> "Why, for goodness sake, is it necessary to answer the phone in English, or to speak 'the slender language' every time when discussing business? Why is saying 'come on' easier than *tyd o'na*, or 'so long' easier than *hwyl*?. . . I am amazed that authors, producers and actors — all claiming that they are good Welshmen — are willing to insult our language like this." (*Y Faner*, 7 February 1986)

> "For too long the whim of individual producers and individual authors has been allowed to devise a policy and to establish a convention concerning the use of English in Welsh programmes." (*Y Faner*, 28 February 1986)

> ". . .the appeal of '*Dinas*' and another programme or two could be increased by weeding the English language out of them." (*Y Cyfnod*, 10 January 1986)

> "The likelihood is that we shall have to suffer some programmes — the fewer the better I say! — which will contain sub-standard Welsh and a jumbled language to please those people who have not learnt at school what constitutes correct language." (*Y Cyfnod*, 29 November 1985)

> "Authors and planners of the series '*Dinas*', you deserve a jolly good thrashing for including so much English in each episode, especially in the episode we saw last week. The words 'End of Part I' would have been just as appropriate at the end of the first half of that episode." (*Y Faner*, 15 November 1985)

This matter also received some attention in the English language press:

> ". . .the criticism came from 'purists' who insist on academic Welsh." (*Western Mail*, 15 November 1985)

> "Vulgarity in Welsh on the principality's television screens is defended by the Welsh fourth channel S4C as part of its special

effort to relate to young viewers in International Youth Year."
(Daily Telegraph, 14 November 1985)

As can be seen, the main burden of the criticism is the occurrence of
English which manifests itself in lexical borrowings and code-switching.
In respect of these features, let us consider two important aspects of the
linguistic situation in Wales: (1) It is diglossic and (2) It is bilingual.

Welsh diglossia

There are distinct high and low varieties of Welsh. The high variety,
known as *yr iaith safonol*, "the standard language", or *yr iaith lenyddol*,
"the literary language", (see Chapters 11 and 12), is found, as is usually
the case with diglossic situations (Ferguson, 1972) in literature and in all
manners of publications, from taxation guidelines to academic journals.
The low variety, known as *yr iaith lafar*, "the spoken language", is the
every-day spoken language of the community, within the family, with
friends, and usually in all contexts where the high variety is inappropriate.

The traditional, highly prescriptive attitude to the use of high and
low varieties of Welsh has been to insist on a rigid demarcation of
function — the low variety being totally unacceptable in written Welsh and
regarded as a corrupt form of the language. This prescriptive attitude is
summed up in the following remarks by a former Professor of Welsh in
the University of Wales:[4]

"The tragedy is (and it is nothing less) that some writers under the
guise of writing living Welsh disown all traditional usage and rule.
In a good novel published recently one finds *mi fues, rwbath, naci,
dwn i'm* and a host of similar corruptions." (Translation, G. E. J.)

Welsh bilingualism

As regards the bilingual situation (similar in many respects to the
diglossic in that the function of the high variety may be taken by one
language and that of the low variety by another), it is linguistic interference
and code-switching, two of the most salient features of bilingualism that
concern us here. Low varieties of Welsh tend to exhibit interference in
the lexicon and on the phonological, morphological and syntactical levels.
High varieties of Welsh, on the other hand, resist interference on all these
levels. For those speakers to whom Welsh constitutes the low variety, and
English the high, the degree of interference and code-switching tends to
be more marked.

In the diglossic context, the *appropriateness* of linguistic choice is important (Ferguson, 1972: 236) and an examination of S4Cs linguistic output shows that it is sensitive to this matter. The factual programmes — news, current affairs, documentaries — all employ a high variety of Welsh (see the last section of this chapter for a discussion of the use of English in one such programme). If a vocabulary likely to be unfamiliar to the audience is employed as, for example, in programmes which take the language into domains usually exclusively English, the commentator/presenter will frequently gloss the Welsh with the equivalent English.

There is, furthermore, evidence that there is a high variety of Welsh developing in the media that accommodates the two main regional varieties of Welsh, namely North Welsh NW and South Welsh SW (see Chapter 5 for further discussion of these). To give one instance, we can look at the variable (au): this is the plural morph that occurs in open final unaccented syllables. In NW it has the variants [ai] and [a]; the [ai] variant is the most formal. In SW it has the variants [ai] and [ɛ] the [ai] being the most formal again. Both the [a] and [ɛ] variants are quite acceptable in contexts which do not require the degree of formality that the [ai]/[ai] variants would indicate. Interestingly, though, newscasters and commentators with a NW accent are showing a tendency to adopt the [ɛ] variant which suggests that it may come to be regarded as more appropriate than the [a] variant, and its adoption by speakers of NW will neutralize its impact as a marker of regional speech.[5]

Low varieties of Welsh occur, as would be expected, in the light entertainment programmes. As was pointed out earlier, the incidence of code-switching to be found in these programmes has attracted a great deal of criticism. As is well known, it is necessary to distinguish between *situational* and *metaphorical* code-switching (Fishman, 1972: 49–50; Gumperz, 1976). Examples of both are to be found on S4C, but the metaphorical is the most common, being used to express irony, satire, humour and also anger and disagreement (cf. Gal, 1979, on Hungarian–German code-switching).[6]

Finally, an extremely interesting aspect of S4C's output is that it reflects and highlights some of the linguistic conventions operating in the bilingual situation. Two interesting ones are:

(1) The mode and manner of a code-shift from English to Welsh, with examples clearly reflecting community norms.

(2) The rules of the code selection between Welsh speakers in the presence of a non-Welsh speaker. The unwritten rule is that Welsh is not usually employed in the presence of a non-Welsh-speaking

third party, and is certainly not offered to a person known to be non-Welsh-speaking. These conventions were quite brilliantly exploited in a recent play on S4C, *Sul y Blodau*, which dealt with the linguistic tensions that arise when monoglot English speakers enter Welsh-speaking communities.

To conclude, S4C's linguistic output reflects very closely the linguistic choices operating in contemporary Wales. It reflects the contrast between low and high varieties of Welsh and highlights the tensions that may arise in a bilingual situation. The media in its extensive variety of programmes draws attention to the matter of the appropriateness of linguistic choice and focuses on the conventions and rules governing these choices.

Clearly, the criticism referred to earlier in this section does suggest that extreme instances of low Welsh with its lexical borrowing and code-switching are not acceptable to the viewers. In the final analysis, however, this criticism, ostensibly directed at the quality of Welsh, may possibly reflect dissatisfaction and frustration on the part of the Welsh speaker with the constraints that the bilingual situation imposes on his language choice. We will turn next to an examination of how one programme copes with these constraints.

The ground rules for English usage in *Y Byd ar Bedwar*[7]

Before the establishment of S4C, Welsh-language television programmes were shared between BBC Wales, and the independent company HTV Wales. Both channels produced a variety of news and current affairs programmes in Welsh, however these were usually restricted in content to Wales and to Welsh-speaking Wales in particular. Because of this, this problem of the use of English in interviews and so forth did not occur very often. S4C however aims to be a complete television service for the Welsh speaker, and as such must present stories and analyses of events not only in Wales, but in the rest of Britain and the world. It became obvious that with such a remit, the problem of dealing with the use of English had to be faced in such a way as to avoid the English dominating the programme concerned, thereby reinforcing stereotypes of the superiority of the English language. In this part of the chapter we will be examining how the producers of one current affairs programme worked out their answer to the problems of English usage noted in the previous section. This programme is *Y Byd ar Bedwar* (The World on Four) produced for S4C by HTV Cymru.

The forerunners to the news and current affairs programmes on S4C were *Y Dydd*, "The Day", *Heddiw*, "Today", and the weekly current affairs analysis programme, *Yr Wythnos*, "The Week". These did not generally use English at all in their broadcasts, therefore a policy on the use of English was lacking. The new requirement on a programme like *Y Byd ar Bedwar* to report on events around the world meant that reports on news in many parts of the world (America, Australia, Canada, etc., as well as the rest of Britain) would be incomplete without the use of a certain amount of English, used by spokesmen, politicians and so on. Two possible answers presented themselves: sub-titles, and using voice-over (that is, providing a Welsh translation spoken over the original English).

The proposal to use Welsh sub-titles when English was spoken did not gain support. As the great majority of viewers to S4C would be Welsh–English bilinguals, the use of sub-titles would suggest that the channel was somehow unaware of this fact, or pretending it was, thereby laying itself open to ridicule. However, if the English was simply left, there was a danger noted above, of it swamping the Welsh language input, and altering the whole *raison d'être* of the channel. Using voice-over was felt to be a better answer to the problem. This method allows the content of the original speaker's utterances to be conveyed to the viewer in Welsh without explicitly denying that viewer's competence in English.

However, voice-over as a technique was naturally unfamiliar to those working on the programme, and there were still worries about its use. For example, what was presented in Welsh on these occasions was second-hand, and there was anxiety about how accurately the original would be conveyed. It was possible that the precise shade of meaning intended by the original speaker might be lost in the translation, this being particularly so when differences in intonation come into play. Also, technical problems arise, for example when the Welsh version is longer (or shorter) than the English, and uncomfortable gaps can result. In such circumstances, viewers may be tempted to follow the original English, or both languages at once, with even more likelihood of the overall meaning being lost. Finally, there was the problem of the amount of time that had to be devoted to translating, and arranging the voice-over, and trying to ensure that it did not impinge overly on the aesthetic quality of the film.

In view of these problems and uncertainties, it was decided that, whereas using voice-over would be the standard response to the occurrence of English in the programme, there would be a flexible approach. When necessary, the original English would be retained if there were sound journalistic reasons. The rest of this section will be devoted to examining a variety of such occasions, and looking at the reasons behind the retention of English in them.

Firstly, we can note occasions that come under the heading of *actuality*. This covers examples when no reporter is used, but when short scenes are shown from conferences, etc. or archive scenes of importance, or when the camera is "eavesdropping" on discussions between people in the news. Secondly, there are occasions when very short stretches (perhaps a single sentence) is used from an interview previously recorded in English. These examples are often so short that using a voice-over is simply not practicable. Another example of when English would be retained would be on dramatic occasions, such as when someone being interviewed used English in an emotional fashion, having broken down in tears, or having being talked into a corner. Here it can be argued that using voice-over would destroy the journalistic effect of the drama being shown on the screen.

Fourthly, we can think of programmes which by their very nature need to retain the English of one or more of the speakers. Examples include programmes about eminent politicians and their attitudes to Wales and the Welsh language. *Y Byd ar Bedwar* produced such a programme on the non-Welsh-speaking Secretary of State for Wales, and used his own words, without voice-over. The programme lasted half an hour, but the English part (when he himself was being questioned) took up only about ten minutes. No complaints were received from viewers about this. With many politicians, their voices and accents are so much a part of their personality, and how they are recognized by the general public (think for example of the present prime minister — Mrs Thatcher), that it is only feasible to leave their comments in English.

There are occasionally legal reasons why it is best not to use the voice-over technique, but leave the original English. For example, were an interviewee to be responding to accusations made against him, or indeed to be making accusations against someone else, and the interview was originally made in English, then it would be the original words that might be needed to be used in any resultant legal action. Therefore, if these words had been "masked" by being subject to voice-over, the company might itself be subject to action. Indeed, the company's lawyers have on occasions refused permission for certain statements to be translated.

Sixthly, there is a category of 'special programmes' involving English locations or personalities. For example, during the miners' strike, at

Christmas 1984, a programme was made concentrating on the links between some of the Welsh mining villages and the ethnic minority community in Brixton, London. In this programme, interviews were conducted in Welsh with miners from Pontyberem, Cynheidre and Betws, but the original Carribean English of Brixton was retained in the London interviews, as this form of English was so much part of the contrast between the two communities that the programme makers wished to highlight.

Similarly, a programme about a Brynaman cinema involved bringing Glenda Jackson, the famous English film actress, to Brynaman to discuss with cinema-goers the reasons why they preferred older sentimental films to anything smacking of the modern. Naturally, as her voice is so much part of her character, she was not subject to a voice-over.

An exceptional case, difficult to categorize, occurred when the Dairycrest factory in Carmarthen was closed. A company spokesman was interviewed in an attempt to answer the strenuous criticism that had greeted this decision. It was felt that in order to capture his arguments properly in this controversial case, it would be better to leave his interview in the original English.

Elections present a particular problem. During the election campaign, all major candidates must be allowed the same amount of time in any one edition of the programme, or across a series of programmes. This means that any voice-over must be carefully used to avoid lengthening or shortening the candidates contributions in comparison with the original English. Also, as some of the candidates are Welsh speakers, an accusation could be made that their own voices are heard by the electorate, but the non-Welsh speakers' are not. An interesting by-product occurred on one occasion, when the over-voicing disguised the fact that one of the candidate's English was far from elegant, but this was totally neutralized in the voice-over!

Finally we can consider the problems of foreign reporting. The general policy is to interview in the local language and then use sub-titles. This of course means relying on translators on most occasions, and one can not be sure of the accuracy of such translations in certain countries. If the people being interviewed understand English (as for example in Commonwealth countries, such as Zimbabwe which featured a lot in the programme in the early days of S4C) then it was decided to use English. This was done in order to get at the truth of the story, and for this same reason the original was retained in the broadcast.

Apart from the above exceptions, the norm on *Y Byd ar Bedwar* is to use voice-over. One factor always taken into account when considering the above exceptions, is the effect any use of English may have on the overall 'Welshness' of the programme. If it is felt that this *is* under threat, then English will not be used. On the whole, this does not happen. However, as a rough rule of thumb, it is generally felt that about five minutes worth of English, scattered through the half hour the programme generally lasts is acceptable, especially when the film is situated outside Wales. As noted in some of the exceptions listed above, this is occasionally exceeded, but only in very special circumstances.

To avoid English altogether would amount on occasions to a form of censorship, and it must be borne in mind that the television journalist's task is different from that of a Welsh language dramatist: his is not to create a situation or a society, but to show it how it is.

Conclusions

This chapter has attempted to look at a few aspects of broadcasting and Welsh. We have shown how, on radio, the type of Welsh used varies in much the same way as styles of Welsh vary in the speech community, and we have noted the importance of this identity between broadcaster and speaker. In turning to television we have examined the problems facing the newly emergent Welsh channel in deciding how to treat the majority language in its broadcasts. Broadcast Welsh, however, has much left to be investigated, and let us hope it is not too long before we see a collection of papers specially dedicated to this theme.

Notes to Chapter 13

1. An earlier version of this section first appeared as a paper by Martin J. Ball (1985c) in the *Journal of Multilingual and Multicultural Development*, Volume 6.
2. An earlier version of this section was presented as a paper, 'Aspects of the Linguistic Output of the Welsh Fourth Television Channel' by Glyn E. Jones at the Colloque Européen, Les Langues moins répandues et les 'Medias' dans la Communauté Européene: Les Problèmes de la Radio-Télèvision, Nuoro, October 1986.
3. G. E. J. is indebted to Mr Emlyn Davies, Programmes' Editor, S4C, for kindly allowing access to S4C's press cuttings file.
4. The remarks by the late Dr Thomas Parry occur in the introduction to R. E. Jones (1975).

5. The existence of an acceptable high variety that can accommodate and yet transcend regional diversity is a boon to S4C. Contrast the detailed planning required in Norway, for example, where two co-existent varieties, Bokmål and Nynorsk, need to be accommodated (see Berg, 1984).

6. Very little work has been undertaken on the topic of code-switching in Welsh. Marilyn Martin-Jones of the University of Lancaster, presented a paper entitled 'Code-switching as a Mode of Discourse: Some Evidence from Bilingual Settings in Wales', at the First International Conference on Minority Languages, University of Glasgow, 1980.

7. An earlier version of this section was presented as a paper by Tweli Griffiths at the Seminar on Welsh and Broadcasting, held at the Welsh Language Research Unit, University College Cardiff in June 1986.

14   Cymraeg Byw

CENNARD DAVIES

The three booklets bearing the title *Cymraeg Byw* ("Living Welsh"), which were published between 1964 and 1970, are an attempt to define the main features of standard spoken Welsh, that form of the language which lies somewhere between conservative literary Welsh on the one hand and the local regional dialects on the other. According to the supporters of *Cymraeg Byw*, the task of the two committees responsible for this work was not to coin a new language but to define one that already existed. The ability of broadcasters, preachers and public speakers to communicate with audiences throughout the country was ample evidence that a form of standard spoken Welsh did exist, but opponents of *Cymraeg Byw* vehemently denied that it in any way resembled the artificial dialect (*tafodiaith ffug*) described in the booklets.

Cymraeg Byw undoubtedly became the burning linguistic issue of the 1960s, for disputes arose not only about the definition of standard spoken Welsh, but also about its function. Should it be written? Should it be used generally or be restricted to learners? As we shall see, these and other arguments had not been satisfactorily resolved by the time *Cymraeg Byw 3* appeared in 1970.

The publication of the three booklets in rapid succession during the mid-1960s must be seen in relation to developments in the field of second-language learning. During this period, teachers of Welsh as a second language felt that they were under a grave disadvantage when faced with competition from the attractive audio-visual courses which were available to teachers of other languages, particularly French. These were based on a scientific analysis of language and it was felt that if similar courses were to be produced in Welsh the defining of a standard spoken form of the language was a necessary prerequisite. In some ways, therefore, *Cymraeg Byw* can be seen as a response to *français fondamental* although its scope was much more limited.

The term *Cymraeg Byw* itself, however, dates from a much earlier period and it was certainly not used initially in connection with second-language teaching. Sir Ifor Williams, Professor of Welsh, at University College, Bangor and one of the outstanding Welsh scholars of this century, is credited with coining the term and he very often used it in drawing attention to the widening gulf between the written language on the one hand and the spoken dialects on the other. To Sir Ifor, bridging that gap posed a challenge which he outlined in a radio talk (Williams, 1935: 56):[1]

> "the sum total of all I have said is that spoken language should be brought closer to the written language in order to ensure a spoken language befitting a nation rather than a commote or parish. After we have achieved this, we should, in my opinion, attempt to modernize book Welsh and make it more flexible, bringing it closer to 'Living Welsh' (*Cymraeg Byw*). At the moment, there exists too great a gap in the middle which must be closed from both sides."

This viewpoint certainly wasn't new as it had been voiced at the end of the last century by the writer and polemicist, Emrys ap Iwan, and more surprisingly, perhaps, by Sir Ifor's predecessor at Bangor, Sir John Morris-Jones. It is true that in referring to Dr John Davies's grammar of 1621, Morris-Jones (1913: v) considered that "the author's analysis of the modern literary language is final; he has left to his successors only the correction and simplification of detail". He had, however, at an earlier date, expressed a markedly different opinion concerning literary Welsh,

> ". . .Welsh has been too conservative. There is nothing in the nature of things that compels us to write forms which are 700 years old. Had the philologists of the last century followed in Edward Llwyd's steps we would have fluent literary Welsh today, and every educated Welshman would speak and write the same language. . . Perhaps one could, by using a little common sense, make literary Welsh much more flexible by applying to it these laws which have influenced our dialects." (Morris-Jones, 1890: 216).

These views were echoed by a succession of distinguished scholars and writers during this century. These include Sir O. M. Edwards, Stephen J. Williams, Henry Lewis, Griffith John Williams and Islwyn Ffowc Elis. There is a high degree of consistency in their observations which can be seen clearly when one compares Sir John Morris-Jones's comments of 1890 with those of Alun Llywelyn Williams in 1951:

> "For practical reasons, as the inflexible literary language is too esoteric, too far removed from the best spoken language, many people have difficulty in reading it. . . It entails bringing the written and spoken forms of the language far closer to each other and at

this point in time that means bringing the literary language closer to the spoken form."

Up until the 1960s the debate had revolved around written Welsh and the concern that it should remain a flexible medium, capable of expressing the complexities of modern life. Indeed, in his BBC radio lecture of 1960, appropriately entitled "*Cymraeg Byw*", Sir Ifor Williams concentrated on the innate richness of the language and its capacity to regenerate itself when faced with changing circumstances. Soon, however, the urgent demands of second-language teachers were to compel scholars to produce specific recommendations in place of the general principles which had hitherto sufficed.

Despite the efforts of such dedicated teachers and course writers as David James (Defynnog), D. O. Roberts and A. S. D. Smith (Caradar), the results of teaching Welsh as a second language to school children and adults in the post-war period could hardly be described as encouraging. The success of such a teacher as W. Elvet Thomas in Cardiff was the exception rather than the rule and this general state of affairs could be explained in a number of ways. The status of Welsh within the society was low; teachers were unsure of their priorities, particularly as the public examinations laid little emphasis on oral skills; the available textbooks were unattractive and badly planned and little thought was given to classroom strategy. Above all, the language taught was generally of a literary nature, bearing little relationship to the Welsh learners would hear spoken around them. Even as late as 1960 it was possible for the following examples to appear in a textbook for adults[2] (possible *Cymraeg Byw* equivalents are given in brackets):

> *Nid oes dim car gennyf i*
> *(Does dim car 'da fi/gen i)*
> *Aethant hwy am dro a daethant hwy yn ôl erbyn tri o'r gloch*
> *(Fe aethon nhw am dro a daethon nhw nôl erbyn tri o'r gloch)*
> *Pe gofynasech i mi dywedaswn wrthych*
> *(Pe baech chi'n gofyn i fi fe fyddwn i'n dweud wrthoch chi).*

The appearance of attractive French courses such as *Tavor* and *Bonjour Line* based on the spoken language seemed to underline the need for change and in April 1964 the Department of Education and Science convened a conference to discuss the use of audio-visual aids in teaching Welsh as a second language. The first paper to be discussed was entitled 'Linguistic and Educational Considerations' and it was clearly stated that the aim should be to teach oral competence. If this was to be achieved, a full description of contemporary spoken Welsh was necessary and it was estimated by experts attending the conference that this would take two to three years. Teachers felt that time wasn't on their side.

The conference was told, however, that following a paper on the state of contemporary Welsh by Professor G. J. Williams at University College, Swansea, a panel had been meeting there for some time under the chairmanship of Professor Stephen J. Williams to discuss the practical implications of *Cymraeg Byw*. It was also revealed that the panel's preliminary recommendations were to be published shortly. The prototype of *Cymraeg Byw* duly appeared later in 1964. In his foreword to the pamphlet, Professor Charles E. Gittins summed up the aim of the panel, thus,

> "The work of the panel aimed to bridge the gap that exists between the literary and spoken language and to offer schools a standard spoken Welsh which would be acceptable throughout Wales to Welsh speakers and 'learners'." (*Cymraeg Byw, Rhifyn 1:* 1964: 3)

When the work of developing *Cymraeg Byw* was taken up by a panel appointed by the Welsh Joint Education Committee, this statement of aims was accepted more or less as it stood. The fact that *Cymraeg Byw* was intended to be used by learners and Welsh speakers alike was to prove a major bone of contention. As R. M. (Bobi) Jones (1964b) put it, "Swansea has decided to fashion a standard spoken language for everyone, not only as a second language". His own opinion was that standard spoken Welsh should be used for learners alone, as the title of his interesting chapter (R. M. Jones, 1964a), in *Cyflwyno'r Gymraeg* entitled, *"Iaith Lafar (Dysgwyr)"* made patently clear. He argued that learners should on no account be faced with a variety of linguistic choices at the outset but should be taught one language which could be spoken, read and written. He then went on to outline the general principles underlying this language. Only one form of a word or structure should be taught initially and the literary form should be given precedence where possible. Irregularity should be avoided at all costs and the forms easiest on the tongue should be adopted.

These principles were put into practice in the pioneering language course that R. M. (Bobi) Jones wrote for adults *"Cymraeg i Oedolion"*. To him the function of standard spoken Welsh was clear,

> "I wish to define the problem of standard spoken Welsh like this — it is the work of simplifying the task of introducing the learner to the living language, be that dialect, a book or what have you. He

will not then have difficulty in understanding any book he might read. . . . . .he needs to cast off any unnecessary burden." (R. M. Jones, 1964b)

In R. M. Jones's view, *Cymraeg Byw* was in no way meant to usurp the role of literary Welsh and the regional dialects but rather to act as a bridgehead into them.

This, however, was not the view taken by other influential bodies. In 1966 the Schools Broadcasting Council for Wales had decided to use *Cymraeg Byw* in radio and television schools' broadcasts for both first- and second-language pupils. There was a strong reaction against this from teachers, particularly against the use of *Cymraeg Byw* in literature accompanying first-language programmes. The furore continued when *Urdd Gobaith Cymru* (The Welsh League of Youth) decided to use *Cymraeg Byw* in "*Cymru'r Plant*", its magazine for Welsh speakers. Indignant letter writers filled the columns of the Welsh language press, one of the most persistent and vehement being the author and schoolmaster, T. Llew Jones. In October 1967 he began an article in "*Y Cymro*" with the *cri de coeur*, "*Mae'n gas gen i Gymraeg Byw!*", "I hate *Cymraeg Byw*". He went on to state that *Cymru'r Plant*" was losing readers mainly because of its "uniform, monotonous language" and that although he accepted the case for using *Cymraeg Byw* with learners it was wrong to impose it upon Welsh speakers. This was a view that was widely held among teachers and writers in a first-language situation but it was by no means the only viewpoint put forward. Whilst many objected to *Cymraeg Byw* being written, others advocated adopting one multi-purpose standard form of language. One of the most enthusiastic advocates of this point of view was Dr Urien Wiliam. In a pamphlet entitled, "*Argymhellion: Gramadeg Cymraeg Modern*", Dr Wiliam (1967: 4) wrote,

> "At the time when there is so much talk of Standard Spoken Welsh (already called '*Cymraeg Byw*') we must avoid the confusion of having two types of standard Welsh — the one spoken and the other written. We must aim at having one standard language which can be spoken in public life, in cultural intercourse, in education and in religion, and which can be written in magazines and newspapers, in forms and practical prose and in creative literature."

If Bobi Jones and Urien Wiliam disagreed with each other regarding the function of *Cymraeg Byw*, the most vociferous opponent of this 'new unauthentic dialect' (Thomas, 1967: 242) was Dr Ceinwen Thomas. In a series of detailed reviews she clearly outlined her objections. Firstly, Dr

Thomas saw no point in coining a new standard dialect as there was one already in existence.

"In their search for a standard spoken language for learners, nobody, as far as I can judge, has thought of examining the language of educated people. But if there is a standard form of language it is the form spoken by educated people. . . It would, I guess, be enough to sit in a conference of cultured Welsh people to convince the most prejudiced that standard spoken Welsh is already a fact, a flexible, unpretentious but also dignified language, as befits a standard language, a language suitable for all purposes — and suitable for learners, be they children or adults. And it is basically one language from North to South despite inherent regional differences." (Thomas, 1966: 177)

The basis of this language is the literary language. "It seeks standards outside itself in the literary language and because of that it is stable, with little tendency to change" (Thomas, 1967: 248). Dr Thomas sees *Cymraeg Byw* as a hotch-potch of forms randomly selected from the dialects and argues that if one had to draw on the resources of the dialects it might have been better to adopt one authentic dialect in its entirety rather than create a new synthesis. This is, however, in her view, completely unnecessary as a standard form of language exists. What is needed is to 'learn its rules and how speakers vary it on ceremonial occasions or when it is used to speak publicly or to converse. That is, we must learn how it works.' (Thomas, 1979: 152). This general ignorance regarding the details of standard spoken Welsh is openly admitted by Dr Thomas. Indeed, she wishes she were able to offer practical assistance,

"Had I the resources, I would send researchers throughout Wales to collect this language from the tongues of ordinary people in order to show how the Welsh-speaking community regards its language and how deeply rooted in the literary language this revered spoken language is." (Thomas, 1966: 178)

In many respects these comments underline the dilemma facing the *Cymraeg Byw* Panel and also the negative nature of Dr Thomas's criticism of its work. Development in the field of second-language teaching made it necessary to act quickly on the Welsh front with very meagre resources and little research at the disposal of the Panel. Secondly, it was necessary to commit the recommended forms of the language to print, an act which their critics studiously avoided. Another factor that becomes evident in following the *Cymraeg Byw* debate is the opposition's lack of appreciation of the nature of the second-language teacher's task.

This point is clearly seen in Dr Thomas's review of "*Cymraeg i Oedolion, Cyfrol* 1", the adult course written by R. M. (Bobi) Jones (1965), (Thomas, 1966). The methodology and underlying philosophy of the course are completely ignored and the reviewer concentrates almost exclusively on the language forms and structures selected by the author. In defending Bobi Jones, Professor Jac L. Williams (Williams, 1967: 83) pointed out that the author's aim was "to provide a bridge for learners, not to set a standard for Welsh speakers".

"*Cymraeg i Oedolion*" marked a turning point in the type of Welsh used in second-language courses and also a basic change in classroom strategy. The emphasis now was well and truly on speaking the language. Although the arguments about various aspects of *Cymraeg Byw* continued, it was widely used in schools and adult language classes during the 1970s and its value soon became apparent to teachers, especially in those areas where there was no living dialect. It was also used in broadcasting and in teaching materials aimed at a nationwide audience.

During this period a large number of people acquired fluency in Welsh via *Cymraeg Byw* and it is worth looking in detail at their linguistic development. Language is a social tool and cannot be learned completely in any classroom. No single teacher can successfully encompass all the dialects and registers of a language and neither can any classroom reproduce all the possible situations in which the learner is going to encounter the language. All a teacher can hope to achieve is to create a bridgehead into the Welsh-speaking society and imbue the learner with enough enthusiasm and instil sufficient confidence to use Welsh at all times. It is that society which provides the "finishing school" and puts its stamp on the language of the learner through a process of assimilation.

It is this process, fundamental to all language acquisition, that has been ignored by critics of *Cymraeg Byw*. The overriding concern of every successful language teacher is to establish a language "platform" in the shortest possible time, thus enabling the learner to put his acquired language to practical use within the linguistic group he is seeking to join. Once this is achieved, the learner inevitably acquires the speech characteristics of that group. It stands to reason, if one accepts this strategy, that the prototype language will be deficient in many respects but it can be justified if it enables the learner to find his way into Welsh-speaking society. Whereas it is conceded that every learner will eventually have to understand *euthum i/ethym i/etho i* and *es i* (differing forms of first-person past tense of *mynd*, "to go") it is maintained that only the latter form is necessary in the initial stages. The crucial question to be asked regarding *Cymraeg Byw* is whether or not it works in practice. Most teachers would by now agree that its virtues far outweigh its defects.

Without doubt, mistakes were made at the outset. Whilst it is legitimate to simplify the choice between various forms, it is unwise to devise new forms under the pretext that the existing ones are too difficult for learners. *Y bachgen un deg un*, "the 11th boy", (lit: "the boy one ten one"), isn't acceptable, despite its attractive simplicity, because it doesn't exist in the spoken language. Over the years teachers have modified *Cymraeg Byw* in the light of practical experience and have found it a useful tool in the initial stages of learning. Speaking is a social function and speech, therefore, is constantly being influenced by external forces. It is obvious to any language teacher that after a period of time the language of his students will have changed considerably under the influence of outside pressures. The teacher has enabled the learner to join the target language group but must accept that it is that group which will ultimately mould his language.

As no critics of the prototype of *Cymraeg Byw* have committed themselves to outlining detailed alternatives, it is difficult to form an overall view of standard spoken Welsh as they see it. If it is the language used in formal public speech or in broadcast talks, experience indicates that this is well within the compass of learners familiar with *Cymraeg Byw*. The same is true of stage dialogue. Take this brief excerpt from *Esther* by Saunders Lewis (1960: 5),

Ahasferus:	'Rwyt ti'n fy syfrdanu i, Esther.
Esther:	Pa ots? Fi piau heno. Yfory, ffarwél.
Ahasferus:	Chei di ddim ffarwelio. Fi piau ti. Heno ac yfory ac wedyn.
Esther:	Haman a'i broclamasiwn?
Ahasferus:	Fedran' nhw mo'th gyrraedd di.
Esther:	Gallan', fy arglwydd, mi allan' fy nghyrraedd i.
Ahasferus:	Ym mhalas y Brenin.
Esther:	Ym mreichiau'r Brenin.
Ahasferus:	Fy mhrenhines i wyt ti. Does gen ti ddim cenedl ond fi.
Esther:	Dydd trallodd y genedl ydy' heddiw. Gan hynny Israeliad wyf innau.
Ahasferus:	Sut hynny?
Esther:	Am fod pob Iddew drwy'r deyrnas yn perthyn imi. Rydw i'n gyfrifol amdanyn' nhw.

This dialogue certainly isn't colloquial nor is it written in the register of Welsh one would use to write a scholarly article. Forms such as *rwyt ti*; *chei di ddim*; *fedran nhw*; *gallan'*; *does gen ti ddim cenedl*, *ydy* and *amdanyn nhw* are precisely those suggested in the *Cymraeg Byw* booklets. They represent a register which can be seen in the work of many modern Welsh writers and which is acceptable when used in conversation.

The first *Cymraeg Byw* publication only dealt with verbs, adjectives and prepositions. The next added sections on nouns, numerals, ordinals, fractions, impersonal forms of the verb and pronouns. Apart from a note on the future tense and some additional recommendations, *Cymraeg Byw* *3* differed very little from the previous booklet except for an interesting article on "The General Principles of Cymraeg Byw" by Mr T. J. Rhys Jones. It is however clear from this third edition that the vexed question of the specific function of *Cymraeg Byw* hadn't been resolved. In his foreword, Mr D. Andrew Davies reiterated what he had said in *Cymraeg Byw 2* namely that both learners and Welsh speakers should use the recommended forms. This is repeated in the section outlining 'Basic Principles', but T. J. Rhys Jones (1970: 12) expresses a very different aim in his article:

> "In formulating *Cymraeg Byw* it was intended to produce an acceptable, flexible, convenient and unoffending language which teachers could confidently and safely introduce to learners, knowing that they could speak it in the presence of any Welsh person or company of Welsh speakers and receive a friendly hearing."

This is the point of view consistently expressed by such advocates of *Cymraeg Byw* as R. M. (Bobi) Jones and the late Professor Jac L. Williams. I would maintain that this would also be the view of most second-language teachers. They would readily acknowledge the importance of eventually mastering literary Welsh and being acquainted with the dialects but would point out that all the registers of language cannot be approached at the same time. Oral competence is the primary objective and that is the sound basis from which mastery of other registers can begin.

The point made by T. J. Rhys Jones regarding 'a friendly hearing' is especially important in the case of Welsh. What he is referring to here is the concept of acceptability. This is important in any second-language situation but as all Welsh speakers are bilingual the consequence of non-acceptability is usually a language switch to English. This can occur for a number of reasons. It happens when a native speaker senses that the L2 speaker isn't completely at ease in the target language, but it can also occur if the learner's Welsh is judged to be too literary in style. 'He speaks like a book' was a criticism often heard in the past, and one suspects that if learners adopted such literary verb forms as *try*, *deffry*, *euthum*, *wrthyf*, and *bûm*, as has been suggested, the reaction of the man in the street would be predictable. Anything that hinders the process of linguistic assimilation is to be avoided and the nature of the language used by the learner is crucial in this context. This is another vital factor which has been ignored by critics of *Cymraeg Byw* not practically involved in second-language teaching.

Time is a great healer and the furore of the 1960s has certainly subsided by now. This has happened partly because *Cymraeg Byw* has proved to be a useful tool and is certainly one of the factors responsible for the far higher success rate in teaching Welsh both to adults and children. The early language models have been modified by teachers in the light of experience, with definite north/south differences emerging both in vocabulary and syntax. These differences have been recognized by the Welsh Joint Education Committee examining board responsible for the new Ordinary Level Examination for adults inasmuch as papers incorporating regional characteristics into *Cymraeg Byw* are now available, together with aural texts more closely related to the language which the learner hears around him.

With the development of radio and television services in the Welsh language, together with the rapid growth of community newspapers (*papurau bro*), people have become more used to hearing and reading Welsh which is less literary in style and more colloquial in nature than the 'pulpit Welsh' which was familiar to the older generation and which also had wide currency throughout the country. It is hoped that these developments will be studied in depth and that the findings will be incorporated into future editions of *Cymraeg Byw*. It is important that the proposed function of standard spoken Welsh is clearly perceived, namely as one of the many registers of Welsh, but the one specifically designated to start the learner on the road to fully mastering the language.

The years following the publication of *Cymraeg Byw 1* in 1964 have been both exciting and fruitful in the field of teaching Welsh as a second language. Radical changes in aims and methodology have coincided with the gradually improving status of the language, the rapidly increasing demand for bilingual education in the anglicized areas and the higher profile of Welsh in the popular media. Every living language is constantly changing and as the demands made upon Welsh have increased so has the nature of the language itself subtly changed. It might appear ironic that Sir Ifor Williams's crusade has made its greatest impact in second-

language spheres but it would be unwise to underestimate the changes
which have occurred in the spoken and written Welsh of native speakers.
These, however, must be the subject of another chapter.

Notes to Chapter 14

1. All quotations are translated from the original Welsh.
2. Examples taken from "Welsh" Bowen & Bhys Jones, 1960.

Part V:
Children's Use of Welsh

15 The development of pronunciation

WYNFORD BELLIN

Introduction

A question that concerns parents, education professionals and professionals like speech therapists is whether there is any standard pattern in the acquisition of pronunciation. Many young children continue to depart from adult pronunciation for a long enough time to create anxiety in adults responsible for their care.

Recent research has made it necessary to recast such apparently straightforward questions. It has become clear that establishing how far a child has reached towards adult-like pronunciation is no simple issue. The complication arises because of gaps between known receptive abilities and capabilities in pronunciation at any given age.

Studies of speech perception in very young children were conducted during the 1970s. It was possible to measure sucking rate in a quiet environment and wait till a stable base rate settled in as a result of no change in stimulation. A change in a speech sound hitherto kept as a stable feature of the background would give rise to a fluctuation in sucking rate. A similar methodology worked with measures of heart rate. So discrimination experiments could be conducted, and crucial distinctions from the point of view of phonology, such as the contrast between voiced and voiceless sounds were registered by young infants, as shown by the effect on sucking rate or heart rate.

It was confirmed that there can be distinctions in reception which are brought out in the small child's speech. So interest in the gap between what children can perceive and what they can produce became more intense.

Children who acquire Welsh

In the case of Welsh-speaking children, many questions about the acquisition of pronunciation receive added interest because of the variety of ways in which children grow up to speak Welsh. For the first time in the history of the Census in Britain, the proportion of Welsh-speaking children rose in 1981, instead of sharing in the general decline of the language. Legislation in the 1960s led to bilingual education schemes, which increased in popularity in the 1970s. The general sociolinguistic situation is described in Bellin (1984a). The situation is such that an increasing proportion of young Welsh speakers attain fluency in the language through the school system rather than from home. For example, in 1985, the proportion of Welsh-speaking children in primary schools in Gwynedd, an area with the highest proportion of Welsh speakers, was over a half (55%). The local authority carries out a kind of census based on teacher's assessments in order to project demand for bilingual secondary schools. But of that 55% a quarter were from homes where Welsh was not spoken.

In schools in Wales, it is common to find children from Welsh-speaking homes where the school uses only English as the medium of instruction, or English for prestige subjects and maybe Welsh for subjects like religious studies. But there are designated bilingual schools, and often primary schools in traditionally Welsh-speaking areas where Welsh is used across the curriculum. The increase in the proportion of Welsh-speaking children is made possible by children from homes where Welsh is not spoken taking part in bilingual primary education.

Interest in Welsh-speaking children has therefore increased for two reasons:

(1)   from the point of view of theory, a sharp distinction is often made between first- and second-language acquisition, and children in bilingual education when Welsh is not spoken at home are of interest in case such a distinction is relevant for the Welsh situation; and

(2)   there are vigorous opponents of Welsh education who regard competence acquired at school as somehow unauthentic, so more needs to be known about acquisition processes in different categories of children.

There are a very few children who continue their education in Welsh, as well as speaking Welsh outside Wales. A number of educational projects for this category have recently initiated, in particular, the running of a primary school in London, where provision is made for the kind of education given in a designated bilingual school in Wales, although there is no continuation at secondary level. In this case the general ambient environment is very unlike Wales, although the school and home environment exercise a joint influence. Since the Census includes questions about knowledge of Welsh only for use inside Wales, there is no knowledge of how many children are brought up to speak the language outside Wales, as happened to two of the children who provided examples of pronunciation for what follows.

Ages and stages in the acquisition of pronunciation

Research reviewed by Stark (1986) still provides a useful guide to what should be expected in vocal development. Very young babies engage in what has been labelled 'reflexive crying', but between three and six months there is an increase in cooing and laughter, followed with considerable overlaps in time spent in what seems to be experimenting with the vocal apparatus, although the safest label is "vocal play".

What begins to engage the linguistic researcher is a period between seven and twelve months when reduplicating babbling occurs with a consonant–vowel (cv) pattern . The author's own daughter, Eirlys, had a strong preference for a voiced alveolar sounding like [d] at this stage. Many children then babble with cv, v and cvc patterns at around 12 months, although Eirlys persisted with preference for cv patterns. Phonetically consistent forms may appear with babbling, but then many children seem to settle into a period of using about 50 words which are confidently related to adult forms by caretaking adults, before a spurt in vocabulary growth.

There is considerable agreement among researchers that thinking in terms of stages and trying to relate them to age can be very misleading. Eirlys followed a phonological pattern just after her first birthday which was of considerable interest because of suggestions about phonological universals (see Bellin, 1984b), but then her brother had followed no such pattern. It seems that Welsh-speaking children, in or out of Wales, will exemplify what has been found in other languages. They will follow distinctive phonological patterns and the age at which change may occur will vary considerably. Only broad generalizations will hold, such as that some classes of sounds like fricatives will be later in appearance than others. But in general, change with age must be gauged by studying the nature of a very varying pattern of speech production. Grunwell (1981) proposed that instead of asking whether a certain stage has been reached at any age, clinicians need to study carefully the variation in young children's speech. A better idea of the level of acquisition reached, according to Grunwell and others, is obtained by trying to decide whether the variation inevitably present is progressive or static.

Phonological processes

There has been much study of young children's deformations of adult word forms when word cominbations begin and vocabulary shows a spurt in growth. The age at which these developments take place can vary considerably. In the case of the author's daughter, Eirlys, it began at 13 months, but it is commonly some months later and often much later still.

Considerable interest has been shown in child deformations of adult word forms such as the following:

[taːni]	/kaːni/	"sing"
[daun]	/gaun/	"gown" (dressing gown)
[dɔlai]	/gɔlai/	"light"
[dadail]	/gadail/	"leave"
[dai duːs]	/kai druːs/	(lit.) "close door".

The child forms are given in square brackets and adult forms in angled brackets. Two phonological processes are exemplified by such forms:

cluster reduction as in [duːs] for /druːs/; and
fronting, or the substitution of a front consonant for a back consonant.

What is of interest about these phonological processes is that they take place when phonological discrimination is present (cf. Bellin, 1984b) and evidence is shown that articulatory patterns for the relevant speech sounds are followed in other environments. For example, when fronting was prevalent a very commonly used form by Eirlys was

[lɯgas]   /lukɪs/   "lucky" (applied to anyone receiving or able to give sweets).

So back consonants were in the repertoire for pronunciation. A build-up of a word combination (cf. Peters, 1986) occurred in the 13th month which did not show fronting. This was in the grandparents' home where coal fires were used and the following effort at a word combination occurred:

gɔ: ... nɔl glɔ: ... glɔ:
(coal) ...(fetch coal) ...(coal).

The attempt at a word combination seemed somewhat precocious at this stage, and also, interestingly, the attempt to avoid cluster reduction, as usually occurred in clusters with /l/, such as in [lɪpi] for "slippers". In the same utterance, fronting of the adult /g/ did not occur. Overall the indications were that, as a rule at this stage, correctly received adult word forms were undergoing phonological processes on the way to being uttered. So when one of Eirlys' deformations like

[waiwo] /bairo/ "biro"

was uttered it may be assumed that first of all a replacement of a liquid with a glide took place, and then the influence of a preference for cvcv word-forms (cf. Bellin, 1984b) was still at work. So consonant harmony resulted in an initial [w] instead of /b/.

Adult words and children's words

Ingram (1986) has brought together much of the work on children's phonological processes, but there remains a considerable problem in deciding how close the child's internal representation of a word is to the adult one. Smith (1973) assumed that children operate from the adult representation of words in pronunciation, and phonological processes intervene between their own grasp of how a form should be pronounced and the way it is actually pronounced.

The problem with assuming that children have the adult grasp of how to pronounce words "internally" arises when deciding how so-called "displaced contrasts" come about. Kiparsky & Menn (1977) give the label "displaced contrasts" to a phenomenon much discussed in the research literature. An example from Eirlys is the following deformation which occurred when fronting was prevalent

[dɔgi] /kɔdi/ "pick up".

If it is assumed that internally she "knew" that the adult form was /kɔdi/, then there could not just have been a single process of fronting, otherwise the deformation would have started with /d/ and the middle consonant would have remained /d/ because consonant harmony (which was prevalent at that time) would have helped. So the deformation might have been [dɔdi].

Since the pronunciation was actually [dɔgi], the only way that would happen starting from an accurate internal representation of the adult form would be as follows:

first of all consonant harmony would result in the form having matching /k/ consonants;

then there would be voicing to a intervocalic [g], as happened with [luɡas];

finally fronting of the initial [k] would occur as normal (see above). The outcome then would be a contrast between the consonants of the adult form even though the contrast is displaced.

Researchers who find such an account too contorted have to insist that despite ability to make distinctions between speech sounds in discrimination experiments, such abilities are not necessarily recruited for phonology. Hence, children do not always internally represent adult forms as models for pronunciation and the gap between what they perceive and pronounce is narrower than usually supposed. These counter-assertions have been made most convincingly by Macken (1980) with re-interpretations of the data presented by Smith (1973).

In the case of Eirlys they fit well, since some of her deformations with substitution of a fricative for a liquid in word-final position seemed to have been influenced by her brother (see Bellin, 1984b) rather than adult forms. She would say

[dadaiv]   /kadair/   'chair'
[taktuv]   /traktɔr/   'tractor'

whereas her slightly older cousin used liquid replacement — [l] for final /r/, and her attempts at 'lemonade' varied between

[lɛmuleid]   [nɛmuleid]   [mɛnuleid]

again at 13 months when disyllabic adult forms gave much less trouble. The attempts suggest lack of clarity about what the adult form "should" be, and other phonological processes suggest only a partial correspondence between internal representations and adult forms.

Younger children and Welsh

Although research on the acquisition of pronunciation generally has led to intricate disputes and uncertainty about the extent of children's mastery of the adult system at any given stage, one thing can be affirmed at least. In Welsh-speaking children, the data of the general disputes are easily paralleled, whatever the circumstances of exposure to the Welsh language, in or out of Wales. They therefore fit easily into the albeit unclear picture of normal development of pronunciation emerging from research activities.

Now when children get older, as happened with Eirlys, peer pressure rather than family pressure can become much stronger. Hence, there was influence of vowel quality from south eastern varieties of English, and this was most obvious in diphthongs, such as a lowering and bringing forward of the vowels in /ai/. On the other hand, where children in Wales have been studied in the pre-school provision that is available through the medium of Welsh, interference patterns from English are very rare. Scope for interference is different, since vowel quality in varieties of English spoken in Wales does not present a considerable contrast, but a longitudinal study of 71 children in groups organized by *Mudiad Ysgolion Meithrin* (see Siencyn, 1985) yielded only one child from a wide geographical spread who did not seem to follow the adult Welsh speakers providing the Welsh-medium activities as the model for pronunciation. In that one case Siencyn describes special circumstances.

Welsh mutations

One of the hallmarks of a Celtic language is the system whereby the initial segments of citation forms of words may change in a wide variety of environments (see also this volume, Chapter 7). The interest of the mutation system for comparing different categories of children is that formal teaching is made impossible by the all-pervasive nature of the environments which condition the phonological changes. Some are purely lexical, some phonological, and in Welsh, as distinct from other Celtic languages, some involve major syntactic categories (see Bellin, 1984b: 168–74). So it is of considerable interest to compare children undergoing a home–school language switch with children from homes where Welsh is spoken. After such a comparison, it was possible to ask whether the much smaller number of London Welsh-speaking children available were more like children from Welsh-speaking homes in a bilingual school, or more like children from English-speaking homes. However, it was necessary to choose some particular environments for testing purposes. The ones chosen were connected with possessive pronouns. Thus the word for 'house' which begins with /t/ may appear as:

dy dŷ, "your (familiar) house" with initial /d/;
ei thŷ, "her house" with initial /θ/;
fy nhŷ, "my house" with initial /nh/.

In most linguistic descriptions of the mutation system, the citation form is treated as the base form, and the other forms are derived by mutation rules. As described elsewhere in this volume (see Chapters 7, 17, and 20), these rules fall into three sets known as soft, aspirate and nasal mutations.

The changes in initial segments are summarized in Table 15.1a. The testing procedures used were oral, but since all the children involved were of school age, and teachers might ask what was going on, conventional spelling was used in the test materials. Table 15.1b can be compared with Table 15.1a for a summary of conventional spelling. An important extension, then, of acquiring the pronunciation of Welsh is to gain some grasp of the way the same lexical item will have 'mutated', and to gain control of the environments in which such changes take place. The reason for picking the particular environments used for the experiments was that possessive pronouns can be regarded as having communicative relevance, whereas other environments conditioning mutation such as those involving

TABLE 15.1   *Welsh consonants and the mutations shown*

Initial segment of citation form	*Soft mutation*	*Aspirate mutation*	*Nasal mutation*
(a) Consonants transcribed			
p	b	f	mh
t	d	θ	nh
k	g	x	ŋh
b	v		m
d	ð		n
g	zero		ŋ
m	v		
ɬ	l		
r̥	r		
(b) Consonants in conventional spelling			
p	b	ph	mh
t	d	th	nh
c	g	ch	ngh
b	f		m
d	dd		n
g			ng
m	f		
ll	l		
rh	r		

gender distinctions would not provide such an obvious relevance for testing purposes.

An elicitation experiment

Children in the investigation

Children in Wales

The children in the investigation attended a Welsh-medium primary school in the Ystalyfera area of Swansea in West Glamorgan. The age range was between five and nine years. There were 12 children from each age group with roughly equal proportions of boys and girls. They were selected at random from enrolment lists. Only a third of the children had parents who both spoke Welsh. However, the basis for categorizing the children was whether they were addressed in Welsh at home, and whether they used the language in reply. The school policy was to teach all children entirely through the medium of Welsh until the age of seven, after which part of the curriculum was taught in English. (See also this volume, Chapter 17.)

Children in London

Of the small number of children available in the Welsh-medium school in London, seven took part in a re-run of the procedure. They were all addressed in Welsh at home.

The elicitation test

An elicitation test with 12 items was devised, using vocabulary judged to be straightforward for the age groups. Each item was a text two or three sentences long. The final sentence in each text stopped with a possessive pronoun, and the child was meant to complete the sentence. The nouns which were targets for completion are given in Table 15.2. Brightly coloured cartoons were prepared — portrayal of the central characters (Dafydd and Siân) for a warm-up item, and then a cartoon for each elicitation item. So, for example, when showing a picture of the central characters with Siân holding a broken doll, the elicitation context was:

Mae Dafydd a Siân	Dafydd and Siân are
yn cweryla. Mae Dafydd	quarrelling. Dafydd has
wedi torri tegannau Siân.	broken Siân's toys.
Mae Siân yn gwaeddu:	Siân shouts:
"Paid â chwarae gyda fy. . ."	"Don't play with my. . ."

where the target was *nhegannau* mutated from the citation form *tegannau*, "toys". (Although translations are given here, the whole investigation was conducted exclusively in Welsh.) In conducting the test, all sessions were recorded, and transcription relied on agreement between two judges.

TABLE 15.2 *Nouns used in the elicitation test*

	Mutation	
Soft	Aspirate	Nasal
pen → *ben* "head"	*pwrs* → *phwrs* "purse"	*pwrs* → *mhwrs* "purse"
te → *de* "tea"	. . .[a]	*tegannau* → *nhegannau* "toys"
cap → *gap* "cap"	. . .[a]	*cap* → *nghap*
brawd → *frawd* "brother"	* * *[b]	. . .[a]
dillad → *ddillad* "clothes"	* * *[b]	*drôr* → *nrôr* "drawer"
menig → *fenig* "gloves"	*menig* [c] (no mutation)	* * *[b]

[a]: no examples were used.
[b]: the consonant never shows this mutation.
[c]: in one case, with the word for 'gloves', the citation form was elicited, since no mutation would be shown in the context.

Results of the elicitation test

Figure 15.1 plots the average number of items where children in an age group in Wales produced the target mutated form, showing the average for Welsh-speaking homes with the symbol w and the average for English-only homes with E. There were no children from Welsh-speaking homes in the youngest group. The results were analysed by comparing the fit of a number of possible regressions. First a simple regression on age was tried, and then extra terms were added in and improvement in fit was tested for significance. As would be expected from the impression given by Figure 15.1, there was a significant regression on age. But the R squared was only 0.33. Adding the effect of home language increased the R squared significantly to 0.83. So parallel slopes can be regarded as the best-fitting regression, instead of a joint regression on age. Both sub-groups improve with age but children from Welsh-speaking homes can be expected to keep a little ahead of the others on this particular set of items. However, only one or two items were implicated in the separation.

The number of children available in London was very small. There were two five-year-olds, four six-year-olds and one seven-year-old. How-

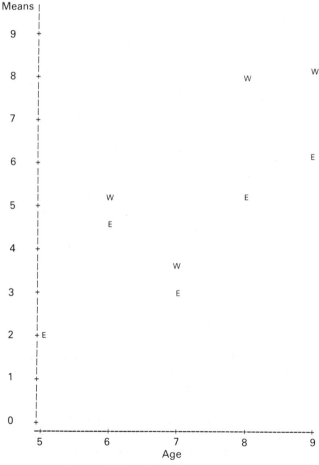

FIGURE 15.1 *Plot of means against age*
w is Welsh-speaking home; e, English-speaking

ever, the central question was whether they were more like their counterparts in Wales, or more like children relying on the school environment for Welsh. This question was addressed by taking the predicted number of correct mutations for each sub-group in Wales from the regression equations. Then it was possible to test how good a predictor a fitted value would be for the London children.

The finding was that the London children were closer to the children from Welsh-speaking homes in Wales, but not significantly so. The chi-square test of goodness-of-fit for prediction of the London results from fitted values for children from Welsh-speaking homes was 6.54 with 6 degrees of freedom. That for prediction of London results from fitted values for English-speaking homes was 9.12 — a poorer fit but not significantly so. Since the Swansea sub-groups were so close together, the absence of significance is not really surprising.

A careful item analysis was conducted using methods described in Bellin (1985) to find whether any particular items from the test were responsible for the slight separation of the Swansea sub-groups. There were two items which distinguished between the language backgrounds. Two was about the number to be expected from looking at the separation between the trends in Figure 15.1. On items requiring *te*, "tea", to mutate to *de* and *cap*, "cap", to mutate to *nghap*, there were different age trends in children from homes where Welsh was spoken and the "immersion" children. (Parallel lines, both improving, in the case of *te/de*, and separate lines with English-speaking homes getting slightly less likely to produce the target for *cap/nghap*.) So it was possible to detect which items had caused the slight separation between the trends in Figure 15.1. However, the numbers from London prevented such a detailed comparison for the children maintaining the language out of Wales.

Conclusions from the elicitation test

The elicitation test established that the children undergoing a home–school language switch were improving with age in the production of mutated forms, in spite of the fact that formal teaching of such rules is neither practical nor part of the curriculum in bilingual schools. (Formal teaching of Welsh as a foreign language occurs only in schools where the medium of instruction is English, although reading, spelling and writing in Welsh obviously have a role in the bilingual school curriculum.)

Careful item analysis of the elicitation test isolated two items where the children who did not speak Welsh at home behaved differently from those who did. It would be surprising if no such items could be discovered. A suggestion as to why those items in particular distinguished the language backgrounds has been made by Dressler (personal communication). In research on Breton, evidence was found that speakers who make use of the language only in specific situations are less likely to produce mutated forms of loan words than other speakers (cf. Dressler & Wodak-Leodolter, 1977). Since the two items distinguishing the language backgrounds in this investigation involve loan words, there may be a reluctance on the part of children from monolingual English homes to submit them to the full mutation system. It is as if they were treated as particularly blatant borrowings. If such a difference in behaviour underlies the results, then these children nevertheless are behaving like speakers whose Welsh was acquired under home or community influence. Lexical imports which have not yet been established as loan words fail to show mutation even in literary registers. The main finding is that all the children improve in control of the phonological changes as they grow older.

Contriving to record spontaneous usage

A common criticism of the kind of elicitation test reported here is that it will underestimate children's ability, since the adult has a definite target form in mind, and will create some test anxiety by the formality of the procedure. Because of such assumptions, the children in Swansea were revisited to try a procedure devised by Mair Rees, a Reading psychology student. The aim of the procedure was to involve children in a game which would require the use of possessives in child-to-child communication, rather than at the insistence of an adult.

The game involved three pairs of identical objects:
two ping-pong balls (involving the mutations *pêl* to *bêl/mhêl*, "ball");
two small cars (involving the mutations *car* to *gar/nghar*, "car");
two bus tickets (involving the mutations *tocyn* to *docyn/nhocyn*, "ticket").
The members of each pair were marked with either a blue or red sticker. Otherwise they were indistinguishable. The game was played between two children seated either side of a small table on which all the objects were positioned. Each child was allocated a colour (red or blue) and told that objects bearing that colour were his/her property for the duration of the game. In the game, a child was asked to turn away from the table, while the partner removed an object. Then the one who had turned away was to look and say which object was missing and whose it was. Taking turns

at removing objects and saying what was missing created opportunities for the phonological contrasts with the voiceless stops to be produced.

Children who played the game

The Swansea school was revisited several weeks after the elicitation test, and four subjects from each of the six- to nine-year-old age groups took part in the game. These children were selected for being close to the median score for their age groups on the elicitation test. Their partners in the game were selected at random from the same class. All sessions were recorded and decisions about whether or not target forms had been produced depended on two judges. The whole procedure was conducted in Welsh.

Results from the procedure with the game

Since the same children from each age group had taken part in the game and the elicitation test, it was possible to compare the likelihood of producing a target form in either situation. The number of children was small, and only the voiced/voiceless distinction on stops was involved. But the main result was clear and surprising.

Comparing the tests

Every child provided six contexts in both the elicitation test and the game where forms showing mutation could have been produced. That meant that the likelihood of producing such forms in the one situation or the other could be compared. Details of the statistics are given in Bellin (1985).

What actually happened was the opposite of what was anticipated. All the six year-olds were better in the formal procedure. Only the oldest children had a higher proportion of target forms in the game procedure — all being more likely to produce mutated forms in that situation assumed to be nearer to spontaneous usage. This was very surprising for two reasons:

(1)   Different procedures often give different results, but their relative difficulty stays stable over age ranges as a rule.

(2) There was so much more adult pressure to produce target forms in the elicitation test.

Since it was never expected that any of the children would be better in the formal test, the results of the youngest children need to be explained.

An admittedly speculative account of how bilingual children deal with the mutation system might account for the surprising superiority of the six-year-old children in the formal test rather than the game. Suppose that bilingual competence has different levels. That is to say, besides practical pronunciation procedures, another level is brought into action when the subject is faced with a linguistic system that pervades phonology, lexicon and syntax, like the Welsh mutation system. There may be a kind of tacit strategic knowledge developing before following the mutation rules in production is tried out.

First of all, an appreciation of what is happening develops at the strategic level. So adult-like pronunciation might be more variable than later on. But the child is sizing up the acquisition task for this aspect of the language. What happened with the formal test was an uncovering of the extent of this strategic-level knowledge. Because the adult elicitation method was so pressing, the strategic-level knowledge alerted children to what was wanted without self-consciousness. Providing the lexical items in the eliciting context, meant that the phonological change was the sole requirement for practical knowledge. Hence, the tacit growing awareness of the system could inform performance on the formal test.

With older children, who are producing the mutated forms in ordinary contexts, there is now reliance on practical production procedures, and any meta-level knowledge comes from awareness of what they are doing in ordinary speech. When a formal elicitation test is administered, it is not tapping a tacit unself-conscious strategic knowledge, but a more conscious awareness of what is going on. The element of self-consciousness may cause unease. Hence, only the oldest children behaved as anticipated, showing superior performance in the less formal game.

Admittedly, proposing that young bilingual children operate with a tacit strategic knowledge before embarking on the every-day use of forms is speculative. But the proposal would help explain the unanticipated results of this investigation.

General conclusions

A simple picture of the normal acquisition of pronunciation cannot be outlined for any language because of the variation between and within children. However, studying children who acquire Welsh in very different contexts reveals a fundamental similarity unless there are very special circumstances. In older children, intricate patterns of mastery of mutation rules seem to be indicated, and these would require further investigation. Nevertheless the similarities between acquisition, even in very different conditions of exposure to the language, continue at later ages. In spite of considerable variation, there seems to be an envelope setting bounds on the variation which moves in a progressive way with continued use of the language even at different ages.

16 The pronouns of address in Welsh

GLYN E. JONES

As in the case with the majority of European languages, Welsh has a binary choice of second-person singular pronoun — *ti* [ti] or *chi* [χi] which will be referred to, in accordance with the accepted convention, as T and V forms respectively. Some dialects of Welsh offer further choices, especially those of south-west Wales which may use the third-person singular masculine and feminine forms *fe* [ve] and *hi* [hi], with a second-person singular reference (see Thorne, 1975/76; 1977a).

The following account of some features of the usage of the TV forms in Welsh is based upon two previous studies (G. E. Jones & Thomas, 1981; G. E. Jones, 1984a) and is confined to choices involving the second-person singular TV forms only.

The usage reported and discussed here is that of three groups of children in the age group 9–11-years-old. The groups are: children from a rural setting whose first language (L1) was Welsh; children from an urban setting also with Welsh as their L1; children from an urban setting to whom Welsh was the second language (L2). The rural children, 45 in number (22 boys (RB) and 23 girls (RG) were from the three neighbouring villages of Llangernyw, Llansannan and Pentrefoelas in Clwyd, North Wales. All had Welsh-speaking parents and were from an overwhelming Welsh-speaking background; according to the 1971 Census the population of each of these three villages was over 80% Welsh-speaking (Jones & Thomas, 1981: 49). The urban L1 children, 56 in total (27 boys (UL1B) and 29 girls (UL1G)) were drawn from three Welsh-medium primary schools in South Glamorgan.[1] Although these children had Welsh-speaking parents, they lived in a highly anglicized urban setting, their parents being recently settled, mainly professional people, members of that emerging group of Welsh-speakers dubbed 'yuppies' (young professional mobiles) in a recent study of the distribution of the Welsh language (Aitchison & Carter, 1985: 43). The urban L2 children, 45 in total (22 boys (UL2B) and 23 girls (UL2G)), although pupils at Welsh-medium schools in South Glamorgan, were, in marked contrast to the rural and urban L1 groups of children, all from a monolingual English background, their parents being non-Welsh-speaking.

In the questionnaire used to elicit the data on the usage of the pronoun of address, each child was required to indicate which pronoun would be employed in a series of interactions which consisted of the child and a specified participant; in one section the child was to indicate how he/she addressed each participant and in another section how the same participants addressed the child.

The participants asked about covered a wide range of interacts, involving kin: parents, siblings, grandparents, uncles, aunts and first cousins; and non-kin: classmates (male and female),[2] teacher, headmaster, minister of religion and strangers. However, because of the marked differences between the urban L2 children and the rural and urban L1 children in their linguistic, social and cultural backgrounds, the number of interactions specified in the questionnaire, through which all the urban L2 could interact through Welsh, was limited to those involving headmaster, teacher and classmates.

Apart from their obvious monolingual English background the UL2 children differed from the UL1 children in socio-economic terms: whilst 80% of the UL1 children clustered at socio-economic groups 1–6, the higher end of the Office of Population Censuses Surveys (1970) 17 point socio-economic groups scale, only 20% of the UL2 children clustered around those points (G. E. Jones, 1984a: 175). Attendance at a place of worship — regarded as a marked feature of the cultural habits of Welsh speakers, was adhered to by over 80% of both the rural and urban L1 groups of children (male and female) (Jones & Thomas, 1981: 31), but by less than 30% of UL2 boys and by 57% of the UL2 girls (G. E. Jones, 1984a: 36). Given the highly anglicized setting in which they live, the absence of Welsh-speaking kin, limited membership of a Welsh-language institution such as the chapel, UL2 children's Welsh-language activities are confined in the main to the school setting, particularly in the case of the boys.

Because of these limitations involving the UL2 group of children, the discussion on the TV usage of all three groups of children will be restricted to the interactions involving classmates, male and female, headmaster and teacher. Despite their limited number, these interacts do provide data on usage involving participants who differ in peer–non-peer terms, status, degrees of intimacy and solidarity, all of which are variables known to be relevant in the choice of address forms (see for example, Ervin-Tripp, 1972; Friedrich, 1972).

To indicate which pronoun of address that would be selected, the children were given three options: *ti*, *chi* or *mae'n dibynnu*, "it depends". The third option was included to allow for any variation that the children might wish to report. Its inclusion, however, multiplied the possible reciprocity patterns. A simple t/v choice (which is the usual allowed in studies of tv usage, for example Lambert & Tucker, 1976) would yield four possible patterns: reciprocal t (rt) that is t sent and received; reciprocal v (rv) that is v sent and received; non-reciprocal tv (nrtv) that is v sent and t received; non-reciprocal vt (nrvt) t sent and v received. The "it depends" option, hereafter referred to as var, added such combinations as reciprocal var (rvar); non-reciprocal t–var (nrt–var) or non-reciprocal v–var (nrv–var) and so on (see G. E. Jones, 1984a: 133). Whilst the inclusion of this third option may have been counter-productive in some respects (see Jones & Thomas, 1981: 32), the extent to which that option was selected by the ul2 children in particular, justified its inclusion, in that it uncovered what would seem to be a marked lack of preference for one particular pronoun over the other, a lack that a simple t/v choice might well not have revealed.

The majority sent and received, and reciprocal forms of address reported, are given in the three flow-charts (Figures 16.1–16.3)[3] and a discussion of the address patterns for the four interactions follow.

Addressing non-peers: Headmaster and teacher

In addressing their non-peers all three groups of children have a clearly evolved *norm* and that is the v form; *chi* is the major form of address sent to headmaster and teacher alike.

These two dyads involve participants with whom the children's relationship would be marked by the constraints of authority, respect, non-intimacy and non-solidarity. In Brown & Gilman's renowned exposition of the underlying semantics of the pronouns of address (Brown & Gilman, 1972), the v form was shown to be the marker of power in terms of superiority, seniority, authority, and of non-intimacy and non-solidarity, hence the children's selection of the v form with these participants is to be expected and is perfectly consistent with v form usage reported for other languages where the t/v choice operates (see Lambert & Tucker's 1976 study).

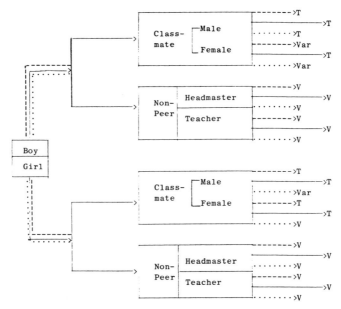

FIGURE 16.1   *Flow chart of the pronoun of address sent*

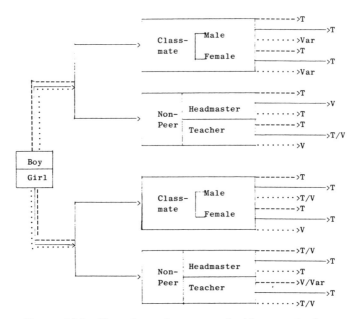

FIGURE 16.2   *Flow chart of pronoun of address received*

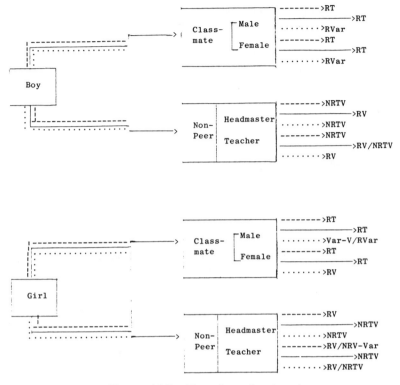

FIGURE 16.3   *Flow chart of reciprocity*

In addressing the children, the patterns reported indicate an urban–rural divide, with headmaster and teacher operating a degree of sex distinction in the rural setting. From headmaster, urban boys, L1 and L2, report receiving T, but rural boys report receiving V; rural girls and UL2 girls, however, report receiving T, with UL1 girls reporting that they receive T and V equally. These patterns show that in the rural, but not the urban setting, headmaster makes a sex distinction sending T to girls, but V to boys.

From teacher, rural boys report receiving T and V equally whilst UL1 boys receive T mostly and UL2 boys receive V mostly; urban girls, L1 and L2, report receiving T and V forms equally but rural girls report T as the majority form received. Again the patterns indicate that in the rural setting, teacher, like headmaster, sends T more often to girls than to boys.

TABLE 16.1   *Majority* sent *and* received *responses for the four interactions*

| | Sent | | | | Received | | | |
| | Classmate | | Head- | | Classmate | | Head- | |
	Male	Female	teacher	Teacher	Male	Female	teacher	Teacher
RB	T	T	V	V	T	T	V	T/V
RG	T	T	V	V	T	T	T	T
UL1B	T	var	V	V	T	T	T	T
UL1G	T	T	V	V	T	T	T/V	V/var
UL2B	T	var	V	V	var	var	T	V
UL2G	var	V	V	V	T/V	V	T	T/V

TABLE 16.2   *Majority* reciprocity *patterns for the four interactions*

| | Classmates | | Headmaster | Teacher |
	Male	Female		
RB	RT	RT	RV	RV/NRTV
RG	RT	RT	NRTV	NRTV
UL1B	RT	RT	NRTV	NRTV
UL1G	RT	RT	RV	RV/NRV–var
UL2B	Rvar	Rvar	NRTV	RV
UL2G	var–V	RV	NRTV	RV/NRTV

This brief study can offer no explanation as to why this sex distinction is made in the rural setting. However, given the semantics of the T and V forms, one can surmise that it might be that the headmaster and teacher select the V form with boys for disciplinary and authoritarian purposes, employing it to mark distance between them, hence reinforcing their now superior status; the selection of the T form with girls might indicate a more paternalistic attitude on the part of headmaster and teacher towards them. On the other hand, it could be a case of the male sex being accorded higher status than the female sex, boys then being addressed with the less familiar, more deferential V form and girls conversely receiving the familiar, less-deferential T form. Clearly a follow-up study is required to explore this matter further.

Addressing peers: Classmates, male and female

A clear L1–L2 divide emerges in the reported pattern. We will take the L1 responses first.

The responses of the rural children and the urban L1 group show quite clearly that T is the preferred form of address they employ when addressing these members of their peer group. UL1 boys, however, reported var as the major option sent to female classmates, hence there is a suggestion that they make a sex distinction here. It should be noted, however, that UL1 girls reported T as the majority form *received* from male classmates which suggests that it is actually the T form UL1 boys send most often to female classmates.

Looking at the reported patterns of the L2 children, the most striking feature is the apparent lack of preference for one form of address over another, particularly in the case of UL2 boys. The UL2 girls do have a preference for the V form when addressing female classmates, but not when addressing male classmates, var being the major pattern reported as sent to them. UL2 girls would therefore seem to be making a sex distinction here. There is a suggestion of a sex distinction in the UL2 boys' reported patterns also: T is reported as the main form of address sent to male classmates, but var to female classmates. It should be noted, however, that although UL2 boys report sending T as the major form of address to male classmates, they report var as the majority option received from male classmates and Rvar emerges as the main reciprocal pattern between them; it would seem therefore that UL2 boys do not have a clear preferred pronominal form of address with their male or female classmates.

Comparing the reported responses of the three groups of children, two features in particular emerge:

(i) A latent sex distinction seems to pervade the urban children's reported patterns, especially in the case of the urban boys. As noted above both UL1 and UL2 boys reported T as the major option sent to male classmates, but var as the major option sent to female classmates. Clearly, then, urban boys have a preference for the T form with male classmates, but not such preference when addressing female classmates. UL2 girls also, as we have noted, differed in their sent patterns between male and female classmates, having a preference for the V form with the latter, but not the former. UL1 girls and the rural children, on the other hand, make no sex distinction, RT being the majority response reported between classmates of both sexes.

(ii) In contrast to the L1 speakers, the L2 children *as a group* lack a clear preference for one form of address over another when addressing classmates.

The responses of the rural children and the UL1 group show that T is the commonest form of address the L1 children employ when addressing classmates of both sexes. This selection of the T form is to be expected since it is the marker of solidarity, and being classmates, and the same age-group, and having a comparable status within the school setting could be taken as tokens of solidarity. The T form is of course the common (but not the exclusive) pronominal form of address employed by similar groups of children in other language communities, as Lambert & Tucker's 1976 study has shown.

Nevertheless, the question that does arise from this Welsh study is, why do the L2 children as a group seem to lack a clear preferred form of address with their classmates.

Obviously, one would not expect that each child in any given group would be on terms of equal intimacy with his/her classmates and we should expect instances of the T/V choice being exploited to express such individual differences. Lambert and Tucker found, for example, that girls in their Puerto Rican survey, selected three alternative patterns, RT, NR,T–U (U: "usted") or RU in addressing female classmates of the same age (interaction 28 in their 1976 study, p. 112), and they remarked "These variations might reflect different degrees of friendliness on the part of our informants. . ." (p. 113). It would be reasonable to interpret the selection of the var option amongst our Welsh informants also as reflecting different degrees of friendliness, and indeed, all L1 children, with the exception of one sub-group, have selected the var option in varying degrees; the exception was rural girls whose choice of the T form would seem to be uncomplicated by factors such as degrees of intimacy and sex differences.

However, whilst the wish to reflect varying degrees of friendliness with classmates might account for the choice of the var option to some degree, it cannot be the only explanation for the *extent* to which UL2 children have selected this option.

Elsewhere (G. E. Jones, 1984a) I have suggested that the UL2 groups' patterns of address are to be viewed as a consequence of their competence as L2 speakers of Welsh and of the nature of the Welsh-language environ-ment in which they are acquiring Welsh. Given their learners' status, a lack of clear norm of address could be viewed as a developmental feature which will disappear as their period of socialization with Welsh-speakers becomes more extensive and their competence improves.[4]

Another contributing factor in the learners' context is that there may be linguistic interference here. Strategies to mark roles and relationships between peers do not in most varieties of English involve a TV choice of the kind offered by Welsh. To the L2 speaker this choice may seem perplexing, especially when it involves one's peers, for the roles and relationships between peers, whether their L1 be English or Welsh in the school-setting, are not necessarily different; however, the means of *expressing* them could be very different. The extensive var responses could therefore reflect the perplexity and possibly the redundancy, the choice offers these L2 speakers.

The selection of the v form as the preferred form of address between L2 girls is also possibly an instance of interference. The Welsh T form has singular reference only, though the v form has singular and plural reference. Functionally, then, it is the Welsh v form that corresponds closest to the English *you* pronoun. By selecting the v form, it could be argued that the UL2 girls are reducing language distance between their L1 and L2 — a common enough trend in bilingual situations (see Baetens Beardsmore, 1982: 101–3).

As regards the circumstances and the context in which these L2 children are acquiring Welsh, this is no doubt a major factor influencing their competence in Welsh. As has already been noted the L2 children's contact with Welsh is severely circumscribed: they lack Welsh-speaking kin, have limited membership of a Welsh-language institution such as the chapel and they live in a highly anglicized society. Furthermore, the school setting to which most of their Welsh-language activities are confined has a very high ratio of L2 to L1 speakers.[5] In this school setting there is some evidence (G. E. Jones, 1984a: 140–1) that there is a code of Welsh being evolved which bears many of the features of the kind of language characteristic of learners, variously referred to as "interlanguage" (Selinker, 1972), "approximative systems" (Nemser, 1971), "learner language systems" (Sampson & Richards, 1973) or, in Welsh, *iaith dysgwyr*, "learners' language". Some of the features of this *iaith dysgwyr* are "wrong" gender attribution, non-observation of mutation rules, simplification of tenses (see G. E. Jones, 1984a: 141), the latter interestingly noted as a feature of Welsh Foreigner Talk by C. James (1986: 48). Given these circumstances, it is not perhaps surprising that most of the L2 children selected var ("it depends") as the major option when reporting their forms of address.

Notes to Chapter 16

1. On the background to these schools see Khleif (1976).
2. In the questionnaire these two participants were described as *merch yn eich dosbarth*, 'a girl in your class'; and *bachgen yn eich dosbarth*, 'a boy in your class'.

3. These are based on the tables below which contain the *majority* responses for each of the four interactions. The actual scores on which they are based are to be found in the Jones & Thomas (1981) study and the G.E. Jones (1984a) study.

4. Susan M. Ervin-Tripp (1974) has shown that the kind of errors committed by younger age-group children in their L2 will have been eradicated in the speech of older age-group L2 speakers.

5. The number of non-Welsh-speaking children admitted to the Welsh nursery schools in the years relevant to our UL2 children is not available, but figures for those who entered the Welsh-medium nursery schools in south Glamorgan in September 1985 are as follows: total number of children admitted, 350; of these 92 were classed as Welsh-speaking, that is L1 speakers, the remaining 258 being classed as 'learners'. Figures supplied by *Mudiad Ysgolion Meithrin* (The Welsh Nursery Schools Movement).

17 The development of the nasal mutation in the speech of schoolchildren

LYNFA HATTON

Introduction

This chapter is based on an investigation conducted at Ysgol Gymraeg, Bryn-y-môr, Swansea, between 1978 and 1980. In these children's speech the nasal mutation seemed to be a fluctuating and inconsistent morphonological phenomenon. It occured more consistently in some grammatical contexts than others, and the exact situation in which responses were elicited seemed to be a very important conditioning factor. Furthermore, the identity of the speaker in terms of age, linguistic background and intellectual ability had a bearing upon the incidence of the nasal mutation. A spectrum of speakers representing such sociological variables was therefore selected and each speaker was recorded in two different situations — in a formal question-and-answer interview and in free conversation with the investigator.

The analysis of the data proved that in general the children were aware of the formalizing process and used more formal patterns of speech in a more formal situation. It was also proved that a child's variation in register depended upon his linguistic background.

Informant selection

Having decided that linguistic background[1] would be the most important factor to consider in this survey, a questionnaire was sent to each family which had a child of junior school age at Ysgol Bryn-y-môr, to obtain information concerning the children's linguistic background. After an analysis of this information, the children were divided into three groups:

(1)   Children with two Welsh-speaking parents;
(2)   Children with one Welsh-speaking parent;
(3a)   Children with monoglot English parents but having a Welsh
       background (i.e. a Welsh-speaking grandparent);
(3b)   Children with no Welsh at all in their family background.

The questionnaires established that the majority of parents in Groups 1 and 2 originated from the area between the rivers Tywi and Neath. It was then decided to further stratify the register according to parents' birthplace and have an additional group which might assist in ascertaining the influence of the school upon the children's language.

The final classification was:

Group (A):   Both mother and father speak Welsh as a first
              language and originate from the Tywi–Neath area.
Group (Bi):   The mother speaks Welsh as a first language and
              originates from the Tywi–Neath area.
   (Bii):   The father speaks Welsh as a first language and
              originates from the Tywi–Neath area.
Group (Ci):   Monoglot English parents but having a Welsh
              background.
   (Cii):   No Welsh background at all.
Group (CHi): Both parents speak Welsh and originate from
              outside the Tywi–Neath area.
   (CHii):   One Welsh-speaking parent and that parent
              originating from outside the Twyi–Neath area.

The children of the school were thus classified into the four groups A, B, C, CH, but further listed according to their class from eldest to youngest within each group. The random sampling technique was used on these lists to give a sample of 20% from each linguistic group.

In order to ensure that such a sample was indeed representative, the index in Table 17.1 was compiled.

By using this index a score was given to each child. This proved a valuable check that the sampling techniques were reliable in that the final sample contained a spectrum of possible scores. The stratified random-sampling technique however was not followed strictly. Such a technique may be perfectly adequate to satisfy the needs of sociologists, but for a linguistic survey of this kind it is too mechanical. After working random tables on the lists of the different groups, nine informants had to be added to the original sample for it to be acceptably representative. The final sample of 26 children was believed to represent a fair cross-section of the children of Ysgol Bryn-y-môr.

Table 17.1

		Points
(A)	*Parents' language*	
	First-language mother	10
	First-language father	10
	Second-language mother	4
	Second-language father	4
	English-speaking mother	0
	English-speaking father	0
(B)	*Parents' use of language*	
	Mother speaking Welsh to child	10
	Father speaking Welsh to child	10
(C)	*Children's use of language*	
	Child speaking Welsh to mother	10
	Child speaking Welsh to father	10
	Child speaking Welsh to brothers/sisters	10
	Total possible	70

The final sample is given in Table 17.2.

Table 17.2

Linguistic group	*Number of children*
A	10[a]
B	7
C	4[b]
CH	5
Total	26

a: The parents of one child in Group A did not reply to my letter. There were no other children of similar background so Group A lost one informant.
b: Also, during the time of my visits to the school one of Group C left the school. It was by then too late to replace him.

Linguistic sampling

The data collected by traditional dialectologists was restricted to one social situation only and it was assumed that this gave a realistic and representative outline of the dialects in question. The interview situation however tends to produce responses which are registrally and stylistically controlled by the question-and-answer framework. It produces examples of careful speech.

Therefore, to be truly representative of informants' usage, the data need to be based on a spectrum of social situations which should therefore produce examples of stylistic variation which occur normally within communities. Sociolinguists since the 1960s have attempted to encompass different registral variation by working on a casual–formal scale and the inclusion of interview responses and examples of spontaneous speech is one common factor in the works of Labov (1966a; 1970; 1972a, c); Trudgill (1974b); Macaulay (1976, 1977) and Milroy & Milroy (1978).

Biondi (1975), Reid (1976) and Romaine (1975, 1979) worked specifically with children and showed that the timing and degree of style-shifting is an interesting phenomenon. Within a bilingual setting I assumed that this would be an important factor to record and analyse, in view of the fact that conflicting views and opinions have been put forward over the last two decades. Labov (1972a) and Wolfram & Fasold (1974) assert that there is very little stylistic variation in the pre-adolescent stage, and that during these years a child is to all intents and purposes a "monostylistic" speaker. Based on their work in Edinburgh, Reid (1976) and Romaine (1979) challenge this viewpoint, arguing that stylistic patterns are fairly well established during primary school years.

In this survey, two components are included:

(i)   Linguistic questionnaire; and
(ii) Casual speech, in order to detect and outline degrees in style shifting if they occurred at all.

The linguistic questionnaire

One thing which is emphasised by sociologists and linguists alike (for example Moser, 1958; Pickford, 1956), about designing a questionnaire is length — a questionnaire should not be too long. As I was working with children and assuming that they would tire easily, it was decided to use a short questionnaire.

According to Welsh Grammar books,[2] the nasal mutation occurs in three situations:

(i)   After the first person singular possessive pronoun, *fy*, for example *fy nghath*, "my cat".
(ii) After the preposition *yn*, "in", which becomes *yng* before *ng*, *ngh*

and *ym* before "m", "mh" for example *Yng Nghaerdydd*, "in Cardiff".

(iii) In the words *blwydd*, "year" *blynedd*, "years" *diwrnod*, "day" after the numerals *pum*, *saith*, *wyth*, *naw*, *deg*, *deuddeg*, *pymtheg*, *deunaw*, *ugain*, *deugain* etc., *can* and the compound numerals containing *un*, *pum*, *saith*, *wyth*, *naw*, *deg*, *deuddeg*, *pymtheg*, *deunaw*.

Therefore these three situations were included in the questionnaire.

The questionnaire is based mainly upon the children giving the Welsh translation equivalents for English examples, but in the second part of the questionnaire, the children were asked to complete a pattern. This was done to ascertain whether there was any difference in these children's patterns when they were dealing with one language only, compared with instances when they were dealing with two languages.

Conversation

Each child participated in five sessions of conversation with the investigator. Once again the sessions were brief in order to sustain the child's interest.

As an introduction to the first conversation, a questionnaire was used,[3] the use of which fulfilled two aims; firstly it was used to overcome the problem of shyness. For a child to speak naturally, he must become accustomed to the investigator. Secondly, it was used to confirm the information about linguistic background which was obtained from the parents, and hopefully to add to it.

Following the questionnaire, the conversation proper was begun by asking the children about their interests, school and friends. In addition, during the second interview, a technique from the work of Griffith (1976) was adopted. The children were given a series of pictures depicting a story (Richardson & Fletcher, 1968) and were asked to relate the story in their own words. This technique succeeded in eliciting speech from even the most shy child.

The results

Following the possessive pronoun *fy*

Linguistic questionnaire

In the analysis of the linguistic questionnaire, the figures obtained from the translation part of the questionnaire are kept separate from those obtained from the pattern-completing.

Translating "My. . ." produced 11 Welsh variations:

(1) *Fy* + nasal mutation[4], for example *fy nghath i* (ø + nasal mutation is also included here. (For example *'nghath i*)
(2) *Fy* + soft mutation, for example *fy gath i*
(3) *Fy* + original consonant, for example *fy defaid i*
(4) *Fy* + aspirate mutation, for example *fy chadair i*
(5) Original consonant + *fi*, for example *brawd fi*
(6) *Fy'n* + original consonant, for example *fy'n dant*
(7) *Fy'n* + nasal mutation, for example *fy'n masged*
(8) *My* + original consonant, for example *my cath*
(9) *Ei* + original consonant + *fi*, for example *ei cath fi*
(10) *Ei* + soft mutation + *fi*, for example *ei gadair fi*
(11) *Ei* + aspirate mutation + *fi*, for example *ei thafod fi*

(Only one person used the three variations (9), (10), (11). Therefore the three are combined in the analysis.)

For analytical convenience, in the results which follow, *Fy'n* was considered as a variation on the pronoun *fy* so (6) above is considered in the same cateogry as (3); likewise (7) above is considered in the same category as (1). Not everyone used each of the above variations. Only one variation was common to all members of the sample — "*Fy* + nasal mutation".

It is interesting to note that no example of the form [ən], the form of the possessive pronoun which was noted by E. C. Rees (1958) in his study of the dialect of the Vale of Loughor, was obtained in this study.

Figure 17.1 shows the average percentage occurrence of the nasal mutation following *fy* for each class in the school.[5] The graph reveals that the nasal mutation in this situation is established in each class. It also reveals the development in the use of the nasal mutation with age — the older the child, the more likely he or she is to use the nasal mutation after the personal pronoun *fy*. The relationship between the use of the nasal mutation and age suggests the influence of formal teaching, that is the influence of the school, upon these children's patterns. It is completely evident from this graph that linguistic development occurs between the ages of seven and eleven. This supports that which Reid (1976) and Romaine (1979) suggest.

The graph also shows that in each age group a higher occurrence of "*Fy* + nasal mutation" was obtained in the second section of the question-

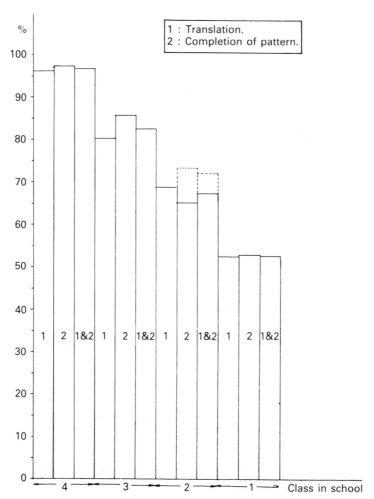

FIGURE 17.1   *Average percentage occurrence of the nasal mutation following* fy *for each class in school*

TABLE 17.3   *The difference in the percentage occurrence of the nasal mutation in the two sections of the questionnaire*

Class	Difference (%)
4	1.14
3	5.67
2	4.38
1	0.49

TABLE 17.4   *Percentage occurrence of nasal mutation following* fy *for each linguistic group*

Group	Fy + nasal mutation (%)
A	60.70
B	77.34
C[5]	46.26
CH	89.65

naire — completion of a pattern. Thus it can be said that these children are more likely to use the nasal mutation when using one language than when using two. However, as Table 17.3 reveals, the difference between the two sections is hardly significant.

Table 17.3 indicates that the difference in the use of nasal mutation between the two sections of the questionnaire increases as one moves up the school from Class 1 to Class 3 but then decreases in Class 4. This decrease in Class 4 can be explained by the fact that the nasal mutation was consistently used after *fy* by the children of the class in both sections of the questionnaire.

The patterns on Figure 17.1 and in Table 17.3 suggest that translation is a less formal situation for these children. Many of them have learnt Welsh as a second language and are more accustomed to translating than completing a pattern. A higher percentage of the nasal mutation was recorded in the more formal of the two situations, that is the completion of a pattern. The evidence in Table 17.3 and Figure 17.1 suggests that formalizing increases with age.

Table 17.4 reflects the correlation between the use of the nasal mutation after *fy* and the linguistic background of the speakers. The children of Group C have monoglot English parents whilst the children of each other group have a varying amount of Welsh in their background. The children of Group C speak no Welsh outside school and the above results show that this group gave the lowest percentage of nasal mutation following *fy*. Thus, with no Welsh in the home, the nasal mutation following *fy* develops at a later age within this group.

However, linguistic background is not the only factor influencing those children's patterns as the results in Table 17.4 prove. The children of Group A have a more thoroughly Welsh background than those of Group B and the majority of Group CH. However groups B and CH were more consistent in their use of the nasal mutation than Group A. A child's ability was not considered during informant selection and as a result the average intelligence of the groups varies. In the detailed analysis of individuals' use of the mutation in her MA thesis (Hatton, 1983), it was proved that use of the nasal mutation following *fy* is also conditioned to a child's intellectual ability. This correlation with ability is reflected in the results in Table 17.4 and partially explains the higher average scores of Groups B and CH. This also shows that linguistic/sociological correlations are not simplistic and more often than not there may be several extra-linguistic factors which may condition a variable although one could be considered the dominant factor. In this particular case linguistic background is a prime factor, but on its own it does not reveal the whole picture.

Conversation

In the analysis of the conversation four variations were obtained:

(1) *Fy* + nasal mutation, for example *fyngwyliau*
(2) *Fy* + soft mutation, for example *fy ddau mamgu*
(3) *Fy* + original consonant, for example *fy beic*
(4) Original consonant + *fi*, for example *tadcu fi*.

Once again, no example of the form [ɛn] was elicited. A number of the examples obtained in the conversation unfortunately began with either a consonant which does not take nasal mutation or with a vowel. However, such examples were included to discover which pattern was used more consistently by these children as they spoke naturally — the possessive pronoun *fy* followed by a noun (e.g. *fy ffrind*) or a noun followed by the pronoun *fi* (e.g. *ffrind fi*).

In Table 17.5, the relationship between age and language patterns is again evident. The norm amongst the older children is to use the more formal patterns, *fy* + noun, whilst the normal amongst Classes 1 and 2 is the less formal noun + *fi*. Two interpretations could be given to the figures in Table 17.5.

(1) The formal pattern *fy* + noun develops in the natural speech of these children sometime between Classes 2 and 3.

(2) It has already been suggested that these children are conscious of formalizing and that this develops with age. Although speaking to the investigator is a less formal situation than answering a questionnaire, the older children appear to react more formally to such a conversation than the younger children and use more formal patterns.

In this particular context, neither interpretation is unrelated nor independent of the other. One sees clearly that *fy* + nasal mutation is a pattern which is learnt as pupils progress along the educational ladder from the lower to the upper classes of the primary school. Secondly it signifies sociolinguistic acculturation with an awareness of formal linguistic patterns and the spread of such prestige patterns into spontaneous speech.

Figure 17.2 compares the occurrence of the nasal mutation following *fy* in the questionnaire with that in conversation for each class.The graph reveals that in each class the use of the nasal mutation is more consistent in the questionnaire than in conversation. This proves that each age group is conscious of formalizing and varies its language patterns according to the formality of the situation.

Figure 17.2 also reveals the correlation between age and use of the nasal mutation in both questionnaire and conversation. In both situations there is unmistakable development in the pattern between the ages of seven and eleven. In reply to the questionnaire, the use of the nasal mutation develops gradually from Classes 1 to 4, while in conversation there is a marked development between Classes 2 and 3. In the detailed

TABLE 17.5   *Average percentage occurrence of the two patterns,* fy + *noun and* noun + fi *for each class*[6]

Class	Fy + *noun* (%)	*Noun* + fi (%)
4	62.16	37.84
3	81.08	18.92
2	11.11	88.89
1	33.33	66.67

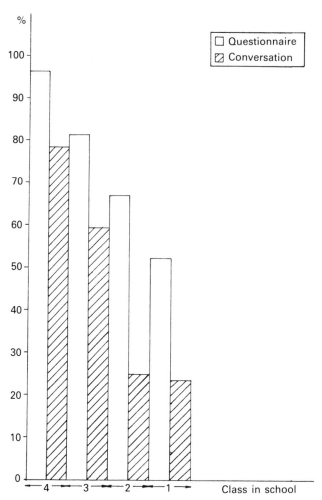

FIGURE 17.2   *Comparison of results from questionnaire and conversation for "fy + nasal mutation"*

analysis of each individual's results (Hatton, 1983) it is suggested that the initial development of the nasal mutation following *fy* occurs during Classes 1 and 2, but inconsistencies persist. Between Classes 2 and 3 the mutation stabilizes in the patterns of the children as exemplified by the fact that what were formerly characteristics of "careful speech" have now spread into spontaneous speech.

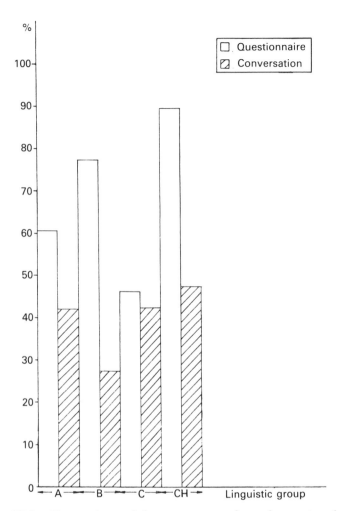

FIGURE 17.3   *Comparison of the percentage of nasal mutation following*
fy *in the questionnaire and in conversation for the linguistic groups*

Figure 17.3 compares the percentage of nasal mutation following *fy*
in the questionnaire and in the conversation for each linguistic group.
From the graph it can be seen that the use of the nasal mutation in the
less formal situation is very similar for each group with the exception of
Group B. The school is the only common factor for Groups A, C and
CH so these results reflect the influence of the formal teaching of the
school on their language patterns, even in an informal situation. In the

case of Group B speakers, the nasal mutation patterns within the immediate family are reflected in their spontaneous speech style. The nasal mutation is in fact an inconsistent feature in the dialects of the area.

Each group is less consistent in its use of the nasal mutation in the conversation than in the questionnaire and is therefore conscious of formalizing. However, notice how slight the difference between the two situations is in Group C's results. The formal patterns of the school are the only influence on the speech of the children of this group and as a result they are monostylistic; they do not have the same variety of register as the children of the other groups.

Following the preposition *yn* "in"

The questionnaire

Six variations were obtained from the children as they translated "In. . .":

(1) *yn* + nasal mutation,[4] for example *Yng Nghaerdydd*
(2) *yn* + original consonant, for example *Yn Talgarth*
(3) *yn* + soft mutation, for example *Yn Frynaman*
(4) *Mewn* + original consonant, for example *Mewn Gorseinon*
(5) *Mewn* + soft mutation, for example *Mewn Dreforus*
(6) *in* + original consonant, for example *In Brynaman*.

Yn + original consonant is the only variation common to each child.
Variations (4) and (5) above are rather unexpected and for analytical convenience, (4) and (5) are considered to be a contraction of *mewn yn*. Examples of (4) above are included with examples of (2); likewise, examples of (5) are considered with examples of (3).

Results

By comparing the results from Table 17.6 with the graph (Figure 17.1) it is completely evident that the nasal mutation following *yn* is far less established in the speech of these children than the nasal mutation following *fy*. According to S. J. Williams (1959), there is a tendency in contemporary spoken Welsh not to mutate place names after *yn* and in some instances to have a soft mutation rather than a nasal mutation. The results in Table 17.6 reflect the tendency not to use the the nasal mutation after *yn*. However, the tendency to use the soft mutation in its place is not strong in the language of these children either.

TABLE 17.6   *Percentage of the occurrence of the different variations for each class*

Class	yn + nasal mutation (%)	yn + original consonant (%)	yn + soft mutation (%)	yn + original consonant (%)
4	37.03	50.00	12.96	0
3	19.84	70.63	9.52	0
2	3.33	92.22	4.44	0
1	4.94	89.5	3.08	2.47

Once again the use of the nasal mutation correlates with age, with the nasal mutation being more productive in the patterns of those children in Classes 3 and 4 than of those in Classes 1 and 2. Indeed the nasal mutation after *yn* is rarely used by children in Classes 1 and 2. Notice the development in the nasal mutation between Classes 2 and 3. This suggests that the basic development in the nasal mutation after the preposition *yn* begins in Class 3.

These results again indicate that linguistic development occurs between the ages of seven and eleven years. The results also reflect the influence of the school's formal education on the children's patterns.

As the figures in Table 17.7 indicate, the norm for each linguistic group is to retain the original consonant after *yn*. As previously noted, S. J. Williams (1959) says there is a tendency in contemporary spoken Welsh not to mutate place names after *yn* so it is likely that the results of groups A, B and CH reflect the influence of their parents on their language patterns by retaining the initial consonant.

However, the home is not the only influence as the use of the nasal mutation by each group is very similar. The school is the only factor common to the four groups, therefore the results also reflect the influence of the school on the children's language patterns. The influence of the school is particularly evident when one considers the results of Group C. Following *fy*, where the nasal mutation continues to be used in contemporary spoken Welsh, Group C's use of the nasal mutation was not as consistent as that of other groups (cf. Table 17.4). However, following *yn*, Group C is more consistent in its use of the nasal mutation than either B or CH. As the children of Group C do not speak Welsh outside school, their patterns reflect the formal patterns of their teachers.

The results in Table 17.7 therefore reflect two conflicting influences on the children's speech in this situation:
(i)   The home, influencing the children not to mutate after *yn*.
(ii) The school, teaching the children to mutate nasally after *yn*.

TABLE 17.7   *Results of the three main variations following* yn *for each linguistic group*

Group	yn + nasal mutation (%)	yn + original consonant (%)	yn + soft mutation (%)
A	17.28	77.77	4.94
B	7.14	84.91	7.94
C	14.81	72.22	5.55
CH	12.22	80.00	7.77

Conversation

The results in Table 17.8 clearly indicate that the nasal mutation following *yn* is rarely used in conversation by these children. The norm in each class is to retain the initial consonant. Thus the nasal mutation following *yn* is far less developed than that following *fy*.

Comparing the above figures with those in Table 17.6, it is seen that the same pattern emerges as in Figure 17.2, namely that there is a higher incidence of nasal mutation following *yn* in the questionnaire than in the conversation in each class. This is further proof that these children are aware of formalizing and vary their speech patterns according to the formality of the situation.

The figures in Table 17.9 clearly indicate that the pattern in each linguistic group is to retain the initial consonant after *yn*. Notice that the highest percentage occurrence of the nasal mutation is found in Group C, the group with no Welsh at home. These results therefore reflect the way in which the home and the school influence the language patterns of these children. Groups A, B and CH are influenced by the dialects of the parents to retain the original consonant after *yn*; they are also influenced by the school to use the nasal mutation after *yn*. Group C have

TABLE 17.8   *Percentage occurrence of variations in speech patterns following* yn *for each class*[6]

Class	yn + nasal mutation (%)	yn + original consonant (%)	yn + soft mutation (%)
4	0	100	0
3	8.89	88.33	2.78
2	0	97.50	2.50
1	4.17	95.83	0

TABLE 17.9   *Percentage occurrence of variations in speech patterns following* yn
for each group

Group	yn + nasal mutation (%)	yn + original consonant (%)	yn + soft mutation (%)
A	2.5	97.5	0
B	0	98.2	1.79
C	16.67	83.34	0
CH	8.33	87.50	4.17

only one influence on their Welsh language patterns, that of the school and so the nasal mutation is more established amongst these children.

A comparison of the figures in Table 17.8 with those in Table 17.6 again reveals the lack of variation in register of Group C. They are the only group in any situation to produce a higher occurrence of nasal mutation in the less formal situation. In whatever situation the children of Group C find themselves, they tend to use the same register, that which reflects the formal teaching of the school, as that is the only register they have when speaking Welsh.

In the words *blwydd, blynedd, diwrnod* following the numerals *pum,*
saith, wyth, naw, deg, deuddeg, pymtheg, deunaw, deugain* etc.

The questionnaire

This section of the questionnaire proved difficult to analyse for a number of reasons:

(i)   variation in the forms of the numerals (e.g. the use of *un deg pump* instead of *pymtheg* etc.);
(ii) other lexical varieties of the forms which mutate;
(iii) answers which did not include the forms which mutate (e.g. *yn saith oed* instead of *yn saith mlwydd oed*);
(iv) confused or incorrect answers.

As a result, a large proportion of answers had to be ignored so that the results for this section are possibly less reliable than those of the other sections. In addition, due to this problem, insufficient data were obtained to satisfactorily analyse the results class by class or group by group; it was only possible to analyse the results of the sample as a whole.

For analysis, the examples of *blwydd, blynedd, diwrnod* and their mutated forms, are classified under three headings:

(i) Numeral + nasal mutation (i.e. the examples of *mlwydd, mlynedd, niwrnod*)

(ii) Numeral + initial consonant (i.e. the examples of *blwydd, blynedd, diwrnod*)

(iii) Numeral + soft mutation (i.e. the examples of *flwydd, flynedd, ddiwrnod*).

TABLE 17.10 *The percentage of examples of the three variations above obtained from the entire sample*

Numeral + nasal mutation	47.34
Numeral + initial consonant	46.81
Numeral + soft mutation	5.85

TABLE 17.11

	Seven years old (%)	For seven years (%)	For seven days (%)
Numeral + Nasal mutation	56.41	50	6.9
Numeral + initial consonant	39.31	45	79.3
Numeral + soft mutation	4.27	4.76	13.79

From Table 17.10 it is seen that a slightly higher percentage of nasal mutation than retention of initial consonant was obtained although the difference was very slight. However, a different result is obtained when one separates the results for the three elements which mutate as shown in Table 17.11. The norm for the sample was to use the nasal mutation of *blwydd* and *blynedd*. However, the nasal mutation of *diwrnod* is extremely rare. These results agree with Samuel J. Evans (1908: 92).

"The nasal mutation takes place after. . .

(iii) The cardinal numerals *pum, saith, wyth, naw, deg, deuddeng, pymtheng, ugain* and its compound, *can*, when followed by:
1. *blwydd, blynedd*. . .
2. *diwrnod*, though this not *infrequently retains its radical initial.*"

Conclusion

This study therefore produced interesting information about the nasal mutation in the language patterns of these children. Firstly, mutating in some situations is more established than in others. For example, in the questionnaire, following the personal pronoun *fy*, the norm in the language of children of every class is to use the nasal mutation. Following the preposition *yn* the nasal mutation is less frequently used and in the speech of some children it is not used at all.

Secondly, the development in the use of the nasal mutation between the ages of seven and eleven is indisputable. This development reflects the influence of the school (that is, the teachers' norms on the patterns of these children). From the results obtained it was possible to establish the time when the different patterns begin to develop in the language of these children. Following *fy* the nasal mutation begins to develop in Classes 1 and 2 while the pattern is quite established by Class 3. On the other hand the initial development of the nasal mutation following *yn* does not occur until Class 3.

Although the development in the nasal mutation may be discussed within the framework of age, it must be remembered that age is not the only factor to consider. Three factors are interrelated in the use of nasal mutation by these children namely, ability, linguistic background and age. None is independent of the others.

The influence of linguistic background is evident when considering their registral variation. The pupils of Group C do not possess the same registral variation as the pupils of the other groups. Group C reflect the formal patterns of the teachers however informal a situation they may be in, while the children of the other groups adapt their patterns of speech according to the formality of a situation.

It has been seen how the use of the nasal mutation develops with age. Also, consciousness of formalizing occurs between the ages of seven and eleven. This was seen in a comparison of the two sections of the questionnaire — translating and pattern completion. Translation was considered to be a less formal situation than pattern completion for these children; a lower occurrence of nasal mutation was obtained in the less formal situation showing that the children were conscious of formalizing.

The consciousness of formalizing was again evident in the comparison of the results obtained from the questionnaire with those obtained from the conversation. The questionnaire was the more formal situation and following both *fy* and *yn* a higher occurrence of nasal mutation was obtained from the questionnaire than from the conversation. There is no doubt that these children adapt their patterns of speech to suit the formality of the situation.

Notes to Chapter 17

1. English linguistic surveys use social class as a factor in informant selection. However, it was felt that social class would not be a relevant factor in this study. See Griffith, 1976 and A. R. Jones, 1969; 1970.
2. The Welsh Grammar books consulted are: Anwyl, 1901; S. J. Evans, 1908, 1909; Morris-Jones, 1913; D. T. Evans, 1915; Morgan, 1952; Williams, 1959; Bowen & Jones, 1960; J. J. Evans, 1960; H. M. Evans, 1961; M. D. Jones, 1965.
3. This was based on the work of M. E. G. Rees (1954). Her questionnaire intended that the children wrote their answers so it was adapted for oral responses.
4. The following were also considered as examples of nasal mutation: c → ng; p → m; t → n.
5. In the second part of the questionnaire, the results of one member of Class 2 (group C) were completely idiolectical. To ignore these results completely would cause an imbalance so the mean of Class 2 with C3 and without C3 was found. This mean is represented by the broken line on the graph.
6. In the tables and graphs relating to the results from the conversation, the results of a child giving only one example were not considered. Placing 100% in a table when this was based on one example only could cause the results to be false and unreliable.

18 Phonological disorders in Welsh-speaking children

SIÂN M. MUNRO

Traditionally, speech pathology has utilized normal language development as the starting point in formulating techniques for assessment and remediation. If this trend is to be continued and extended, so that Welsh-speaking children are better catered for, more information needs to be made available regarding the normal development of the Welsh language. As most of these children also have some degree of English, this need for information is extended to the development of Welsh–English bilingualism, the relationship between the two languages being an important aspect of acquisition. Such information then provides a potential yardstick for describing abnormal acquisition.

However, descriptions of the patterns of disordered speech and language do not provide an explanation of *how* each child achieved these patterns. One method of attempting such an explanation is by applying some procedure which will look at the strategies adopted by a child and which will be sufficiently fundamental to serve both languages. The search is for a general set of organizational principles which will account for aspects of children's abnormal language behaviour.

The study upon which this chapter is based (Munro, 1985) was concerned with principles of this nature. Although the original study dealt with various levels of language performance, including the grammatical, its main concern was with segmental phonology. Owing to limitations on space, it is the latter level which is highlighted here, though, of course, many of the methodological issues originally presented during the phonological analysis were also pertinent to the analyses at other linguistic levels. These issues were many and varied but were encapsulated in the following aims:

(i) to obtain data directly from clinical contexts;
(ii) to determine acceptability or otherwise of a child's patterns from a bi-rather than a monolingual standpoint, thereby considering collective competence;

258

(iii) to avoid direct translation from English materials.

The emphasis, then, was on assessment, though implications for remediation were also considered.

The two subjects chosen were from one area of Wales, namely the
Swansea Valley (Cwmtawe). Selection was restricted to this area because
its speech patterns were those most familiar to the author, thus facilitating
the necessary distinction, during assessment, between regional variation
and idiosyncracy. Previous experience had suggested that the clinical
population was no different from other parts of Wales, therefore restriction
of the study to one such region was not considered to be rendering the
results inapplicable to the country as a whole. The dialectal and accent
characteristics of Cwmtawe Welsh and English were described in the
original work but are not included here.

Similarly, the details of data selection cannot be described although
some of the main points are included as they constitute important aspects
of any approach to clinical phonological analysis, particularly in bilingual
contexts. One of the first criteria in selecting data was that they should
provide the basis for a phonetic analysis involving a description of speech
without reference to its linguistic functions. In order to ensure that the
sample was comprehensive, further criteria were applied namely: that a
particular phoneme should be sampled word-initially, -medially and
-finally, that it should be elicited by several stimulus words in order that the
effects of varying contexts were considered, and that decisions regarding
correctness of production should be based on more than a single response
per phoneme type.

The responses were elicited from a picture-naming task, there being
186 English words and 182 Welsh, including lexical borrowings. The status
of borrowed words is controversial and it may be argued that words
borrowed from English should not have been included in the Welsh
section. However, many of the words were totally integrated into the
Welsh language and had been for many years, particularly in anglicized
areas like Cwmtawe. Where native Welsh forms existed as 'competitors'
to borrowed forms the former were usually selected.

Phonetic transcription of whole words ensured that any additional
information about a consonant or consonant cluster was noted. However,
despite such efforts to gain as comprehensive a set of information as
possible, some consonants and clusters were not incorporated, for example
those never/infrequently occurring in particular word-positions or those
which could not easily be illustrated. Also avoided were separate categories of stimulus words reflecting a division of word-medial consonants into

those which were syllable-initial and those syllable-final. (Although this exclusion is only briefly mentioned here, the original study contained detailed discussions of the controversies regarding the manner of syllable division and of its possible significance in clinical terms.)

Of course, any study of developing phonology could not concern itself only with inventories of speech sounds, one had also to consider the distribution of segments in words and processes which might affect that distribution. Furthermore, an indication was required as to whether the segments were used contrastively. In other words, a phonological analysis was needed, hence the reason for phonetic transcription of whole words rather than of individual speech sounds, isolated from their contexts.

Even with this provision, a limitation remained which was the result of adopting the three-position format, that is the procedure was word-oriented. As words do not appear as separate entities but as a sequence of syllables, and as articulation of single words is not truly representative of a child's abilities, the study provided additional information via a sample of continuous speech for each subject.

Phonetic transcriptions were made by the author during the picture-naming sessions in order to make maximum use of visual information. As this was not feasible during spontaneous conversation, transcriptions from tapes were made as soon as possible after the recording. In both cases, impressionistic transcription was made, this being a particularly detailed record, suitable for clinical purposes.

Having completed the transcriptions, preliminary analyses were undertaken which were termed "phonetic" analyses. This term was applied as it was largely concerned with identification and description of the speech sounds produced by the subjects; as the full pattern-forming capabilities of the speech sounds were not investigated at this stage, the term "phonetic" was felt to be appropriate. The distinction was, of course, an artificial one as phonetic and phonological approaches are usually intermingled but the distinction was retained in order to distinguish between earlier and later analyses.

Consonants and vowels were analysed separately, but in view of the absence of significant difficulty with vowel production[1] for both subjects, remaining sections dealt only with consonant production. With reference to these consonants, the effects of grammatical and lexical complexity were scrutinized but were found to be of little relevance.

The preliminary phonetic analyses (and later approaches) were largely based on the work of Grunwell (1977) though modifications[2] for the requirements of bilingual contexts were the concern of the current author. One such modification arose in calculating the correspondences between adult target phonemes and subjects' realizations (see Figures 18.3, 18.4,

18.7 and 18.8); Grunwell combined several types of realizations under the term "zero" correspondence as follows: (i) nil, (ii) [ʔ], (iii) tentative, and (iv) non-English.

The examples given by her of type (iv) were [ɬ] and [x]. To label these as zero correspondences for Welsh–English bilingual children would have been unfair. While it might have been argued that [ɬ] and [x] did not appear in the English of adult Welsh–English bilinguals (excluding borrowing) and were therefore 'foreign' to it, the exposure of the children to these phonemes and the potential for intrusion from one language to another created a different relationship between target inventories and children's realizations.

Results

During the preliminary analyses, separate profiles were presented for each language. The main reason for this was that when dealing with language-learning problems in bilingual children, an important distinction has to be made between a limited exposure to one of the languages which would detrimentally affect only that language, and a true pathology which affects any and all languages attempted. As speech therapy is concerned with the latter, separate considerations of each language were required initially in order to make this fundamental distinction.

Subject (S1): Nigel – chronological age 8 years 9 months

The following figures show s1 Nigel's profiles in the two languages. Figure 18.1 and 18.2 refer to the realization of individual target phonemes and do not include consonant clusters. The inventories for Welsh and English were similar, with the range of audible units being largely restricted to liquids, glides and nasals. As might be expected with such limited inventories, there was no intrusion from one language into another.

The formulation of the inventories for s1: Nigel highlighted some of his basic inadequacies, but only in a limited way. A further perspective was gained by comparing his phonetic units with the corresponding adult targets (see Figure 18.3 and 18.4). While there are arguments for considering the independent nature of abnormal child phonologies (see later) there remains, inevitable, a dependency of the child's patterns upon those of the adult.

	Bilabial	Labiodental	Dental and alveolar	Palatal	Glottal
Stop					ʔ[2 3] [h]
Nasal	m		n		
Liquid			l		
Fricative		(v)[1]			h
Frictionless continuant		ʋ[2] [ʔ]			
Glide	w			j	
Non-audible release	m⌐[2] [ʔ]				

1. [v] four tokens.
   Note: Tokens are considered to be limited if they number five or less.
2. Diacritics [ʔ], [h] denote infrequent phonetic variants.
3. [ʔ] occasionally occurs with [m⌐] in the configuration [m⌐ʔ] as realization of target bilabial or labiodental phonemes.

FIGURE 18.1 *Complete phonetic inventory for* s1: *Nigel – Welsh*

Again, Welsh and English were similar, the most striking similarities being the large number of correct realizations for target /m/ and /n/, and the weighting towards [ʔ] and nil realizations. Differences between the languages in the numbers for these and other correspondences were frequently due to differences in the number of tokens. In both languages, there was variability in the realizations, including some language-specific variability, but the latter were not so marked, in numerical terms, as to suggest that s1: Nigel was differentiating between the two languages with respect to those particular correspondences. In the original study, further correspondences were calculated to reveal any patterns associated with word-position. Also, correspondences for consonant clusters were analysed.

Subject 2 (S2): Rhodri – chronological age 5 years 8 months

The procedures resulting in Figures 18.1 to 18.4 inclusive were repeated for s2 Rhodri.

	Bilabial	Labiodental	Dental and alveolar	Palatal	Glottal
Stop					ʔ⁴
Nasal	m	(ɱ)²	n	(ŋ)¹	
Liquid			l		
Fricative		(v)¹			h
Frictionless continuant		ʋ³ [ʔ]			
Glide	w³ [ʔ]			j	
Non-audible release	m̚³ [ʔ]				

1. [ŋ], [v] one token each.
2. [ɱ] five tokens.
3. Diacritic [ʔ] denotes infrequent phonitic variant.
4. [ʔ] quite frequently occurs with [m̚] in the configuration [m̚ʔ] as realization of target bilabial or labiodental phonemes.

FIGURE 18.2 *Complete phonetic inventory for* s1: *Nigel – English*

The inventories of speech sounds realizing individual target phonemes were different from those for Nigel in that the number and range of realizations for Rhodri were far less restricted. Despite these variations, there were similarities between the two subjects in terms of consistency between Welsh and English at this stage of the analysis for, (correct) realizations of those phonemes peculiar to the Welsh target systems ([x] and [ɬ]) appeared only in his Welsh inventories.

Rhodri's realizations for certain targets were variable and there were some inter-language differences. In fact, further analyses indicated that the lack of consistency was related to word-position. Significantly, variability was also evidenced in relation to targets which Rhodri was quite capable of articulating, for example /n/, /f/ and /v/ were always realized correctly in both languages, but there was also a high percentage correspondence between these consonants and various other target phonemes, notably fricatives. It should be pointed out that lack of correspondence was not invariably due to error on Rhodri's part. There were several instances suggestive of accent variation.

TARGET

Target \ Child's realization	m	n	v	l	w	ʊ	j	h	ʔ	mˀ	mˤ	Nil	Total
h									9			1	10
j						2							2
w					8	2							10
r/g			1		3	16	2	1	4	1		9	37
l				15								9	24
ɬ				1				1	9			4	15
ʃ									8			2	10
z									1				1
s								2	9			6	17
χ								1	2			3	6
ð						1	4	1				3	9
θ							2	1	1	1		2	7
v			3			6			2			4	15
f								1	5			2	8
ŋ	3											1	4
n		57					2		3			10	72
m	28								1				29
dʒ									3				3
tʃ									4			2	6
g									11	2		5	18
k				1					34	1		2	38
d		1							27	2		14	44
t									21	2		4	27
b		3							10	13	3	2	31
p	2								3	9	2	2	18
Total	33	61	4	17	11	27	10	8	167	31	5	87	

CHILD'S REALIZATION

FIGURE 18.3 Overall correspondences for s1: Nigel – Welsh

		p	b	t	d	k	g	tʃ	dʒ	m	n	ŋ	f	v	θ	ð	s	z	ʃ	ʒ	l	ɹ	w	j	h	
CHILD'S REALIZATION	m	3	4	1						22																30
	ɱ	1	2						1	1																5
	n				1						63	14									1					79
	ŋ											1														1
	v																					1				1
	l																				31			1		32
	w													1								1	9			11
	ʋ													4								15	8	1		28
	j										1					7		1				1		7	2	19
	h			7				1	1								2	1								12
	ʔ	12	9	31	24	21	8	9	5	1			5	4		13	21	5	8	2		2			11	191
	m̚	1	3										5	3	2											14
	mʔ		12										5	1												18
	Nil	7	3	24	7	13	9	1	2	1	4		6	2	2	4	16	20	2		4				5	132
		24	33	63	32	34	17	11	9	25	68	15	21	15	4	24	39	27	10	2	36	20	17	9	18	

FIGURE 18.4 *Overall correspondences for* SI*: Nigel – English*

	Bilabial	Labio-dental	Alveolar with Labio-dental	Dental and Alveolar	Alveolar with Palatal	Palatal	Velar	Velar with Alveolar	Uvular	Glottal
Stop	p b			t $_{[\neg]}$ $^{[h]}$ d ^{5} $_{[\neg]}$			k g			ʔ
Stop with liquid								kl¹		
Stop with fricative			tf³							
Stop with glide					dj¹					
Nasal	m			n			ŋ³			
Liquid				l						

				ð¹	χ	h¹
Fricative	f v			ð¹	χ	h¹
Lateral Fricative				ɬ⁵		
Affricate				tʃ¹		
Frictionless continuant	ʋ					
Rolled				r²		
Glide	w⁴		j³			

FIGURE 18.5 *Complete phonetic inventory for s2: Rhodri – Welsh*

1. [ð],[h],[tʃ],[dj],[kl] one token each.
2. [r] two tokens.
3. [j],[ŋ],[tʃ] three tokens.
4. [w] four tokens.
5. Diacritics [⎕], [ʰ] denote infrequent phonetic variants.

	Bilabial	Alveolar with Bilabial	Labio-dental	Alveolar with Labio-dental	Dental and Alveolar	Alveolar with Palatal	Palato-alveolar	Palatal	Velar	Glottal
Stop	p[w] b [4]				t d				k[ʋ] [4] g	ʔ
Stop with Fricative				tf¹ dv¹						
Stop with Glide		tw¹				dj²				
Nasal	m				n				ŋ[ɡ]³ [4]	
Liquid					l					
Fricative			f[ᵇ] [4] v		θ¹ ð¹		ʃ²			
Affricate					tʃ					
Frictionless Continuant			ʋ							
Rolled					r¹					
Glide	w							j³		

1. [r], [θ], [ð], [tw], [tʃ], [dv] one token each.
2. [ʃ], [dj] two tokens each.
3. [ŋ], [j] three tokens each.
4. Diacritics [ʷ], [ᵇ], [ʋ], [ɡ] denote infrequent phonetic variants. They refer to sequential rather than simultaneous articulations.

FIGURE 18.6 Complete phonetic inventory for s2: Rhodri – English

While the above analyses served to measure the degree of correspondence between (adult) target phonemes and subjects' realizations of them, they did not take into account the number of words distinguished by any particular phonemic contrast and thus the pattern-forming aspects of the child's phonology. Whether a child's difficulties are due to lack of articulatory skill and/or abnormal *organization* of speech sounds, the nature of the resultant phonological pattern is of fundamental importance in both diagnosis and intervention. The further analyses (see later) were selected because they were very much concerned with such phonological issues and because they had implications for the assessment of bilingual children.

As stated previously, the analyses were based on the work of Pamela Grunwell. Her thesis (1977) concluded that the most insightful methods were the analysis of phonological simplifying processes and a description of the child's speech as an independent phonological system. One of the advantages of the processes approach was that it could frequently deal with errors in a more principled manner. For instance, realizations on the type of correspondence analyses given above could appear to be quite diverse but could, in fact, be related to the same underlying simplifying processes.

Analysis of the child's phonological system also had advantages, mainly that it highlighted the *function* of sound patterns. This introduced the notion of contrastivity and thereby the communicative implications of the abnormal patterns.

Furthermore, these analyses could account for both intra- and inter-language variations in speech sound emergence. They were, therefore, conceived of as building on 'common denominators' and, as such, were particularly useful in cross-linguistic studies and consequently bilingualism. The search for commonality had been the basis of much research into universality, a tradition continued in this study. One's aim was to investigate a link between languages which would not only be unifying in relation to bilingualism, but would also provide a basis for comparing normality with abnormality.

In my original work (Munro, 1985), various approaches to universality were discussed as was the relationship between universality on the one hand and rules and strategies on the other. It was decided that if a rule was broadly defined as a principle to which a procedure conformed, then one's approach to processes and systems could be said to be rule-based, but the use of rules did not imply adherence to a generative framework. It was also decided that a charactertistic was deemed to be universal if it was considered to be generally available to children of differing languages, though that characteristic might be present in varying degrees.

TARGET

TARGET \ CHILD'S REALIZATION	p	b	t	tʃ	d	dj	k	kl	g	tʃ	m	n	ŋ
h													
j													
w													
r/r̥												1	
l					1								
ɬ													
ʃ													
z													
s													
χ							3						
ð													
θ			1										
v													
f													
ŋ												2	2
n											5	70	1
m											33		
dʒ					1	1							
tʃ				3									
g		6			1				22				
k	6	1	2				36		1				
d		2			52				1				
t	1		25										
b	1	33											
p	20	1											
Total	28	43	28	3	56	1	39	1	24	1	38	73	3

CHILD'S REALIZATION

CHILD'S REALISATION

	f	v	ð	χ	ɬ	l	r	w	ʊ	j	ʔ	Nil	Total
									1		4		5
										3			3
					1				4	1			6
		16				2	2		17		1	4	43
				1	30							2	34
	15				6	1							22
	9				1								10
			1										1
	26				2								28
	2			9									11
		7											7
	9												10
		16							1		1		18
	11												11
													4
		1									5		83
													33
													2
													4
											1		31
	2										1		49
		1										2	58
													29
													34
													21
Total	74	41	1	9	10	34	2	4	20	3	7	14	

FIGURE 18.7 *Overall correspondences for s2: Rhodri – Welsh*

TARGET / **CHILD'S REALISATION**

Realisation	Total	h	j	w	ɹ	l	ʒ	ʃ	z	s	ð	θ	v	f	ŋ	n	m	dʒ	tʃ	g	k	d	t	b	p
p	29																						5		24
b	37																			1		1		34	1
t	49																				2		47		
tʃ	1							1																	
tw	1																		1						
d	33																	2		3		27	1		
dv	1																	1							
dj	2																	2							
k	34																				30	4			
g	10																			9		1			
tʃ	7																		7						
m	24													1	3	20									

	n	ŋ	f	v	ʃ	l	r	w	ʊ	j	ʔ	Nil	Total
											7		7
											3		3
								12					12
				9	1	1		2	8				21
						32							32
						2							2
			10				1						11
			15										15
			20		2								22
			3		1								4
			5										5
			7					1					8
			20										20
	12	4					1						17
	45				1					1			50
													20
					2								7
													8
													13
	1												33
													28
		1											59
													34
													25
Total	58	4	56	36	2	35	1	14	11	3	7	1	

FIGURE 18.8 Overall correspondences for s2: Rhodri – English

Furthermore, in the light of continuing controversy, no claims could safely be made for any psychological status for the rules discussed but this did not signify dismissal of a psychological model *per se*. Children's perception of their phonological errors (see Munro, 1985) suggested that a psycholinguistic model of language was required which would account for various aspects of information-processing. In this model, linguistic constructs were seen as dependent on cognitive skills such as classification, hierarchization, etc., which were not limited to language but appeared elsewhere in non-language behaviours. Given the fundamental nature of these cognitive operations it seemed reasonable to assume that children of all languages brought them to bear on the task of language learning, thereby allowing for the existence of cognitive universals.

Thus, children would be predisposed to develop language(s) according to a universal developmental pattern, accounted for in the study of "formal" universals namely: statements on the form of rules of language (Grunwell's "minimal design features"). Of course, any one language would build upon these rules in a variety of ways; variations would also arise from differences between children in terms of rule application. Despite these variations, there were elements which were considered non-inferential, constant across languages ("substantive" universals) and which were therefore less abstract than those ingredients implied within formal universals.

Having considered the theoretical basis of universality, its possible relationship to phonological simplifying processes was discussed, followed by an account of these processes in children acquiring various languages. After referring to some of the international studies, the next stage was a rather more detailed account of processes evidenced in the normal acquisition of Welsh, data having been obtained from several sources:

> my own data (one child);
> Welsh Language Research Unit, Cardiff, based on the work of Harrison and Thomas (1975) (three children); and
> Bellin (1984b) (two children).

As all six children were also simultaneously acquiring English (to differing degrees) they provided suitable yardsticks against which to compare s1: Nigel and s2: Rhodri.

To summarize briefly, evidence from the six linguistically normal simultaneous bilinguals suggested that their use of phonological simplifying processes was similar to that of monolingual (English) children. Not only did the same processes appear but there was also a parallel in the variability between children from similar linguistic backgrounds, that is, the same processes were available but children selected from them in different ways. Furthermore, although the six children had different language dominance patterns, there was no marked difference in the nature and timing of the processes in their two languages.

The final aspect of universality to be discussed was its relevance in considering the child's phonological system. Various theoretical arguments were debated before concluding that a child's phonological system was to be regarded as a self-consistent one, not merely an imperfect version of an adult's. Such a claim appeared to account for otherwise inexplicable aspects of phonological acquisition and for the gradualness of phonological change.

Analysis

The analysis of such a system consisted of a statement of phonotactic possibilities, a statement of the sets of contrastive phones[3] at each place in the word-structure and a statement of the feature compositions of contrastive phones. One of the advantages of using distinctive features was their proposed universality, their ability to account for phonemic contrasts in all languages and/or combinations of languages.

Having completed the analyses, the subjects' systems were assessed for their normality (or, at least, their adequacy) by ensuring that certain basic requirements were met. To this end, the formal and substantive universals mentioned earlier were brought into effect. Such an assessment, comparing a system with universal properties, treated two languages as a unified system and therefore a combination of Welsh and English data.

TABLE 18.1 s1: *Nigel's simplifying processes*

	English	*Welsh*
Cluster Reduction:	smile [mɔ̃ĩl]	*smocio* ['mõʔɒ̃]
	flour ['lãũə]	*glas* [lã:]
Consonant Harmony:	yawning ['jɔ̃jɪn]	*ffarmwr* ['mˀãmõm]
	thumb [mˀɔ̃m]	*blino* ['nɪ̃nõ]
Final Consonant	up [ə̃]	*gwyneb* ['wĩnɛ̃]
deletion:	leg [lɛ̃:]	*lawr* [lãũ]
Metathesis:	skipping ['mˀĩʔĩn]	*trwyn* [nʊ̃ĩ]
	crab [mˀʔæ̃:]	*cornel* ['ʔɒ̃lɛ̃]
Gliding:	orange ['ɔ̃wĩ]	*môr* [mõ:w]
	there [jɛ̃:]	*menyn* ['mẽjĩn]
Fronting:	penguin ['ɱẽnĩn]	*llong* [ʔɒ̃n]
	ring [ʊ̃ĩn]	*angel* ['æ̃nɛ̃l]
Favourite Articulation	cushion ['ʔʊ̃'ʔĩn]	*trwsus* ['ʔũ̃ʔĩ]
(Use of glottal stop):	jacket ['ʔã̃ʔĩ]	*cysgu* ['ʔĩ̃ʔĩ]

[mˀ] signifies a consonant with non-audible release used by s1: Nigel in realizing target labial consonants.

TABLE 18.2 *Summary of* S1: *Nigel's simplifying processes*

Cluster Reduction	Major — delayed (i.e. frequently reported in chronologically younger, normal children)
Consonant Harmony	Minor — very delayed
Final Consonant Deletion	Major — very delayed
Metathesis	Minor — deviant (i.e. does not appear very often in normal development)
Gliding	Minor — very delayed
Fronting	Minor — very delayed
Favourite Articulation	Major — deviant

TABLE 18.3 S2: *Rhodri's simplifying processes*

	English	*Welsh*
Cluster Reduction:	afraid [feɪd]	*prynu* [ˈpəni]
	stove [foˑv]	*cyffro* [ˈkəfɒ]
Consonant Harmony:	plug [pləb]	*pedwar* [ˈpɛbwar]
	number [ˈməmbə]	*mewn* [mɪʊm]
Metathesis:	goat [dok]	*taclu* [ˈkləti]
	bucket [ˈbətɪg]	*wilber* [ˈlɪmbɛ]
Favourite Articulation:	sun [fən]	*tri* [tfiˑ]
(use of [f] and [v])	that [væt]	*sêr* [feˑv]

TABLE 18.4 *Summary of* S2: *Rhodri's simplifying processes*

Cluster Reduction	Major — delayed
Consonant Harmony	Major — very delayed
Metathesis	Minor — deviant
Favourite Articulation	Major — deviant

The adoption of a level of processing common to both languages was recognized as controversial and discussed in detail at several points in the original thesis.

Although one was considering entities common to both languages, language-specific characteristics were not ignored but were incorporated at several stages.

Subjects' simplifying processes

Data for S1: Nigel indicated that seven processes were operating. Examples are given in Table 18.1. Analysis of the processes provided an explanation for some of the realizations appearing in the correspondence tables and was particularly useful in explaining variability. The status of these simplifying processes could be summarized by considering their relative strengths and by relating them to processes evidence in normal phonological acquisition. s1: Nigel's summary is given in Table 18.2. The procedure was repeated for Rhodri and his results are given in Tables 18.3 and 18.4.

Subjects' phonological systems

The two languages were united whenever possible, language-specific patterns being stated as and when necessary. Patterns that were occurring in both languages but were more predominant in one were also incorporated into the analysis.

S1: Nigel

Firstly, the phonotactic structure of mono-, di-, and multi-syllabic words was analysed. Although s1: Nigel was able to make attempts at a variety of consonant (c) – vowel (v) sequences, there were few complex (cc) sequences in the data and those that did occur involved only a limited range of consonants. The proportion of language-specific sequences increased along with the number of syllables per word. This was attributed to the nature of the target languages.

Table 18.5 *Contrastive phones word-initially for s1: Nigel*

Contrastive phone	Target(s) for which phone is contrastive	
m	m	
n	n	
l	l	
j	j	
ʔ	t d k g tʃ dʒ s z ʃ	
	ɬ* h	
ʊ	r*	v
mˀ	p b f	θ*
	Welsh only	English only

* These three account for language-specific patterns in Nigel's system because they are also language specific in the adult systems.

Table 18.6   *Contrastive phones word-medially for s/: Nigel*

Contrastive phone	Target(s) for which phone is contrastive	
m	m	
n	ŋ	
l	l	
ʔ	t d k g s ʃ	
m˺	f	
n	—	n
ʔ	θ χ ɬ	tʃ dʒ z ʒ *
m˺		b
	Welsh only	English only
w	w	
j	j	

* The specificity demonstrated in this row tends to parallel the pattern in the target languages concerned for the phonemes specified are either exclusive to or far more common (word-medially) in that language.

Next, contrastive phones were analysed according to word-position.

Word-initial: for both languages
|m|, |n|, |l|, |ʋ|, |j|, |ʔ|, |m˺|

were contrastive. (Vertical brackets are used to signify the establishment of contrastivity in the child's system.) Overlapping occurred, that is variable realizations from an apparently random interchange of phones which are contrastive in the child's system. Although these overlapping phones were distributed differently in the two languages, it was, by and large, the same group of phonetic elements which served the two languages. If one considered adult targets, language-specific patterns became more obvious (see Table 18.5).

Word-medial: Contrastive phones were |m|, |n|, |l|, |ʔ|, |m˺|, |j|, |w|, but the last two were contrastive for Welsh only. Both the number of contrastive phones and the degree of overlapping were smaller than demonstrated word-initially (see Table 18.6).

Word-final: Nil realizations were not included when contrastivity was calculated. Therefore, the elimination of a large number of Nil realizations word-finally left very few tokens so that contrastivity could not be established with confidence, except in the case of |m|, |n|, |l|. These were

Table 18.7   s1: *Nigel's minimum distinctions word-initially and -medially*

		Labial	Apical	Dorsal	Glottal
(a)	*Word-initially*				
	Stop				ʔ
	Nasal	m	n		
	Approximant	ʋ	l	j	
	Non-audible*	m˥			
(b)	*Word-medially*				
	Stop				ʔ
	Nasal	m	n		
	Approximant	[[w]]	l	[[j]]	
	Non-audible*	m˥			

* It could be argued that this should not be adopted as a distinctive feature but it is necessary in order to give a clear account of s1: Nigel's phonological system.

Table 18.8   s1: *Nigel's minimum distinctions word-finally*

	Labial	Lingual
Nasal	m	n
Approximant		l

contrastive for both languages with no language-specific patterns. Although |n| and |l| were contrastive, they alternated to quite an extent with Nil.

In all word-positions there also appeared phonetically different segments that did not seem to operate contrastively (variants).

The third stage in analysing a subject's phonological system was to identify contrastive features, that is the minimum distinctions accounting for the system of contrastive phones. They were incorporated whether they served one or both languages, but points at which only one language made use of a particular distinction were marked by [[ ]].

For s1: Nigel, the minimum distinctions required word-initially and word-medially are given in Table 18.7a and b, and word-finally in Table 18.8.

The fourth stage of this analysis was a comparison of previously presented data with universal properties. Having accounted for the patterns within the child's system in terms of properties that were claimed to be universal, it was also necessary, for clinical purposes, to assess the normality of that system, for example its stability and symmetry. This further involvement of universality was, to a large extent, concerned with the formal universal properties, the principles of organization of systems. Once again, concentration on such fundamental aspects enabled one to view the bilingual's languages as a single system.

With regard to the communicative adequacy of this single system, the small inventory of contrastive phones, particularly word-finally, resulted in a marked degree of actual and potential homophony, for example

[ʔî] *tŷ*/*tri*/*cig*/tea/see/etc.
[ʊɔ̄:] *bord*/wall

Overlapping of contrastive phones lead to some unpredictability, for example

[ʊā], [ʔwāh] *gwallt*
[jɛ̃], [ʔɛ̃ʰ] there.

In all word-positions there was non-contrastive variability which involved some phonetic diversity. However, this variability was not entirely random and could not be said to result in asystemic patterns. There was also some asymmetry, particularly word-initially and medially (see Table 18.6 and 18.7). Of course, the single system approach was in danger of masking asymmetry for, by uniting two languages, one could "fill the gaps", as seen in the word-medial grid. This was counterbalanced by marking language-specific patterns and by relating asymmetries to the respective adult languages. It was by considering this relationship with reference to medial /w/ and /j/ that a type of asymmetry peculiar to bilingualism was detected. The /w/ and /j/ were present only in s1: Nigel's Welsh system and therefore were absent from his word-medial English system but not from the corresponding target English system. Thus, he could be said to be exploiting the resources of feature contrasts in one language but not in the other.

S2: Rhodri

This subject attempted a greater variety of sequences than s1: Nigel and did not demonstrate Nigel's limitations with regard to cc sequences. In this respect, Rhodri was different from many children with phonological problems for there were quite a number of complex 'terminations' (word-final). The analysis of disyllables required a separate section devoted to the greater proportion of cvcvc sequences in Welsh. This was not due to any peculiar systemic modifications on Rhodri's part, but to the higher percentage of target cvcvc sequences in Welsh.

s2: Rhodri also had a greater variety of contrastive phones than s1: Nigel.

Table 18.9 *Contrastive phones word-initially for s2: Rhodri*

Contrastive phone	Target(s) for which phone is contrastive	
p	p	
b	b	
t	t	
d	d	
m	m	
n	n	
l	l	
w	w	
ʔ	h	
f	f s ʃ	
v	v	
v/ʋ	r/r̝	ɹ
f		θ
f/ɬ	ɬ	
	Welsh only	English only

Word-initial

|p|, |b|, |t|, |d|, |m|, |n|, |f|, |v|, |l|, |w|, |ʔ|.

These were contrastive for both languages. There were quite a number of non-contrastive variants and some overlapping of contrastive phones, though the latter was not as widespread as for s1: Nigel.

In considering the adult target systems, one found two interesting patterns that is both [ɬ] and [f] occurred with equal frequency for Welsh-specific target /ɬ/, and [ʋ], [v] occurred equally for Welsh /r/ or English /ɹ/. As each pair appeared to operate contrastively, each was presented (see Table 18.9) as a unit composed of two items. However, they could not be said to be in complementary distribution for their appearance was not context-conditioned and they did not occur in mutually exclusive contexts.

The language-specific section was due entirely to language-specific characteristics of the target languages.

Word-medial: Once again, [v] and [ʋ] appeared to occur as a unit and were therefore included as such in the list of contrastive phones:

Table 18.10   *Contrastive phones word-medially for s2: Rhodri*

Contrastive phone	Target(s) for which phone is contrastive	
p	p	
b	b	
t	t	
d	d	
m	m	
n	n	
l	l	
f	f s ʃ	
v	v	
v/ʋ	r/r̪	ɹ
	Welsh only	English only
k		k

|p|, |b|, |t|, |d|, |k|, |m|, |n|, |f|, |v|, |l|, |v/ʋ|.

Compared with many children with phonological problems, s2: Rhodri had developed a larger number of contrastive phones than might have been anticipated for this place in word-structure.

There was some overlapping of the phones, notably within and between the group of contrastive stops, also the contrastive liquids and nasals

Word-final: The contrastive phones were:

|p|, |b|, |t|, |d|, |k|, |g|, |m|, |n|, |f|, |v|, |l|, |χ| and |v/ʋ|.

Although s2: Rhodri's system word-finally was surprisingly well developed within the context of clinical phonology, it was still susceptible to overlapping. With the exception of /ŋ/, language-specific patterns were due to the specificity of the target languages.

Moving on to analysis of contrastive features, word-initially and word-medially the minimum sets are given in Table 18.12a and b, word-finally in Table 18.13.

No changes were required in the framework in order to encompass |χ| and |g| word-finally (see Table 18.13).

The appraisal of s2: Rhodri's communicative adequacy showed that he had restricted phone inventories at all places in word-structure but not

Table 18.11   *Contrastive phones word-finally for s2: Rhodri*

Contrastive phones	Target(s) for which phone is contrastive	
p	p	
b	b	
t	t	
d	d	
k	k	
g	g	
m	m	
n	n	
f	f s θ	
l	l	
n		ŋ
f	ɬ	z
v	ð	
v/ʋ	r/ɾ̥	
	Welsh only	English only
χ	χ	

Table 18.12   s2: *Rhodri's minimum set word-initially and -medially*

		Labial		Lingual		Glottal
(a)	*Word-initially*					
	Stop	p	b	t	d	ʔ
	Nasal		m		n	
	Approximant		w		l	
	Fricative	f	v			
(b)	*Word-medially*					
	Stop	p	b	t	d	[[k]]
	Nasal		m		n	
	Approximant		ʋ		l	
	Fricative	f	v			

nearly as restricted as for s1: Nigel. Furthermore, the inventories were not markedly different in size depending on word-position. Although his system was obviously inadequate, it had quite a degree of contrastive potential. However, the stability of his system was affected by the overlapping of contrastive phones and consequent unpredictability, for example

Table 18.13

	Labial	Apical	Dorsal
Stop	p b	t d	k g
Nasal	m	n	
Approximant	[[ʋ]]	l	
Fricative	f v		[[χ]]

['tebɒt], ['pedɒt], *tebot.*

Non-contrastive variation contributed further to the lack of predictability, examples including:

['tegɛf], ['kedɪl], *tegell.*

With regard to organization of the feature contrasts word-initially, there was a degree of symmetry in the "Stop", "Nasal" and "Approximant" sections of Table 18.12a, if |ʔ| was disregarded. Correlations existed between the features of "Stop", "Nasal", "Approximant" on the one hand and "Labial", "Lingual" on the other. However, asymmetry and uneconomical use of feature contrasts was implied by the addition of |f|, |v| and |ʔ|.

A very similar picture was presented word-medially but the replacing of |ʔ| by |k| on the grid was significant as it was specific to Rhodri's English. This could not be related to absence of /k/ in adult, target Welsh and was therefore regarded as a gap in his system.

Some of the asymmetry which existed word-finally could be attributed to the respective adult systems. Nevertheless, there remained 'real' instances of failure to exploit the contrastive potential of the system.

Discussion

A distinction is made in speech pathology between delayed and deviant patterns in abnormal phonologies. Frequently, the distinction is not a clear one for the patterns may co-exist in the same individual; furthermore, extremely delayed patterns are regarded by some as a type of deviance. Where the foregoing analyses of systems and their comparison with universal properties was concerned with organizational principles, subjects' deficiencies were regarded as deviant as they were deficiencies in very basic design features. For instance, both subjects demonstrated paradigmatic deviance namely: asymmetrical sets of contrasts and uneconomical use of contrastive potential, though both facets were far more marked for s1: Nigel. His system was also deviant with regard to syntagmatic aspects such as predominance of simple phonotactic structures.

Further asymmetry with failure to exploit contrastive resources was evidenced for Nigel and Rhodri in that phones which were normally contrastive for Welsh and English were contrastive in only one of the languages within their systems. Obviously, this was a type of deficiency not referred to by Grunwell (1977) as it related solely to the bilingual context. the query which arose was whether this deficiency, labelled as a type of asymmetry in the analyses, should also be regarded as deviant. In addition to the universal aspects of phonological systems already utilized, further principles related to co-existing languages had to be considered. It was tentatively suggested that one of these principles was that in simultaneous bilinguals the sharing of rules and/or structures by the two languages was reflected in like-acquisition (Kessler, 1971; Swain, 1972). Occasions when that principle was not applied could, perhaps, be regarded as pockets of deviance.

Another interesting point about both subjects was that their systems did not seem to "favour" the dominant language. This was in sharp contrast to the superiority demonstrated in the dominant language at other levels (morphology, etc.).

Leaving aside these aspects related exclusively to bilingualism and returning to the notion of the system as a whole, it was possible to compare each subject with other children reported to have phonological problems. Grunwell (1977) described her (monolingual) subjects as presenting with phonological "disorder", a term which implied almost completely unintelligible speech resulting primarily from consonantal deviations, a chronological age above four years, normal hearing for speech, average or low average intelligence and adequate verbal comprehension and expressive language. All these criteria applied to both subjects although s2: Rhodri was not as lacking in intelligibility as s1: Nigel.

Phonotactically, s1: Nigel demonstrated several signs of disorder, namely infrequent use of consonant clusters, restricted range of word-final consonants, high-frequency occurrence of |ʔ| and a strong tendency to open syllable structure. Other significant signs included overlapping of contrastive phones, marked asymmetry and failure to realize the contrastive potential latent in the system.

s2: Rhodri also showed overlapping and some asymmetry with failure to exploit contrastivity but in other respects his system was quite different from those considered to be disordered. For instance, he was phonotactically quite sophisticated by comparison and there were only minimal

differences in size between phone inventories at different places in structure.

Having looked at possible deviant aspects of the subjects' phonological systems,[4] their relationship to phonological simplifying processes was
considered. For s1: Nigel, the processes effecting simplification of phonological structure to the greatest extent were Cluster Reduction and Final
Consonant Deletion. Simplification of the phonological system was
effected, to an extent, by the Gliding process in that it interferred with
the establishment of contrastive phones for several targets, but /ɹ/ and
/ð/ in particular. Fronting also had some effect. However, it was the
pervasive use of |ʔ| word-initially and medially (see Favourite Articulation)
which had the most drastic effect on the system of contrastive phones.

For s2: Rhodri, too, Favourite Articulation had a very limiting
effect on the system while his Cluster Reduction effected simplification of
structure although, as stated previously, quite a degree of complexity was
retained despite the latter process. Consonant Harmony was quite marked
in the data for s2: Rhodri, and was regarded as a process simplifying
structure because it resulted in phonetically more uniform sequences of
consonants and because the harmonized target consonants were usually
found to occur in other contexts, that is they were not actually lacking in
the child's system.

Overall, s1: Nigel demonstrated far more deviant patterns than s2:
Rhodri and was more likely to be classified as "phonologically disordered".

Notes to Chapter 18

1. s1: Nigel's vowels were nasalized but the lowered soft palate did not
   mask their characteristic formant patterns and so his vowel realizations
   could be said to be phonemically equivalent to the non-nasalized
   targets.
2. Another modification (not related to bilingualism) is the adoption of
   the word as the unit of analysis in Munro (1985); Grunwell's (1977)
   approach mainly uses the syllable.
3. This term was adopted by Grunwell (1977), the reason for its preference over "phoneme" when referring to the child's system being that
   the latter term was usually used in a monosystemic rather than a
   polysystemic framework of the kind applied by Grunwell.
4. Following the analyses described, the original thesis discussed the
   relationship between phonology, bilingualism and cognitive processing. It also discussed the effects of such relationships on phonological
   therapy. Unfortunately, it is not possible to include such details here.

Part VI:
Theoretical Implications

19 Language variation and social stratification: Linguistic change in progress

ROBERT OWEN JONES

This chapter will be concerned with the question of linguistic variation and will consider methods by means of which one can delineate and account for such heterogeneity within a Welsh–Spanish bilingual community. The emphasis however will not be on bilingualism as such, but upon variables within the Welsh vernacular which are at times attributable to the effects of Spanish acculturation pressures, but which at other times arise out of the sociological make-up of the Welsh-speaking community itself. The question of linguistic variation however, is approached from a sociolinguistic and dialectological standpoint. Such variation has always been a basic tenet of dialect studies in spite of other tendencies, fashions and attitudes found in traditional and mainstream linguistics. Traditional descriptions and analyses have always been based on abstract forms — those patterns which were considered to be correct or literary and prestigious forms. In Wales such an emphasis is not exceptional since Welsh linguistic descriptions in common with the European linguistics tradition were based upon the classical Alexandrian framework and so took linguistic homogeneity as its norm. As noted by Chambers & Trudgill (1980: 145)

> ". . .throughout the history of linguistics, linguists have tended to act as if language is not variable. Most linguistic theories have started from the assumption that variability in language is unmanageable or uninteresting or both. Consequently there has been a tendency to abstract away from the variable data that linguists inevitably encounter, in order to begin the analysis at a more homogeneous level."

Dialectology on the other hand has always emphasized the hetero-geneous nature of speech communities and therefore it is not the study of abstractions, but it intentionally attempts to come to terms with linguistic reality within specific areas and communities. It is not the study of possible or supposed patterns, it does not restrict itself to the study of patterns which are considered to be correct, pure or prestigious;[1] it is not the study of static, unchanging or standard phenomena, but neither is it solely the study of odd, peculiar forms which have restricted distributions (see Bagley Atwood, 1963; Petyt, 1982; Wakelin, 1972). It is in fact the study of language in its human context. This can mean a study of the co-variance of linguistic structure with geographical localities as was the case in early traditional dialectology (see Viereck, 1973), or a study of the co-stratification of the linguistic and the social within specified localities as exemplified since the 1960s with the growth of sociolinguistics.[2] Linguistic geography attempted to describe variation, but due to its sampling methods resulted in over-generalized statements ignoring intra-dialect variation which is as integral a part of linguistic heterogeneity as inter-dialect variation is. Sociolinguistics on the other hand focuses its attention on those features which are variable within a community and which can, on the synchronic plane, draw attention to features that are changing in the language. Such studies can throw light on the distribution of variables within communities but also upon the mechanism of linguistic change itself which traditionally has been the domain of diachronic linguistics.[3]

Traditionally sound change was studied by comparing the sounds of one period with those of another period — two historically distinct periods. What such studies entail however is the comparison of base forms with the results of change — a before and after study. It was not a study of the progression of change, of the nature nor of the mechanics of change. Such studies could not say anything about the change itself, its spread through the community and its various realizations through the linguistic systems of those speakers. They dealt with two assumed static states or periods in the history of a language and ignored the interim period when change was manifestly operative in the language. Such an emphasis on the results of linguistic change rather than upon the progression and mechanism of change itself arises from the ideas and methodological framework of the neo-grammarians of Leipzig.

They held that language change was abrupt and complete and did not leave residual forms and therefore there was no point in studying the process of change. Their main concern was to order and systematize the linguistic and historical data at their disposal and part of that attempt was to evolve a framework which would explain linguistic change. They contended that a systematic study of language would of necessity reveal and explain every linguistic change in the history of a language. This viewpoint was in direct contrast to that of Rudolf von Raumer (1856) who held that the process of linguistic change could not be simply stated because it did not necessarily conform to set patterns.

> "We ascertain that the sounds of words have changed when we compare the older state of language with the more recent. The process of change itself however has not yet been investigated enough. If we penetrate deeper into the darkness which in many ways veils these questions we find a huge multitude of highly different processes at work. And what is even more troublesome, we find that to isolate these processes becomes ever more difficult. . ." (R. von Raumer in Lehmann 1967: 72)

In 1875 Karl Verner published an article which postulated an approach which later became the mainstay of the neo-grammarian methodology. There had to be a rule which would explain the exceptions of the rule, and it was the task of the grammarian to discover this rule. Verner (and the neo-grammarians) held that every sound change occurred mechanically and affected all given items at the same time.[4] Therefore within this framework variables could not co-occur at the same point in time. Change was characterized by universal uniformity. Karl Brugmann concludes in 1878:

> "First every sound change inasmuch as it occurs mechanically takes place according to laws that admit no exceptions" (Osthoff & Brugmann in Lehmann 1967: 204)

They were simply asserting that sound change affected everyone within communities at the same point in time and all items which could potentially change would be affected. This viewpoint of course over-simplified the linguistic situation, because it ignored the possibility of variableness, of exceptional patterns and even contradictory patterns amongst the speakers of a language. The bases for such hypotheses were abstract linguistic forms. It was taken for granted that uniform linguistic patterns existed at two points in time. All that such a framework could accomplish however was to present a catalogue of formulae which could account for change but could not deal with the details of what actually occurred in the language in specific communities resulting in what we call "change".

> "We should beware however of confusing the image which must result from such a method with the linguistic reality. The representation of the evaluation of language as consisting in a succession of

discrete states is no more a true reflection of the situation. . . .
However many language states are considered over a given period
their succession will never provide a true picture of the unbroken
continuity of language in time. . . . It is thus due to the limitations
of our methodology that we are faced with the rather absurd situation
that language evolution, although observable retrospectively in its
results, appears to totally elude observation as a process while it is
actually taking place." (Bynon, 1977:2)

Even modern linguists of this century have consistently declared that one
cannot observe language in the process of change (Bloomfield, 1933: 347;
Hockett, 1958: 439; Postal, 1968: 70). Sociolinguistic studies since the
1960s however have shown that one can profitably study those features
that are variable and that in certain cases those variable patterns are in
fact examples of change occurring at that point in time. In the works of
Labov, Milroy, Macaulay, Trudgill, Romaine etc. the emphasis has been
upon the study of variability — from person to person, but also a study
of the variableness which naturally occurs within the linguistic repertoire
of the individual. They have in fact shown that synchrony and diachrony
intersect in such studies in apparent time.

In the linguistic data gathered in Gaiman, Chubut during 1973–74
variables abound.[5] One could superficially explain such phenomena by
suggesting that this may be a dialect melting-pot situation. In R. O. Jones
(1983) I have shown how important it is to have a valid and representative
sample of speakers and how this can ultimately explain the distribution
of the web of variable forms in current usage. The data were based
upon the speech of a stratified random sample of the Welsh-speaking
community. As described in R. O. Jones (1984), 244 informants were
stratified according to age, sex, religious patterns, educational background
and cultural affiliations. These then form the basis for a classification into
two status groups A and B within each age block — except amongst the
young. All the young people and children fitted into Group B as defined
in terms of the above-mentioned features.

Group A speakers were Welsh in orientation and active in the Welsh
chapels. They had Welsh cultural affiliations and they formed a dense
social network group in that they socialized almost exclusively within
Group A. Within the community they were considered as representing
the core of Welsh life and as being distinctive in their Welsh identity.
Group B were outward looking. They did not constitute a cohesive unit
and seemed to be on the periphery of Welsh life in terms of religion,
education and cultural affiliations. Members of this group were Argentine

rather than Welsh in their orientation. Such divisions in terms of age and social status proved to be important factors in the distribution of certain variables within the speech of Gaiman.[6]

There are two variable realizations for the /x/ phoneme namely [x] and [x̩]. The expected Welsh norm [x] occurs in the speech of the old in Groups A and B, then in the middle-aged in Group A, but in the middle-aged Group B [x̩] is the norm and remains so in the speech of the younger generations irrespective of status grouping. The same pattern is shown in the occurrence of aspirated and unaspirated variants of /p/, /t/, /k/. Status grouping is irrelevant in the older group and in the young middle-aged group. The former consistently use aspirated [pʰ] [tʰ] [kʰ] and the latter group use the unaspirated [p] [t] [k]. Within the middle-aged group however the social identity of speakers is a relevant conditioning factor. These variations therefore are not random features or free variation phenomena, but are strictly distributed within the age framework and within one age group according to social status. In R. O. Jones (1984) (h) is shown to be correlated with age, social identity and stylistic context. It was also shown that the incidence of (h) could be further conditioned by the linguistic factor; the incident of (h) varied according to the morpho-phonological shape and grammatical function of different lexical terms. The distribution of variables can therefore be quite complicated and this may be further exemplified by consideration of the distribution of /a/ and /e/ in final unstressed syllables within the community.

When one considers spoken Welsh dialects one has a binary division into those that allow /a/ and /e/ in final unstressed syllables and those that restrict the distribution of /e/. In the north west and in the south east /a/ occurs in the final unstressed syllable where "e", "ai", "ae" and "au" occur in orthography and which are realized in the north-east, the midlands and the south-west as /e/. In Gaiman both /e/ and /a/ occur in the final unstressed syllable but it would be wrong to assume that the pattern there is identical to what one gets in the north-east, the midlands and south-west dialects of Welsh. When one examines the distribution of /a/, /e/ in parallel lexical sets and different grammatical categories a very different picture emerges as shown in Table 19.1.

In Gaiman /a/ consistently occurs where the other two groups have /a/ but, both /a/ and /e/ may occur in the lexical items where the north-west and the south-east have /a/ and where the other group has /e/. This would suggest a case of dialect mixing, an explanation which would seem quite plausible considering the historical background of the area. Such a statement however is far too generalized in that it assumes that /a/ and

TABLE 19.1   *Distribution of /a/ and /e/ in final unstressed syllables*

Written		NW/SE	SW/NE	Gaiman	
Noun singular					
"bread"	*bara* (a)	/a/	/a/	/a/	
"chair"	*cadair* (ai)	/a/	/e/	/a/	/e/
"support"	*cynhaliaeth* (ae)	/a/	/e/	/a/	/e/
"light"	*golau* (au)	/a/	/e/	/a/	/e/
"morning"	*bore* (e)	/a/	/e/	/a/	/e/
Noun Plural					
"things"	*pethau* (au)	/a/	/e/	/a/	
"nails"	*ewinedd* (e)	/a/	/e/	/a/	/e/
Verb–Noun					
"to hold"	*cynnal* (a)	/a/	/a/	/a/	
"to play"	*chwarae* (ae)	/a/	/e/	/a/	/e/
"to start"	*dechrau* (au)	/a/	/e/	/a/	/e/
"to read"	*darllen* (e)	/a/	/e/	/a/	/e/
Adjective					
"soft"	*meddal* (a)	/a/	/a/	/a/	
"thin"	*tenau* (au)	/a/	/e/	/a/	/e/
"high"	*uchel* (e)	/a/	/e/	/a/	/e/

/e/ are in free variation or at best are distributed in the lexis in a random fashion. Traditional dialectology treated such linguistic variation as free variation but as Chambers & Trudgill (1980: 60) noted: "this type of variation is usually not free at all, but is constrained by social and/or linguistic factors".

Further study of the data within the generation and status group framework illustrates that this is not a case of dialect mixing nor indeed a case of a patternless distribution of the two phonemes in question. Viewed within the generation spectrum one concludes that what one has here is a native Gaiman system exhibiting variableness due to the fact that it is currently changing. The fact that older speakers of both Groups A and B have identical patterns led me to take those patterns as the native or typical ones, those that had evolved in a South-American Welsh system at the time when the present older generation were children. At that time chapel, Sunday School, Welsh education and Welsh cultural activities were dominant influences upon the life of the community and these had a uniform effect not only sociologically but also linguistically upon this age group. In the speech of the old one gets /e/ in final unstressed syllables for orthographic "ai", "ae" and "au" in singular nouns,

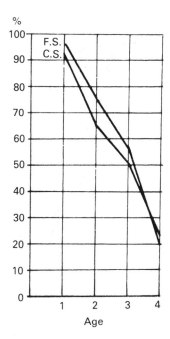

FIGURE 19.1   *Decrease in the use of /e/ in the generation framework*

verb–nouns and adjectives but /a/ for the noun plural morpheme "au". Orthographic "a" is always /a/ and orthographic "e" is always /e/. In this age group therefore the grammatical function of a word can condition the occurrence of /a/ and /e/ in final unstressed syllables. This is not the case in the Welsh dialects of Wales. In the other generation groups in Gaiman one notes a tendency to have /a/ in the very instances where the older generation had /e/. The phoneme /e/ is being replaced by /a/ and at an increasing rate when viewed along the generation axis. Figure 19.1 exhibits generation and stylistic variability in the occurrence of /e/.

In the speech of the older generation (Class 1) /e/ is the norm in the speech of the young (Class 4) /a/ is the norm and /e/ is the exception. In casual speech there is a difference of 68% between the incidence of /e/ in the speech of the older generation and that of the young. In formal style there is an increase in the use of /e/ in every age group but the greatest increase was recorded in the speech of the middle-aged. This is an important factor to bear in mind because later in this discussion it is shown that this generation is really the instigator of change. It would appear therefore that the incidence of /e/ is generation-bound but the

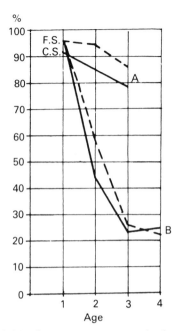

situation is not as simple as that. The overall tendency is to replace /e/ by /a/ at an increasing rate as one progresses from the old to the young. The progression of change however is not at the same rate in the two status groups within each generation as exemplified in Figure 19.2.

There is a decrease in the use of /e/ along the generation axis but note that the Group A age groups are very similar to each other — there is only a decrease of 11% from Group 1A to Group 3A. In Group B however there is a sharp decrease of 70% from Group 1B to Group 3B. Figure 19.2 shows clearly that generation 2B is the spearhead of the change. There is a drop of 48% from the patterns of Group 1B to those of Group 2B. Retaining /e/ is definitely a Group A marker, and in the 2A and 3A group patterns we seem to have two competing forces — the conservative influence of their status groups which would be in favour of retaining /e/ and the influence of peer group patterns which progress towards replacing /e/ by /a/. This would seem to illustrate a point made by Milroy & Milroy (1985b: 62): ". . .a strong close-knit network may be seen to function as a conservative force, resisting pressures to change from outside the network". This is a clear indication that the speakers' sociological background is a key factor in assessing and understanding speech patterns.

It is interesting to note that Groups 1A and 1B patterns are identical which is not the case within other age groups. I suggest that a mixing or interweaving of the different geographical Welsh dialect patterns had already occurred and had stabilized into a Patagonian system in the speech of this generation. The conformist influence of Welsh medium education, of Welsh non-conformity, of Welsh culture and social networks operating when they were children resulted in a fairly uniform system amongst this age group.[7] Professor R. Le Page (1979) noted a similar pattern of stabilization in Belize in spite of the heterogeneous nature of the community. In her study of variables in Belfast L. Milroy (1980: 180) reaches a similar conclusion:

> ". . .it seems that cultural and linguistic focussing are associated with a close-knit network structure and can take place if the conditions are right at any stratum of society."

When the present middle-aged were children the close-knit chapel-orientated social order was rapidly disintegrating and social Groups A and B even emerged amongst the children. Those who were Group B did not come under the conformist influence of the chapel and its associated social and cultural activities and dialect features prevalent in the speech of grand-parents at that time re-asserted themselves in the speech of this group. Close social networks operating amongst Group A speakers explains the low rate of change as one progresses from the older speakers to the young middle-aged speakers. James and Lesley Milroy noted a similar pattern in Belfast:

> ". . .the degree to which individuals approximate to a vernacular speech norm seems to correlate to the extent to which they participate in close-knit networks. It should not be surprising that a close-knit group tends to be linguistically homogeneous." (Milroy & Milroy 1978: 23)

Social Group 2B started a process which was carried on by younger generations mainly through the process of lexical diffusion.[8]

> "Lexical diffusion: the theory that a diachronic sound change may spread gradually through the lexicon of a language, rather than affecting all the relevant words at the same time, and to the same extent." (Hudson, 1980: 169)

This example disproves the neo-grammarian assumption that sound change affects all the relevant words in a language simultaneously. Not all /e/ in final unstressed syllables were replaced by /a/. Instead the change occurred in certain lexical items in the speech of one group and spread to more lexical items in the speech of the next generation. Hooper (1976) discussed the possibility of change spreading gradually from the familiar items to the less familiar items. It is suggested that frequency of occurrence of certain words might be a factor in the diffusion of change. That may indeed be one factor in the spread of /a/ in Gaiman but such a hypothesis was not systematically examined. The spread of /a/ however is not only conditioned by the age of the speaker and his status group but also by the linguistic environment. The grammatical identity of a lexical item has a bearing upon the diffusion of /a/. As Figure 19.3 shows the rate of occurrence of /e/ in different parts of speech can vary substantially in every one of the seven age/status groups. Within Groups A there is a decreasing incidence of /e/ as one progresses from adjectives to singular nouns to plural nouns and finally to verb–nouns.

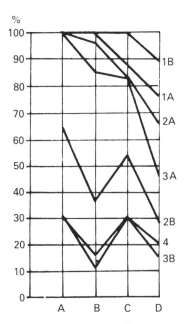

FIGURE 19.3   Use of /e/ in different parts of speech.
A, adjective; B, singular nominative; C, plural nominative; D, verb–noun.

The category which showed the greatest degree of weakening along the age axis was the weakest category in the speech of Group 1A, the

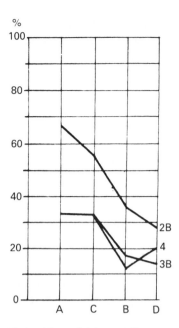

FIGURE 19.4   *Use of /e/ in different parts of speech.*
A, adjective; B, singular nominative; C, plural nominative; D, verb–noun.

verb–noun — a reduction from 75% in Group 1A to 49% in Group 3A. Within Group B the categories which showed the highest occurrence of /e/ in the speech of the older generation, exhibit the greatest degree of change in the speech of the other generations. In fact within Group B the scale of highest/lowest occurrence of /e/ in terms of grammatical categories is changed from adjective, singular noun, plural noun, verb–noun in Group 1B to adjective, plural noun, singular noun, verb-noun in Group 2B, but to adjective, plural noun, verb–noun, singular noun in Groups 3B and 4. Therefore in relative terms the category that exhibits the most radical change is the singular noun class. The resultant pattern as shown in Figure 19.4 records a fairly similar rate of occurrence for all grammatical categories in the speech of the younger generation.

The graph in Figure 19.4 is much shallower for Groups 3B and 4 in comparison with the patterns of Group 2B. In the speech of Group 2B there is a difference of 38% between the occurrence of /e/ in the adjective class and in the verb–noun class. In the speech of Groups 3B and 4 the difference between the highest incidence in the adjectives and the lowest incidence in the singular noun category is 18% in one and 13% in the other. It would appear that the grammatical category of items is a decisive factor in the occurrence of /e/ in the speech of Group 2B but is hardly relevant in the speech of the younger generations since /a/ is now the dominant variable in all grammatical categories.

What does all this show? It certainly illustrates that linguistic variability is not a simple matter. It cannot be explained merely in terms of the age factor. The social background of the speaker has a bearing upon his linguistic patterns. But in addition grammatical and lexical factors need to be borne in mind if one is to understand how change is realized and progresses within the linguistic repertoire of each age and status group. This would seem to fit within the lexical diffusion framework proposed by Wang (1969). The change is indeed phonetically abrupt. There did not appear to be a phonetic inter-stage between /e/ and /a/. No examples of more open allophones of /e/ were recorded, but in each case one had a clear transfer from /e/ to /a/. The change is gradual and works its way through the lexicon at different rates of progression according to the grammatical category of different lexical items. Chen (1972) notes similar characteristics in the Chinese dialect of Shuang feng. What he has to say about phonological change in that dialect seems to ring true for the situation in Gaiman:

> "When a phonological innovation enters a language, it begins as a minor rule affecting a small number of words. . . . As the phonological innovation gradually spreads across the lexicon however, there comes a point when the minor rule gathers momentum and begins to serve as a basis for extrapolation. At this critical cross-over point the minor rule becomes a major rule and we would expect diffusion to be much more rapid. The change may however reach a second point of inflection and eventually taper off before it completes its course leaving behind a handful of words unaltered." (Chen, 1972: 474)

The rate of change can vary considerably within a community. It can start slowly, progress with a sudden increase, followed by a slower rate once more. This was called an "S-curve model" by Chen (1972: 475). This is the pattern in Gaiman as shown in Figure 19.5 and Table 19.2.

The change progresses very slowly within Group A but within Group B there is a substantial change from Group 1B to Group 2B, a lesser change from Group 2B to Group 3B and Group 4 and this is the case in the four grammatical categories. The rates of occurrence of /e/ in the different parts of speech exhibits the following rates of change by comparing the two extremes on the generation axis. Within Group B adjectives 66%, singular nouns 86.5%, plural nouns 67%, verb–nouns 70%. Within each part of speech however as Table 19.3 shows, the greatest decrease in the occurrence of /e/ occurs from Groups 1B to 2B. The slowing down then occurs in the next two generation groups.

The fact that a lexical diffusion of phonological change operates in Gaiman becomes clearer still when another possible variable constraint is

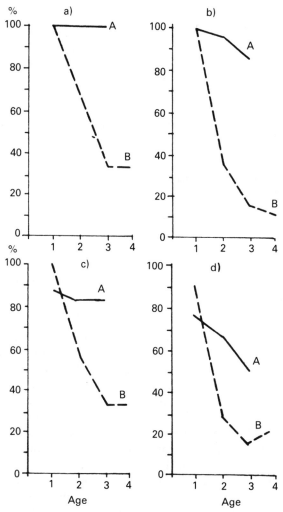

FIGURE 19.5   *Rate of change in the different part of speech in the generation framework*
A, adjective; B, singular nominative; C, plural nominative; D, verb–noun.

TABLE 19.2

Group	Adjective	Nom. Singular	Nom. Plural	Verb–Noun
1A	100	100	87.5	75
2A	100	96.5	83	65.5
3A	100	86	83	49
1B	100	100	100	90
2B	66.6	36	55	28.5
3B	33	16.5	33	15
4	33	13.5	33	20

TABLE 19.3

Rate of decrease	Group 1B–2B (%)	Group 2B–3B (%)	Group 3B–4 (%)
Adjective	33	33	0
Nominative singular	64	19.5	3
Nominative plural	45	22	0
Verb–Noun	62	13	+5

considered, that is the orthographic symbol representing the variable. We may conveniently make a binary division here into (e) words and ("ae", "ai", "au") words. In the speech of Groups 1A and 1B all of these will tend to be realized by /e/ in all grammatical categories.

Within Group A /e/ in (e) words is consistently retained amongst all speakers along the age axis. In Group B on the other hand there is substantial decrease of /e/ in (e) words — a 65% drop in occurrence between Groups 1B and 4. In ("ae", "ai", "au") words the same patterning pertains within the two social groups but the rate of change is not the same along the generation axis within the two status groups. There is a gradual drop of 12% from Group 1A to 2A but a 71% drop from Group 1B to 2B. On the other hand from Group 2A to 3A, the rate of change accelerates to 27% whereas in the Group B it decreases from 24 to 0%. We may therefore conclude that the orthographic shape of a lexical item can condition the progression of change. Within Group A speakers, orthographic "e" inhibits change and even in Group B certainly slows down the rate of change whereas in "ae", "ai", "au" words the change is to all intents and purposes complete.

Figure 19.6 however, does not show that differentiation according to orthographic shape may be further conditioned by grammatical category as shown in Tables 19.4 and 19.5 below.

Within Group A in (e) words there is hardly any change within the generation framework — a mere 2% in verb–nouns, 4% in plural nouns.

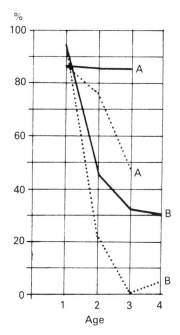

FIGURE 19.6 /e/ in "e" words (full line) and in "ai", "ae" and "au" (dotted line)

TABLE 19.4 /e/ in lexical items with the orthographic "e"

Group	Singular noun (%)	Plural noun (%)	Verb–Noun (%)
1A	100	87.5	75
2A	100	83	73
3A	100	83	73
1B	100	100	90
2B	41	55	40
3B	33	33	30
4	27	33	30

TABLE 19.5 /e/ in lexical items with the
orthographic "ae", "ai", "au"

Group	Singular noun (%)	Verb–noun (%)
1A	100	75
2A	93	58
3A	72	25
1B	100	90
2B	31	17
3B	—	—
4	—	10

In Group B the greatest decrease occurs in the singular noun category
and the change is at its steepest from Group 1B to Group 2B. In all
grammatical categories however the end result is basically the same — a
decrease from a consistent use of /e/ in Group 1B to a low (27–33%)
incidence in Groups 4A and B. In the ("ae", "ai", "au") lexical items
Group A speakers exhibit a decrease of 28% in the use of /e/ between
Groups 1A and 3A in singular nouns. In (e) words no decrease at all was
recorded. In the verb–nouns in the ("ae", "ai", "au") words a 50%
decrease in the use of /e/ was recorded between Group 1A and Group
3A. In (e) words the decrease was 2%. In Group B the same tendencies
as in (e) words operated but in these words the change was complete in
singular nouns from Group 1B to Groups 4A and B and in the verb–noun
it was a drop from 90 to 10%.

In both categories of words the greatest rate of change was recorded
from Group 1B to Group 2B and then the slowing down took place. It
was interesting to note that with some of the other variables as well,
generation 2B seems to be the instigator of the change. These are indeed
instances of a sociocultural change being mirrored in the linguistic patterns
of the community.[9]

Language change is not a simple process. The diffusion of change is
not dependent on whim or fashion but can be correlated with contemporary and non-contemporary sociological factors. In some communities variables arise when change is instigated from 'above', starting with the higher
social order and spreading down to lower classes. More often than not
this kind of change involves the spread of prestige forms through communities. The Gaiman community is rather different in that all of the variables
analysed are examples of change initiated at a lower sociocultural level

which are gradually spreading upwards, from status Group B to status Group A. In the Gaiman community such a process was inevitable — it is one of the hallmarks of a language death situation. The prestige Welsh patterns characteristic of Group A do not really have status or importance outside the chapel-orientated social network. Group A have a respected status within the 'Welsh' community only and not necessarily so in the wider Argentinian context. Group B speakers are Argentine-orientated and their range of registers in Welsh are very limited. The younger speakers are basically what Nancy Dorian has called semi-speakers, but their restricted control of the language is not regarded with alarm by their elders. The decline of the Welsh chapel and the closure of *Yr Ysgol Ganolraddol* which at one time set the linguistic norms, has meant that there is no longer a recognizable 'standard' nor are there institutions which can uphold this standard. It is quite clear that social stratification and linguistic patterns are two sides of the same coin. Suzanne Romaine summarizes most effectively the points which I have attempted to convey:

"Unless our analyses are equally responsive to both social and linguistic factors in an integrative fashion then we run the risk of presenting a lop-sided view of the speech community as a whole." (Romaine, 1982: 5)

Notes to Chapter 19

1. This is in complete contrast to the study of "language". John Morris-Jones (1921: v) expresses the importance of pure and correct forms as follows, "The written language has been corrupted not only under the influence of false etymological theories but in the opposite direction by the substitution of dialectal for literary forms. . . the value of the tradition is that it represents the language in a form which was everywhere recognized as pure and of which the various dialects represent different corruptions."
2. W. Labov, 1963; 1964; 1966a,b,c,d; 1968; 1969b; 1970; 1972b; 1973a,b; Labov, Cohen, Robins & Lewis, 1968; Levine & Crockett, 1967; Shuy, Wolfram & Riley, 1967; Trudgill, 1978; Wolfram, 1969.
3. As expressed by Milroy & Milroy (1985b) ". . .observed synchronic variation can be viewed as the counterpart of change in the diachronic dimension".
4. Petyt (1980: 56): "The Neo-grammarian view would be that a particular sound change would operate over a certain area, affecting every word whose phonological structure was such that it could undergo this change".
5. 'Socio-dialectological Survey of Welsh in Chubut' supported by the Social Science Research Council. See R. O. Jones, 1973; 1976; 1979; 1983; 1984 and 1983–84.
6. These status groups are defined in terms of Welshness, ethnoculture identity and affiliations rather than in terms of socio-economic grouping.

7. At the beginning of this century the chapel in each area acted as the hub of spiritual. cultural and social life. The three aspects were delicately intertwined and such networks enforced linguistic norms as well as moral and behavioural patterns which gave the community its own distinct identity. When they were children it was the norm to attend Sunday School, go to the Band of Hope and attend other mid-week meetings. All went to the *eisteddfodau* and the *cyrddau cystadleuol*. If they did not go to chapel then they would be social outcasts. At that time also, the Welsh were very much aware of the fact that they had to retain their social identity as Welshmen in a Latin world. This common background resulted in all members of this generation having similar patterns.

8. In Sommerfelt (1962: 72–5) it is shown that changes can spread slowly through a language word by word. He exemplified such a process by reference to dialects of Welsh. He showed that the change from /xw/ to /hw/ was happening on the synchronic level spreading from area to area, from one age group to another but also from word to word. He makes another salient point ". . .les changements ne s'aperent pas au même moment dans tous les mots en question". The first to examine the concept systematically however was Wang in 1969. In Wang & Cheng (1970) it is concluded that, "A closer look at changes in progress and a more careful examination of large quantities of residual forms lead us to conclude that most (not necessarily all) types of phonological change are phonetically abrupt but lexically gradual. . . words change their pronunciations by discrete perceptible increments (i.e. phonetically abrupt) but severally at a time (i.e. lexically gradual) rather than always in a homogeneous block".

9. The third and fourth decade of this century was a period of great social change in Chubut. The chapel-bound structure gradually lost its hold on the Welsh-speaking community. Children were brought up who did not have control over the same range of registers in Welsh as their elders had, because their social networks extended outside the Welsh community. As pointed out by Milroy & Milroy (1985b: 75): "Linguistic change is slow in populations established and bound by strong ties, rapid when weak ties exist in populations".

20 Variation in consonant mutation — where do the variable rules go?

MARTIN J. BALL

Variation and grammatical theory

For many sociolinguists, the study of linguistic variation needs not only to show which linguistic and non-linguistic variables interact, and to what extent. It is also necessary to account for these patterns within a theoretical grammatical framework. As Labov (1966a) states, in his preface to one of the classical early works of sociolinguistic analysis:

> "*sociolinguistics* is. . . frequently used to suggest. . . the comprehensive description of the relations of language and society. This seems to me an unfortunate notion, fore-shadowing a long series of purely descriptive studies with little bearing on the central theoretical problems of linguistics or of sociology." (Labov, 1966a: vii)

He makes it clear that it is his intention "to solve problems" (p. vii) in the analysis of the patterns of linguistic variation he observed.

Trudgill (1974b: 4) also makes the point that "one of the main aims of research of this type is to shed light on various aspects of linguistic theory. Studies which are able to do this are obviously of more value than those that are not."

Given, then, the desirability of incorporating the results of studies of variability into grammatical theory, the next question that arises is, which theory? Since the 1950s linguists have been faced with a wide range of competing theories and variations of theories, some of which might well appear more suited to dealing with sociolinguistic factors than others. It is not necessary for our purposes to examine all of these theories, however, as this paper will adopt a transformational approach.

Transformational generative (TG) grammar has deliberately eschewed dealing with linguistic variation. As Radford (1981: 2) states, "linguistics is. . . primarily concerned with competence", and *competence* is defined as "the fluent native speaker's knowledge of his language". Linguistic variation is assigned to *performance*: "what people actually say". Indeed, Chomsky (1965) in his classic account of TG, explicitly states that performance should be excluded from his approach to grammar:

> "Linguistic theory is concerned primarily with an ideal speaker-listener, in a completely homogenous speech-community." Chomsky, 1965: 3)

He further adds, "to study actual linguistic performance, we must consider the interaction of a variety of factors, of which the underlying competence of the speaker-hearer is only one" (p. 4). Chomsky, therefore, is not saying performance should not be studied, only that TG was not intending to do that.

The rules of TG then are proposed as a description of a homogenous version of a language, variability being assigned to performance, or more recently perhaps to an area termed "pragmatics", but still not brought into the theory.

We have already referred to the fact that many sociolinguistic studies have attempted to integrate their results into a theoretical framework. Many different approaches have naturally been taken, but, considering the discussion above, it is perhaps surprising how many of these have chosen a TG framework with which to work. We will discuss below how this has been adapted to cope with variation data, but the reason for working through the TG paradigm is simply because it is the most influential of the modern schools of linguistics and has much of value within it. As Labov states, regarding TG's failure to account for heterogeneity, "the critique of the conventional linguistic methods just given must not be taken as a suggestion that they be abandoned" (Labov, 1972a: 201).

In the third section of this Chapter below, we will be discussing how to characterize variation in Welsh mutation usage theoretically, and for this purpose we also will be using a transformational framework, for the reasons noted above. However this framework is used with changes developed by sociolinguistics, and these are discussed in the following section.

Some ways of characterizing linguistic variation

Labov's New York study

Labov (1966a) was the first really major linguistic study to attempt any kind of theoretical input. This study was primarily concerned with phonological variation, and its final section ("synthesis") attempts a description of the structure of the New York City vowel system. This work was undertaken before the development of generative phonology, as expounded in Chomsky & Halle (1968), so a rule-based analysis was not undertaken. Rather, an adaptation of the traditional phonemic analysis is attempted, which is termed "variance analysis". This technique involves the examination of how much overlap occurs with the allophones (variants) of differing phonemic units. Utilizing this method for the analysis of casual speech, and the more traditional "contrastive analysis" for the examination of more careful speech, phonemic analyses were worked out for different groups of speakers. These are plotted onto complex "three-dimensional" diagrams, that attempt to show the vowel systems of New Yorkers in terms of style, class as well as phonetic environment. No attempt is made at any quantification of variability, and the resulting diagrams are extremely complex. Nevertheless this is an interesting initial attempt to characterize variation within the framework of an existing theoretical approach.

Trudgill's Norwich study

Trudgill's investigation of Norwich English (Trudgill, 1974b) was undertaken in 1971, after the publication of the first major account of generative phonology (Chomsky & Halle, 1968). Trudgill felt, therefore, that his attempt to deal theoretically with his data "can most usefully be constructed within the theoretical framework of generative phonology" (Trudgill, 1974b: 134). However, he does not make great use of the variable rule, developed by Labov (1969a), but rather concentrates on the notion of the "diasystem". This approach has some similarities to the panlectal approach of researchers such as Bailey (1972), but Trudgill claims that panlectal approaches are not justifiable, as they are too broad: widely differing varieties of a language should not be grouped together on psycholinguistic grounds if for no other reason, as they cannot be said to be internalized in any way by speakers. His diasystem, however, is an attempt to account for an internalized set of alternations, accessible to

Norwich speakers. He claims therefore, that "the incorporation of different Norwich speech forms into a single system is not simply. . . an intellectual exercise" (Trudgill, 1974b: 135).

The aim of Trudgill's diasystem is to produce all forms of Norwich English from a common underlying base. In order to achieve this, a single underlying systematic phonemic system is proposed, on which operate different types of phonological and phonetic rules, some of a variable nature (based on Labov, 1969a), to produce the different actual pronunciations of Norwich speakers. The diasystem as proposed by Trudgill has not been commonly used since, though the term 'community grammar' used more recently by many sociolinguists, has obvious connections with Trudgill's notion. A community grammar can be envisaged as attempting to account for all the linguistic variability within one speech community through variable rules.

Labov's variable rules

The previous section dealt with an attempt to describe a diasystem, and noted that some of the rules established were "variable rules". Rules of this type were first suggested by Labov (1969a), and were clearly an attempt to adapt generative phonology to enable it to deal with the data on language variation, which was being collected in ever increasing amounts at this time.

Labov's topic was the contraction and deletion of the copula in non-standard black English, and the problem of accounting for this within the framework of a generative phonology. Indeed, he states,

". . .this paper is directed at the methodological problem which seems to me of overriding importance in linguistics at the moment: to connect theoretical questions with a large body of inter-subjective evidence which can provide decisive answers to those questions." (Labov, 1969a: 757)

He proposes to do this in the following way: "the notion 'rule of grammar' is enlarged to include the formal treatment of inherent variation as a part of linguistic structure" (p. 715). This implies that rules must be drawn up that account for variability where this occurs, as well as rules that are categorial for all speakers. If variable rules are incorporated into a generative approach "it will be possible to enlarge our current notion of the 'linguistic competence' of a native speaker" (p. 736), and therefore variation need no longer be classed with other types of performance "errors".

The way such rules would work is explained by Labov in relation to the contraction and deletion processes of black English:

"First is an input variable which sets the overall frequency with which the rule is selected. Second, there are variable constraints which differentiate the frequencies with which the rule applies according to the syntactic and phonological features of the environment. . . and third, of course, there are extra-linguistic features such as age, sex, ethnic group, social class, and contextual style." (Labov, 1969a: 733)

In this paper, however, these extra-linguistic factors are not explicitly brought into the rule schema.

Labov draws up a set of rules, some categorial, some variable, which account for the patterns of use of the copula in this vernacular, and states, "there is no doubt that the variable rules presented here show a great advance in accountability over the use of 'free variation' (Labov, 1969a: 737). However, he is also in clear support of the basic generative approach to phonology, and he believes "that our findings give independent confirmation of the value of generative techniques" (p. 761).

Development of the variable rule

Labov's ideas about variable rules were further developed in Labov (1970) and Labov (1972a), though the latter considered also the work of Cedergren and Sankoff (written 1972, though published 1974).

Cedergren & Sankoff (1974) suggested several modifications to Labov's original variable rule format. Most important of these was the provision that constraints on rule operation should be characterized as being independent of each other. Labov (1972: 231) feels "this hypothesis is of the greatest importance to linguistic theory, for it provides the first strong justification for the linguist's assembly of individual rules into rule schema".

Cedergren & Sankoff (1974) also are the first to bring numerical and statistical data into the format of the rules, and Labov (1972a) follows this by attempting to characterize the effect of some of the non-linguistic variables.

Following these developments much work has been done involving the variable rule concept: both theoretical and practical. Collections such as Fasold & Shuy (1973) and Sankoff (1978) both contain studies of the concept. The methodology was developed to such an extent that computer programs were made available for the calculating of raw data, and transformation into variable rules showing the relative strengths of different constraints. The most recent of these programs — VARBRUL 3 — is described in Rousseau and Sankoff (1978), though as Fasold (1978: 94) points out, "a great many variable rules can have constraint hierarchies correctly assigned on the basis of horizontal tree displays alone".

The use of variable rules has not been restricted to phonological variation, though most work has been done in this area. Guy (1973) gives a good survey of applications of variable rule methodology up to that time.

Variation and mutations

Variable usage of Welsh consonant mutations

The initial consonant mutation system of Welsh has been discussed from a theoretical viewpoint in Awbery (1975). The mutations are three separate sets of phonological changes affecting word initial consonants, triggered not phonologically, but, idiosyncratically, by various syntactic or morphological environments. The soft mutation SM — or lenition — changes voiceless stops and liquids to voiced, voiced stops to voiced fricatives (exception: /g/ which is deleted), and /m/ to /v/. The aspirate mutation AM — or spirantization — changes voiceless stops to voiceless fricatives. The nasal mutation NM changes stops to homorganic nasals (aspirated nasals corresponding to the voiceless stops).

SM has the greatest number of triggering environments, the other two types having fewer triggers, and/or triggers occurring with less frequency. Ball (1984b, and this volume, Chapter 7) conducted a detailed investigation into the use of these mutations, concluding that AM in most of its triggering environments was used very rarely, though factors of style and speakers' acculturation rating (Welsh *versus* English cultural loyalties) and amount of formal Welsh language education, had roles to play in the variation patterns. NM was next most commonly affected, while SM remained virtually categorial for most of the environments studied. Exceptions to this in the case of SM tended to involve linguistic variation: SM was virtually categorial for example in the context of preposition+noun, but variable with preposition+place name. Other triggering environments referred to in the discussion below include (standard Welsh mutation usage shown in brackets following the trigger): *tri*, "three", (+AM); *a*, "and", (+AM); *ei*, "his", (+SM), *ei*, "her", (+AM), feminine nouns (cause SM to following adjectives, receive SM from preceding determiners).

Where do the variable rules go?

As noted above, variable rules — within the framework of transformational generative grammar — have been proposed for both phonological and syntactic variation, and for areas (such as copula contraction and deletion) which are on the borderline between the two. These variable rules, then, can be "fitted-in" either to a generative phonological account or, within syntax, to one of the several different types of rules of syntax, depending on the exact nature of the variation (though arguments exist as to whether syntactic variation can be dealt with in terms of variables, see Lavendera, 1978).

As regards the variable nature of mutations noted above, the question arises, where would variable rules for mutations go? As Awbery (1975) asks: are the mutations syntax or phonology? In this context of variable rules, my answer for most of the mutating environments studied above is, in the normal sense of those terms, neither.

The claim of phonology is, on the surface, a strong one: the result of the application of mutation is a sound change, and one that is, usually, phonemic. On the other hand, these sound changes are triggered by a particular syntax: for example the position of a mutating word. To some extent morphology (for example use of a non-periphrastic verb causes mutation to a following direct object), and lexis (gender in nouns), can also be seen as having parts to play here.

However, in order to resolve this problem we need to examine more closely the theory into which we are trying to fit this variation. For the purposes of this discussion, we will be using the extended standard theory of transformational syntax, as described most comprehensively in Radford (1981). Many developments, not all of them non-controversial, have taken place outside this theory (particularly in the area of interest here: the lexicon), but this account is a relatively clear and well understood version of transformational theory, and is easily acccessible in published work.

In the extended standard theory, the syntactic component consists of various types of rules (branching rules, lexical insertion rules, transformational rules), together with a lexicon, which contains the words of the language categorized syntactically, semantically, morphologically and phonologically. Other rules and components are also included (see Radford, 1981: 390), but need not concern us here.

The phonological component is a separate entity, but phonological rules can be triggered from the syntactic component, and so is not totally independent.

In terms of mutations therefore, as Awbery (1975) points out these can best be characterized as phonological rules triggered from somewhere within the syntactic component. The question remains, where? The majority of the triggers examined in this study point to the lexicon. Mutations that occur after specific words are clearly features peculiar to those words. Even mutations dependent on gender can be specified in the lexicon, for example through a lexical redundancy rule specifying:

(1)   [+noun, +fem] → [+mut, +SM]/___ [+adj]

(where [+mut] is a lexical feature meaning 'causes mutation to following word', and the specific mutation is characterized afterwards), or:

(2)   [+det] → [+mut, +SM]/___ [+noun, +fem].

Mutations on the negatives of non-periphrastic verb forms, for example:

(3)   *Gwelais i John* → *Welais i ddim John*
      "I saw John" → "I didn't see John"

seem most economically characterized as being triggered by the particles *ni* or *na*, which are later deleted variably — their retention being a mark of literary or formal Welsh.

It is true that some mutations appear not to be storable in the lexicon, for example object of a non-periphrastic verb, but these appear to be a minority of types.

For our purposes then, we can state that the mutations that most interest us originate in the lexicon, as sub-categorization features of particular lexical items. These features will then trigger off the relevant phonological rule at a later state in the derivation. If the mutations originate in the lexicon, it is only a short step to the view that variation in mutations should somehow be characterized as being within the lexicon. Variable rules within the phonology will not be adequate for this purpose. They would work if the mutations were uniformly variable, but as was found in Ball (1984b) variation in the use of mutations can be related to the different mutation triggers. The only way the variation could be characterized within the phonology would be for each trigger to be uniquely categorized in respect of its own version of a mutation, and to have different phonological rules (variable or categorial as the case may be) for each trigger. This of course would be grossly uneconomical, lack simplicity and run counter to our intuitions.

Variation in the lexicon

The variable rules discussed earlier were all concerned with phonological or syntactic variation. We have here proposed, however, variation that exists within the lexicon, specifically within the sub-categorization features of lexical entries. As far as the author is aware, although studies of lexical variation have been undertaken (e.g. Sankoff, Thibault & Bérubé, 1978), no-one has yet needed to characterize that variation in the way it is suggested is needed for mutations.

It is difficult to see how the concept of a rule, variable or categorial, can apply to the assigning of sub-categorization features to a lexical item. The features are considered inherent, as can be seen in Radford's (1981: 125) description of a syntactic feature: "any lexical item of category X will be sub-categorized with respect to the type of X-phrase it can occur in". Not much room for variation is given in that statement. Strict transformationalists do not in any event admit variability into their derivations, but it must be admitted that it is not easy to see how the assigning of a set of features to a lexical item could be done variably.

The solution would seem to lie either in the use of some kind of variable features, or in adapting other lexical rules to a variable format. To take the second point first; Radford (1981) describes the lexicon in extended standard theory as consisting of lexical entries, containing syntactic, morphological, semantic and phonological features; together with two main sets of rules: redundancy rules (dealing with both feature and word-formation — that is morphological — redundancy) and restructuring rules (which deal with variability in the syntactic behaviour of certain lexical items). From this description it would seem unlikely that redundancy rules could easily be used to capture the variability we have examined (again [+mut] would need to be characterized separately for each trigger). Their primary purpose, as with all redundancy rules, are as devices for promoting descriptive simplicity. However, the restructuring rules briefly described by Radford (1981) may well be adaptable for our purpose.

Radford (1981) gives the following as an example of a restructuring rule:

(4) [v take [NP advantage] [PP of [NP someone]] → [v take advantage
     of] [NP someone] (adapted from Radford (1981: 137)).

This accounts for the different syntactic structures this construction can
appear in, that similar surface structures would not be able to fulfil. It is
only a short step from this to a rule variably altering the feature specification of a lexical item, or the effect of that feature specification. An
example (shown here as a categorial rule for exemplification of such a
usage could be shown as:

(5) *tri* [+quant, +mut, +AM] → [+quant]

or for a trigger such as *tri*, with its generally low mutation triggering, the
above rule reversed could well be better motivated, at least for some
varieties of Welsh.

    Radford describes these rules as being "somewhat idiosyncratic and
highly lexically governed" (Radford, 1981: 138), a description which would
fit in well with our needs.

    The alternative proposal envisaged variable features, an idea not
previously used to my knowledge. These could be characterized within
arrow-brackets (the notation suggested by Labov (1969a) for any variable
constraint in a rule), and the precise nature of any variable application
of each type of feature fully specified in redundancy rules. In other words,
different types of AM usage (near categorial as in *ei*, "her", or varying
according to style and acculturation group as in *a*, and many others) would
have to be noted in the optional features. An example might be seen as
follows:

(6) *a* [+conj, ⟨+Mut, +AM2⟩, . . .].

This entry means that *a* optionally causes AM, and the type of variation
is further specified under a redundancy rule for AM, variability pattern 2.
This redundancy rule can be drafted in a similar pattern to the variable
rules already discussed.

    It is not easy to choose between these alternative solutions at this
stage. The restructuring rules present the simplest answer: existing rules
being simply adjusted slightly to a new role. Intuitively, however, the
notion of variability inherent in the feature specifications of the lexical
items themselves is perhaps more appealing.

    It would appear also, that variable features would offer the most
elegant solution to the problem of different usage patterns between prepo-
sition+noun and preposition+place name noted above. The mutating

prepositions can be categorially marked [+mut], with place names marked with an optional feature ⟨+blocks mut⟩. This also justifies separating the general feature of causing a mutation, [mut], from the specific mutations which are entered into the phonology: [SM], [NM], [AM], as this blocking feature of place names may well apply to all types of mutation. The use of restructuring rules to capture the place-name distinction would necessitate a more complex formulation.

Examples

Whichever of the two proposals in the previous sub-section is accepted, eventually a form of variable rule is needed (as a restructuring rule, or a feature redundancy rule).

Any variable rule can have variable conditioning on its application in terms of its linguistic environment (for example X will occur less often in the environment A____B, than in the environment C____D), and/or in terms of sociolinguistic factors (i.e. age, sex, class, etc.). For example, Labov (1972a) shows a rule for the variable deletion of the copula in black English vernacular, that is conditioned by linguistic environment:

$$(7) \quad z \rightarrow \langle \emptyset \rangle \begin{bmatrix} +\text{Pro} \\ +\text{cons} \end{bmatrix} \#\# \underline{\quad} \#\# \begin{bmatrix} +\text{Vb} \\ +\text{fut} \\ +\text{NP} \end{bmatrix} \text{(Labov, 1972a: 229).}$$

He also shows a rule for the variable (-ing) (whether or not the final nasal is velar), which is governed by non-linguistic factors:

$$(8) \quad \begin{bmatrix} -\text{cont} \\ -\text{tense} \\ -\text{ant} \end{bmatrix} \rightarrow \langle \emptyset \rangle \begin{bmatrix} +\text{voc} \\ -\text{cons} \\ -\text{stress} \end{bmatrix} \begin{bmatrix} +\text{nasal} \\ +\text{cor} \end{bmatrix} \underline{\quad}$$

$$\text{po} = \text{a.(SEC)} + \text{b.(style)} + \text{c. (Labov, 1972a: 240)}$$

This last line shows the overall probability operating on the rule above it, and that this probability is derived from socio-economic class factors and style factors, and possibly other, unspecified factors. The numerical aspect of these rules need not concern us here, (the full data are shown in Ball, 1984b) the rules shown below are only in outline without numerical form (as done, for example, by Labov, 1972a).

It is clear then, that for most of the variables we have studied, rules of the second type above will be necessary. It is therefore possible to construct a restructuring rule for *a* as follows:

(9)   *a* [+conj, +mut, +AM. . .] → [+conj]⟨+mut, +AM⟩
       po = a.(acculturation) +b.(style) +c.

A variable such as personal pronoun *ei* (masculine) showing categorial usage in the context +noun, but variable usage when +verb, would obviously need linguistic environment to be incorporated:

(10) *ei* [+pron, +masc, +mut, +SM] →
       [+pron, +masc] ⟨+mut, +SM⟩/____ [+vb]

Though, as noted above for prepositions, a variable feature analysis could perhaps account for this differently.

These examples show, therefore, that variation can be accounted for within the lexicon in a relatively straightforward manner. It is possible therefore to capture, within this theoretical framework, the patterns of variability that have emerged from the study of the initial consonant mutation system of Welsh. Variation within the lexicon is obviously not restricted to the highly individual mutation features of the Celtic languages, and it could well be necessary to account for variation in gender assignation to nouns in many languages through devices such as those suggested in this chapter.

Contributors

Martin J. Ball. Senior Lecturer in Sociolinguistics, Department of Behavioural and Communication Studies, Polytechnic of Wales.

Wynford Bellin. Lecturer in Psychology, University of Reading.

Cennard Davies. Principal Lecturer in Welsh, Department of Arts and Languages, Polytechnic of Wales.

Tweli Griffiths. Producer, 'Y Byd ar Bedwar', HTV Cymru, Cardiff.

Lynfa Hatton. Welsh Department, Ebbw Vale Comprehensive School.

Berwyn Prys Jones. Translation Department, The Welsh Office, Cardiff.

Dafydd Glyn Jones. Senior Lecturer in Welsh, University College of North Wales, Bangor.

Glyn E. Jones. Head of the Welsh Department, University College, Cardiff.

Robert Owen Jones. Head of the Welsh Department, University College, Swansea.

Siân Munro. Senior Lecturer in Speech Pathology, School of Speech Therapy, South Glamorgan Institute of Higher Education, Cardiff.

Anna E. Roberts. Senior Translator, Gwynedd Health Authority.

Alan R. Thomas. Professor, Department of Linguistics, University College of North Wales, Bangor.

Siân Elizabeth Thomas. Announcer, Sianel Pedwar Cymru (Channel 4 Wales), Cardiff.

References

AITCHISON, J. & CARTER, H. 1985, *The Welsh Language 1961–1981. An Interpretive Atlas*. Cardiff: University of Wales Press.

ANWYL, E. 1901, *A Welsh Grammar for Schools: Part 1 Accidence*. London: Swan Sonnenshein & Co. New York: Macmillan.

ATWOOD, E. B. 1963, Methods of American dialectology. *Zeitschrift für Mundartforschung,* 30, 1–30.

AWBERY, G. M. 1975, Welsh mutations: syntax or phonology? *Archivum Linguisticum (New Series),* 6, 14–25.

—— 1976, *The Syntax of Welsh. A Transformational Study of the Passive*. Cambridge: Cambridge University Press.

—— 1982, A bibliography of research on Welsh dialects since 1934. *Cardiff Working Papers in Welsh Linguistics,* 2, 103–19.

—— 1984, Phonotactic constraints in Welsh. In M. J. BALL & G. E. JONES (eds), *Welsh Phonology: Selected Readings*. Cardiff: University of Wales Press.

—— 1986, *Pembrokeshire Welsh*. Caerdydd: Amgueddfa Werin Cymru.

AWBERY, G. M., JONES, A. E. & SUGGETT, R. 1985, Slander and defamation: a new source for historical dialectology. *Cardiff Working Papers in Welsh Linguistics,* 4, 1–24.

BAETENS BEARDSMORE, H. 1982, *Bilingualism: Basic Principles*. Clevedon: Multilingual Matters.

BAILEY, C. -J. N. 1972, The integration of linguistic theory: internal reconstruction and the comparative method in descriptive analysis. In R. STOCKWELL & R. MACAULAY (eds), *Linguistic Change and Generative Theory*. Bloomington: Indiana University Press.

BAKER, C. 1984, *Aspects of Bilingualism in Wales*. Clevedon: Multilingual Matters.

BALL, M. J. 1976, *Towards a Description of the North Welsh Monophthongs*. Unpublished MA dissertation, University of Essex.

—— 1984a, Phonetics for phonology. In M. J. BALL & G. E. JONES (eds), *Welsh Phonology. Selected Readings*. Cardiff: University of Wales Press.

—— 1984b, *Sociolinguistic Aspects of the Welsh Mutation System*. Unpublished PhD thesis, University of Wales.

—— 1985a, An error recognition test as a measure of linguistic competence: an example from Welsh. *Journal of Psycholinguistic Research,* 14, 399–407.

—— 1985b, Phonological variation in the personal pronouns of Welsh. *Cardiff Working Papers in Welsh Linguistics,* 4, 25–30.

—— 1985c, Radio Cymru: Programme style and linguistic variation. *Journal of Multilingual and Multicultural Development,* 6, 157–64.

—— 1986, The reporter's test as a sociolinguistic tool. *Language in Society,* 15, 375–86.

—— (forthcoming) *Welsh Phonetics*.

BALL, M. J. & JONES, G.E. (eds) 1984, *Welsh Phonology. Selected Readings.* Cardiff: University of Wales Press.

BELL, A. 1982, Radio: the style of the news language. *Journal of Communication,* 32, 150–64.

BELL, R. T. 1976, *Sociolinguistics: Goals, Approaches and Problems.* London: Batsford.

BELLIN, W. 1984a, Welsh and English in Wales. In P. TRUDGILL (ed.), *Language in the British Isles.* Cambridge: Cambridge University Press.

—— 1984b, Welsh phonology in acquisition. In M. J. BALL & G. E. JONES (eds), *Welsh Phonology: Selected Readings.* Cardiff: University of Wales Press.

—— 1985, The linguistic competence of bilingual children in Welsh medium schools. *Child Language Seminar Papers: 1985,* 131–47.

BERG, H. 1984, The Norwegian Broadcasting Corporation, minority languages and broadcasting. *Journal of Multilingual and Multicultural Development,* 5, 243–47.

BEVAN, J. T. 1971, *Astudiaeth Seinyddol o Gymraeg llafar Coety Walia a Rhuthun ym Mro Morgannwg.* Unpublished MA thesis, University of Wales.

BIONDI, L. 1975, *The Italian-American Child: His Sociolinguistic Acculturation.* Washington DC: Georgetown University Press.

BLOCH, B. 1948, A set of postulates for phonemic analysis. *Language,* 24, 3–46.

BLOM, J. P. & GUMPERZ, J. J. 1972, Social meaning in linguistic structure: code-switching in Norway. In J. J. GUMPERZ & D. H. HYMES (eds), *Directions in Sociolinguistics. The Ethnography of Communication.* New York: Holt, Rinehart & WINSTON.

BLOOMFIELD, L. 1933, *Language.* London: Allen and Unwin.

BOWEN, E. G. 1950, The Celtic saints in Cardiganshire, *Ceredigion,* 1, 3–17.

—— 1964, *Daearyddiaeth Cymru fel Cefndir i'w Hanes.* Caerdydd: Cyhoeddiadau'r BBC.

BOWEN E. G. & JONES, T. J. RHYS 1960, *Teach Yourself Welsh.* London: English Universities Press.

BOWEN, I. 1908, *The Statutes of Wales.* London: Unwin.

BROWN, R. & GILMAN, A. 1972, The pronouns of power and solidarity. In P. P. GIGLIOLI, (ed.), *Language and Social Context.* Harmondsworth: Penguin.

BYNON, T. 1977, *Historical Linguistics.* Cambridge: Cambridge University Press.

Cymraeg Byw, Rhifyn 1, 1964, Published on behalf of the Education Faculty of University College, Swansea by Llyfrau'r Dryw.

—— Rhifyn 2, 1967, Welsh Joint Education Committee.

—— Rhifyn 3, 1970, Welsh Joint Education Committee.

CARSTAIRS, A. 1983, Paradigm economy. *Journal of Linguistics,* 19, 115–28.

CEDERGREN, H. J. & SANKOFF, D 1974, Variable rules: performance as a statistical reflection of competence. *Language,* 50, 333–55.

CHAMBERS, J. K. & TRUDGILL, P. 1980, *Dialectology.* Cambridge: Cambridge University Press.

CHEN, M. 1972, The time dimension: contribution toward a theory of sound change. *Foundations of Language,* 8, 457–98.

CHESHIRE, J. 1982, *Variation in an English Dialect: A Sociolinguistic Study.* Cambridge: Cambridge University Press.

CHOMSKY, N. 1957, *Syntactic Structures.* The Hague: Mouton.

—— 1965, *Aspects of the Theory of Syntax.* Cambridge, Mass: MIT Press.

CHOMSKY, N. & HALLE, M., 1968, *The Sound Pattern of English.* New York: Harper and Row.

Coleg Llyfrgellwyr Cymru, 1978, *Termau Llyfrgell a'r Byd Llyfrau.* Llanbadarn fawr.

COPPLESTONE-CROW, B. 1982, The dual nature of the Irish colonization of Dyfed in the Dark Ages. *Studia Celtica,* 16/17, 16–23.

CURRIE, H. C. 1952, A projection of sociolinguistics: The relationship of speech to social status. *The Southern Speech Journal,* 18, 28–37.

DARLINGTON, T. 1902, Some dialectal boundaries in mid-Wales. *Transactions of the Honourable Society of the Cymmrodorion (1900–01),* 13–19.

DAVIES, E. J. 1955, *Astudiaeth Gymharol o Dafodieithoedd Dihewyd a Llandygwydd.* Unpublished MA thesis, University of Wales.

DAVIES, J. J. GLANMOR 1934, *Astudiaeth o'r Gymraeg llafar Ardal Ceinewydd.* Unpublished PhD thesis, University of Wales.

DAVIES, L. 1969, *Astudiaeth Seinyddol gan gynnwys Geirfa o Dafodiaith Merthyr Tudful a'r Cylch.* Unpublished MA thesis, University of Wales.

DE CAMP, D. 1958–9, The pronunication of English in San Francisco. *Orbis,* 7, 372–91; 8, 54–77.

DEUCHAR, M. 1983, Review of CHESHIRE, J. 1982, Variation in an English dialect: a sociolinguistic study. *Times Higher Education Supplement,* 26 August 1983, 13.

DITTMAR, N. 1976, *Sociolinguistics. A Critical Survey of Theory and Application.* London: Edward Arnold.

DRESSLER, W. & WODAK-LEODOLTER, R. 1977, Language preservation and language death in Brittany. *International Journal of the Sociology of Language,* 12, 33–44.

ERVIN-TRIPP, S. M. 1972, On sociolinguistic rules — alternation and co-occurrence. In J. J. GUMPERZ & D. H. HYMES (eds), *Directions in Sociolinguistics. The Ethnography of Communication.* New York: Holt, Rinehart & Winston.

—— 1974, Is second language learning like the first? *TESOL Quarterly,* 8, 111–27.

EVANS, D. TECWYN 1915, *Yr Iaith Gymraeg: ei Horgraff a'i Chystrawen.* Liverpool: Hugh Evans & Sons.

EVANS, H. MEURIG 1961, *Llwybrau'r Iaith.* Llandybie: Llyfrau'r Dryw.

—— 1974, *Dilyn Cymraeg Byw.* Abertawe: Christopher Davies.

EVANS, J. J. 1960, *Gramadeg Cymraeg.* Llandysul: Gwasg Gomer.

EVANS, S. J. 1908, *The Elements of Welsh Grammar.* Newport: John E. Southall.

—— 1909, *Studies in Welsh Phonology.* London: David Nutt, Newport: John E. Southall.

FASOLD, R. W. 1978, Language variation and linguistic competence. In D. SANKOFF (ed.), *Linguistic Variation. Models and Methods.* New York: Academic Press.

FASOLD, R. W. & SHUY, R. W. (eds), 1973, *Analyzing Variation in Language.* Washington DC: Georgetown University Press.

FERGUSON, C. A. 1972, Diglossia. In P. P. GIGLIOLI (ed.), *Language and Social Context.* Harmondsworth: Penguin.

FISCHER, J. L. 1958, Social influences on the choice of a linguistic variant. *Word,* 14, 47–56.

FISHMAN, J. A. 1970, *Sociolinguistics: A Brief Introduction.* Rowley, Mass: Newbury House.

—— 1972, The sociology of language. In P. P. GIGLIOLI (ed.), *Language and Social Context.* Harmondsworth: Penguin.

FLETCHER, P. & GARMAN, M. (eds), 1986, *Language Acquisition: Studies in First Language Development.* 2nd edition. Cambridge: Cambridge University Press.

FRIEDRICH, P. 1972, Social context and semantic features — the Russian pronominal usage. In J. J. GUMPERZ & D. H. HYMES (eds), *Directions in Sociolinguistics. The Ethnography of Communication.* New York: Holt, Rinehart & Winston.

FRIES, C. C. & PIKE, K. L. 1949, Coexistent phonemic systems. *Language,* 25, 29–50.

FYNES-CLINTON, O. H. 1913, *The Welsh Vocabulary of the Bangor District.* London: Oxford University Press.

GAL, S. 1979, *Language Shift: Social Determinants of Linguistic Change in Bilingual Austria.* New York: Academic Press.

GIGLIOLI, P. P. (ed.), 1972, *Language and Social Context.* Harmondsworth: Penguin.

GIMSON, A. C. 1962, *Introduction to the Pronunciation of English.* London: Edward Arnold.

GLEASON, H. A. 1955, *An Introduction to Descriptive Linguistics.* New York: Holt, Rinehart & Winston.

—— 1961, *An Introduction to Descriptive Linguistics.* 2nd edition. New York: Holt, Rinehart & Winston.

GOODE, W. J. & HATT, J. R. 1952, *Methods in Social Research.* New York: McGraw-Hill.

GREGORY, M. 1967, Aspects of varieties differentiation. *Journal of Linguistics,* 3, 177–99.

GRIFFITH, W. LLOYD 1976, Iaith plant Llŷn. In J. L. WILLIAMS (ed.), *Ysgrifau ar Addysg 6.* Caerdydd: Gwasg Prifysgol Cymru.

GRIFFITHS, D. W. 1975, *Astudiaeth Eirfaol o Gymraeg llafar Llanfair Caereinion.* Unpublished MA thesis, University of Wales.

GRIFFITHS, H. M. (1981–86), Ardaloedd gweinyddol 1284–1980. In H. CARTER (ed.), *Atlas Cenedlaethol Cymru.* Caerdydd: Gwasg Prifysgol Cymru.

GRUNWELL, P. 1977, *The Analysis of Phonological Disability in Children.* Unpublished PhD thesis, University of Reading.

—— 1981, *The Nature of Phonological Disability in Children.* Academic Press: London.

—— 1982, *Clinical Phonology.* London: Croom Helm.

GUMPERZ, J. J. 1962, Types of linguistic community. *Anthropological Linguistics,* 4, 28–40.

—— 1968, The speech community. *International Encylopedia of the Social Sciences,* 381–86. London: Macmillan.

—— 1976, *The Sociolinguistic Significance of Conversational Code-switching.* Working Paper 46, Language Behavior Research Laboratory, University of California, Berkley.

GUMPERZ, J. J. & HYMES, D. H. (eds) 1972, *Directions in Sociolinguistics. The Ethnography of Communication.* New York: Holt, Rinehart & Winston.

GUY, G. R. 1973, Use and application of the Cedergren-Sankoff variable rule program. In R. W. FASOLD & R. W. SHUY (eds), *Analyzing Variation in Language.* Washington, DC: Georgetown University Press.

HALL, R. A. Jr 1950, *Leave Your Language Alone!* Linguistics Press, Republished 1960 as *Linguistics and Your Language.* New York: Anchor.

HALLIDAY, M. A. K. 1972, Sociological aspects of semantic change. *Proceedings of the 11th Congress of Linguists,* 853–88. Bologna: Il Mulino.

HARRIS, Z. S. 1951, *Structural Linguistics.* Chicago: Phoenix.

HARRISON, G. & THOMAS, C. 1975, *The Acquisition of Bilingual Speech by Infants.*

Final Report on SSRC Grant HR2104/1.

HATTON, L. 1983, *Astudiaeth o rai Patrymau llafar Plant 7 i 11 oed yn Ysgol Bryn-y-Môr, Abertawe*. Unpublished MA thesis, University of Wales.

HAWKINS, P. 1984, *Introducing Phonology*. London: Hutchinson.

HOCKETT, C. F. 1958, *A Course in Modern Linguistics*. New York: Macmillan.

HOOPER, J. B. 1976, Word frequency in lexical diffusion and the source of morpho-phonological change. In W. CHRISTIE (ed.), *Proceedings of the Second International Conference on Historical Linguistics*. Amsterdam: North Holland.

HUDSON, R. 1980, *Sociolinguistics*. Cambridge: Cambridge University Press.

HYMES, D. H. 1972, Models of the interaction of language and social life. In J. J. GUMPERZ & D. H. HYMES (eds), *Directions in Sociolinguistics. The Ethnography of Communication*. New York: Holt, Rinehart & Winston.

INGRAM, D. 1986, Phonological development: production. In P. FLETCHER & M. GARMAN (eds), *Language Acquisition: Studies in First Language Development*. Cambridge: Cambridge University Press.

IPA 1949, *Principles of the International Phonetic Association*. London: IPA.

JAMES, C. 1986, Welsh foreigner talk: breaking new ground. *Journal of Multilingual and Multicultural Development*, 7, 41–54.

JONES, A. R. 1969, *Oral Facility in Bilingual and Monoglot Children*. Unpublished MA thesis, University of Wales.

—— 1970, *Oral Facility in Bilingual and Monoglot Children*. Pamphlet 18, Education Department, University College of Wales, Aberystwyth.

JONES, D. 1950, *The Phoneme, its Nature and its Use*. Cambridge: Heffer.

JONES, G. D. 1962, *Astudiaeth Eirfaol o Gymraeg llafar Rhosllanerchrugog*. Unpublished MA thesis, University of Wales.

JONES, G. E. 1983, *Astudiaeth o Ffonoleg A Gramadeg Tair Tafodiaith ym Mrycheiniog*. Unpublished PhD thesis, University of Wales.

—— 1984a, L2 speakers and the pronouns of address in Welsh. *Journal of Multilingual and Multicultural Development*, 5, 131–45.

—— 1984b, The distinctive vowels and consonants of Welsh. In M. J. BALL & G. E. JONES (eds), *Welsh Phonology. Selected Readings*. Cardiff: University of Wales Press.

—— 1984c, Atodiad i 'The Linguistic Geography of Wales'. *Cardiff Working Papers in Welsh Linguistics*, 3, 97–103.

—— 1985a, Hala dechreunos — A knitting assembly in Breconshire? *The Society for Folk Life Studies*, 23, 116–18.

—— 1985b, Bera — a Brycheiniog word. *Brycheiniog*, 21, 69–72.

—— 1985c, A word geography of Brycheiniog. Some preliminary remarks. *Cardiff Working Papers in Welsh Linguistics*, 4, 101–18.

—— (forthcoming), Ffin y llafariad ganol yng Nghanolbarth Cymru. *Studia Celtica*.

JONES, G. E. & JONES, A. forthcoming a, Atlas geirfaol Brycheiniog. Rhai sylwadau a chasgliadau. *Bulletin of the Board of Celtic Studies*.

—— forthcoming b, *Atlas Geirfaol Brycheiniog*.

JONES, G. E. & THOMAS, P. W. 1981, The pronouns of address in Welsh: A pilot study. *Cardiff Working Papers in Welsh Linguistics*, 1, 29–59.

JONES, M. D. 1965, *Cywiriadur Cymraeg*. Llandysul: Gwasg Gomer.

JONES, R. E. 1975, *Llyfr o Idiomau Cymraeg*. Abertawe: Gwasg John Penry.

JONES, R. M. 1964a, Cyflwyno'r Gymraeg. In J. L. WILLIAMS (ed.), *Ysgrifau ar Addysg 3*. Caerdydd: Gwasg Prifysgol Cymru.

—— 1964b, Iaith lafar safonol. *Baner ac Amserau Cymru*, 29 October, 5

November, 12 November.
—— 1965, *Cymraeg i Oedolion*. Caerdydd: Gwasg Prifysgol Cymru.
—— 1979, The present condition of the Welsh language. In M. STEPHENS (ed.),
The Welsh Language Today. 2nd edition. Llandysul: Gomer.
—— 1985a, Cymraeg llenyddol llafar. *Y Traethodydd*, 140, 146–61.
—— 1985b, Cyweiriau'r iaith lenyddol. *Barddas*, 92–3, 23–4.
JONES, R. M. & THOMAS, A. R. 1977, *The Welsh Language. Studies in its Syntax
and Semantics*. Cardiff: University of Wales Press.
JONES, R. O. 1967, *A Structural Phonological Analysis and Comparison of Three
Welsh Dialects*. Unpublished MA thesis, University of Wales.
—— 1973/74, Amrywiadau geirfaol yn nhafodieithoedd Cymraeg y Wladfa. *Studia
Celtica*, 8/9, 287–98.
—— 1976, Cydberthynas amrywiadau iaith â nodweddion cymdeithasol yn y
Gaiman Chubut, sylwadau rhagarweiniol. *Bulletin of the Board of Celtic
Studies*, 27, 51–64.
—— 1979, *Tyred Drosodd. Galwad y Wladfa*. Caernarfon: Gwynedd County
Library.
—— 1983, *Astudiaeth o Gydberthynas Nodweddion Cymdeithasol ag Amrywiadau'r Gymraeg yn y Gaiman, Dyffryn y Camwy*. Unpublished PhD thesis,
University of Wales.
—— 1983/84 Patrwm newid ieithyddol yng Nghymraeg y Wladfa. *Studia Celtica*,
18/19, 253–67.
—— 1984, Change and variation in the Welsh of Gaiman, Chubut. In M. J. BALL
& G. E. JONES (eds), *Welsh Phonology: Selected Readings*. Cardiff: University
of Wales Press.
JONES, T. 1932/4, A bibliography of the dialects of Wales. *Bulletin of the Board
of Celtic Studies*, 6, 323–50; 7, 134–36.
JONES, T. J., RHYS 1970, Egwyddorion cyffredinol "Cymraeg Byw". In *Cymraeg
Byw, 3*. Y Bontfaen: D. Brown a'i Feibion.
—— 1977, *Teach Yourself Living Welsh*. Sevenoaks: Hodder and Stoughton.
KESSLER, C. 1971, *The Acquisition of Syntax in Bilingual Children*. Washington
DC: Georgetown University Press.
KHLEIF, B.B. 1976, Cultural regeneration and the school: An anthropological
study of Welsh medium schools in Wales. *International Review of Education*,
22, 177–92.
KIPARSKY, P & MENN, L. 1977, On the acquisition of phonology. In J. MACNAMARA,
(ed.), *Language Learning and Thought*. New York: Academic Press.
LABOV, W. 1963, The social motivation of a sound change, *Word*, 19, 273–309.
—— 1964, Phonological correlates of social stratification. *American Anthropologist*
66, 6, ii, 164–76.
—— 1966a, *The Social Stratification of English in New York City*. Washington
DC: Center for Applied Linguistics.
—— 1966b, Hypercorrection by the lower middle class as a factor in linguistic
change. In W. BRIGHT (ed.), *Sociolinguistics*. The Hague: Mouton.
—— 1966c, The linguistic variable as a structural unit. *Washington Linguistics
Review*, 3, 4–22.
—— 1966d, The effect of social mobility on linguistic behavior. *Social Inquiry*,
36, ii, 186–203.
—— 1968, The reflections of social processes in linguistic structures. In J. FISHMAN
(ed.), *A Reader in the Sociology of Language*. The Hague: Mouton.

—— 1969a, Contraction, deletion and inherent variability of the English copula. *Language*, 45, 715–62.

—— 1969b, The logic of non-standard English. *Georgetown Monographs on Language and Linguistics*, 22, Washington DC: Georgetown University Press.

—— 1970, The study of language in its social context. *Studium Generale*, 23, 30–87.

—— 1972a, *Sociolinguistic Patterns*. Oxford: Basil Blackwell.

—— 1972b, *Language in the Inner City*. Philadelphia: University of Pennsylvania Press.

—— 1972c, Some principles of linguistic methodology. *Language in Society*, 1, 97–120.

—— 1973a, The linguistic consequences of being a lame. *Language in Society*, 2, 81–115.

—— 1973b, The social setting of linguistic change, In T. SEBEOK (ed.), *Current Trends in Linguistics, 11*. The Hague: Mouton.

LABOV, W., COHEN, P., ROBINS, C. & LEWIS, J. 1968, *A Study of the Non-Standard English of Negro and Puerto Rican Speakers in New York City (I and II)*. Final Report, Cooperative Research Project 3288, US Office of Health, Education and Welfare, Washington DC.

LAMBERT, W. E. & TUCKER, G. R. 1976, *Tu, Vous, Usted. A Social-Psychological Study of Address Patterns*. Rowley, Mass: Newbury House.

LASS, R. 1984, *Phonology*. Cambridge: Cambridge University Press.

LAVENDERA, B. R. 1978, Where does the sociolinguistic variable stop? *Language in Society*, 7, 171–82.

LEHMANN, W. P. 1967, *A Reader in Nineteenth Century Historical Indo-European Linguistics*. Bloomington: Indiana University Press.

LE PAGE, R. B. 1979, review of HYMES, D., *Foundations in Sociolinguistics: an Ethnographic Approach*. London: Tavistock Publications, and DITTMAR, N., *A Critical Survey of Sociolinguistics: Theory and Application*. New York: St Martins Press. *Journal of Linguistics*, 15, 168–79.

LE ROUX, P. 1924, *Atlas Linguistique de la Basse Bretagne*. Rennes and Paris.

LEVINE, L. & CROCKETT, H. J. 1967, Speech variation in a Piedmont community: postvocalic-r. In S. LIEBERSON (ed.), *Explorations in Sociolinguistics*. The Hague: Mouton.

LEWIS, D. G. 1960, *Astudiaeth o Iaith lafar Gogledd-orllewin Ceredigion*. Unpublished MA thesis, University of Wales.

LEWIS, J. E. 1911, *A History of Wales*. London.

LEWIS, R. 1972, *Termau Cyfraith (Welsh Legal Terms)*. Llandysul.

LEWIS, SAUNDERS 1960, *Esther*. Llandybie: Llyfrau'r Dryw.

—— 1968, Rhagair. In *Problemau Prifysgol*. Llandybie: Llyfrau'r Dryw.

LLOYD, J. E. 1911, *A History of Wales*. London.

LYONS, J. 1968, *Introduction to Theoretical Linguistics*. London: Cambridge University Press.

—— 1970, *New Horizons in Linguistics*. Harmondsworth: Penguin.

McDAVID, R. I. 1948, Postvocalic-r in South Carolina: a social analysis. *American Speech*, 23, 194–203.

MACAULAY, R. K. S. 1976, Social class and dialect in Glasgow. *Language in Society*, 5, 173–88.

—— 1977, *Language, Social Class and Education: A Glasgow Study*. Edinburgh: Edinburgh University Press.

MACKEN, M. A. 1980, The child's lexical representation: the 'puzzle-puddle-pickle' evidence. *Journal of Linguistics*, 16, 1–17.

MACNAMARA, J. (ed.) 1977, *Language Learning and Thought*. New York: Academic Press.

MATTHEWS, P. 1974, *Morphology. An Introduction to the Theory of Word Structure*. Cambridge: Cambridge University Press.

—— 1981, *Syntax*. Cambridge: Cambridge University Press.

MIDDLETON, M. 1965, *Astudiaeth Seinyddol gan gynnwys Geirfa o Gymraeg Ardal Tafarnau Bach*. Unpublished MA thesis, University of Wales.

MILROY, J. & MILROY, L. 1978, Change and variation in an urban vernacular. In P. TRUDGILL (ed.), *Sociolinguistic Patterns in British English*. London: Edward Arnold.

—— 1985a, *Authority in Language*. London: Routledge and Kegan Paul.

—— 1985b, Linguistic change, social network and speaker innovation. *Journal of Linguistics*, 21, 339–84.

MILROY, L. 1980, *Language and Social Networks*. Oxford: Basil Blackwell.

MORGAN, T. J. 1952, *Y Treigladau a'u Cystrawen*. Caerdydd: Gwasg Prifysgol Cymru.

MORIN, Y. -C. & KAYE, J. D. 1982, The syntactic bases for French liaison. *Journal of Linguistics*, 18, 291–330.

MORRIS, W. M. 1910, *A Glossary of the Demetian Dialect of North Pembrokeshire (with special reference to the Gwaun Valley)*. Tonypandy: Evans and Short.

MORRIS-JONES, A. 1926, *The Spoken Dialect of Anglesey*. Unpublished MA thesis. University of Wales.

MORRIS-JONES, J. 1890, Cymraeg Rhydychen. *Y Geninen*, 8, 214–23.

—— 1891, Cymraeg (yr iaith). *Y Gwyddoniadur Cymreig (2nd edition)*, 3, 48–79.

—— 1913, *A Welsh Grammar, Historical and Comparative. Phonology and Accidence*. Oxford: Clarendon Press.

—— 1921, *An Elementary Welsh Grammar*. Oxford: Clarendon Press.

—— 1931, *Welsh Syntax. An Unfinished Draft*. Cardiff: University of Wales Press.

MOSER, C. A. 1958, *Survey Methods in Social Investigation*. London: Heinemann.

MUNRO, S. 1985, *An Empirical Study of Specific Communication Disorders in Bilingual Children*. Unpublished PhD thesis, University of Wales.

MYRDDIN BARDD (J. JONES) 1907, *Gwerin-Eiriau Sir Gaernarfon. Eu Hystyr a'u Hanes*. Pwllheli: Richard Jones.

NEMSER, W. 1971, Approximative systems of foreign language learners. *International Review of Applied Linguistics*, 9, 115–23.

Office of Population Censuses and Surveys 1970, *Social and Socioeconomic Classifications*. London: HMSO.

—— 1982, *Census 1981. County Report. Powys. Part 1*. London: HMSO.

ORTON, H., SANDERSON, S. & WIDDOWSON, J. 1978, *The Linguistic Atlas of England*. London: Croom Helm.

OSTHOFF, H. & BRUGMANN, K. 1878, Morphologische Untersuchungen auf dem Gebiete der indogermanischen Sprachen, I. English Translation in W. P. LEHMANN, (ed.).

PARRY, T. 1944, *Hanes Llenyddiaeth Gymraeg*. Cardiff.

—— 1955, *A History of Welsh Literature*. Oxford: Trans. by H. Idris Bell from the Welsh.

PEATE, I. 1925, The Dyfi Basin: a study in physical anthropology and dialect distribution. *Journal of the Royal Anthropological Institute*, 1925, 58–72.

PETERS, A. M. 1986, Early syntax. In P. FLETCHER & M. GARMAN (eds), *Language Acquisition: Studies in First Language Development*. Cambridge: Cambridge University Press.

PETYT, K. M. 1980, *The Study of Dialect. An Introduction to Dialectology*. London: André Deutsch.

PHILLIPS, V. 1955, *Astudiaeth o Gymraeg llafar Dyffryn Elái a'r Cyffiniau*. Unpublished MA thesis, University of Wales.

PICKFORD, G. R. 1956, American linguistic geography: a sociological approach. *Word*, 12, 211–33.

POSTAL, P. 1968, *Aspects of Phonological Theory*. New York: Harper & Row.

PRIDE, J. B. & HOLMES, J. 1972, *Sociolinguistics*. Harmondsworth: Penguin.

PRYCE, W. T. R. 1978, Welsh and English in Wales, 1750–1971. A spatial analysis based on the linguistic application of parochial communities. *Bulletin of the Board of Celtic Studies*, 28, 1–36.

PUTNAM, G. N. & O'HERN, E. M. 1955, The status significance of an isolated urban dialect. Supplement to *Language*, Language Dissertations 53.

QUIRK, R., GREENBAUM, S., LEECH, G. & SVARTVIK, J. 1972, *A Grammar of Contemporary English*. London: Longmans.

RADFORD, A. 1981, *Transformational Syntax*. Cambridge: Cambridge University Press.

REES, ALWYN D. 1979, The Welsh language in broadcasting. In M. STEPHENS (ed.), *The Welsh Language Today*. 2nd edition. Llandysul: Gomer.

REES, E. 1958, *Tafodiaith Rhan Isaf Dyffryn Llwchwr*. Unpublished MA thesis, University of Wales.

REES, M. E. G. 1954, *A Welsh Linguistic Background Scale*. Pamphlet 2, Education Department, University College of Wales, Aberystwyth.

REES, R. 1936, *Gramadeg Tafodiaith Dyffryn Aman*. Unpublished MA thesis, University of Wales.

REES, W. 1968, The mediaeval Lordship of Brecon. An address presented to William Rees by the Brecknock Society. *Brecknock Museum Publications*. 1–53.

REID, E. 1976, *Social and Stylistic Variation in the Speech of some Edinburgh Schoolchildren*. Unpublished M Litt. thesis, University of Edinburgh.

RICHARDS, M. 1938, *Cystrawen y Frawddeg Gymraeg*. Caerdydd: Gwasg Prifysgol Cymru.

RICHARDSON, G. & FLETCHER, N. 1968, *Histoires Illustrées*. London: Edward Arnold.

ROBERTS, A. E. 1973, *Geirfa a Ffurfiau Cymraeg llafar cylch Pwllheli*. Unpublished MA thesis, University of Wales.

ROBERTS, M. E. & JONES, R. M. 1974, Iaith lafar. In *Cyfeiriadur i'r Athro Iaith, Rhan II, D–N*. Cardiff, University of Wales Press.

ROLANT, EURYS 1984, Cymraeg iach. *Y Traethodydd*, 139, 78–92.

ROMAINE, S. 1975, *Linguistic Variability in the Speech of some Edinburgh Schoolchildren*. Unpublished MLitt thesis, University of Edinburgh.

—— 1979, The language of Edinburgh schoolchildren: the acquisition of sociolinguistic competence. *Scottish Literary Journal*, 9, 55–61.

—— 1980, What is a speech community? *Belfast Working Papers in Language and Linguistics*, 4, 41–59.

—— 1981, The status of variable rules in sociolinguistic theory. *Journal of Linguistics*, 17, 93–119.

—— 1982, *Sociolinguistics: Variation in Speech Communities.* London: Edward Arnold.

ROUSSEAU, P. & SANKOFF, D 1978, Advances in variable rule methodology. In Sankoff, D. (ed.).

ROWLANDS, E. I. 1981, Dosbarthu'r rhagenwau personol. *Bulletin of the Board of Celtic Studies,* 29, 419–31.

RUDDOCK, G. 1969, *Astudiaeth Seinyddol o Dafodiaith Hirwaun ynghyd â Geirfa.* Unpublished MA thesis, University of Wales.

SALESBURV, W. 1546, *Oll Synnwyr Pen Kembero Ygyd.* Facsimile reprint edited by J. Gwenogvryn Evans, 1902. Bangor: Jarvis and Foster. London: J. M. Dent.

SAMPSON, G. P. & RICHARDS, J. C. 1973, Learner language systems. *Language Sciences,* 9, 18–24.

SAMUEL, O. 1971, *Astudiaeth o Dafodiaith Gymraeg cylch Y Rhigos.* Unpublished MA thesis, University of Wales.

SANKOFF, D. (ed.) 1978, *Linguistic Variation. Models and Methods.* New York: Academic.

SANKOFF D., THIBAULT, P. & BÉRUBÉ, H. 1978, Semantic field variability. In D. SANKOFF (ed.), *Linguistic Variation. Models and Methods.* New York: Academic Press.

SELINKER, L. 1972, Interlanguage. *International Review of Applied Linguistics,* 10, 209–31.

SHUY, R. W., WOLFRAM, W. & RILEY, W. 1967, *A Study of Social Dialects in Detroit.* Washington DC: Office of Education.

SIENCYN, S. W. 1985, *Astudiaeth o'r Gymraeg fel Ail Iaith yng Nghylchoedd Meithrin Mudiad Ysgolion Meithrin.* Unpublished MEd thesis, University of Wales.

SMITH, N. V. 1973, *The Acquisition of Phonology: a Case Study.* Cambridge: Cambridge University Press.

SOMMERFELT, A. 1925, *Studies in Cyfeiliog Welsh. A Contribution to Welsh Dialectology.* Oslo: I Kommission Hos Jacob Dybwald.

—— 1962, *Diachronic and Synchronic Aspects of Language.* The Hague: Mouton.

SOUTHALL, J. S. 1892, *Wales and Her Language.* London & Newport: J. Southall.

STARK, R. 1986, Prespeech segmental feature development. In P. FLETCHER & M. GARMAN (eds), *Language Acquisition: Studies in First Language Development.* 2nd edition. Cambridge: Cambridge University Press.

STEPHENS, M. (ed.) 1979, *The Welsh Language Today.* 2nd edition. Llandysul: Gomer.

SWAIN, M. 1972, *Bilingualism as a First Language.* Unpublished PhD thesis, University of California.

SWEET, H. 1884, Spoken North Welsh. *Transactions of the Philological Society,* 1882–4, 409–84.

THOMAS, A. R. 1958, *Astudiaeth Seinegol o Gymraeg llafar Dyffryn Wysg.* Unpublished MA thesis, University of Wales.

—— 1959, Ffonemau llafarog tafodiaith Dyffryn Wysg. *Bulletin of the Board of Celtic Studies,* 18, 265–70.

—— 1961, Ffonemau cytseiniol tafodiaith Dyffryn Wysg. *Bulletin of the Board of Celtic Studies,* 19, 193–201.

—— 1973, *The Linguistic Geography of Wales.* Cardiff: University of Wales Press.

—— 1975, Dialect mapping. *Orbis,* 24, 115–24.

—— 1976, Derivational complexity in varieties of contemporary Welsh. In R. A. FOWKES (ed.), *Celtic Linguistics 1976*. International Linguistic Association.

—— 1977, A cumulative matching technique for computer determination of speech areas. *Germanistische Linguistik*, 3/4.

—— 1978, Dialect mapping and models of pronuncation. *Publication of the 29th Annual Georgetown Round Table on Languages and Linguistics, International Dimensions of Bilingualism.*

—— 1980, Areal Analysis of Dialect by Computer: A Welsh Example. Cardiff: University of Wales Press.

THOMAS, B. 1980, Cymrêg, Cymraeg: cyweiriau iaith siaradwraig o Ddyffryn Afan. *Bulletin of the Board of Celtic Studies*, 28, 579–92.

THOMAS, C. 1961, *A Phonological Conspectus of the Welsh Dialect of Nantgarw, Glamorgan.* Unpublished MA thesis, University of London.

—— 1966, Review of JONES, R. M. 1965, *Y Traethodydd*, 121 (3rd Series, 34), No. 521, 174–80.

—— 1967, Review of *Cymraeg Byw, Rhifyn 2. Llên Cymru*, 9, 242–49.

—— 1974, The verbal system and the responsive in a Welsh dialect of south-east Wales, *Studia Celtica*, 8/9, 271–86.

—— 1979, Y tafodieithegydd a "Chymraeg Cyfoes". *Llên Cymru*, 13, 113–52.

THOMAS, P. W. 1982, Putting Glamorgan on the map. *Cardiff Working Papers in Welsh Linguistics*, 2, 73–101.

—— 1984, Glamorgan revisited. Progress report and some emerging distribution patterns. *Cardiff Working Papers in Welsh Linguistics*, 3, 119–47.

THORNE, D. 1971, *Astudiaeth Seinyddol a Morffolegol o Dafodiaith Llangennech gan gynnwys Geirfa.* Unpublished MA thesis, University of Wales.

—— 1975/6, Arwyddocâd y rhagenwau personal ail berson unigol ym Maenor Berwig, Cwmwd Carnwyllion. *Studia Celtica*, 10/11, 383–87.

—— 1977a, Arwyddocâd y rhagenwau personol ail berson unigol yng Nglyn Nedd (Gorllewin Morgannwg), Hebron (Dyfed) a Charnhedryn (Dyfed). *Bulletin of the Board of Celtic Studies*, 33, 389–98.

—— 1977b, *Astudiaeth Gymharol o Ffonoleg a Gramadeg Iaith lafar y Maenorau oddi mewn i Gwmwd Carnwyllion yn Sir Gaerfyrddin.* Unpublished PhD thesis, University of Wales.

—— 1984, The correlation of dialect and administrative boundaries in Welsh: a review. In M. J. BALL & G.E. JONES (eds), *Welsh Phonology. Selected Readings.* Cardiff: University of Wales Press.

—— 1985, *Cyflwyniad i Astudio'r Gymraeg.* Caerdydd: Gwasg Prifysgol Cymru.

TRUDGILL, P. 1974a, *Sociolinguistics: An Introduction.* Harmondsworth: Penguin.

—— 1974b, *The Social Differentiation of English in Norwich.* Cambridge: Cambridge University Press.

—— (ed.) 1978, *Sociolinguistic Patterns in British English.* London: Edward Arnold.

—— 1986, *Dialects in Contact.* Oxford: Basil Blackwell.

Uned Iaith Genedlaethol Cymru 1976, *Gramadeg Cymraeg Cyfoes/Contemporary Welsh Grammar.* Y Bontfaen: D. Brown a'i Feibion.

—— 1978, *Cyflwyno'r Iaith Lenyddol.* Y Bontfaen: Hughes a'i Fab.

VERNER, K. 1875, Eine Ausnahme der ersten Lautverschiebung. *Zeitschrift für vergleichende Sprachforschung auf dem Gebiete der indogermanischen Sprachen*, 23, ii, 97–130.

VIERECK, W. 1973, The growth of dialectology. *Journal of English Linguistics*, 7, 69–86.

VON RAUMER, R. 1856, Die sprachgeschichtliche Umwandlung und die naturge-schichtliche Bestimmung der Laute. *Zeitschrift für die österreichischen Gymna-sien*, 353–77.

WAKELIN, M. F. 1972, *English Dialects. An Introduction*. London: Athlone Press.

WANG, W. S. -Y. 1969, Competing changes as a cause of residue. *Language*, 45, 9–25.

WANG, W. S. -Y. & CHENG, C. C. 1970, Implementation of phonological change. The Shuang-feng Chinese case. *Proceedings of the Annual Regional Meeting of the Chicago Linguistics Society*, 6, 552–9.

WATKINS, T. A. 1951, *Tafodiaith Plwyf Llansamlet*. Unpublished MA thesis, University of Wales.

—— 1955, Linguistic atlas of Welsh dialects. *Orbis*, 4, 32–42.

—— 1961, *Ieithyddiaeth. Agweddau ar Astudio Iaith*. Caerdydd: Gwasg Prifysgol Cymru.

—— 1968, Llafar llenyddol Cymraeg. In T. JONES (ed.), *Astudiaethau Amrywiol a Gyflwynir i Syr Thomas Parry Williams*. Caerdydd: Gwasg Prifysgol Cymru.

WEINREICH, U. 1953, *Languages in Contact*. The Hague: Mouton.

—— 1954, Is a structural dialectology possible? *Word*, 10, 388–400.

WEINREICH, U., LABOV, W. & HERZOG, M. 1968, Empirical foundations for a theory of language change. In W. P. LEHMANN & Y. MALKIEL (eds), *Directions for Historical Linguistics*. Austin: University of Texas Press.

WILIAM, U. 1967, *Argymhellion: Gramadeg Cymraeg Modern*. Llandysul: Gwasg Gomer.

WILLIAMS, A. LL. 1951, Y rhwyg rhwng llyfr a llafar. *Baner ac Amserau Cymru*, 22. August 3.

WILLIAMS, A. E. 1986, *Termau Archifau*. Caernarfon: Gwasanaeth Archifau Gwynedd.

WILLIAMS, I 1926, Rhagair, In *Tŷ Dol (Henrik Ibsen)*. Bangor: Evan Thomas.

—— 1935/46, Cymraeg llwyfan. In *Meddwn I*. Llandybie: Llyfrau'r Dryw.

—— 1960, Cymraeg Byw. *BBC Radio Lecture*.

WILLIAMS, JAC L. 1967, Sylwadau ar adolygiad. *Y Traethodydd*, 122 (3rd Series, 35), No. 523, 80–85.

WILLIAMS, S. J. 1959, *Elfennau Gramadeg Cymraeg*. Caerdydd: Gwasg Prifysgol Cymru.

—— 1980, *A Welsh Grammar*. Cardiff: University of Wales Press.

WOLFRAM, W. 1969, *A Sociolinguistic Description of Detroit Negro Speech*. Wash-ington DC: Center for Applied Linguistics.

WOLFRAM, W. & FASOLD, R. W. 1974, *The Study of Social Dialects in American English*. Englewood Cliffs, NJ: Prentice Hall.

Index